GW00703415

The British Colonial Experience
1800-1964

The British Colonial Experience 1800-1964
The Impact on Maltese Society

Edited by

Victor Mallia-Milanes

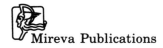Mireva Publications

Published under the auspices of
The Free University:
Institute of Cultural Anthropology/
Sociology of Development
Amsterdam

First published in 1988
by Mireva Academic Publications Enterprises (M.A.P.E.) Limited
of Tower Street, Msida, Malta
under the auspices of the
FREE UNIVERSITY OF AMSTERDAM
Phototypeset and electronically paged on
Schoolbook 10/12 pt by
Mariner Phototypesetters Limited
Marsascala, Malta
and printed and bound by
Interprint Limited
Marsa, Malta

Cataloguing in Publication Data
The British Colonial Experience, 1800-1964: The Impact on Maltese Society
1. Malta — History-1800-1964
2. Malta — Social life and customs
I. Mallia-Milanes, Victor

945.8508

ISBN 1 870579 01 1 (hardback)
ISBN 1 870579 02 X (paperback)

For Mary

Contents

Contents

Notes on Contributors

Joseph Bezzina   Lecturer in Church History
Faculty of Theology, Malta

Jeremy Boissevain   Professor of Social Anthropology
State University, Amsterdam

Salvino Busuttil   Professor of Economics, UN
Economic Adviser to St Vincent
and the Genadines (1986), and
Director-General Foundation for
International Studies, University
of Malta

Carmel Cassar   *Formerly* St Edward's College,
Malta

Arthur G. Clare   *Formerly* Department of Economics
New Lyceum, Malta

Dominic Cutajar   Assistant Curator of Fine Arts,
Malta

Denis de Lucca   Senior Lecturer in History of
Architecture, Architectural Theory,
and Professional Practice
University of Malta

D.K. Fieldhouse   Vere Harmsworth Professor of
Imperial and Naval History, and
Fellow of Jesus College Cambridge

Emmanuel Fiorentino   Art and Design Centre, Malta

Henry Frendo   Associate Professor of Modern
History
University of Malta
Formerly Department of Politics,
La Trobe University, Melbourne

Oliver Friggieri   Associate Professor of Maltese

Literature and Literary Theory
University of Malta

Stephen Howe Tutor in Politics and Development
Studies
Ruskin College, Oxford

Adrianus Koster Senior Lecturer, Institute of
Cultural Anthropology and
Sociology of Development
Free University, Amsterdam

Victor Mallia-Milanes Lecturer in Early Modern History
University of Malta

Peter Serracino Inglott Professor of Philosophy and Head
of Department of Philosophy
University of Malta

Godfrey Wettinger Associate Professor of Medieval
History, and Head of Department
of History
University of Malta

Ann Williams Lecturer in Mediterranean Studies
University of Exeter

Edward L. Zammit Associate Professor of Industrial
Sociology and Chairman, Workers'
Participation Development Centre
University of Malta

List of Illustrations

Acknowledgements

The publishers are grateful to the following persons and institutions for permission to reproduce photographs and other illustrations.

Revd Fr. Joseph Bezzina
Mr Mario Buhagiar
Mr David J. Camilleri
The Capuchin Church, Floriana
The Cathedral Museum, Gozo
Mr Dominic Cutajar
Mr Joe Friggieri, jun.
Mr Tony Gatt
Museum of Fine Arts, Valletta, Malta
The Parish Church of St Dominic, Valletta
Mr Tony Terribile

Plates appear between page 256 and page 257

Conventions

References: To reduce the length of the footnotes, only the author's name and a shortened title of the work cited are generally given. Full details are provided in the bibliography.

Currency: The currency mentioned in the text is generally the pound sterling (£), which subdivided into twenty shillings (20s), and each shilling into twelve pence (12d.) There are occasional textual references to the *scudo* (subdivided into 12 *tari*, and each *tari* into 20 *grani*) which was allowed free circulation until late in the nineteenth century. It was equivalent to approximately 1s. 8d.

Weight (avoirdupois): Occasional textual references are also made to the pound (lb), which was equivalent to approximately 453 grams; and to the *rotolo*, equivalent to approximately 792 grams.

List of Abbreviations

AAM	Archiepiscopal Archives, Valletta, Malta
AEG	Episcopal Archives, Gozo
AES	Archives of the Congregation of Extraordinary Ecclesiastical Affairs, Vatican City
AIM	Archives of the Inquisition, Malta
AOM	Archives of the Order of St John, National Library of Malta
ASP	Archivio di Stato, Palermo
ASV	Secret Archives of the Vatican, Vatican City
CG	Debates of the Council of Government of Malta. Malta, Government Printing Press, 1877-1922
CO	Colonial Office Papers. Public Record Office, London
Driberg Papers	Driberg Papers, Christ Church, Oxford
FCB Papers	Fabian Colonial Bureau Papers, Rhodes House, Oxford
Gov.	Correspondence to the Governor of Malta. Palace Archives, Valletta, Malta
Hansard	British Parliamentary Debates.
Lib.	Library Manuscripts Collection. National Library of Malta
MGG	Malta Government Gazette
NAV	Notarial Archives, Valletta, Malta
NLM	National Library of Malta
PA	Parish Archives
PAV	Palace Archives, Valletta, Malta
PP	Parliamentary Papers

PRO	Public Record Office, London
Reg. Batt.	Baptismal Register
WO	War Office memoranda and despatches. Public Record Office, London
SB	Secretariat of Papal Briefs
SCC	Sacred Consistorial Congregation
SS	Secretariat of State

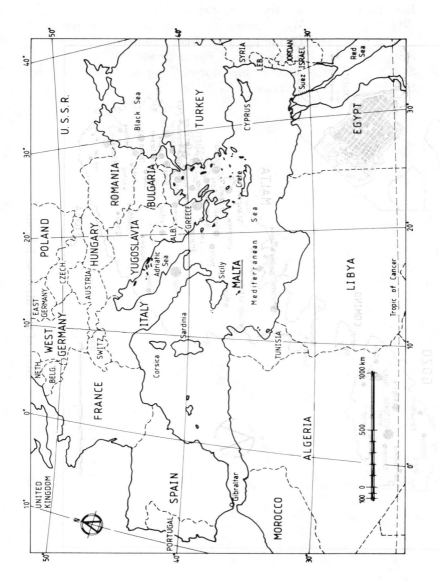

Map of the Mediterranean

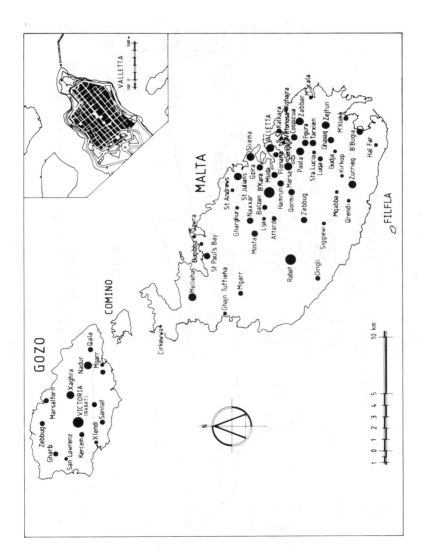

Map of the Maltese Islands

GOZO

Zebbug
Gharb
Marsalforn
San Lawrenz
Xaghra
Kercem
VICTORIA
(RABAT)
Xlendi
Nadur
Sannat
Qala
Mgarr

COMINO

Cirkewwa

MALTA

Mellieha
Bugibba
St Paul's Bay
Ghajn Tuffieha
Mgarr
St Andrew's
Gharghur
St Julians
Sliema
Naxxar
Gzira
Mosta
Lija
Balzan
B'Kara
Msida
VALLETTA
Attard
Hamrun
Floriana
Mqabba
Qormi
Marsa
Senglea
Kalkara
Cospicua
M'Xajra
Zabbar
M'Skala
Dingli
Qrendi
Rabat
Zebbug
Paola
Fgura
Tarxien
Zejtun
Sigtjewi
Sta Lucia
Luqa
Ghaxaq
Gudja
Kirkop
M'Xlokk
Zurrieq
B'Bugia
Hal Far

FILFLA

VALLETTA

0 1 2 3 4 5   10 km

Foreword

The impact a colonizing power has on the societies which it controls has always been a controversial question and the answers given for any particular territory will never be agreed. In principle the impact may range between two extremes: the imperial impact may be very slight indeed, superficial and transient; or it may be profound, completely restructuring the dependent society and cutting it off from its roots. One aim of the contributors to this book is to place Malta within this spectrum.

Approaches to this problem are likely to vary in two main ways: over time and as between the colonizing power and the colonial people.

To consider first the time factor, until perhaps the second or third decades of the twentieth century most modern European imperial countries were proud of their colonial achievements and tended to claim that they had had a 'civilizing mission' in their overseas possessions. Success in this mission was necessarily measured by the extent to which they suppressed what they regarded as undesirable attitudes, institutions, and practices in the colonies and replaced them by 'civilized' or 'Christian' values. On the other side of the divide, it was common in the earlier stages of the alien occupation for members of the colonial élite to be profoundly impressed by what their new rulers brought with them, often because it was assumed that these imports explained the success of the colonizers. These élites thus attempted to mould themselves in the image of the colonial power, adopting its language, education, and often its values: classic examples include members of the Indian upper classes during the later nineteenth century and Francophile West Africans well into the twentieth century.

During the middle decades of the twentieth century, however, belief that the European impact was an unqualified good waned on both sides of the colonial equation. On the imperial side it retained much of its force among the vulgar; but, from at least the early 1920s, it was increasingly held among anthropologists and those administrators in closest contact with subject peoples that radical reconstruction of colonial societies and their beliefs destroyed much that was valuable and might leave a dangerous cultural and psychological vacuum. One political consequence of this was the adoption of 'indirect rule' as a guiding principle in British administration in Africa, whose aim was to preserve indigenous structures under an imperial umbrella. Although after 1945 there was a revival of a 'modernizing' ethic among the colonial powers, this can be seen primarily as a response to demands for political and economic 'development' by colonial subjects: the only forms of development the western powers knew were their own.

On the other side of the water, the main solvent of earlier enthusiasm for the consequences of alien occupation was the growth of something we conventionally call nationalism, but which in many cases is better thought of as resentment at alien domination without necessarily implying a sense of common interest and experience. Paradoxically one of the earliest expressions of such nationalism among the élites was for greater equality with the Europeans, including the opportunity to adopt their lifestyles: for example, after 1945 the intelligentsia of French West Africa opposed the creation of colonial universities on the ground that these would be inferior to those of France to which many of them had gone or hoped to go. Moreover, the demand for political freedom implied in the first instance that the colonies should be given the political rights and institutions of the imperial state. Political democracy and the rule of law were therefore transported to the African colonies in the very last years before independence; and at the same time most Europeans, and probably most Africans, assumed that these imports were in themselves desirable and might be retained indefinitely.

Once into the new world of independence, however, every ex-

colony – and one must now look at the whole ex-colonial world,
not merely that part given independence in the 1950s and 1960s
– has tended to review its colonial inheritance in the light of
its own past and present. At this stage the critical determinant
seems to have been whether the pre-colonial form of a particular
society was significantly different from what it became during
the colonial experience and how much of that earlier inheritance
survived. Again one can postulate two extremes. At one end of
the spectrum there are the ex-colonies formed by European
settlers who were sufficiently numerous to swamp the
indigenous people. The obvious first example of such ex-colonies
was the United States which, despite the superficially different
format of its post-independence constitution and structure, in
fact retained most of the essentials of England in the
seventeenth and eighteenth centuries. In different degrees other
comparable examples are Canada, Australia, New Zealand, and
many of the Latin American States. At the other extreme many
African colonies had been occupied for little more than half a
century, within the life-span of many alive, when the colonial
flags were pulled down. For them, by contrast with most colonies
of white settlement, the colonial experience, at least in
retrospect, was one of humiliation. They had a strong instinct
to reject the style and symbols of western influence, to rediscover
their lost past: hence, for example, the adoption by Nkrumah
of 'Ghana' in place of 'The Gold Coast' as the name of his new
State. Hence, also the increasingly common use among the
westernized indigenous élite of traditional dress (pioneered in
India much earlier by Gandhi) and indigenous language,
together with the rejection of western forms of government and
law. In these and many other ways Afro-Asian societies have
attempted to rewrite their own history to deny that there was
an imperial impact.

This, of course, is to write fiction. The imperial impact is
immutable, even though its superficial forms can be altered at
once and its effects will wear thin over time. Every post-colonial
State and society bears the imprint of its colonial experience and
is different from what it might have been had it never become
a dependency. For the historian of modern European colonialism
of the distant future it will be as fascinating to disentangle the
threads which lead back to the colonial past of Africa, Asia, and

Latin America, as it has been for historians of the post-
Roman world to pin-point the continuing influence of Roman
law and culture on western Europe and the Mediterranean.
The function of a Foreword is to pose questions, not to
provide answers. In terms of the approach adopted above
the critical question is how Malta fits into this general
theory of the impact of empire on dependent societies.
Seen from the standpoint of the general historian of modern
imperial systems, Malta is not unique but belongs to a
restricted category – that of very small territories within
the European world whose culture and religions are those
of western Christendom and thus has much in common with
the parent State; but whose inhabitants, though ethnically
not very different, speak a different language from that of
the imperial power and whose laws and institutions have
a long and distinguished history. In the British experience,
the only other comparable colonies have been Gibraltar
and, for limited periods, Minorca and the Ionian Islands.
Like them Malta was acquired in the course of the interminable
international struggles of the period before 1815 and then
retained mainly to keep France out, rather than because
Britain wanted or needed it. In course of time, however, a
function was found for Malta as the main Mediterranean
naval base west of Alexandria, and it retained this function
and utility into the 1950s.

This fact was likely to be decisive for the way Britain
handled Malta. Had the aim continued to be merely negative – to deny it to France (or later Italy) – the British
would not have had to contrive any significant 'policy' for
the island: they could merely have treated it as a loose
protectorate on the later model of, say, Tonga. Because
they needed to use it and its inhabitants, policies were
necessary.

What these were and what impact they had on the Maltese
are the questions which this book attempts to answer. Each
writer approaches the same problem from a different slant
and reaches different conclusions. Inevitably their subject-
matter is specific to Malta, since all history is specific.
But the problem, as I have tried to suggest, is of much
wider importance because it is common to all imperial

systems at all times. This book is therefore a valuable contribution to the general history of modern European imperialism.

Jesus College,   *D.K. FIELDHOUSE*
Cambridge

Editor's Preface

British Malta can hardly be said to have been neglected by historians; its political history, in particular, possesses a respectable literature.[1] Without trying to underrate the value and importance of such works, no attempt has, unfortunately, been made to study the period through a total or near-total approach. The long years I have been teaching the subject at Advanced Level, together with the difficulties I encountered, have prompted me to try and remedy this deficiency. The result is the present volume, which has taken the form of a collective work, drawing together a team of specialist contributors. Together they will explore, through their essays, the extent to which Maltese society, in some of its major aspects, had been modified by the impact of its long British colonial experience.

Change is, therefore, the overall theme of the book – the slow departure from old habits, a small Mediterranean island society yielding, in imperceptible stages, to a perhaps unintended process of Anglicization. 'It is by indirect and for the most part unintended influence,' wrote Sir Henry Maine in 1880,[2]

that the British power ... metamorphoses and dissolves the ideas and social forms underneath it, nor is there any expedient by which it can escape the duty of rebuilding upon its own principles that which it unwillingly destroyed ... We do not innovate or destroy in mere arrogance. We rather change because we cannot help it. Whatever be the nature and value of that bundle of influences which we call Progress, nothing can be more certain than that, when a society is once touched by it, it spreads like a contagion.

Writing in 1820, W.I. Monson observed that, within the short span of two decades, the actual presence of the British on the island of Malta was already rendering the place 'pleasing to an English eye'.[3]

The cleanliness and regularity of the streets (of Valletta), the moderate height of the houses, combined with the view of our troops on guard, our manufactures in the shops, and our language almost universal, gave the town an English look. ... This little country is, indeed ... fast nationalising, though there are still some who remember with affection old times. The spirit of chivalry has yielded to the genius of commerce; and the change is, in my opinion, too violent. Mercantile pursuits seem to monopolise their minds; for it has given a turn to the well known industry of the natives.

A few years earlier, George Whitmore, too, recorded his impressions of the island, fast experiencing 'a strange change from the darkness visible of former days'.[4]

The streets presented such a variety of costumes that the carnival itself could not exceed it, while every vacant spot under the shelter of awnings or arcades was filled with stalls and merchandise. It had been the endeavour of Sir Alexander Ball to remove sundry nuisances which were not tolerated in other civilized cities but had obtained a footing at Valletta. For this purpose he erected places for public conveniences, to prevent the general defilement of the streets, and stuck up a notice to the effect in Italian and English over the entrance of the city on the sea side.
He also prohibited the owners of hogs from turning them loose in the town. The convents opposed this measure so strongly that the point was conceded to their pigs ...

It was a foretaste of the profound structural changes that Maltese society was to experience through the 164 years that separated the end of the revolutionary upheaval in 1800, against the French administration of General Vaubois, from the island's attainment of Independence in 1964. During this period, writes Brian Blouet,[5] transformation

took place in a society which was highly individual and the new social patterns which emerged were distinctive and Maltese: the islands retained their character and personality.

The student of nineteenth- and twentieth-century Malta would do well to ask himself how much of this change has been total, how much of it emerged as a natural historical development, independent of the British influence, and how much of it was artificially imposed, or created, to suit the needs of the colonial power. Certain elements of continuity in Maltese society – indigenous traits in its habits of mind, lifestyle, customs and traditions, and in the character of what is left of the rural landscape — have survived both the ravages of time and the insensitive assault of modernization. These elements — the Braudelian 'constants' — that still look proudly primitive, would be fairly easily recognized today by either Alexander Ball or Giorgio Mitrovich.

A survey in the form of the present book cannot claim to be either exhaustive, or 'perfectly balanced'. No contribution in this collection, for example, deals directly with the political or constitutional development of British Malta, although aspects of both issues emerge frequently in the essays. The first three chapters are of an introductory nature: the origins of Maltese nationalism; a general view backwards of Maltese politics through the ages; and Britain's role in the Mediterranean during the period under review. All the other thirteen papers in the book[6] attempt to study the development of important aspects of Maltese society under the influence, or pressure, of British colonialism. These range from the structure of everyday life and patterns of behaviour to Church-State relations and the nature of the local economy; from the question of identity and nationhood to Malta's fate within the British imperial decolonization; from her developing art and architecture to literature and other dimensions.

My first, and greatest, debt of gratitude must be to the sixteen distinguished scholars who have contributed to this volume, which is as much the product of their effort as of mine. I also owe a great debt both to Professor D.K. Fieldhouse of Jesus College, Cambridge, for having so generously accepted to write a Foreword, and to the Institute of Cultural Anthropology/Sociology of Development of the Free University of Amsterdam which very kindly offered to have this work published under its auspices.

Many special thanks are due, too, to my colleagues on the editorial board of *Hyphen:* Louis J. Scerri, Joe Zammit Ciantar, and Charles Caruana Carabez. The idea of publishing a book on Malta to commemorate the tenth anniversary of our Journal was originally theirs. Louis J. Scerri's interest in the present book, his encouragement, and his advice and criticism have helped me a great deal. He has also provided the index. I am also grateful to David Cremona and Mario Buhagiar for kindly accepting to go through most of the text, indicating errors and inconsistencies which had escaped my attention, and suggesting improvements.

I hope this book will finally convince my wife that the long hours I have had to spend every day away from her were all in a good cause.

NOTES

[1] See, for example, the works by Henry Frendo, Hilda Lee, Joseph M. Pirotta, Edith Dobie, A.V. Laferla, and others, in the Bibliography.
[2] H.S. Maine, *Village-Communities in the East and West,* 237-8.
[3] W.I. Monson, *Extracts from a Journal,* 124-5.
[4] *The General: The Travel Memoirs of General Sir George Whitmore,* ed. Joan Johnson, 32.
[5] B. Blouet, *The Story of Malta,* 2nd ed., 197.
[6] Chapters 7 and 8 of the book have originally appeared in *Hyphen* ii, 5 (1981), 195-211, and ii, 6 (1981), 235-55.

1

VICTOR MALLIA-MILANES

The Genesis of Maltese Nationalism

Historians have traditionally considered the Maltese revolution
of 1798 against the French Government of General Vaubois as
'a brief but glorious episode'.[1] This definition errs in
perspective. It ascribes to the revolution, which dragged on for
two years, two attributes which are alien to its real place and
significance in Maltese and British colonial history. The
dramatic events which were sparked off on 2 September were
neither of an episodic character, nor were they in any sense
isolated from the historical continuity of nineteenth- and
twentieth-century Malta. Rather, in the perspective of the
longue durée, the revolution constituted in its totality 'the initial
traumatic event' which 'acted as a catalyst' for the emergence
of the long, structural movement of nationalism and
independence.[2] The history of subsequent years was a logical
development of these years: for, the moment the national leaders
thought that their victory over the French was a *fait accompli,*
the Maltese Congress was dissolved; Captain Alexander Ball,
in whom the Maltese rebels 'had found a leader who seemed able
to weld their isolated endeavours into a coherent movement',
was recalled to his naval duties; and Major-General Pigot was
invested with full executive powers on the island. The Maltese
leaders' expectation of being entrusted with political power was
frustrated, their hopes thwarted by disappointment. The
'cession' phenomenon was desecrated, dwindling into one of
'conquest'.

Was it for this that we took up arms and made our brave stand against
the tyranny of France?[3]

Not unlike the French, the British had entered Malta 'as friends, to establish themselves as masters.'[4] It was this tragic twist of fate, following so closely and so abruptly on the recent revolutionary experience, that ushered the nascent Maltese nationalist movement into a new dimension by unleashing forces that would irresistibly create and deepen new antagonisms. From the 1820s onwards, the pervasive influence of the Italian refugees on the island, both through their actual presence and through their profuse literary and political activities, would soon evolve into an intimate Romantic association with the bourgeois sectors of the local community and give rise to a forceful ideological response to the identification of parallel social conditions, grievances, and needs then obtaining in British Malta.[5]

At what stage in its historical development can Malta be said to have begun 'to take on a sense of national consciousness'? In 1798 a small intellectual minority succeeded in mobilizing popular forces in the urgency of overthrowing a regime in the general interest. They awakened the local inhabitants to an acute consciousness of the betrayal on a national level and, in so doing, they prepared an 'ideological framework for unity' against any other form of political aggression in the future. They created at once an awareness of what was sacredly theirs by right, and a state of readiness to defend it. In September 1798 this sense of national consciousness, restricted to the educated few, received the moral approval and physical support of the unrefined masses in a combined effort to assert their collective identity – a deed which Ernest Renan would have called 'tangible' and 'solid'.[6] What appeared to have been at first a spontaneous rural protest, primitive in kind, in the remote capital of the island, soon developed into an organized armed revolt on a national scale.

Over 150 years earlier, in a brave attempt to establish the identity of the Maltese people, his countrymen, Gian Francesco Abela had published his erudite *Della descrittione di Malta.*[7] Though inaccurate in many respects, it was the first history of the glorious past and an account of the rich legacies of a society which had hitherto been noted mainly for its cultural archaism and economic backwardness.[8] Abela dispelled this perhaps not altogether unfounded impression. Once its euphoric distortions and misconceived notions are with reverence discarded,[9] his narrative neatly sums up in an integrated whole all the major elements which made of the Maltese people a 'social homogeneity', a potential nation.[10] These elements included: an unassuming, compact archipelago within a European cultural sphere of influence; a native common language of Semitic origins, which recent research has shown to have been employed in some early form of literary exercise in the fifteenth century;[11] a profound attachment to Roman Catholicism, their focus of national unity, whose cults and catacombs, shrines, priests, and church bells had left through the ages an indelible imprint on the indigenous mentality; common institutions which were associated in the popular mind with a modicum of political freedom and civil liberties; ancient customs, traditions, and heroic folk memories; in short, a common past, recalling historical experience of great sacrifices and grand moments of patriotism. Essentially, these elements constituted the 'grand solidarity' of the Maltese community as one distinct people, a latent force lending itself to an unrealized potential. But the slow, painful process of its realization had in fact begun, perhaps unnoticed, years earlier and only gathered momentum during the latter half of the eighteenth century.

Tension is known to have prevailed in Malta between the absolute Prince Grand Master and the inarticulate, largely illiterate, majority of the population, very often under the politico-spiritual guidance of the secular clergy, ever since the accession to the magistracy of the austere Jean Parisot de la Valette in 1557.[12] His relentless suppression of municipal rights, his curtailment of individual freedom, and his remorseless extortion of taxes had set the style and pattern for later magistracies. This forceful intrusion upon the individual and the indigenous community as a whole occasioned the gradual alienation of the ruled from the knightly ruling class of foreigners. During the next two centuries, such tension was accentuated by the cumulative effect on Maltese society of a consistent demographic growth, general social and economic improvements, the slow rise of a prosperous bourgeois class, and the gradual infiltration into the island in the late eighteenth century of enlightened ideas of liberty and equality, revolutionary notions of government, and physiocratic theories of trade, by way of knights, nobles, and merchants.[13]

However, it is not until the social historian of Malta has diligently scrutinized the dusty, archaically catalogued, records of the *Castellania* (the Order of St John's Criminal Court of Justice), and other related documentation, in order to determine the nature, frequency, and pattern of popular revolts and disturbances, their economic and political content, the social composition and motives of the rioters, and the impulses which had stung them into violent action, that we shall be able to ascertain with credibility this gradual process of realization. At present, the only evidence available is fragmentary, limited to a few, isolated, though fairly vociferous, occurrences. Joseph Callus, one of the island's national heroes, is the earliest known victim of such overt opposition to the knights' regime. His daring petition of grievances to Philip II of Spain, denouncing the authoritarian character of la Valette's government as an ubiquitous erosion of his countrymen's ancient rights and privileges, led him to the gallows in 1561.[14] The popular uprising in Gozo in 1603 against the high-handed treatment of the 'governor', who represented 'the person and authority' of the Grand Master on that island, was another instance.[15]

In 1637 an outburst of popular anger was precipitated by Grand Master Lascaris's decision to impose a widely resented tax on income to finance the Floriana fortifications. The clergy of the rural parishes maintained that the Maltese people had been exempted from such taxation by right of ancient royal concessions and objected to the Order's style of government in general. Although actual violence was averted, the wide national resistance offered to the tax collectors succeeded in securing its immediate object. From a direct tax on income, it was converted into an indirect levy on edibles.[16] Again in 1638, in an effort to reclaim traditional privileges, a certain Antonio Sardo, on behalf of his fellow Maltese, exposed Lascaris's 'misgovernment' in a *cahier de doleance* to Philip IV of Spain.[17] Another emotional upheaval was provoked by a similar attempt in 1671 to raise through taxation some 100,000 scudi, this time to finance the Cottonera fortifications, which were to prove, it has been too rightly observed, 'a bottomless pit which swallowed up everything the Treasury could scrape together'.[18] Once more, an economic grievance which had begun, as in 1715,[19] as a demand to ease economic burdens, extended into the political sphere, involving clerical immunity and fruitless appeals to Rome against denials of ancient rights and privileges.

As the eighteenth century wore on, spontaneous popular riots grew more frequent and began to assume a more articulate manifestation. Ange Goudar, [20] writing in 1776, identified six different uprisings in Malta in the span of fifteen years between 1760 and 1775. On at least one occasion the temper of the people was such that words like 'Poveri Maltesi, in che miserie vi ha portato questo Gran Maestro' were daubed on the Magistral Palace in Valletta.[21] Others even threatened a 'Sicilian Vespers'.[22] If Giorgio Cavalcabò's observations are anything to go by, the political atmosphere was becoming so tense that knights dared not move out of the city of Valletta and peasants dreaded the very idea of having to spend the night there.[23] The revolt of the clergy in 1775[24] was symptomatic of a growing general discontent among the various sectors of society – knights, priests, slaves, merchants, and peasants – with the absolute power of the 'prince', a rebellious feeling of insubordination and disillusionment, pervasive and widespread. In 1796 Antonio Miari, the Venetian Republic's representative in Malta, feared the imminent outbreak of a serious revolt, and was quick to report it to his accrediting authorities:[25]

For several days in these parts certain disturbances have been noticed and some fears entertained, caused by certain inflammatory bills, which have been affixed even upon the doors of the Magistral Palace.

In January 1797 another (or was it perhaps the one Miari had feared?) attempt at revolution by the Maltese people was discovered. The ringleaders were either condemned to death or exiled. One of them was Mikiel Anton Vassalli, an intellectual young man with strong nationalist feelings, and a severe critic of the Order, who sought to 'dispel the darkness of ignorance'. His death sentence was later commuted to life imprisonment in Fort Ricasoli, after his having disclosed the names of his fellow conspirators. Vincenzo Barbara was another.[26] Were the Maltese becoming increasingly conscious of their traditional servile attitude and gradually trying to repudiate it?

Napoleon's conquest of Malta in June 1798 was the logical culmination of a subtle process of Gallicization of the island.

During the course of the eighteenth century, a special
dominance-dependence relationship had been cultivated between
France and Malta, through which the former succeeded in
politically dominating the Order and keeping it economically
dependent on her. Considering the Order's constitutional
hostility towards Islam, this was necessary policy for France in
her consistent drive towards gaining and sustaining commercial
supremacy in the Levant and, in so doing, she undermined in
imperceptible stages the reason for the Order's existence.[27]

Malta offered France, as it did all other Christian powers,
spacious natural harbours for shelter and safe anchorage,
transit-trade facilities, a ready source for the recruitment of
sailors and soldiers, sumptuous warehouses, arsenals, efficient
quarantine services, and free hospitalization. But it was the
preponderance of French knights, the numerical superiority of
French sailors and privateers over subjects of all other
nationalities, who regularly and consistently availed themselves
of these services, the commercial ties which Maltese merchants
thought it favourable to their interests to foster with French
merchants, and the Common Treasury's increasing dependence
on the *responsiones* accrued from the three French Langues of
Auvergne, Provence, and France, which long before June 1798
had virtually turned the island into a French colony.[28] From
1765, for example, the Maltese began to enjoy the right of
citizenship before French tribunals.[29] But the slow process of
change through Gallicization ran deeper.

The lengthy period of prosperity which eighteenth-century
Malta had experienced, marked by sustained demographic
growth, economic development, social stability, and general
improvement, had aroused among sections of the community
new hopes, new desires, and new expectations, irresistibly
accompanied by the stirrings of restlessness already noted.
Concurrently, French influence had extended its sway still
further in the field of social and cultural life, defying with
surprising comfort, as it were, the massive network of
impenetrable fortifications. Enlightened ideas, manners,
fashions, and refined tastes flowed from the shores of France
to those of Valletta alongside Frenchmen and French
merchandise and found easy assimilation among the polite
society of the capital, where the Maltese collaborated with the

knights in fashionable academic circles and refined cultural activities.[30] Such familiarity not only strengthened their aspirations. It provided the necessary psychological climate to nourish among the same social milieu a corresponding belief in their value capabilities. 'The glamour and glitter of society in Malta' in the years preceding the fall of the Bastille, claims Ryan,[31] are reflected in the wills of individual knights and in the number of private libraries and rare collections of early books and manuscripts over the island. They are equally evidenced in the impressively elegant private buildings and noble public edifices 'embellished within and without with all that art and money can supply'.[32]

Regrettably, however, very few contemporary writings provide light for an understanding of Maltese thought of the period. Notwithstanding the exclusive environment of the educated few, the innate conservatism and increasingly authoritarian character of the Order, the pervasive influence of the Inquisition and the intellectually abhorrent sense of apprehension it engendered, the rigorous application of censorship, the domineering influence of the Roman Catholic Church over all forms of education, and the physical insularity of the country – all these factors rendered the development of new, liberal, unorthodox thought and the spread of political ideas critical of the Order's style and method of government, if not perhaps altogether impossible, certainly difficult.

The outbreak of revolution in France in 1789 undermined Grand Master De Rohan's enlightened programme of 'social reconstruction'.[33] With the nationalization of all the knights' possessions in that kingdom three years later and an inevitable deterioration in the Order's relations with the new Republic after the abolition of the monarchy, there was a sudden halt in the island's prosperity, a sharp economic downswing, and a consequent decline in value capabilities.[34] The initial kindly disposition of the same respectable sectors of society to Napoleon's brief sojourn in Malta in June 1798[35] lay within the logic of rational expectations. The efficiency and benevolence of the early phase of the new administration, epitomized in the declaration that 'all inhabitants of Malta are equal. Their talents, merit, patriotism, and their attachment to the Republic shall alone establish any difference between them',[36]

8   VICTOR MALLIA-MILANES

contrasted sharply with the 'arrogance, tyranny, and oppression'
of the Order's.[37]

To the politically conscious sectors of Maltese society the
débâcle of June 1798, located within the context of Napoleon's
professions of intent, signified the breaking of the fetters on the
exercise of their rights, the daybreak of their future. If only for
a short moment, Napoleon meant the triumph of their
expectations, the fulfilment of their desire to break loose from
their previous condition, the futility of which the June days were
vociferous enough evidence. The Maltese people had inherited
from their past a subservient attitude. The Order's paternal
government had rendered them obedient and lacking in political
self-reliance. Those, it has been claimed, [38] who had conceived
the project of conspiring against the Order had neither the
influence, the power, nor the means to realize it. Napoleon
succeeded in catalysing what would have presumably taken
much longer to materialize; for it was only *after* the islands had
fallen into French hands that the Maltese are said to have
betrayed their open hostility to the Order.[39] Until then, claims
Miége,[40] they had remained 'passive spectators of events',
implying a slackening of revolutionary impulse. But was it, in
fact, the threatening presence of French cannon and an imposing
French fleet in the harbour that explain Grand Master
Hompesch's decision to capitulate? Was it his certain knowledge
of treachery within the Order? Or was it, rather, the ultimatum,
presented to him by the defiant people's representatives at the
moment when he had not the strength to subdue them, either
to capitulate or, failing that, to face a popular insurrection?[41]

Napoleon had not only shown the way. At a deeper level, the
traumatic events which he set in motion were a lesson in
psychological regeneration. They were a timely and potent fillip
to the Maltese leaders' value expectations. To the clear-minded
observer, the French occupation was an indication of the
feasibility of building in Malta a new political system different
from the Order's. This awareness grew in intensity in direct
proportion to the increasing realization that the initial hopes
were after all an illusion, until it developed into a subconscious
impulse to make possible what had just been proved feasible.
Napoleon promised the Maltese what he had only two years
previously promised the Italians. 'Your property, your religion,

and your usages will be respected,' he had told the Italians in 1796.[42] To the Maltese, on 12 June 1798, he declared that they would continue to enjoy 'as in the past the free exercise of the Apostolic and Roman Catholic Religion', that they would 'preserve their property, and the privileges they now possess', and that 'no extraordinary contributions' would be imposed.[43] The Maltese, like the Italians, soon learned that neither General Vaubois, nor his garrison, had entertained any intention of upholding Napoleon's pledge. Malta, like Italy, 'was a country to be sacked and pillaged' by the self-styled liberators.

The genuineness of Maltese aspirations and the crude realism of French politics proved irreconcilable. Napoleon's enlightened political philosophy was alien to the style of life in Malta. His thorough reorganization of society[44] was a blow — crisp, sudden, and decisive — to the islanders' deeper values: their stability and security, their strong family attachment and profound sense of honour, their pride in traditional loyalties, their staunch Catholic convictions combined with their deep-rooted fanaticism, the devout practices of their faith which held an intimate relationship with whatever sense of national integrity and identity they entertained, their thrift and frugality. Napoleon's relentless violation of values, which completely paralysed their aspirations, was inevitably bound to generate reaction, an essential prerequisite for historical change. The form and content of most of his forceful impositions and the accelerated pace with which they were carried out shattered all hopes of relaxation. The cumulative effect of his ruinous economic measures, [45] dictated by an urgent search for new sources of revenue, his insensitive religious reforms[46] inspired by an 'enlightened' spirit of anticlericalism and irreligiosity, the uncompromising arrogance of the behaviour of French troops,[47] and the psychological impact of thwarted expectations that the evils which had hitherto afflicted Maltese society would be cured, provoked a deep spiritual restlessness, a general mutinous commotion throughout the island. This widespread disenchantment manifested itself in the prolonged, determined rebellion to regain the threatened characteristic Maltese way of life, to reassert its past in an attempt to reassure itself of a better future. The bold initiative of 2 September 1798, precipitated by confirmed rumours of the French disaster at

Aboukir Bay towards the end of August,[48] was occasioned by
the short-lived French attempt to sell by auction the immovable
property of the Friars Minor at Rabat and despoil the Carmelite
Church at Mdina.[49]

The events that signalled the outbreak of revolution are
common knowledge; their outline need here be only briefly
given. The circulation of wild rumours of the latest French order
for the closure of Mdina church alerted the country people
beyond endurance. On Sunday 2 September, large crowds
clustered at Rabat and Mdina. Before long, Louis Masson, the
French officer in command of the old capital and the first to earn
the contempt and hostility of the angry mobs, was murdered.
The next day, the furious mood of the villagers was raised to
a higher pitch by a few shots from the garrison that had already
decided to surrender. The garrison was butchered, their bodies
burned 'on a nearby hill'. Other French sympathizers, including
an elderly knight 'identified with the shameful capitulation of
11 June', met the same fate. Throughout the country the
tricolour was hauled down. On top of the old medieval bastions
of Mdina, majestically overlooking a wide expanse of
countryside, the Maltese red and white flag was hoisted in a
gesture of triumph and vindication. After this violent affray,
all the French troops on the island ignominiously retreated in
safety within the bastions of Valletta and the harbour cities.

One aspect which has not been given due consideration by
historians is the relevance of the attempted conspiracy of
January 1799 to the revolution as a whole. This abortive attempt
had at least one fundamental importance. It widened the
dimension of the insurrection of 2 September. It lent a sense of
all-inclusiveness, of breadth and collectiveness to the villagers'
action by demolishing the obstacles which had physically divided
the people into two distinct camps, those within and those
outside the Valletta fortifications. It welded the two sides in a
'mystical union' and gave the revolution a truly national
character. A 'national-popular movement' appears to have
developed.

It is within such a context that Dun Mikiel Scerri should be
properly viewed. Estranging him from the essential reciprocity
of his role in action would only succeed in marring the true
image of the man. The moment he is divorced from the vital

participation of his fellow countrymen within and outside Valletta, his stature in historical reality — as distinct from popular Romantic fiction — would inevitably collapse, his meaning would become unintelligible, his significance negligible. Scerri's recognized position in Maltese history is comprehensible only in association with the totality of the revolution, as an integral part of an organic whole. Divested of all philosophical rhetoric, the message which he conveyed through his secret correspondence with Canon Francesco Saverio Caruana was simple, clear, and unmistakable.[50] He identified himself with the fears and aspirations of the people. His infectious enthusiasm for the realization of their deepest desires, his simplicity, and his intensity of feeling gave Maltese nationalism stimulus and inspiration. Though at times he showed trepidation at what appeared to him an unnecessary delay and irresolution among the village leaders, which gave him the impression that their faith in the success of their task was faltering, he strove through his letters to mobilize their nationalist sentiments and love towards their fatherland by emphasizing the virtues of patriotism: sacrifice, steadfastness, and unyielding determination against the overwhelming odds that surrounded them on all sides, and by warning them against the resistance that patriotism would necessarily encounter. His correspondence was not lacking in political content. His was a positive assertion of his love of the *patrie*, his faith in the ideal of liberty, his hope of freedom, the urgency of the public good, and his belief in the sanctity of conspiracy against despotic rulers, and in its redemptive effects. What bound the Maltese together on either side of the fortified walls of the city was a 'sentiment of sacrifice' which they shared in one 'grand solidarity'.

One of the French rationalist writers, the Abbé Sieyès, had declared in 1789 that

the nation exists before all things and is the origin of all things ... In whatever manner a nation wills, it is sufficient that it does will; and its will is always the supreme law.[51]

The Maltese revolution of 2 September 1798 and the subsequent siege were a clear assertion of this new principle of national sovereignty. In 1798 the Maltese *had willed* a complete

and absolute change of government. The exercise of their
sovereignty was evident in their actions and deliberations. Two
days after the general insurrection of 2 September, a provisional
revolutionary government was established with the name of
National Assembly. Its work appears to have been at first
difficult. There were elements of pride, prejudice, and
personality, which made for discord and division within the
leadership. On 11 February 1799, under Captain Alexander
Ball's influence, the Assembly was reformed into a
democratically elected, representative National Congress. It was
composed of 22 delegates elected by the heads of families in every
village or casal, together with Bishop Labini's vicar to represent
the clergy, and one judge. At once, writes Temi Zammit,[52] the
congressmen, assuming as of right full sovereign authority —
deliberative, political, legislative, and executive —

took steps to distribute food to the people, to collect funds, to maintain
order, and to administer justice, for which purpose the tribunals at
Notabile were reconstituted.

On 5 September they placed themselves under the protection
of the pro-British Ferdinand IV of Naples, proclaiming him their
legitimate sovereign. Proposed by Francesco Saverio Caruana
— the voice not only of the people, as Ball called him, but also
of realism in the Assembly — this was for the time being
necessary policy. It was the only means, in circumstances such
as those currently obtaining in Malta, to secure food provisions
and military supplies. At every stage the Maltese deputies
claimed to be acting 'on behalf of the entire Maltese nation'.[53]

On 5 September 1800 the French capitulated. The
achievement of the Maltese was neatly summed up in Brigadier-
General Thomas Graham's address, dated June 1800.[54]

Brave Maltese
Without arms, without the resources of war, you broke asunder your
chains. Your patriotism, your courage, your religion, supplied all
deficiences. Your energy commanded victory, and an enemy formidable
to the best-disciplined armies of Europe yielded in every point to your
unexampled efforts, and hid their disgrace behind the ramparts. The
gallant battalions of Casals have ever since confined them there, with
a vigilance and patience worthy of the cause of freedom.

The sheer enormity of their task combined with the obvious

economic and technical limitations of Maltese society. This realism was acknowledged in the second great exercise of the people's sovereignty. They *willed* great-power protection to preserve the gains of their revolution. By 6 January 1799 the Maltese had already expressed their desire 'to be under the English'.[55] Ball claimed that they had 'a great dislike to the Russians' and an equally 'great antipathy ... to the Neapolitan King'. They had recognized in Great Britain a more powerful protector, a more useful ally in their attempt 'to liberate themselves from the French'.[56] On 31 March 1799 the congressmen petitioned Ferdinand 'to accord [their] request of transferring the sovereignty of these two islands to His Britannic Majesty'.[57] After the capitulation they were still determined, as they declared in an 'Appeal' to Charles Cameron, the Civil Commissioner, on 19 October 1801, 'not to submit to any other power than Great Britain' − not even to the likely return of the Order of St John. They were prepared, they claimed, 'to perish under the walls of their city if they cannot maintain their liberty and independence'.[58]

Earlier that year, Cameron announced that King George III had granted the Maltese 'full protection and the enjoyment of all [their] dearest rights'.[59] To the public mind, these 'rights' were believed to have been traditionally invested in such national institutions as the *Consiglio Popolare* and the *Università*. The basis of this 'belief' may, indeed, be partly or wholly mythical; nonetheless, in terms of pure popular psychology, what matters is not whether such beliefs correspond to historical truth, as the Royal Commission of 1812 had tried to find out, but whether they are genuinely embedded in emotional reality. In the mid-1770s, for example, Canon Vittorio Gristi, Chancellor of the Holy Office of the Inquisition, recorded in his unpublished memoirs that he had noticed a close relationship between the increasing autocracy of Grand Master Pinto and a corresponding decline in the autonomy of the local *Università*, the overriding image of a people stripped of the last vestiges of their rights and privileges.[60] This belief was not confined solely to the sacred realms of tradition. During the uneasy Amiens years, when Britain's retention of the island was far from certain, the British representatives felt themselves inclined to promote 'the development of self-government' in

Malta 'in order to neutralize the influence of France on the island'.[61] George Whitmore is more specific in his memoirs.[62]

It favoured the policy of Great Britain to please and flatter the Maltese to the utmost − their future destiny was not yet sealed, and it was a primary object to reconcile them and those who were soon to be their avowed masters. Their public games and the great functions of the Roman Church were not only patronized by the presence of the Protestant authorities, but we refrained from appropriating the ecclesiastical structures which devolved on us from the Knights of St. John.

Was Cameron's proclamation an unwittingly cynical reverberation of Napoleon's fatal promises, one that would lead the people in unexpected directions?

No discrepancy existed, however, between Maltese nationalism and loyalty to Britain as protector. A balance had been struck between the two, the basis of which appears to have lain in the 'neutral attitude' of the Maltese towards a 'necessary subordination'. But the balance proved fairly precarious. Even before the war had broken out again in May 1803, the British authorities were revealing what appears to have been a belated acknowledgement of the injudiciousness of Pitt's decision to reject De Rohan's offer of Malta as a naval base in the early 1790s.[63] They were now realizing that the island's 'value had become too great ... to accept a compromise over its future'.[64]

After their experiences in 1798-1801, the French knew that any major move in the eastern Mediterranean had to be considered excessively risky so long as Britain held Malta. For Britain the evacuation of Malta would mean the loss of its only advanced base and would be tantamount to a return to the black year of 1796 when the Mediterranean as a whole had had to be abandoned. Britain had not a single ally in southern Europe. The commercial ports formerly most used by merchants, notably Livorno and Ancona, remained closed and under French control. Consequently the ministers refused to implement their undertakings at Amiens to evacuate Malta, although this gave the French propaganda advantages.[65]

It was, ironically, Britain's reluctance to honour the terms of the Treaty of Amiens, itself the cause of so much umbrage within the Maltese national leadership, and which had evinced so many 'protestations of attachment' to the new protector, that destroyed the balance. The new role assigned to Malta would be one based on its significance as a fortress, a concept that would allow no recognition of popular sovereignty. 'The Maltese,' says Lee,[66] 'were not prepared for this development of policy'. Once more, the 'solvent' of the Maltese' loyalty to their protector was their becoming aware, for the second time within the span of five years, that their interests were different from those of the metropolis'[67] – a perfect replica of 1798.

The revolution of 1798 had no lasting effect on the economic or social structure of Malta. Over the next century and a half, change in these spheres would be slow and protracted, presumably because the British had not come to Malta, as they had done in India, in search of markets, but to gain a strategic and military advantage over their rivals. The only structural change was effected at the level of the island's political culture. By the time the Maltese found themselves on the threshold of their long British colonial experience, a value-system, expressing the deeper aspirations of the people, had already been identified. The forces of nationalism had been set in motion.

NOTES

[1] See, for example, V. Denaro, *The French in Malta,* 65.
[2] For a brilliant exposition of the relationship between the 'event' and 'structural change', E. Le Roy Ladurie, 'The "Event" and the "Long Term"' in *Social History: the Case of the Chouan Uprising',* 111-31.
[3] *Appeals of the Nobility and People of Malta,* 79-80.
[4] W.I. Monson's remark on the French. *Extracts from a Journal,* 132.
[5] On the Italian refugees in Malta during the Risorgimento, B. Fiorentini, *Malta rifugio di esuli e focolare ardente di cospirazione;* G. Mangion, *Governo inglese, Risorgimento italiano ed opinione pubblica a Malta;* V. Bonello, B. Fiorentini, L. Schiavone, *Echi del Risorgimento a Malta.*
[6] E. Renan, *Qu'est-ce qu' une nation ?,* 27.
[7] Published in Malta in 1647.
[8] See, for example, the Order of St John's Eight Commissioners' Report of 1524, reproduced in I. Bosio, *Dell'Istoria della Sacra Religione,* iii; J. Quintin, *Insulae Melitae Descriptio.*
[9] On Abela and his work, *Gian Francesco Abela: Essays in his Honour;* N. Dennis, *An Essay on Malta;* A.T. Luttrell, 'Girolamo Manduca and Gian Francesco Abela: Tradition and Invention in Maltese Historiography', 105-32.
[10] For a definition, L.L. Snyder, *Varieties of Nationalism: A Comparative Study,* 25.
[11] See, G. Wettinger, M. Fsadni, *Peter Caxaro's Cantilena: A Poem in Medieval Maltese.*
[12] G. Wettinger, 'Early Maltese Popular Attitudes to the Government of the Order of St. John', 266, 273-4.
[13] J. Montalto, *The Nobles of Malta,* especially chapter xix.
[14] A. Mifsud, 'Papi, Fortificazioni e Tasse nel Passato di Malta', 420; P. Cassar,

Medical History of Malta, 17-19; id., 'A Medico-Legal Report of the Sixteenth Century from Malta', 354-9; S. Zarb, 'Matthew Callus', 50-62; J. Galea, 'Matthew Callus: A Myth ?', 63-8.

[15] V. Mallia-Milanes, 'In Search of Vittorio Cassar: A Historical Approach', 249-50.

[16] See, A. Hoppen, *The Fortification of Malta by the Order of St. John,* 148-9; Mifsud, 241; V. Borg, *Fabio Chigi, Apostolic Delegate in Malta,* 51-4; A. Koster, *Prelates and Politicians,* 24.

[17] Wettinger, 263.

[18] E. Schermerhorn, *Malta of the Knights,* 209.

[19] Hoppen, 150.

[20] *Reflexions sur la dernière émeute de Malthe,* cited after F. Venturi, *Settecento riformatore,* iii, 14-16.

[21] P. Fava, 'A Reign of Austerity', 50.

[22] Ibid.; R. Cavaliero, *The Last of the Crusaders,* 155.

[23] See Venturi, 14-16.

[24] Cavaliero, 216.

[25] V. Mallia-Milanes, 'The Order of St. John 1793-1798', 105-106.

[26] C. Testa, *Bejn iż-Żewġ Naħat tas-Swar,* i, 94; F. Panzavecchia, *L'Ultimo Periodo della Storia di Malta,* 343-7. On Vassalli, A. Cremona, *Vassalli and His Times;* P. Cassar, *The Quest for Mikiel Anton Vassalli;* J. Cassar Pullicino, 'M.A. Vassalli in 1798-99'.

[27] See, for example, J. Godechot, 'La France et Malte au XVIIIe Siècle', 67-79.

[28] Hoppen, 158; Cavaliero, 48, 275; Godechot, 67.

[29] AOM 272, ff.61-64, 'Lettere Patenti del Re di Francia, Luigi XV, con le quali gli abitanti di Malta vengono naturalizzati regnicoli di Francia', 12 July 1765.

[30] See F.W. Ryan, *The House of the Temple, passim.*

[31] Ibid., 132-3.

[32] J.H. Cooke, *Sketches written in and about Malta,* 14.

[33] Ryan, 134.

[34] Mallia-Milanes, 'The Order of St. John 1793-1799', 104-105.

[35] See Bosredon Ransijat's letter to Napoleon, 17 July 1798, in W. Hardman, *A History of Malta during the period of the French and British occupations,* 90.

[36] Ibid., 81; Ryan, 319.

[37] Hardman, 1.

[38] A. Mifsud, *Origine della sovranità inglese su Malta,* 30.

[39] Ibid.

[40] M. Miége, *Histoire de Malte,* iii, 61.

[41] See Giuseppe Maria Capodieci's *relazione,* in G.V. Ellul, 'The French Invasion of Malta', 7-20, and, especially, 12.

[42] J.E. Driault, *Napoleon en Italie,* 2.

[43] Hardman, 61.

[44] Ibid., 74; see also H.P. Scicluna, *Actes et Documents pour servir à l'Histoire de l'Occupation Française de Malte.*

[45] Bosredon Ransijat, *Journal du Siège et Blocus de Malte,* 279; Denaro, 59-61.

[46] Ibid., 46-54.

[47] F. Cutajar, *L'occupazione di Malta nel 1798,* 19, 31.

[48] Denaro, 54.

[49] Cavaliero, 245 *et seq.*

[50] For Scerri's correspondence, Testa, ii, 383-99, 401, 405-410.

[51] E. Sieyès, *Qu'est-ce que le tiers Etat ?* See also P. Bastid, *Sieyès et sa pensée.*

[52] T. Zammit, *Malta,* 263.

[53] Hardman, 113.

[54] Ibid., 305; Zammit, 389.
[55] Ball to Nelson, in Hardman, 162, 176, 187.
[56] Ibid., 192-5.
[57] H. Lee, *Malta 1813-1914*, 15.
[58] Hardman, 406-407.
[59] Zammit, 391.
[60] AIM, 'Giornale Istorico' (1775-6), an anonymous manuscript attributed to Canon Vittorio Gristi.
[61] Lee, 16.
[62] *The General: The Travel Memoirs of General Sir George Whitmore*, ed. Joan Johnson, 31.
[63] Mallia-Milanes, 'The Order of St. John 1793-1798', 99-101.
[64] J.R. Jones, *Britain and the World 1649-1815*, 278; A. Cobban, *A History of Modern France*, ii, 41-2.
[65] Jones, 278-9.
[66] Lee, 17.
[67] D.K. Fieldhouse, *The Colonial Empires*, 103.

2

GODFREY WETTINGER

The Nature of Maltese Politics, c. 870-1964

No sooner is one historical myth laid to rest than another arises to take its place. Now that the two-thousand-year constant faithfulness of the Maltese people to the Christian religion has been shown to be legendary,[1] a new belief is growing up to the effect that the history of the Maltese Islands has been one of constant colonialism for at least the last two thousand years, a condition that was terminated only by the achievement of independence during the latter part of the twentieth century. In fact, all the past history of the Maltese Islands is normally regarded by the Maltese man-in-the-street, and especially by the politician, as a long undistinguished period of colonialism, with the local inhabitants in a position of inferiority and dependence vis-à-vis the foreign ruler.[2] A moment's reflection, however, should convince anyone that this is merely the reflection backwards down the centuries and millennia, back to Roman and Punic times at least, of beliefs which had become a habit in the long years of British rule during the nineteenth and twentieth centuries. For a proper understanding of Maltese and other history, it is obviously essential to refrain from using criteria utterly foreign to the period or people involved. Nineteenth century colonialism had important features which distinguished it from any other previous systems of government or, indeed, any other previous type of colonialism.[3] This was also the time when national consciousness was rapidly rising to its triumphant peak during the second and third decades of the twentieth century.[4] Contemporary colonialism became merely the rule of one people over another, not that of a State over another, or that of a dynasty over its subject peoples or another dynasty. Incidentally, in any case, none of the latter have normally been considered as varieties of colonialism.

No particular conceptual problem arises for the whole of the British period. Malta, like Great Britain, was subject to the British Crown, and nationalism was certainly less rampant as an ideology in Great Britain than in most other European countries of the time.[5] But even then,[6] it is clear that the local Maltese population and the members of the armed forces of Great Britain were quite distinctly set off against each other, the former being always politically and, for long, also socially in a position of inferiority to the others, and very few of the Maltese were themselves sufficiently well-off economically to be able to aspire to a position of economic equality with the British settlers.[7] The latter were themselves exiguous in number since there was really little reason for them to stay on the island unless they had an official job to perform, except for the English merchants who took refuge in the island during Napoleon's Continental System. After some years under the War Department, Malta was relegated permanently to the Colonial Office, whose administration was at best paternalistic, at worst domineering and churlish. The attitude of the population at large, on the other hand, ranged from critical and resentful alienation for some to fawning acceptance of the inevitable and mercenary servility for the others.

Political nationalism in Malta itself, in the sense of the fight for political rights over and against the foreign ruler, took a double form: an insistence on internal self-government, at first by appeals to supposed medieval rights conceded by the Aragonese rulers, and also an obstinate resistance to British cultural assimilation and an openness to Italian cultural influences not very different from the antagonism of Bulgars and other Slav peoples of the Balkans to Turkish rule and their opennness to Russian cultural and even political penetration. On the other hand, internal tensions which had been building up for centuries, now became evident in more than one sphere of life. There were the natural differences between town and village inhabitants with their different exposures to foreign influences, those between industrial and farming attitudes to work, those between the few rich and the many who were, for much of the time, desperately poor. There were, in particular, the abrasive differences between the traditionalists and those who were more open to new ways of life and thought, mainly between those brought up in the local version of Italianity and those who, rightly or wrongly, embraced Anglicization with all that it entailed.

The occupation of Malta by the French in 1798-1800 was too brief for the establishment of a permanent *modus vivendi* to be arrived at.[8] Certainly, while a section of the population together with some knights looked on the new rulers as harbingers of better things with the abolition of the nobility and slavery and the passing of various secular laws, the rest looked on with unabated suspicion, resorting to open rebellion at the first opportunity. That led to a couple of years of bitter fighting, in some respects taking on the nature of a civil war, accompanied with summary executions, the exiling of opponents, and the collapse of the island's population figures.

The 268 years of rule of the Order of St John over Malta had a unique juridical character.[9] While the local population found itself in a permanent position of inferiority and dependence, the Order claimed, and largely exercised, for most of the time, a sovereign authority over the Maltese Islands. It would be highly imprecise to claim that Malta was a colony during any part of this period. Of course, the Order depended for its survival on financial subventions from its landed property situated abroad throughout what remained of Catholic Europe, but there was no constitutional dependence on any part of the whole of Europe except for the shadowy maintenance of a feudal subjection to the King of Sicily which became increasingly meaningless with the fading away of feudal concepts. It was, however, precisely to this feudal subjection that the early political leaders of Malta looked for protection against the autocracy of the Grand Master until the tragic history of Joseph Callus in 1561 revealed its weakness in the world of real politics.[10] The Order was also spiritually subject to the authority of the Pope, a position which became politically of supreme importance during the troubles that occurred towards the end of the rule of Grand Master de la Cassière as well as during the eighteenth-century appeals to Roman tribunals of Greeks who had been plundered by vessels flying the flag of the Order. It enabled the Maltese clergy to oppose the Grand Master by sheltering under the protection of the Papacy.[11] They received only very limited support, however, from that quarter, just sufficient to earn them a great increase of political stature so that, during the seventeenth and eighteenth centuries, they became the chief spokesmen of political discontent.[12] The nobility and other lay opponents of the Order either left the island on the Order's arrival in 1530 or allowed themselves to be cowed into submission or even subservience, although elements among them segregated themselves at Mdina, living their life apart from that of Valletta, the new centre of affairs.[13]

In fact, very little is known for certain or in detail of the islanders' attitude to the coming of the Order.[14] An early clerical political agitator, Dun Filippu Borgia of Birkirkara (1567-1649), claimed that he had heard from his maternal grandmother that it used to be said that the Order would not remain in Malta more than a hundred years, after which it would go to Sardinia where it would end in a puff of smoke, while the Maltese would go to the town of Pulici in Sicily.[15] According to this writer, the common people who were disgusted with their native nobility gave their free consent to the coming of the Order, while the nobility opposed it. The people had long been praying that a ruler would arrive who would maltreat the nobles as much as the commoners, and prognosticating that 'A sparrow hawk would come out of the east, and it would put the peregrine falcon to flight away from its nest'.

It would therefore appear that the main opposition to the Order's rule over Malta came at first from the nobility, and only later from the populace by then under the leadership of the clergy protected by their privileges and the Papacy. On the whole, however, the Order's rule was autocratically benevolent in character and disaffection was generally quite restrained, flaring up only on the rarest of occasions as in the 1630s and in 1775. The year 1575 saw the establishment of the Inquisition in Malta, with the Inquisitor also acting as nuncio in the island.[16] This led, as is generally well-known, to the development of a three-cornered power struggle, the local political game henceforth centring around the relations of the Grand Master, the Bishop, and the Inquisitor, with the local notables lining up behind one or other of the three contenders.

The rule of the Order also saw a complete transformation of the island's economy, with the Order consistently pumping in large sums of money for defence and naval purposes, eventually resulting in the construction of five towns around the harbours with their massive fortifications and imposing administrative buildings.[17] The multiplying factor in the economics of the islands was no doubt responsible for the concurrent changes that were also transforming all the larger villages, though the smaller ones tended instead to languish, or even die out. On the other hand, one can argue that the dead hands of the Grand Master, the Bishop, and the Inquisitor where private initiative was concerned were largely responsible for the retarded mental and cultural development of the islanders, who were largely isolated from what was happening on the continent of Europe whether in the religious or in the political spheres. Thus Lutheranism, after some initial success in the first half of the sixteenth century, was stamped out and Malta's religious development became largely a matter of conformity, formalism, and folklore.[18] Only a small section of the population seems definitely to have fallen under the influence of the French *philosophes* and the Enlightenment of the eighteenth century.[19] Certainly the latter were to vie with the local clergy in their opposition to the Order towards the end of its rule but their relative weakness is revealed by their inability to counteract the opposition of the clergy to the reforms which were introduced by the French in 1798.[20]

One might imagine that the clergy were even more dominant in Maltese political life during the pre-1530 period. It does not, however, seem to have been so at all. That was, in fact, a period when public affairs were managed largely by the small landed class living at Mdina who held feudal and non-feudal land. Though the Church's spiritual influence was held in check only by the great ignorance of the inhabitants in religious matters and the prevalence of popular superstition, it was not allowed any direct or indirect role in the exercise of political power on the island. Thus the clergy could not, by the laws of the Sicilian kingdom, attain to any of the municipal or royal offices, they did not represent the villagers in the town council, and, in fact, attended meetings themselves only when specially summoned for the purpose to discuss matters which involved their Order

directly, except for the Bishop or the Vicar General who attended
normal meetings though the former was not normally resident
on the island. In 1427-8 the clergy acted as peace-makers
between the island rebels and the royal court: they certainly
were not ringleaders so far as one can see.[21] The town notables
themselves on that occasion seem to have succeeded in raising
the whole island against their rector or governor, Consalvo
Monroy, in spite of the evident alienation of the country people
from those of Mdina.[22]

Foreigners were sometimes marked out for adverse comments,
especially Catalans. In 1463 the Catalan merchants were
accused of harassing their local debtors,[23] but in 1411 the
section of the population that favoured the Catalan monarchy
worsted its opponents after serious tumults which led to the
death of at least one person and the outlawing of another, the
victorious side shouting triumphantly *Vivat Rex Aragoniae.*[24]
Perhaps this was because it was still too close to the Age of the
Tyrants, the time when the whole Sicilian kingdom was
dominated by four great nobles, Malta itself falling under the
control of a count or marquis instead of remaining under the
direct control of the Crown.[25] This, in fact, seems to have been
the most constant aim of the Maltese throughout the Later
Middle Ages. It is first heard of in 1198 when the Empress
Constance first promised the Muslim and Christian
municipalities of Malta and Gozo that their islands would never
again be enfeoffed but would remain on the royal domain.[26]
The promise was broken soon afterwards. It was renewed by her
son, the great Emperor Frederick II, *stupor mundi,* and
subsequently by the Aragonese kings in 1283, 1350, and
1397.[27] The last similar promise was made in 1428 after the
Monroy episode.[28] This time it was not to be broken until 1530
when the islands were granted to the Order precisely as a free
and unencumbered fief. Mere rumours in 1451 that the islands
were about to be granted to the Spanish Order of Montesa were
enough to arouse the wrath of the local notables in the town
council.[29]

Throughout the Later Middle Ages, Malta and Gozo formed
integral parts of the Sicilian kingdom even when enfeoffed as
a county or marquisate. Again it would be wrong to think of
Malta's status then as that of a colony, although the island was

to see a steady stream of settlers from Europe landing on its shores, marrying local girls, and eventually becoming absorbed among the local population, thus helping powerfully in the constant Latinization of the local population which, however, must have had a largely Moorish character for most of the time.[30] Constitutionally, Malta's position *vis-à-vis* Sicily was one of dependence *de facto* but of equality *de jure*, because both islands belonged to the same dynasty, and it was that which counted then. Malta depended on Sicily for its food supplies[31] and for its ultimate defence.[32] Otherwise, however, it went largely its own way except in so far as the Crown was concerned: in all administrative matters in Malta and Gozo, as in every other Sicilian municipality on the royal domain, the final authority was always that of the King and his officials at Palermo. Every part of the kingdom was exploited for the sake of the commonwealth.[33] There was no Colonial Office, of course, at Palermo in charge of places like Malta, Gozo, Pantelleria, or Djerba, because the concept itself did not exist.[34] The Maltese at the time seem actually to have desired a greater strengthening of their ties with Sicily or, to be more precise, with the Sicilian Crown in order to escape the exactions and vexations of their local gentry and local grandees or overlords, the Counts or even the rectors or governors like Monroy. There was therefore no idea at all that Malta should have its national autonomy because the idea would have been anachronistic.[35] On the other hand, there was no awareness of any particular Italianity, or even Sicilianity at that, in the Maltese people at all at the time. The desire to form part of the royal domain had nothing to do with it.[36] When their ultimate sovereign resided at Bruxelles or Barcelona they were not at all averse to petitioning him there, bypassing the Viceroy at Palermo, though they still had to have his answer and royal commands put into effect from Palermo, the centre of government. They sometimes called their own language their *lingua materna*,[37] otherwise referred to by them more vaguely by such phrases as *ut vulgo dicitur* or *ut vulgariter,* while they referred to Italian in the Italian way as the *volgare.*

Practical problems of geographical distance and the constant operations of the Tunisian corsairs made it advisable for the Maltese authorities in practice to enjoy a greater measure of

autonomy than most if not all Sicilian towns, though Messina
was usually held up in Malta as the model municipality to aim
at, insisting that Malta should be treated as an actual street
of Messina.[38] The town council of Malta habitually discussed
defence matters, the provision of cannon, and the equipment of
the town militia.[39] The inhabitants were allowed to have their
own local courts of appeal on the island to obviate the necessity
of local people going on the long and dangerous trip to Palermo
to pursue their appeals.

Locally, much of the power struggle revolved during the
fifteenth century around the continual bickerings between the
island's municipality and its officials on the one side and the
Castellan of the Castle-by-the-Sea and his garrison together with
the surrounding inhabitants, especially those of Birgu, on the
other.[40] Some members of the local nobility were strongly
entrenched at Mdina, others held offices like that of *Secreto* and
Castellan which provided them with a power base of
considerable relative strength. Marriage arrangements
frequently occurred between these important personages and
members of their families, but rarely brought peace for more
than a short time.[41] The Crown bought support locally by
means mainly of the grant of crown lands, especially from 1372
onwards,[42] a process that was carried to such lengths that,
quite early in the fifteenth century, some grants had to be
revoked to retain sufficient income for the Crown to provide for
the expenses of keeping garrisons on both islands.[43]

Throughout most of the last 140 years that preceded the
coming of the Order, the main political problems seem to have
revolved around sharing out the municipal offices that had to
be vacated and filled every year.[44] This annual event was
frequently accompanied by accusations of the abuse of power
by the outgoing officials, allegations which were regularly
examined by the incoming ones at first, and later investigated
thoroughly by a royal official, the *sindicaturi,* sent over for the
purpose, presumably because the older system was no longer
functioning as it should. On occasion, parish priests were asked
to inform their parishioners that they had to present their
complaints at a given date for a hearing and possible redress.[45]
It was sometimes requested that the town mayor, or *hakem,* had
better be a foreigner.[46]

Church-State quarrels did occur during the fifteenth century, but they were concerned mainly with such matters as the opposition to the claims of the Bishop over the property of deceased clergymen leading in 1479 to the placing of the whole town council under an interdict,[47] the unfortunate choice by the Bishop of a young foreign clergyman who did not know Maltese,[48] or the continual long absences of the Bishop from his diocese.[49] Conflict between laymen and clergymen centred on such matters as the payment of tithes[50] — a problem also met with during the fourteenth century,[51] payment of first-fruits to the parish clergy,[52] allegations that the people were not properly provided with the church services they needed. Confrontation with the Papacy occurred in the early sixteenth century over the papal advowson to ecclesiastical benefices on the island because the Pope frequently preferred foreign ecclesiastics around him to local ones who could better administer to the people.[53]

In pre-Aragonese times, under the Angevins, the Suabians, and even the Normans, Malta's connection with Sicily was already one of a purely dynastic nature. No active and explicit colonization is known to have occurred throughout those periods. The settlement of some townsmen from Celano, a town in the Abruzzi, can be shown to have been a mere exiling in chains of persons who had fallen out of favour with the Suabian authorities.[54] Though it is recorded that at least one of them actually died in Malta, eventually the survivors were pardoned and allowed to leave. In any case, they are not likely to have numbered more than a few score at most. They certainly left no perceivable sign of themselves on the island and its inhabitants or their language.[55] The arrival of free European Christians presumably started in Norman times, from 1127 onwards — the earliest possible date for the re-establishment of Christianity and of a Christian regime on the island. Such settlers are likely to have been predominantly of male sex, their children born locally adopting the local form of spoken Arabic, literally their mother's tongue, as their language of preference and, in all probability, as the only one they knew properly in most cases.

It was during this period that occurred the beginning of the second decisive change of the last thousand years in Malta's cultural set-up, the gradual switch from an Islamo-Arabic to a

Christian European but Semitic- (i.e. Arabic) speaking culture.[56] This must have been the main political as well as religious problem for the whole of the twelfth and thirteenth centuries. It is recorded to have led to at least one murder of a Muslim during the reign of King Roger who died in 1156 and the placing of the Christian communities under an obligation to pay an annual fine not forgiven until 1198. Gradually Islam was worn down, until finally, around 1249, its last exponents who refused baptism were sent into exile to Lucera, possibly after a last-fling rebellion.[57] This left the Jews as the only non-Christian community in Malta. Possibly some friction existed here as in Sicily between members of the Greek form of Christianity and those of the Latin, the ex-Muslims themselves in Sicily apparently preferring to adopt the Greek rather than the Latin rite, which was the rite of their rulers and erstwhile persecutors.[58]

This was also the time when Malta first began to be given to Counts, apparently in recompense for their services to the rulers of Sicily as Lords High Admiral.[59] That the inhabitants did not approve of the arrangement has already been noted above. It should, however, here be added that Henry Piscatore was a redoubtable leader of his Maltese men in fighting abroad in Crete as well as in Tripoli (Lebanon) and was himself accompanied by Provençal troubadours.[60] He was of Genoese extraction, like others of his house, leading possibly to a great increase and consolidation of Genoese influence in the island, about which however not much is known. Certainly, Pisans and Genoese who met in Maltese waters did not look well on each other.[61]

Going further back to the so-called Arab, really Muslim, period, the main political issues would have centred around the relations between Christians and Muslims for the time that any of the former survived after the arrival of the Arabs around A.D. 870.[62] After the final disappearance of Christianity, the chief remaining problems, dimly perhaps documented if only the modern historian could refrain from reading more into his sources than is warranted by their precise words, is the mutual relationship of the free and unfree inhabitants. Complete equality was not obtained by the latter before they undertook to help them repel the Byzantine invasion of 1048 otherwise unrecorded. Malaterra's own account of the taking of Malta by Count Roger the Norman in 1090 does not refer to any local Christians. The only internal socio-political strife Malta seems to have had during the late eleventh century therefore appears to have been mainly limited to that caused by the existence of a relatively large slave community of Christian captives brought here by the local Muslim corsairs, the Jewish community itself being probably too small, and in any case unlikely, to cause any particular problem to the Muslim authorities. There might, on the other hand, have been Muslim sectarian conflict between Shiites and Sunni, seeing that the Shiite Fatimids ruled over this part of the Mediterranean for some considerable time.

The local Government was certainly headed by a *qa'id* or military governor and was normally subject to the Emirs of Sicily. Malta was therefore part of the Sicilian State under Muslim rule, the connection being at least in part a dynastic and in part a religious one. Here again it would be highly inappropriate to talk of colonialism in the nineteenth-century sense. This, however, does not mean that Muslims did not settle on the island in sizeable numbers. This would have been colonialism in the classical sense. The status of any unconverted indigenous inhabitants who remained in Malta after 870 could only have been that of the *dhimmi* at best, so well known in Islamic literature,[63] and it could very well have been worse. It is not excluded that they were expelled. Possibly they were reduced to the status of *ghabid,* though the *ghabid* of 1048 seem to have been completely Islamicized by then.[64] No authentic information is available of the details of the day-to-day running of the relations between the chief authorities in Malta and Gozo and their superiors at Palermo.[65] Between 1090 and 1127 Malta could have stuck to the agreements reached with Count Roger the Norman in 1090, recognizing his suzereignty and that of his son, King Roger, but possibly not steadfastly enough because the latter found it necessary to reassert his authority by a complete reconquest of the islands in 1127.

Looking back on the whole period, one is struck by the endless variation in the status of the islands ranging backwards from that of a nineteenth-century type colony, governed by the State authorities of a separate country almost two thousand miles away, to that of a largely autonomous State with a self-perpetuating oligarchical type of government of foreigners originating from most of the countries of Catholic Europe, faintly reminiscent of other oligarchical types of government of foreigners who ruled over Egypt, the Mamelukes, and over Tunisia and Algeria, the foreign *taifas*.

This was preceded by the status of an integral part of the kingdom of Sicily, frequently cut off from direct rule from Palermo by the use of a feudal nexus, in any case Malta's link being a dynastic one which also placed her for long periods under tutelage of the kings of Aragon, and for a brief one that of the Angevins and the Suabians. For a century Malta recognized the suzereignty of the Norman rulers of Sicily and before that that of the Muslim dynasties who preceded them and the Muslim caliphs of the Middle East. For most of the time, autonomy was not even an objective, and when it was the political philosophy behind it, when there was any, it was utterly foreign to the ideas of the nineteenth century. And for all the time, the play of local politics was circumscribed in ways particular to each period with very little that was continuous between one era and another. Only by a thorough understanding of this can one hope to grasp the full scope of the Maltese political scene down (or up) the centuries. Merely reading our past history with the eyes and ideas, and ideals, of the nineteenth and twentieth centuries will only confuse our minds and falsify our history.

NOTES

[1] Articles by A. Mayr, E. Rossi, A. Luttrell cited in G. Wettinger, 'The Arabs in Malta'.

[2] The numerous commemorative articles issued on the anniversaries of Independence or Freedom provide plenty of evidence of this view.

[3] D.K. Fieldhouse, *Economics and Empire*, with its excellent reading lists, is a good account of one of colonialism's main aspects.

[4] H. Kohn, *Nationalism: its Meaning and History*.

[5] Nationalism, of course, exists in England in less overt forms, and has spread in its more normal pattern in Ireland, Scotland, and Wales.

[6] Of course, it is not possible here to give a complete bibliography even of the best books on British Malta. These should suffice: E. Dobie, *Malta's Road to Independence*; H. Frendo, *Party Politics in a Fortress Colony*; J.M. Pirotta, *Fortress Colony: the Final Act*; see also B. Blouet, *The Story of Malta*.

[7] Two perceptive, even if sometimes haughty, accounts from the British point of view: *Malta, painted by V. Boron, described by Frederick W. Ryan*; and E. Shepherd, *Malta and Me*.

[8] A. Mifsud, *Origine della sovranità inglese su Malta;* W. Hardman, *A History of Malta during the period of the French and British occupations;* unfortunately, C. Testa's *Maż-Żewġ Naħat tas-Swar,* though carefully written, lacks detailed documentary references.

[9] All things considered, A.P. Vella's *Storja ta' Malta,* ii, is the best recent synthesis for Malta's history under the Knights from the point of view of the Maltese inhabitants.

[10] J. Galea, 'Matthew Callus: a Myth?'; S.M. Zarb, 'Matthew Callus'.

[11] G. Wettinger, 'Early Maltese Popular Attitudes to the Government of the Order of St. John'.

[12] P. Callus, *The Rising of the Priests;* see also V. Borg, *Fabio Chigi, Apostolic Delegate in Malta,* for information of suspicions of clerical involvement in the troubles of 1633.

[13] J. Montalto, *The Nobles of Malta.*

[14] R. Valentini, 'I Cavalieri di San Giovanni da Rodi a Malta: trattative diplomatiche'.

[15] Wettinger, 'Early Maltese Popular Attitudes'.

[16] A.P. Vella, *The Tribunal of the Inquisition in Malta;* A. Bonnici, *Maltin u l-Inkwiżizzjoni f'Nofs is-Seklu Sbatax.*

[17] Blouet, *The Story of Malta.*

[18] No adequate treatment exists of these more abstract elements of religion.

[19] R. Cavaliero, *The Last of the Crusaders;* C. E. Engel, *L'Ordre de Malte en Méditerranée.*

[20] A. Cremona, *Vassalli and his Times.*

[21] Wettinger, 'Early Maltese Popular Attitudes'.

[22] G. Wettinger, 'The Pawning of Malta to Monroy'.

[23] 'quod mercatores Cathalani vexant populum pro debitis indebito modo et non consueto', 7 March 1463, NLM, *Università* 11, ff. 181, *et seq.*

[24] ASP, *Protonotaro del Registro,* vol. 18, ff. 332^v *et seq.*

[25] I. La Lumia, 'I quattro vicari'.

[26] C. Schroth-Kohler, T. Kolzer, H. Zielenski, 'Zwei staufische Diplome fur Malta aus den Jahren 1198 und 1212', 519-20.

[27] H. Bresc, *Un monde méditerranéen: economie et societé en Sicile,* 682, 733-4, 785, etc.

[28] R. Valentini, 'Ribellione di Malta e spedizione alle Gerbe come conseguenze dell'inefficienza della flotta aragonese nel Mediterraneo'.

[29] NLM, *Università* 11, f.70.

[30] Wettinger, 'The Arabs in Malta', esp. 95-6.

[31] Id., 'Agriculture in Malta in the Late Middle Ages', esp. 13-18; A. Mifsud, 'L'approvigionamento e l'Università di Malta'.

[32] G. Wettinger, 'The Militia Roster of Watch Duties of 1417'.

[33] For all this, of course, the standard authority now is Bresc, *Un monde méditerranéen.*

[34] Bresc does, however, argue that Sicily, and therefore no doubt Malta, formed part of the economic periphery of the industrial and trading activity centred on Barcelona, and thus suffered from an unfair trading situation.

[35] H. Koht, 'The Dawn of Nationalism in Europe'; Gaines Post, 'Two Notes on Nationalism in the Middle Ages'.

[36] Bresc reports that Maltese persons at Trapani were regularly referred to as *nation maltaise* towards 1440. *Un monde méditerranéen,* 379.

[37] G. Wettinger, 'Linguistic Pluralism and Cultural Change in the Maltese Islands during the Middle Ages'.

[38] *Capitoli* granted at Barcelona, 2 January 1460. NLM, *Università* 3, doc. 10.

[39] NLM, *Università* 11, *passim.*

[40] Much of this is evident from the published and unpublished *Capitoli* or pleas for the redress of grievances that the inhabitants periodically addressed to the Crown from about 1410 onwards.

[41] Only detailed psephographical studies can adequately bring out the whole picture of the continual family manoeuverings during the fifteenth century.

[42] H. Bresc, 'Documents on Frederick IV of Sicily's Intervention in Malta: 1372'.

[43] R. Valentini, 'Il patrimonio della Corona in Malta fino alla venuta dell'Ordine'.

[44] The lists in G.F. Abela, *Della descrittione di Malta*, 422-43, are frequently erroneous: they must be emended by information from Maltese and Sicilian archives, the latter of which also contain much information on Gozitan officials.

[45] Thus the proclamations of 16, 18, 21 August 1479 asked all those who had any complaint against the retiring town mayor and his judge to appear before the jurats with their grievances.

[46] *Capitoli* of 24 March 1449.

[47] NLM, *Università* 11, ff. 417ᵛ *et seq.*, entries from 2 May 1480 onwards. See especially entry dated 9 June 1490, a discussion in the town council on the excommunication pronounced by the Bishop on the persons who attended the meeting of 2 May. Ibid., f. 426ᵛ.

[48] NLM, *Università* 11, ff. 471-73, town council meeting of 28 January 1481.

[49] Viceroy to Bishop, 31 August 1517. ASP, *Real Cancelleria*, 253, ff.358ᵛ-359ᵛ.

[50] Court papers have survived in some cases. See G. Wettinger, *The Jews of Malta in the Late Middle Ages*, doc. 98.

[51] G. Cosentino, *Codice diplomatico di Federico III Aragonese*, 488.

[52] A. Mifsud, 'Sulle nostre Decime', doc. II, 172.

[53] 'Indulto del Papa Leone X ... che i Beneficii non si diano a stranieri ma a' naturali dell'Isola', NLM, *Lib.* 494, f. 102ᵛ.

[54] 'In nostra constitutus presentia retulisti quod quondam Andreas Bacconensis, pater tuus, pro devotione quam gerebat circa Romanam ecclesiam a Frederici fautoribus captus et tamdiu apud Maltam in vinculo detentus extitit donec ibidem post plurimas angustias expiravit,' Perugia, 24 April 1252. Bibliotheque des Ecoles Françaises d'Athenes & de Rome, *Registres d'Innocent IV*, ed. E. Berger, iii, doc. 5693. This document was kindly pointed out to me by Mr J.T. McPartlin.

[55] The *Cantilena* of Peter Caxaro has only one word of Romance origin. The word 'wâri' is derived directly from medieval dialectal Arabic as it is recorded in the early fourteenth-century if not late thirteenth-century *Vocabulista in arabico* 212, meaning 'retro'; cf. A. Cassola, 'On the meaning of *Gueri* in Petrus Caxaro's *Cantilena'.*

[56] Maltese writers are usually chary of admitting the Arabic affiliation of the Maltese language and have been preferring the word *Semitic* instead, but that word is far less exact and in scholarly works unpardonably so.

[57] H. Bresc, 'Mudejars des pays de la Couronne d'Aragon et Sarrasins de la Sicile normande: le probleme de l'acculturation'; id., 'Società e politica in Sicilia nei secoli XIV e XV', 273.

[58] Bresc, 'Mudejars', 55.

[59] E. Mazzarese Fardella, *I feudi comitali di Sicilia dai Normanni agli Aragonesi.*

[60] D. Abulafia, 'Henry Count of Malta and his Mediterranean Activities'; J.M. Brincat, 'Le Poesie "Maltesi" di Peire Vidal'.

[61] A.T. Luttrell, 'Malta e Gozo: 1222-1268'.
[62] Wettinger, 'The Arabs in Malta', and the authorities cited there.
[63] Cf. Cahen, 'Dhimma'.
[64] Cf. Daniel Pipes, *Slaves, Soldiers and Islam*.
[65] G. Vella, *Codice diplomatico di Sicilia sotto il governo degli Arabi*.

3

ANN WILLIAMS

Britain and the Mediterranean, 1800-1960

Already in the eighteenth century Britain's policy in the Mediterranean was being shaped partly by her relations with other European powers and partly by her economic interests in an increasingly wider world. The Peace of Utrecht (1713), a series of treaties disposing of the problems of the Spanish Succession Wars, gave Britain Gibraltar (captured in 1704) and Minorca (captured in 1708). Anglo-French rivalry was a dominant issue in the Seven Years War. The unsuccessful attempt of Admiral Byng to relieve Minorca after French troops had landed on the island was the prelude to the second struggle in 1756. There was already concern too about Russian ambitions in the Mediterranean and about the state of the Ottoman Empire.

The coalitions against Napoleon marked a clear appreciation of the importance of the Mediterranean. The smaller states were drawn into positive alliances with the larger ones. Tuscany and Sardinia joined Britain, Russia, Austria, and the Ottoman Empire in 1799. Napoleon's expedition to Egypt and his dramatic annexation of the country disturbed Britain, particularly because the overland route to India was already important in her thinking.

The changing relationship with Malta in these years, perhaps, illustrated the slow beginnings of 'an attitude to empire': Russia's ambition to gain influence in Malta and the Mediterranean through the Order of St John was quickly appreciated by France who moved into the island. England was much slower to see that it was no longer possible just to free

Malta without taking over herself. The dispatches of Nelson and Captain Ball during the blockade illustrated the course of the debate.[1] In October 1798, Lord St Vincent had seen the British role as primarily a naval exercise:

First, [he listed] the protection of the coasts of Sicily, Naples and the Adriatic, and in the event of war being renewed in Italy, an active co-operation with the Austrian and Neapolitan armies. The cutting off of all communication between France and Egypt, that neither supplies nor reinforcements may be sent to the army at Alexandria. The blocking up of Malta, so as to prevent provisions being sent into it, the co-operating with the Turkish and Russian squadrons that are to be sent into the Archipelago.[2]

The implication was that these interests existed only for the duration of the war with France and that afterwards it would not be necessary to maintain a garrison in the island. However, changing attitudes in the course of the conflict against Napoleon encouraged the British to remain in Malta. Its proclamation as a Crown Colony in 1813 marked a new stage in Britain's Mediterranean policy. As the voice of the Government of India grew stronger for the protection of communications through the Mediterranean, Malta became more important; the Crimean War and the opening of the Suez Canal were two major milestones on this route.

In the eastern Mediterranean, the closely-linked issues of the overland routes to India and the support of the Ottoman Empire in whose territories they lay, became more pressing, and once again the voice of the Indian administration was dominant. 'During the nineteenth century, it forged South Asia into a single unit for defence purposes by means of annexations, alliances, and the exercise of influence, and extended that unit into the Middle East.'[3] Its methods were successful. Support of emerging, nationalist movements was all right if it were the Greeks in 1821; all British statesmen had had a classical education. Muhammad Ali's ambitions in the 1830s to unite Egypt and Syria seemed more dangerous. Britain and France were temporarily in agreement in their desire to see his power limited to Egypt and the Sudan. Palmerston was anxious that Britain should maintain her presence by diplomacy and naval presence alone. Only in the Crimean War in 1854 did she resort to belligerence to restrain Russia from gaining naval access to the Mediterranean. The Peace of Paris encouraged Britain to hope that the Ottoman Empire would accept constitutional reform and become an acceptable ally, but fear of growing nationalism within the empire led to renewed agression. Egypt was demanding more attention. The opening of the Suez Canal in 1869 and Disraeli's purchase of the Khedive's shares in the waterway in 1875 led a year later to Anglo-French Dual Control of Egypt's finances. Britain and France were increasing their power in the Mediterranean. France began her conquest of Algeria in 1830 and went into Tunisia in 1881. Britain gained another island, Cyprus, in 1878. The businessmen of both countries were extending loans and supporting enterprises throughout the Mediterranean area. The British Government, the great supporter of *laissez-faire*, did not want it to be supposed that she interfered in order to protect financial investors. Gladstone, looking back in 1884 on the increased involvement in Egyptian affairs, stressed: 'Our policy was not a policy for the benefit of a number of creditors or bond holders, or whatever you call them, but it was a policy of an Imperial character, and with the minimum of interference to maintain the position of that important country so important in the chain of our communications.'[4]

In the last decade of the century Britain's enthusiasm for the 'good old Turk' was dampened by the atrocities in Armenia and Bulgaria. Salisbury, who became Prime Minister in 1886, exercised a dominant influence on foreign policy and his major concerns were to reduce French influence in Egypt and to help Russia out of Constantinople. The Mediterranean situation was complicated by the ambitions of newly-united Italy and her rivalry with France.[5] It was imperative too to reach an agreement with Germany in Africa. By 1890 Salisbury was ready to move back into the Upper Nile provinces and to appreciate that Germany, with whom he had been negotiating to keep the peace in the Mediterranean, was more of a threat than an ally. After the clash of arms at Fashoda in 1898, Britain moved to better relations, and finally to the Entente of 1904 with France which gave the latter predominant influence in Morocco, a new source of Mediterranean unrest. Britain herself gained a free hand in Egypt. Anglo-German rivalry became the dominant constraint of the new century. The outbreak of the

First World War led Britain into a new phase of commitment
in the Mediterranean and particularly in the Middle East. The
Ottoman Sultan joined Germany, thus giving the allies the
opportunity to plan for the eventual demise of the vast Ottoman
Empire. They began a series of negotiations and secret treaties
to settle the Arab provinces. The Sherif of Mecca, the Amir
Hussein, in correspondence with the British High Commissioner
in Egypt, Sir Henry McMahon, was promised Arab independence
with the reservation that the largely Christian areas west of
Damascus, Homs, Hama, and Aleppo were excluded, an
arrangement which did not mention Palestine. At the same time
Britain and France were making other arrangements for the
division of the spoils. In November 1915, Sir Mark Sykes and
M. Georges Picot drew up their agreement. Sykes obviously did
not consider the Hussein-McMahon letters binding because the
Sykes-Picot plan put the area from Gaza to Kirkuk in the British
sphere and that from Damascus to Mosul in the French, with
Palestine under international administration. Russia put in a
claim to control Constantinople.

The military situation in the Middle East changed in June
1916. The Arab Revolt occurred and Hussein, with British
financial and military help, raised the Arab tribes who moved
northwards from Arabia to join General Allenby. Allenby,
appointed Commander-in-Chief of the Egyptian Expeditionary
Force in 1917, took Palestine and Syria with Arab help. The
British position in Mesopotamia was strengthened when
Baghdad was taken in March 1917 and at the end of the war
she held a dominant place in the eastern Mediterranean.

Meanwhile, the diplomatic situation had changed
dramatically. In March 1917 the Tsarist regime in Russia was
overthrown, and the Bolsheviks repudiated the treaties of their
predecessors, and also themselves became involved in civil war,
so the Allied Powers felt no obligation to the postwar
Mediterranean. In April 1917 the United States came into the
war, and proved very critical of the secret plans for the
dismemberment of the Ottoman Empire. A further thread was
woven into the tapestry in November 1917 when in the Balfour
Declaration the British Government stated that 'His Majesty's
Government view with favor the establishment in Palestine of
a national home for the Jewish people and will use their best

endeavours to facilitate the achievement of this object.'[6]

All these conflicting promises were impossible to reconcile, and the Versailles Peace Conference did not settle the outstanding issues in the eastern Mediterranean. The Turkish leader Kemal Ataturk pushed on with his conquests and was finally able to get his Government recognized at Lausanne in 1923 and, as an important corollary, the supplementary regime of the Straits ensured an open passage through the Straits for international shipping. One of Britain's major concerns throughout the nineteenth century was settled satisfactorily, although in fact Britain had backed the wrong horse, Greece. The Arabs were not so fortunate; the Allies did not feel they were able to rule themselves, and the new League of Nations and its Permanent Mandates Commission made arrangements for their administration. Britain was given a mandate over Palestine; France administered Syria and Lebanon. Transjordan, part of geographical Syria, had been occupied by British and Arab troops at the end of the war, and it was eventually given to Hussein's son, the Amir Abdullah. His brother Feisal eventually became King of Iraq.

Both Jordan and Iraq lay under British tutelage. Britain and France had emerged clearly from the First World War as the major powers in the Mediterranean. France had already, before the war, become a colonial power in the area and Britain was now committed to a paternal presence too. Egypt had been burdened with large numbers of British and imperial troops and heavy requisitions of food had been made during the war. A strong nationalist opposition arose under Saad Zaghlul, and his arrest in 1919 caused a revolt. Lord Allenby was sent out as High Commissioner and at the end of 1919 the Milne Mission was promised to look into the position of Egypt. This unrest was mirrored by the *Sette Giugno* disturbances in Malta. The solution in Egypt was the abolition of the Protectorate in the declaration of February 1922 which made the country an independent state with its own rulers. Britain, however, retained the right to maintain troops to defend Egypt and the Canal and to control the Sudan.

The Middle East continued to be the pre-occupation of the twenties and Britain was lulled into reassurance by the disunity of the opposition. Even the punitive measures against the murderers of Sir Lee Stack in Egypt in 1925 failed to arouse response. Although the Jews were already settling in Palestine at the expense of the indigenous Arabs, the communities did not come into open conflict until the 1928 Wailing Wall incident. The more amenable Transjordan was given its own government in 1928 with British tutelage over finance and foreign policy. An Anglo-Iraqi treaty was signed in 1922 and in January 1931 the mandate was officially terminated. Good relations with Iraq were important for the growing oil industry, although Britain still regarded its exploitation as a company rather than a Government affair. Further afield, but still defending the route to India, Aden became a Crown Colony and treaties were signed with the Gulf States.

The third decade of the twentieth century was to give Britain a much rougher ride. The rise of Fascist Italy, Egypt's neighbour in Libya, increased the anxiety for the stability and protection of Egypt. Abyssinian problems led to a greater acceptance of Anglo-Egyptian interests and the 1936 Treaty authorized the stationing of British troops 'in the vicinity of the Canal' for its defence. In Palestine the effects of German Fascism were felt with greatly increased Jewish immigration from 1932 onwards. The result 'dispelled for good the British hope of muddling through in Palestine.'[7] Violence became endemic and Lord Peel's Commission in 1937 recommended partition. The open sore of Palestine was affecting Britain's relations with all the Arabs, although the day of reckoning was postponed by the Second World War.

The Middle East was not Britain's only concern in the thirties. Mussolini's rise to power meant that Italy again had to be treated seriously. Italian irredentists, who had for some time viewed Malta as part of Italy, were strengthened by the Fascists who spoke of a new Roman empire in the Mediterranean, the mare nostrum. Ambassador Grandi, Italy's representative at the Court of St James, in 1932 called Malta 'the Italian gem of the Mediterranean.' He hoped for the support of the British Fascist Party, but they remained firmly nationalist in declaring the islands British.[8]

The Duce's propaganda department took great pains in the thirties, particularly in Egypt and the Levant where they saw hostility to the British, in encouraging local discontent, and stressing Italy's 'right of priority' in the Mediterranean. In the western basin Pan-Fascists had visions of the linking of the Italian communities in Corsica, Tunisia, and Malta. Malta was even granted 'representation' in the Italian parliament on the eve of the Second World War.[9] Mussolini hoped that by the extension of Italy's influence and ultimately control over Corfu and the Balkans, and with increased settlement leading to more control over Egypt, Britain would be forced to recognize Italian supremacy in the Mediterranean and so ensure that British ships would have to ask permission for their movements in the area.

Britain's response to this was one of vacillation. Her strategic planners, looking at her global commitments, were doubtful if she could defend both her Far Eastern and her Mediterranean sectors, and were half prepared to sacrifice the latter.[10] In the 1935 crisis over Abyssinia she both reneged on her commitment to the League of Nations and also appeased Italy's aggression in the Hoare-Laval Pact of December 1935, which gave Italy part of Ethiopia immediately and the right of economic expansion and settlement in another zone. In spite of a public outburst in Britain against this cynical move, Mussolini took over Ethiopia.

There was concern, too, in the mid-thirties over Spain. Strategically she was well-placed in the western Mediterranean to dominate trade and communications in and out of the Sea, and Britain and France had 'striven for generations to keep her weak, amiable, and neutral.'[11] The violent Civil War which broke out in 1936, and the expansionist ambitions of Italy and Germany in Spain ended these hopes. Officially the British Government did not want to intervene and hoped for stalemate. The British volunteers could make an unofficial anti-Fascist gesture.

In January 1937, Britain made 'a gentleman's agreement' with Italy to maintain the *status quo* in the Mediterranean. It did not last. In 1937 Italy fortified Pantelleria and, a year later, her ambitions in Albania became obvious. The latter conquest had a great effect in swinging British Government policy against Mussolini's regime.

It was clear to both Britain and France that Italy was an uncertain quantity and that they must share the responsibility of protecting their interests in the Mediterranean. By the late thirties oil production in the Middle East was increasing in importance.[12] Both economic and strategic reasons demanded that the seaway should be kept open. France had no naval base east of Bizerta. At the beginning of January 1939, the new base at Mers-el-Kbir was begun. The French planned to base their Mediterranean strategy on the triangle Toulouse-Bizerta-Mers-el-Kbir (the last was necessary because Franco's success in Spain left this flank exposed). Britain had a line Gibraltar-Malta-Alexandria-Cyprus-Palestine, although in the last three she was by no means a welcome occupying force.

As events moved towards war, France and Britain continued this co-operation. It seemed clear that the Mediterranean and North Africa would be important if Italy could not be persuaded to remain neutral. At the other end of the Mediterranean, it was hoped that Turkey would remain friendly and unengaged. (The Italian invasion of Albania persuaded her to sign a tripartite treaty with Vienna and Britain in September 1939.) As a contingency plan it was agreed to divide the Mediterranean into eastern and western spheres separated by the Straits of Messina, the British taking care of the former, including Malta, and the French, the latter, including Tripoli.[13] In the event, the collapse of France put the whole onus on Britain as Vichy Governments were set up in French North Africa and the French Levantine mandates. The immediate anxiety that the Germans would take possession of the French fleet and block the Mediterranean was settled by the British, with reluctance, scuttling the ships in July 1940.[14]

In the eastern Mediterranean the British, with the Free French, invaded Syria in June 1941 to prevent German use of its air bases. Britain assured General de Gaulle that France's predominance over other European powers in the area would be prescribed, though Syria and Lebanon had been promised independence.[15] In Palestine, fortunately for Britain, the Jews had agreed, as Ben Gurion said, to fight 'this war as if there were no White Paper (the May 1939 document promising independence within ten years and limited Jewish immigration) and the ... White Paper as if there was no war.' Arab response was mixed; the Mufti and his supporters joined Germany, the majority remained neutral.[16] Egypt took no active part, but the Middle East Supply Centre caused hardship among the population.

North Africa was important militarily in two phases of the Second World War. The initial Italian offensive in 1940 against Egypt was not conclusive and, in the spring of 1941, Rommel's Deutsche Afrika Korps came to their aid. The Germans had also invaded Greece and Yugoslavia in 1941. The lowest ebb of British fortunes in the Mediterranean was reached in 1942 when Malta lay under siege and Tobruk had fallen. In November 1941, an Allied force of British and Americans invaded North Africa and, a year later to the month, the fall of Alamein marked a change in fortunes. Security in North Africa persuaded many doubters in the Middle East to keep a more friendly neutrality towards the British, and it provided a base for the counter offensive against the Fascists in Italy.

The world of 1945 was a poor and divided one. The wider issues of global diplomacy and the Cold War were reflected in the Mediterranean. Britain, for a brief while longer, was predominant in the Middle East as France had withdrawn from the Levant and was preoccupied with her internal security and her North African empire. Although she granted India independence, the route through the Canal was still important for the preservation of Commonwealth links and trade and for the passage of oil tankers. She felt that the presence of her troops was necessary to keep open the seaway, an illusion that the Suez crisis was to dispel. The oil industry had developed extensively in the latter part of the war and, although it was an international concern, Britain had a great interest in its protection. The Iraq fields and the pipeline to the Mediterranean made her anxious to see stable regimes in Iraq and Syria.[17]

The dominant figure of the postwar period was Ernest Bevin who 'presided over foreign and 'Imperial' affairs with a grasp of detail as well as a command of general policy in a manner unparalleled since Lord Curzon.'[18] He was in favour of non-intervention in the Middle East and of getting the United States to bear much of the cost of supporting the area. The Truman Doctrine, proclaimed in March 1947, saw Greece and Turkey as the potential sources of danger.[19] They were included in the North Atlantic Treaty Organization formed in 1949. Bevin himself had a grand design to establish a Pax Britannica in the eastern Mediterranean, linking Egypt, Cyrenaica (gained after

Italy's defeat), Iraq, and Transjordan, giving them sovereign authority, while they contributed military strength to the region, now that Britain could no longer rely on India as a manpower reserve.[20] The plan foundered on the disunity and tension of the Middle East. King Abdullah of Jordan was murdered in Jerusalem. Violent revolts broke out in Iraq in 1948.

Palestine, which Bevin had no desire to keep, could neither be held nor relinquished without violence. In April 1947, Britain put the thorny problem before the United Nations Assembly, and the United Nations Special Commission on Palestine (UNSCOP) recommended the partition into an Arab and a Jewish State and the ending of the British Mandate in 1948. In May of that year the State of Israel was announced. The Arab-Israeli war which followed left Arab refugee camps in the Gaza strip, a divided Jerusalem, and an enmity between the two peoples which no longer had any hope of reconciliation. It was a further slide downhill in Britain's decline of power in the Middle East.

In the central Mediterranean, Britain had taken on commitments in Libya and, in 1949-51, was preoccupied in arranging its independence while retaining an air base in the country. The proposals for the integration of Malta with Britain in the nineteen-fifties looked, for a brief period, as if it were heralding a new era in British colonialism with the island sending representatives to the British Parliament in London.[21] Malta, instead, moved towards independence in 1964, as is discussed elsewhere in this book.

The fifties saw increased United States and Russian tension in the Mediterranean. Mr Dulles stressed the importance of the 'Northern Tier' states after the Musaddiq incident in Iran in 1951 had shown the vulnerability of Britain in the face of nationalist uprisings. In February 1955, Turkey and Iraq made a pact of mutual co-operation (the Baghdad Pact), which was later joined by Britain, Pakistan, and Iran to counter Russian influence in the area. In Egypt, where Britain still had an important base, an army junta organized a bloodless coup and overthrew the King and the Constitution in 1952, and two years later Gamal Abdel Nasser took over control. He negotiated the end of the 1936 treaty with Britain and the withdrawal of British troops within a period of twenty months. The riots in Amman, the dismissal of Glubb Pasha in March 1956, the hostility felt for Nasser by the British Prime Minister Anthony Eden, the withdrawal of funds from the Aswan High Dam project, the nationalization of the Canal, and the Suez débâcle of 1956 are still being debated. The opening up of the British official documents for the period in January 1987 is confirming the muddle and perfidy of British policy.[22] More than ever it is clear that 1956 marked publicly the decline that had already taken place.

NOTES

[1] W. Hardman, *A History of Malta during the period of the French and British occupations*, 161-335.
[2] Quoted in Hardman, xxii.
[3] E. Monroe, *Britain's Moment in the Middle East*, 12.
[4] Parliamentary Debate (19 February 1884), quoted in D.C.M. Platt, *Finance, Trade and Politics in British Foreign Policy*, 170.
[5] C.J. Lowe, *Salisbury and the Mediterranean*, deals with the diplomatic manoeuvres of the decade.
[6] A. Williams, *Britain and France in the Middle East and North Africa*, 52.
[7] Monroe, 85.
[8] D. Mack Smith, *Mussolini's Roman Empire*, 88.
[9] M. Muggeridge (ed.), *Ciano's Diary*, 34.
[10] L.R. Pratt, *East of Malta, West of Suez*, analyses the concerns of the Chiefs-of-Staff Committee and their influence in these years, particularly 8-28.
[11] E. Monroe, *The Mediterranean in Politics*, 221.
[12] Monroe, *Britain's Moment*, 95. Only one-twentieth of the world's total supply came from the Middle East in 1938, but its loss would have been significant.
[13] I.S.O. Playfair, *The Mediterranean and the Middle East*, i, 28.
[14] Ibid., 131-8.
[15] A.H. Hourani, *Syria and Lebanon*, gives the text of the letters, 371-2.
[16] Williams, 29.
[17] Ibid., 111.
[18] Wm. R. Louis, *The British Empire in the Middle East*, 3.
[19] J.C. Hurewitz, *Diplomacy in the Near and Middle East*, ii, 273-5.
[20] Louis, 106.
[21] E. Dobie, *Malta's Road to Independence*, 165-73, and D. Austin, *Malta and the End of Empire, passim*.
[22] R. Rhodes James, *Anthony Eden*, uses Eden's papers extensively, and Keith Kyle, who is producing a book on Suez using the official documents opened up in January 1987, spoke of the machinations of British policy in this period at a Symposium of the Society for Mediterranean Studies, 'Suez Thirty Years After' held at St Anthony's College, Oxford, in March 1987.

4

JOSEPH BEZZINA

Church and State in an Island Colony

When we took possession of Malta, the great majority of the inhabitants of that island were Roman Catholics, and it was promised and proclaimed to the people of Malta that we would respect and protect their religion. In one of the proclamations of General Pigot, that officer declared that it was his duty as well as his inclination to insure to the Maltese people full protection for their religion and their property. Indeed, in every declaration on the part of the Crown of England with reference to the island of Malta, there was an open and solemn declaration that the religion of the Maltese should be confirmed, maintained, and respected.[1]

This declaration by Lord Russell in the House of Commons on 15 August 1853 defines Britain's policy regulating Church-State relations in Malta. To secure their position in the island, the British were increasingly conscious of the need to acknowledge an interdependence between the civil and religious authorities. This survey[2] seeks to outline the development of these relations and analyse those events that at times strengthened them, at times weakened them. With self-government in 1921, these relations entered a new phase: the colonial powers retreated in the background and their position was taken by the political parties and the Malta Parliament. These developments were to condition further these relations.

I The Official Policy Towards Religion

On 5 September 1800, as soon as the British took formal possession of Malta and Gozo, Sir Ralph Abercromby,

Commander-in-Chief Mediterranean, informed the Maltese that
'all rights, privileges, and immunities in Church and State were
to be preserved.'[3] Major-General Henry Pigot later re-affirmed
these British intentions.[4]

In accepting British protection, the Maltese did not forfeit any
privilege. The Declaration of Rights of 15 June 1802, signed by
the members of the National Congress that had been convened
during the French blockade,[5] affirmed that the King of Great
Britain was to uphold and protect their religion; that no other
temporal sovereign should be permitted to interfere in matters
spiritual or temporal; and that other religions were to be
tolerated.[6]

The British never agreed fully with the articles of this
declaration, but neither did they disregard them. The first Civil
Commissioner was instructed 'to meet [the Maltese] wishes, to
show [himself] indulgent even in their prejudices, and to omit
no fair opportunity of conciliating their affection and ensuring
their fidelity'.[7] In a country where the life of the people
revolved around the Church, this meant co-operation in religious
affairs. The Royal Commission of 1812 concluded that the time
was not yet ripe to abolish certain priviliges; that 'would
undoubtedly draw down the indignation of an angry priesthood
and, through their means, create a considerable degree of
discontent among the people'.[8]

Such a policy was confirmed in 1813 in Lord Bathurst's
instructions to Sir Thomas Maitland, the first Governor: 'The
free exercise of religious worship to all persons who inhabit and
frequent the island is to be secured.' No material alterations
were proposed.[9] The third section of a supplement to these
Royal Instructions further expounds on ecclesiastical affairs.[10]

Within the context of such provisions, often considered as
Malta's first Constitution, Governor Sir Henry Cavendish
Ponsonby thought it superfluous to publish the Emancipation
Act in Malta in 1829: 'as no Acts of Parliament, imposing
disabilities on Roman Catholics, had ever been in force in Malta,
and Roman Catholics had been eligible to all offices except the
Governor.'[11] This policy of religious liberty had been
established 'as a necessary feature of the imperial system'[12]
evident in Canada (1774), Martinique and Santo Domingo (1794),
the Cape, and other colonies (1815).[13]

The British believed in 'religious neutrality' as 'the corollary of a policy of toleration and protection for all institutions unless objectionable on grounds of public policy'.[14] In Malta and Gozo they went slightly further. They not only respected the liberty of the Church; to some extent, they also protected her from proselytism. A Biblical Society, founded in 1814 through the interest of the Church Missionary Society, was forbidden to designate itself 'of Malta' and restricted in the distribution of parts of the Bible in Maltese. Nonetheless, shortly afterwards, two missionary groups, the American Missionary Society and the Society of English Independents, were permitted to own and operate a printing press at a time when the Press was not yet free, though they were forbidden to print anything in Maltese.[15] Notwithstandingly, the Papal Secretary of State was to be assured of the British intention 'to protect the Roman Catholic religion against the attempts of any Society or class of persons, provided the forms and practices constantly observed in the British Dominions were not violated'.[16] It was not before 1 November 1844 that the Anglicans opened a church in Malta, and they never had one in Gozo. As the local Roman Catholic establishment was not supported by the Government, previous attempts to persuade the latter to build a church out of its own expenses had been rejected.[17] The Archbishop of Malta was also accorded military honours which were declined to the Anglican Bishop of Malta and Gibraltar whose See was erected in 1842.[18]

Liberty, protection, and co-operation formed the basis upon which the British directed Church-State relations in the twelve Constitutions granted to Malta between 1813 and 1964. The norms outlined in 1813 were re-iterated in substance in the Constitutions of 1835, 1849, 1887, and 1903. The British appreciated the strategic significance of Malta and Gozo in imperial defence and succeeded in winning over the confidence of the people largely by securing every respect to their religion. This, of course, went hand in hand with the concept of religious toleration: everyone's right to follow one's conscience and practice one's religion.

Of outstanding relevance were the 1921 and 1964 Constitutions.[19] The former, granting self-government, laid down the following two provisions:

1. All persons in Malta shall have the full liberty of conscience and the free exercise of their respective modes of religious worship.
2. No person shall be subject to any disability, or excluded from holding any office, by reason of his religious profession.[20]

The first affirms the right to freedom of conscience and worship, the second prohibits religious discrimination.

The *Assemblea Nazionale di Malta*, the body set up to defend and work for the right of the Maltese to self-government, had originally suggested to the British Government to include a provision declaring that the religion of Malta and Gozo is the Roman Catholic one. Such proposal was not intended to impose Catholicism,[21] yet the request was rejected on the grounds that the Constitution was not the proper document to define a country's religion. As a symbolic gesture of protest against the Colonial Government, and as a re-affirmation of the general local feeling, the first legislation of Parliament was precisely the Religion of Malta Declaration Act of 4 March 1922. It declared the Roman Catholic Apostolic Religion as the religion of Malta, recognizing the special historical and social status of Roman Catholicism in these islands.[22] Subsequent Constitutions (1936, 1939, 1947, 1959, and 1961) left the matter undisturbed.

The Independence Constitution (1964) recognized Roman Catholicism as the religion of Malta:

1. The Religion of Malta is the Roman Catholic Apostolic Religion.
2. The State guarantees to the Roman Catholic Apostolic Church the right freely to exercise her proper spiritual and ecclesiastical functions and duties and to manage her own affairs.[23]

The right to full freedom of conscience was also affirmed and religious discrimination was prohibited.[24]

The major difference between the 1921 and 1964 Constitutions lies not so much in the recognition which the latter grants to the special status of the Catholic Religion in Malta, as in the specific guarantee of freedom which it gives to the local Church. The desirability of giving this constitutional guarantee had been discussed to no avail in connection with the Constitution of 1921. However, the differences of opinion then were of minor importance in practice, because it was generally assumed that Parliament should not restrain the legitimate freedom of the Church in any way. The socio-political context in the 1960s was, as will be shown further on, completely different. The Church was playing a very active role and it exerted its influence in the drafting of those constitutional articles.[25] The autonomy that the Church had invariably enjoyed during the 164 years of colonial rule became finally entrenched in the Constitution which laid down the fundamental principle for the regulation of healthy relations between Church and State.

II CO-OPERATION IN PRACTICE

Sir Thomas Maitland probably professed no religion, but, in accordance with his instructions, he did his best to keep good relations with the Church. Yet it was a matter of time before the British, urged especially by political pragmatism, commenced to force the religious establishment of Malta to conform with that of Catholic European countries, such as Austria, France, and the Two Sicilies.

These changes were facilitated by another fact. After two hundred years of almost complete interruption, official contacts between the Holy See and the British Government were resumed at the Congress of Vienna (1815) between Cardinal Consalvi, the Papal Secretary of State, and Lord Castlereagh, the British Foreign Secretary. These contacts became increasingly necessary as a result of the growing importance of Catholics in Ireland and Canada, and the establishment of English rule in Malta and the Ionian Islands. These developments made possible some private missions to Rome, including one by Maitland himself in mid-1920. In several encounters with Consalvi, the Governor discussed ecclesiastical affairs related to the Ionian Islands and Malta.[26] Probably as a result of some tacit agreement, on 25 June 1822 Maitland imposed the Mortmain Law,[27] which forced the Church to sell off bequests of property within one year of acquisition.

This development signals the beginning of a British colonial ploy in its dealings with the Church in Malta. Instead of discussing matters with the local hierarchy, whom they considered too conservative, the British dealt directly with Rome. This gave them a twofold advantage: they would present the local authorities with a *fait accompli,* and they could therefore avoid opposition that could easily build up during lengthy discussions. This ploy was subsequently resorted to by Maltese leaders during the self-government era as well as after independence.

In 1825 Earl Bathurst, Colonial Secretary, in a private communication to the Governor, aired the idea that 'some arrangement [should] be made with the Holy See by which an accredited agent from Rome, in the nature of a Nuncio, should be fixed as a resident in Malta'.[28] The idea did not materialize and further contacts had to be carried out in Rome. It was on one such mission by Sir Frederick Hankey, Chief Secretary, that Governor Ponsonby in 1828 got Rome's acquiescence for two important enactments: the restriction of Ecclesiastical Courts' jurisdiction (including that of the pro-Vicar of Gozo) to spiritual matters,[29] and the abolition of the right of sanctuary in criminal cases.[30] The Vatican's yielding to British diplomatic pressure was probably intended to avoid obstacles to the promulgation of the Emancipation Act. Henceforth, the Governor's satisfaction at the fact 'that this material change has been favourably received by the population at large' was rather premature.[31] Only bishops could not be taken to Court.

With little effort, the British had succeeded in dismantling all ecclesiastical immunities – something which one Grand Master after another had attempted to and failed. The abolition of Ecclesiastical Courts, to the indignation of many, soon led to an increase in clandestine marriages. On 7 September 1831 the Governor, after a request by the Church, enacted legislation for their effectual restraint.[32]

The British also co-operated with the Church in education which had been entirely imparted according to religious principles and had for a long time 'exclusively in the hands of the Catholic clergy'.[33] In 1845 some Jesuits were given a tacit permission in their individual capacity for the opening of the Saint Paul Boarding School, destined to raise considerably the standard of education in Malta.[34] In 1859, when it was rumoured that radical changes were being contemplated for the University and the Lyceum, the Governor assured the Archbishop that he would be consulted before any alterations were carried out:

I shall be always most happy to avail myself of any information and

assistance that Your Grace may afford me in connection with this most
important subject ... and in which a question of the interests of the
Roman Catholic religion may be involved.[35]

Several burial laws were also enacted in agreement with the
Church. On 3 May 1869 burials were prohibited in the inner-
port area: Valletta, Floriana, and the Three Cities.[36] An
extension of the prohibition to all villages, discussed in the
1890s, met with great opposition from the country people who
opposed interment outside their churches.[37] The practice was
eventually discontinued. Burials within churches and crypts
were finally prohibited on 18 October 1974.[38]

III INITIAL PROBLEMS

Church-State relations were of course not always that cordial.
A major problem concerned the right of presentation of
candidates to the Malta bishopric and the appointment to several
ecclesiastical offices which the British claimed for themselves.
    One of the earliest issues was the Conventual Church of St
John. As it had previously belonged to the Order, the Colonial
Office considered it, and all its treasures and possessions, as
Government property. It was, however, ruled out that the church
should be appropriated for Anglican worship. These assumed
rights went against both the foundation deed and previous
enactments. On 23 November 1577 Grand Master Jean de la
Cassière had laid down that if the Order relinquished Malta the
Conventual Church would revert to the local clergy.[39] On 13
June 1798 Napoleon handed over the church to Archbishop
Vincenzo Labini[40] who, on 30 August, provisionally obtained
the title of Co-Cathedral for the church. The British, however,
solidly maintained their claim, creating several problems that
persist to this day. Maitland ordered that the throne on the right
of the high altar, previously reserved for the Grand Master, was
to remain there with the coat-of-arms of the British Sovereign
'clearly displayed as a sign of his authority in the islands.[41]
Eventually a second throne was erected on the opposite side for
the Archbishop.
    The Oath Question constituted another major issue.[42] After

the Emancipation Act, British Roman Catholic subjects holding public offices were obliged to take an oath not to disturb or weaken the Protestant religion. The oath was first imposed in Malta on 2 January 1839.[43] The Vatican held that it could not be approved and a petition for its replacement was lodged. After many terse exchanges, and some wise suggestions by Governor More O'Ferrall, the Colonial Office, on 13 January 1848, accepted a new formula and the question came to an end.[44]

The discussion on the freedom of the press, first suggested by the Royal Commission of 1836, also created much acrimony.[45] The fears of Archbishop Caruana that the Catholic religion and the Church would be 'ridiculed' were of no avail even though they were backed by the Vatican. Nor were the memoranda signed by hundreds of priests and the objections of the Kingdom of the Two Sicilies much considered.[46] Newspapers began to be published in 1838 and freedom of the press was granted on 14 March 1839, though a law of libel slightly narrowed this newly-gained freedom.

Another dispute arose in 1845 when, without any consultation with the Archbishop or the Colonial Secretary, Governor Stuart passed an ordinance in the Council to regulate 'the administration of certain pious foundations and the revision of the accounts of such administration'.[47] The law would have invested the Civil Courts with the right to audit the accounts of administration and to remove administrators if their registers proved defective. Faults there may have been, but the Governor exceeded the limits of his authority, discrediting the British in Malta and causing indignation in the Colonial Office.[48] The Governor was adamant; however, the Archbishop avoided this interference by establishing a mixed commission of laymen and ecclesiastics to supervise the administration of Church foundations.[49] The ordinance was shelved.

A long arduous dispute involving also the Anglican Church began with the promulgation of the new Criminal Code where, in the chapter concerning offences against religion, the Roman Catholic religion was described 'dominant', the other religions 'dissentient' from Roman Catholicism.[50] After years of heated arguments, involving the Archbishop of Malta and the Anglican Bishop as well as members of the Council of Government and the House of Commons, the Code was enacted by an Order-in-

Council on 30 January 1854 with the relevant chapter omitted.[51]

This breach in relations widened when, by letters patent of 30 July 1857, all ecclesiastics were excluded from the Council of Government.[52] No official reason was given, but the Government knew that opposition to its policies by priests in the Council could easily degenerate in a worse opposition by the people. This is precisely what happened and the British eventually had to give in.

The Risorgimento did not fail to affect local Church-State relations. The unification of Italy meant the end of the Pope's temporal power, and the Maltese, in line with the Catholic world, fully backed Pius IX's claims for the Papal States. They could not but show displeasure at the backing accorded by the British Foreign Secretary to the unification of Italy and especially at Governor Le Marchant's declared support to Lord Russell and open sympathy with the Italian cause.[53] The presence in Malta of many revolutionaries and their irritating press marred the situation further.[54] Yet, at the worst of the crisis, the Pope sought British protection and Her Majesty's Government informed him that Malta would be at his disposal if the need arose.[55]

Church-State relations were further tried during the discussions on the marriage question.[56] The validity of marriages, even as a legal contract, was in Malta based on Canon Law as enacted in the Council of Trent. In 1889, the Simmons-Rampolla agreement had affirmed that a marriage between two Catholics or between a Catholic and a non-Catholic would only be valid if celebrated according to the rites of the Tridentine Decrees. All other marriages remained subject to Civil Law. Back in 1865, Sir Adrian Dingli, the Crown Advocate, had expressed much the same views when he declared that *consuetudo abrogatoria* marriages between Anglicans celebrated in Malta had constantly and universally been reputed legal and valid.[57]

The Colonial Office thought otherwise and decided to settle the question by specific legislation binding all colonies. On 27 June 1892, the Foreign Marriage Act declared valid those mixed marriages contracted under certain conditions;[58] this implied a deviation from the former agreement and both priests and people considered the enactment a defiance to papal authority. Nothing happened initially but, on 6 March 1896, the Governor informed the Archbishop that local legislation concerning the Act would soon be enacted.[59] Malta was ablaze. Three mammoth meetings of protest were organized on 8, 15, and 22 March. The British began to fear that the agitation would endanger public peace and the matter was allowed to drop. Civil Marriage was finally introduced by the Maltese Socialist Government on 12 August 1975.[60] Notwithstanding wide and vociferous protests, it remains the only valid form before the State.

IV   The Right of Presentation to the Malta Bishopric

The problem that most severely strained Church-State relations before the 1921 Constitution concerned the right of presentation to the Malta bishopric.[61] Aware that 'he who rules the soul rules everything',[62] the Colonial Government did its utmost to elect a bishop of its own choice.

In granting Malta and Gozo to the Order of St John, Emperor Charles V had established that, whenever the See became vacant, the Grand Master was to nominate three ecclesiastics of the Order so that the sovereign or his successors would choose one for confirmation by the Pope. Their wish was almost always met with. On 30 April 1807, Archbishop Labini, the last bishop elected under the Order, died. The ecclesiastical authorities informed King Ferdinand III of Sicily who, on 12 June, presented his candidate to the Pope.[63] The Civil Commissioner of Malta, Alexander Ball, questioned the proceedings[64] but approved the candidate, Ferdinando Mattei, a Maltese. Mattei was elected Bishop on 18 September and, like his predecessors and successors, he was granted the title of Titular Archbishop.

The Royal Commission of 1812 argued that, should the islands be officially taken over by Great Britain, the right of presentation would automatically pass to the new sovereign, the King of England,[65] very conveniently forgetting that the Knights of St John were also a religious order. When Mattei died on 14 July 1829, Governor Ponsonby claimed the right with the Papal Secretary of State that very day.[66] There was full agreement on the candidate, Francesco Saverio Caruana, but the See remained vacant for more than nineteen months. The right was also claimed, for ulterior motives, by the King of the Two Sicilies. The British were offended and sent Sir Frederick Hankey to Rome in November 1830. As a result of diplomatic pressure, Caruana was eventually elected on 28 February 1831. On the same occasion, Pope Gregory XVI conceded a further British request: Malta was formally separated from the Metropolitan See of Palermo on 20 June 1831.

A complication could ensue if London and Rome disagreed on the candidate. Such a problem arose in 1837, when the Holy See disregarded the recommendation of the Government to a canonry as had been the custom. The Colonial Secretary was amazed that the Vatican was upsetting the *modus vivendi* reached earlier and by which 'the spiritual pretentions of the Pope [had been harmonized] with the rights and obligations of the British Crown'.[67]

In the beginning of 1838, Governor Bouverie promulgated an ordinance 'declaring appointments to Ecclesiastical Offices or Benefices by a foreign power, without the approbation of the Governor, to be invalid'.[68] This was little short of direct defiance of papal authority. The Bishop, naturally, did not apply to the Governor to convalidate bulls, and subsequent ones remained dormant. On 22 March 1838, Rome instructed Archbishop Caruana to suspend the bull of the canonry with the implicit hope that the Governor would suspend his ordinance. He, however, persisted in his stand even when several parish priests, to the general indigation, could not be installed. In July 1838, Sir Hector Greig, the Chief Secretary, and Archdeacon Salvatore Lanzon proceeded to Rome in an attempt to break the deadlock. The Governor, however, refused a very practical suggestion by the Vatican authorities that in future an agreement be reached on the candidate before the issue of the bull.[69] Eventually a partial understanding was reached: the person receiving a bull of appointment was to petition the Governor for approbation.

Yet the central issue, the possibility of an unwanted candidate, remained. It soon came again into the limelight when the authorities refused to agree to the appointment of a coadjutor to the ailing Archbishop Caruana. In October 1844 the *sostituto* of the Papal Secretary of State, Monsignor Francesco Capuccini, travelled to London to work out a solution.[70] Only a chain of partly unrelated circumstances favoured a solution.

The Irish Members in the House of Commons, always ready to espouse causes akin to their own, became very much interested in the Maltese dispute. They succeeded in exerting very valuable pressure. The Peel administration also began to show a greater degree of malleability in the hope that the Vatican would use its 'moral influence in a paternal and convenient manner' to silence the Irish liberal priests. Finally, in mid-1846 there was a change of Government. On 30 June Lord Russell became Prime Minister and, three days later, Earl Grey became Secretary of State for the Colonies. The change brought more interest in colonial affairs and the Maltese dispute was treated more seriously.

On 16 June, a fortnight before Russell's election, Giovanni Mastai Ferretti, the partly-liberal Bishop of Imola, was elected Pope as Pius IX. In a matter of weeks he enlisted the support of Richard More O'Ferrall, a Member of the House of Commons. The Papal Secretary of State requested him to intervene in the Maltese dispute.[71] He obliged and succeeded in convincing the Colonial Office that the choice of candidates to the bishopric and other offices by the Pope would certainly be made 'with the anxious desire to make it acceptable to Her Majesty's Government'.[72] On 21 April 1847 Publius Maria dei Conti Sant was elected Coadjutor Bishop. Commonsense had finally prevailed. Unofficial discussions between the two Governments before the final appointment to the bishopric proved to be the wiser procedure.

This is what was in fact done in 1856 before the election of Archbishop Gaetano Pace Forno. The British representative in Rome, R.B.P. Lyons, again did his best, unsuccessfully, to assert further the rights of the State. While reiterating that no appointment would ever be made before informing the British Government, he pointed out that no right of veto to appointments could ever be recognized or granted by Rome.[73]

The dispute surfaced again in the 1880s. It was being rumoured that the Vatican was considering the appointment of the Apostolic Administrator Antonio Buhagiar as Bishop of Malta.[74] The other candidate, Mgr. Pietro Pace, Bishop of Gozo, was preferred by the Governor, Sir Lintorn Arabin Simmons. After much argument, Pace was transferred to the Malta bishopric on 11 February 1889. Yet it would be, to say the least, inaccurate to attribute his election solely to British pressure. Pace was an acknowledged able leader both locally and in Rome, where he was held highly in Curia circles;[75] his proven pro-British leanings, contrary to Buhagiar's real or supposed Francophile dispositions, did the rest.

The improving relations between Britain and the Holy See led to further discussions on this and other problems. These took place at the Vatican between Simmons, who had resigned the local governorship and proceeded to Rome as Envoy Extraordinary and Minister Plenipotentiary of Britain, and Cardinal Rampolla, Papal Secretary of State.[76] As regards episcopal appointments, the agreement reached did not go an iota further than the 1857 Lyons-Antonelli agreement. The Vatican could not, and in fact did not, pay the least heed to the claimed veto. Any affirmation about the acquiescence of the Vatican on this point in official and other correspondence[77] betrays a misunderstanding of the agreement and of the policy followed by the Vatican at that time.

In the late 1930s the problem arose once more. The candidate to the Malta bishopric, Mgr. Michael Gonzi, Bishop of Gozo, was not acceptable either to the British or to the local Government.[78] Gonzi had accepted the Gozo bishopric in 1924, presumably in the hope that the appointment would serve as a stepping-stone to Malta. When the Vatican moved in that direction in 1936, it found the concerted opposition of Sir Harry Luke, Lieutenant-Governor, and of Lord Strickland, leader in the Council of Government: they considered him too politically involved and pro-Italian, a rather dangerous disposition at the time.[79] However, during the Second World War, he showed his dedication to the Allied cause and the Colonial Office abandoned its stand. Gonzi became Archbishop on 19 December 1943.

The Holy See, on this occasion, resorted to delaying tactics and eventually convinced the British to accept an unacceptable man. The incident that supposedly altered the British stand, the gathering of grain — a reference to an early 1942 episode, when Gonzi convinced the Gozitan farmers to hand over their hoarded grain to the Government — was certainly blown out of all

proportions by both sides.[80] In truth, Vatican diplomacy had
proved itself successful once more.

V A CASE OF CO-OPERATION: THE ESTABLISHMENT OF THE DIOCESE OF GOZO

An outstanding episode of co-operation between Vatican and
British diplomacy took place during the long campaign of the
priests and people of Gozo to establish a separate diocese from
Malta. It was one of the major religious events during colonial
rule and in which the British co-operated with Rome in a very
exceptional way.[81]

The establishment of an independent diocese for Gozo and
Comino was first unsuccessfully requested on 30 October 1798
just after the expulsion of the French from Gozo. On 30
December 1836, the Gozitans tried again. Governor Bouverie
made it clear that he was 'not averse from recommending such
request to the favourable consideration of His Majesty,
[keeping] in view the spiritual advantages of the Gozitans'.[82]
Yet further progress was halted by Archbishop Caruana and his
successors, who were unwilling to accede to a curtailment of
their sphere of pastoral care.

The question was again taken up in the 1850s by Father Pietro
Pace, a young Gozitan priest who was to become Archbishop of
Malta in 1889; and (Sir) Adrian Dingli, an eminent Gozitan then
slowly establishing himself as the *de facto* Governor of Malta.
Through British co-operation, they succeeded in reaching their
aim.

It became clear to one and all in 1860 that the Vatican had
understood the necessity of a separate diocese for Gozo, and that
the opposition of the Maltese hierarchy was unjustifiable. The
Vatican, however, was unwilling to take a decision without a
clear approval by the British, with whom they were then striving
hard to keep the best of relations to convince them from taking
sides in the thorny question of Italian unification. That approval
was sought on 12 September 1860. Lord Russell, the Foreign
Secretary, immediately communicated the request to the
Colonial Office which in turn asked Governor Le Marchant
'whether there is any reason to object to the proposed

appointment of a bishop'.[83] The Governor discussed the matter with Crown Advocate Dingli and, on 25 October, he drafted his letter of approval.[84]

After further considerations, the Colonial Office conveyed the approval to the Foreign Office. Notwithstanding the many difficulties created in similar circumstances closer home, the Foreign Office, having clearly understood the difficulties of the Vatican and of the Gozitans, decided to pose no problems. On 21 November 1860, Lord Russell acceded to the proceedings and duly informed Odo Russell, the British representative in Rome, about the whole matter.[85] Early in December, Odo Russell passed on the British approval to Cardinal Antonelli, the Papal Secretary of State.

Only after this unequivocal reply did the Vatican begin to tackle seriously the other related problems. In the meantime, Odo Russell continued to give his 'most careful and earnest attention to Sir Gaspard Le Marchant's clear and able instructions so as to be ready to carry them out as favourable opportunities occur'.[86] This diplomatic attention proved to be of no little help and the Vatican finally conceded to the wishes of the Gozitans. On 16 September 1864, Pius IX created Gozo and Comino a separate diocese directly subject to the Holy See.[87]

Shortly afterwards, the first bishop, Monsignor Michele Buttigieg, invited the Sicilian Jesuits to run the Seminary and a boarding and day school. This was inaugurated on 4 November 1866 and it soon achieved a considerable reputation. The sons of the best Gozitan families and many intellectually talented boys from Malta and even from Sicily attended this school. Boys were prepared to proceed for the priesthood or to sit for the matriculation examinations. For almost half a century, the school, which still survives, exerted a particular influence on the social and intellectual life of the Maltese.[88]

VI THE CHURCH AND THE QUEST FOR SELF-GOVERNMENT

The quest of the Maltese for self-determination is rooted in the Declaration of Rights of 1802. Their claims were initially based on a false notion of the institutions of medieval government: the *Università* and the *Consiglio Popolare*.[89] The Church had taken an active part in these institutions and, officially or through individual clerics, it was also dragged into the quest for political rights.

The first political agitation under the British was led by William Eton, an English civil servant. According to Eton, the Constitution desired by the Maltese at that time, while allowing the Church a separate assembly, precluded it from taking any decision, even in ecclesiastical matters, without the participation of the lay element of the proposed *Consiglio*.[90] Anticlericalism is apparent elsewhere in his political thought, but his ideals were short-lived.

The movement was revived in 1832 by the formation of the *Comitato Generale Maltese*: it was led by Camillo Sceberras and Giorgio Mitrovich and included representatives of the clergy. Owing to its pressure, the advisory Council of Government, an institution suggested as early as 1813, was established in 1835.[91] As in 1813, the Archbishop was to be one of the official members but, as the Vatican counselled him to desist from taking part, he declined his seat. According to George Lewis, one of the 1836 Royal Commissioners, the clergy's interest and influence in politics had 'considerably declined of late years'.[92]

It was a hibernation enforced by circumstances. Of the eighteen members who were to form the Council of Government according to the 1849 Constitution, eight were to be elected directly by the people. Three of those elected were ecclesiastics: Father Filippo Amato, the Titular Bishop Annetto Casolani, and Mgr. Leopoldo Fiteni.[93] As a result, Church-State issues, previously arranged confidentially between the ecclesiastical and colonial authorities, could now become public with the consequence that relations could be put in greater jeopardy. As already outlined, this is precisely what happened during the discussion of the Criminal Code and this eventually led to the exclusion of the clergy from the Council.

Neither was their presence to prevent any encroachment on the Church's legitimate rights necessary, thought Governor Le Marchant. For with 'thirteen out of eighteen members of the Council being Roman Catholics, there is not the slightest ground for fearing that any just and reasonable claims of that Church could, under any circumstances, fail to be attended to'.[94] However, after a lot of pressure from various quarters, the

Colonial Office submitted the question to a referendum. The majority was found to be in favour and, by letters patent of 29 April 1870, ecclesiastics were readmitted to the Council, though no more than two could be members at the same time.[95]

Priests continued to play a significant part in the Council and in the Maltese quest for self-government. Their role increased with the emergence of the Language Question and the foundation in 1880 of the pro-Italian and anti-reformist party soon to be known as the *Partito Nazionale*. Under its Gozitan leader, Fortunato Mizzi, it fought Anglicization and demanded a new constitutional order with the weapon of *italianità*. The party attracted many professionals and easily won the support of many ecclesiastics, one reason being that the British had wholeheartedly backed the Risorgimento, which was partly directed against Church and Pope. It is no wonder that the only priest elected in the 1880 election, Father Emmanuel Debono, was an anti-reformist. The direct and indirect support of the clergy to the party 'with a defined and distinct platform ... [and] a vision of Malta as a nation'[96] was not insignificant.

Three priests were again elected to the Council in the 1888 election, the first after the 1887 Constitution. The priest who was to play a most prominent part in politics, Mgr. Ignazio Panzavecchia,[97] entered the political scene in 1891 as a representative of the clergy, one of the four classes of special electors created by this Constitution. He continued to play a significant role even after 1898, when priests were barred from the Council by Archbishop Pace so as to prevent any disturbance in Church-State relations by their active participation in debates. Priests were eventually also barred by the 1903 Constitution. When, in 1911, Governor Sir Leslie Rundle bluntly opposed the Maltese request for a Council with a majority of elected members, Panzavecchia became the head of the abstentionist wing of the *Partito Nazionale* — members resigned *en masse* soon after being elected in order to ridicule the Constitution and to press for wider constitutional liberties.

At that time the situation had been further precipitated by Manwel Dimech,[98] an anticlerical and anti-imperialist self-made man who, through his activities and writings, succeeded in challenging both the Church and the colonial authorities. Notwithstanding his early criminal record and his many extreme positions, he is symptomatic of the underlying anxieties and tensions. The offended authorities soon succeeded in eliminating the man, now venerated by the local Left as the first Maltese Socialist. He died in exile in 1921.

The First World War brought a short-lived economic revival and tranquillized the situation for a few years. Soon afterwards, on 25 February 1919, seeing that their strong verbal protests were of no avail, the Maltese political leaders convoked *L'Assemblea Nazionale di Malta* to petition for self-government. The Assembly met under Sir Filippo Sceberras, but the veteran Panzavecchia not only played a leading role; he also assisted in the formulation of the liberal draft Constitution.[99]

The political and economic situation was becoming intolerable and, on 7 June 1919, rioting broke out in Valletta. The tragedy was not greater owing to the intervention of Panzavecchia and Bishop Angelo Portelli, the Vicar-General, who calmed the crowds and urged them to disperse. The *Sette Giugno* riots were an expression of the grievances created by the political and economic situation in the first two decades of the twentieth century.

By letters patent of 14 April 1921, the British Government decided to give Malta a Parliament with wide self-governing powers. Priests became eligible as candidates once more. The *Unione Politica Maltese,* a party of moderate Nationalists led by Panzavecchia, won a relative majority in the October election and Lord Plumer, the Governor, invited Panzavecchia to form a Government. Conscious that fulfilling the role of priest and premier might be too problematic — even if Austria was led by Ignaz Seipel, a priest — Panzavecchia refused, and suggested Party Senator Joseph Howard as Malta's first Prime Minister. In the first Parliament, four of the thirty-two members of the Legislative Assembly and five of the seventeen members of the Senate were priests. Of the first four, one was from Gozo—Alfonz Hili, Archpriest of Rabat, the first and only priest ever to be elected from that island.[100]

The clergy had been the spokesmen of the Maltese since the times of the *Consiglio Popolare.* They succeeded in gaining for the people many rights in the distant and not so distant past. They decided to proceed in that role even under the new Constitution, though such participation led them well into the secular field. Their presence in Parliament, noted a Vatican official, was in conformity with the Constitution of the land and all norms of Canon Law were rigorously observed. There is no evidence to support the accusation that priest-parliamentarians had abused of their mandate or had failed in the performance of their civil and religious duties.[101] The Royal Commission of 1931 was not surprised by the prominent part played by priests in politics.[102]

Nonetheless, as a result, Church and State became more interwoven. Unavoidably, this furnished an occasion for controversy and friction.

VII   CONFRONTATION AND CONFLICT

The 1921 Constitution was certainly a very important step in the Maltese process of state formation. During this process, two distinct groups that had for long been slowly developing consolidated themselves in the local political arena: one consisting of an anti-British party of professionals and the majority of the clergy which sought ever more liberal Constitutions for Malta under the battle-cry of *italianità*, and another consisting of a pro-British group of middle-class men with a minority of the clergy supporting it.[103] In the 1921 Parliament, there were members of the clergy on both sides.

The *Unione Politica Maltese*, with the support of other parties, was in Government from 1921 to 1927; after 16 January 1926, following its union with the *Partito Democratico Nazionalista*, it became known as the Nationalist Party. In August 1927, the pro-British Constitutional Party won the election. The Prime Minister, Lord Strickland, was determined to give more importance to the English language in education and the courts at the expense of Italian, but he had the drawback of a minority in the Senate.

On 11 June 1928, the Estimates Appropriation Bill was defeated in the Senate, the two ecclesiastical members voting with the Opposition. Several demonstrations were organized against the clergy and the controversy soon developed into a full-blown confrontation between Church and State.[104]

The Church in Malta was then led by Archbishop Maurus

Caruana, a Benedictine monk who had lived in Scotland for the greater part of his life, and in Gozo by Bishop Gonzi, who between 1921 and 1924 had been a member in the Senate on behalf of the pro-British Labour Party. Notwithstanding their seemingly common interests with Strickland's party, a conflict followed.

The antagonism of Strickland to the Church, more specifically to the Bishop of Gozo and the clergy of that island, was deep-rooted. In 1921, the Gozitan parish priests and clergy had wholeheartedly favoured Enrico Mizzi and his *Partito Democratico Nazionalista* to the political detriment of the Constitutional Party. Mizzi occasionally even attended informal parish priests' meetings, though it is an exaggeration to affirm, as Bishop Gonzi is quoted to have done,[105] that he customarily presided such meetings.[106] To Strickland's indignation, Mizzi's party, which contested Gozo with only four candidates, won the four Gozo seats — an unbeaten record. Strickland's attacks continued in his newspapers during the following years:[107] for this he excused himself on the false premise that his real intention was the promotion of religion and the same Church. By 1928, he was expecting that the Bishops take a precise stand against the participation and interference of the clergy in politics and to direct the clergy's representatives in the Senate 'to support the Government of every and any party in questions of routine and procedure and especially in financial matters'.[108]

This was the crux of the Church-State confrontation that exploded in 1928. Several anticlerical demonstrations, fanned by the Constitutional Party newspapers and sustained by other extreme elements, took place in July. On 15 August, Archbishop Caruana publicly condemned the anticlericalism manifest in these demonstrations and announced the setting-up of a weekly newspaper in Maltese, the *Leħen is-Sewwa*, to counteract these attacks.[109] Since its first issue, on 1 September 1928, this paper has played a prominent role in all Church-State issues.

The situation was further marred by the Carta incident. Father Felice Carta, the Provincial of the Franciscan Conventuals, ordered the transfer of a subordinate, Father Guido Micallef, to a Sicilian convent. Owing to the latter's Stricklandian leanings his transfer was termed a banishment for political motives and the Government intervened to put off his departure.[110] Relations were further exacerbated in January 1929 when three visiting Anglican bishops were allowed to organize conferences in the Throne-Room of the Governor's Palace. Many protests followed.[111]

In the meantime, Strickland, in line with the old-established British colonial ploy to side-step the local Church authorities, attempted to deal directly with Rome. Together with his deputy, Sir Augustus Bartolo, he travelled to Rome hoping to see the Pope. They only succeeded in getting an informal meeting with the Secretary of State.[112] On 23 February 1929, the Secretary of State, Cardinal Gasparri, begged the British Government through its representative at the Vatican, Sir Henry Chilton, so 'that suitable instructions may be given to the authorities of Malta, with a view of reassuring the Holy See as likewise the conscience of the Catholics of the island'.[113] In reply, the Minister suggested the sending of an Apostolic Visitor.

The Vatican complied, sending a higher-ranking Apostolic Delegate, Mgr. Paschal Robinson, who studied the Malta situation between 3 April and 2 June 1929. On 16 June, he presented his report in which, according to Sir Ronald Graham, British Ambassador to Italy, Robinson advised reconciliation.[114] This was certainly the whole purpose of his mission, but he could not conceal his conclusions:

It is not an exaggeration to say that at present Malta is subjected to a regime of terror and inquisitorial despotism, in which the opposition is disarmed and its papers gagged, the Church menaced, justice suspended, the Constitution in danger, the country in turmoil, Church and religion openly vilified.[115]

The report caused a sensation. And the confrontation continued both locally and through diplomatic channels. The British, through Governor Sir John Du Cane, became inevitably involved and generally supported Strickland.[116] Pope Pius XI on the other hand, in a speech to a Maltese pilgrimage on 22 August 1929, fully upheld the Bishops' stand and invited all Maltese Catholics to back their pastors.[117] The Opposition press, in the meantime, used the report to its ends, precipitating matters further. The two sides had taken up their stand: Strickland, argued the ecclesiastics, was meddling with religion and causing havoc in the religious sphere and so the British should intervene to stop him; Strickland, on the other hand, was convinced that he had a right to intervene to annihilate what he perceived as anti-clerical opposition.

The British once more aired the idea of a concordat. A concordat for the regulation and settlement of ecclesiastical affairs had been initially suggested in the late 1820s by Sir Frederick Hankey on one of his missions to Rome. Yet there was no real need for a concordat. Strickland twice suggested a similar agreement: in 1889 during the Simmons-Rampolla talks when he was Chief Secretary to the Government, and again in 1929 during Mgr. Robinson's visit.[118] Commented the Apostolic Delegate:

A superficial examination of these notes [for a concordat] is enough to understand the mentality and the Erastian policy of Strickland, who craves at all costs to make the Church subservient to the State and to reduce bishops and priests to mere Government civil servants.[119]

The conflict finally broke out on 1 May 1930 with the publication of the Election Pastoral Letter. After enlightening Christians on their rights and duties at election-time, the Bishops felt duty-bound to forbid Catholics to vote for Strickland and his candidates or to stand in election on behalf of the Constitutional Party.[120]

Events precipitated in quick succession. On 3 May Governor du Cane proclaimed a state of emergency and suspended the elections on the false premise that elections had lost their freedom. Demonstrations and counter-demonstrations followed. On 24 June, James McDonald, the British Prime Minister, informed the House of Commons that owing to the intervention of the Vatican in the temporal affairs of Malta, the Government had reluctantly decided 'to sanction a temporary suspension of the [1921] Constitution'.[121] Full legislative and executive powers were placed in the hands of the Governor.

In April 1931 a Royal Commission was sent to study the political situation. Lord Askwith, its Chairman, revealed years later that 'the Commission's *chief object* was to settle the dispute with the Church, and privately he said that his aim was to build a bridge over which the Vatican could cross'.[122] The Foreign Office wanted at all costs to restore relations with the Holy See — otherwise the advancement of the Empire with millions of

Catholic subjects would be in jeopardy.

The Commission recommended the re-activation of elections, eventually called for 11-13 June 1932. In the meantime, Strickland had lost much of the British support and, convinced by close friends, he decided to break the deadlock. He apologized to the Bishops who, on 3 June, withdrew the sanctions against him.[123] The election was won by the Nationalist Party, with the last priest-politician, Mgr. Enrico Dandria, elected in their ranks. He was made Minister of Education but died within a month, on 3 July.[124]

Events on the European and international scene were at that time rapidly worsening. With the Nationalist Party in Government, the Language Question became a central issue once more. The British, seriously afraid of an alignment with Fascist Italy, suspended the Constitution once more in November 1933.[125]

Church-State relations receded in the background. During the Second World War, the Church and the Maltese went out of their way to further the Allied cause and, after 1945, these cordial relations between Church and State were preserved for several years.

VIII FROM INTEGRATION TO INDEPENDENCE (1956-64)

The Church in Malta grew considerably in the twentieth century.

Englishmen were apt to point critically at the number of priests, monks and nuns to be seen in the street. Few of them understood that these people were the doctors, lawyers, nurses, welfare workers, teachers and civil servants and the like, who operated a Welfare State based upon voluntary offerings and dedicated service.[126]

This comment by Eric Brockman mirrors the astonishment of the British when they came in contact with the Church in Malta. They were especially amazed how a Church, that unlike their own was not state-financed, could support such a large number of personnel and institutions 'entirely from funds supplied by the people themselves'.[127] The steady increase in population and a slowly-recovering economy had led to a great expansion of the Church's activity in the educational, charitable, and social fields. For the good of the whole community, the Church had opened several primary, secondary, and trade schools; increased the number of homes for poor and abandoned orphans; and ran two modern well-equipped hospitals.[128]

The cordial relations between the British and the Church were consolidated during the war and, after the settlement of the Gonzi succession, they continued almost unruffled to the end. Difficulties, however, cropped up in the 1950s. By this time Malta was moving towards a two-party system: the Nationalist Party, with membership from the professional and upper classes of society together with some from the middle and rural classes; and the Malta Labour Party, with support from the workers and the middle class.[129] In February 1955, the latter party, under the leadership of Dom Mintoff, won the election. The campaign had focused on the Integration issue.[130]

The possibility of integration with Britain had first been thought up by Mabel Strickland, daughter of Lord Strickland who had died in August 1940, in a leader in the *Times of Malta* of 15 April 1943. However, when both the Colonial Secretary, Sir Oliver Stanley, and Cardinal Hinsley of Westminister showed her that it might adversely affect the position of the Maltese and the Church, she abandoned the idea. It was taken up by Mintoff in 1950 and, after becoming Prime Minister, he conveyed to the British a formal request for integration.[131]

The Opposition parties held that integration was a step back in Malta's road to self-government and vehemently opposed the proposal. The Church was assured by Mintoff that its position and rights would be safeguarded and initially took no sides. After a round-table conference favoured the idea, Mintoff decided to hold a referendum on the matter on 12—13 February 1956.

On 21 January, with the full backing of Cardinal Tardini, the Papal Secretary of State, Archbishop Gonzi and Bishop Joseph Pace of Gozo issued a historic joint Pastoral Letter. They declared that the guarantees on the position and rights of the Church, which they had insisted to be included in the new Constitution or in an annexed official document, had not been granted. So they admonished the Maltese to do their duty as Catholics.[132]

British Prime Minister Sir Anthony Eden, who backed Malta's Integration, considered the pastoral 'moderate'.[133] Not so

Mintoff, who publicly criticized the Bishop's stand. A furious battle of words followed on their respective newspapers. On 1 February, all Catholic organizations unanimously decided not to vote in favour of integration unless the said guarantees were obtained. Church authorities suggested to the Governor to postpone the referendum.[134] The British Government, it became known years later,[135] also favoured this postponement. Mintoff, however, refused – with the consequence that the result proved very indecisive. This was also the verdict reached in the House of Commons during a heated debate on 26 March. When religion was discussed, the members disagreed on whether the change would be beneficial or detrimental.[136] Integration was eventually shelved and full independence demanded.

Church-Government differences created by the Pastoral Letter were patched up for some time, but the second major Church-State confrontation was building up. It broke out on 29 April 1958 when Archbishop Gonzi broadcast on Rediffusion (the local cable radio network) to condemn violence by Labour supporters the previous day.[137] He was accused by Mintoff, who had tendered the resignation of his Government on 21 April, of unpatriotic behaviour. Other minor incidents followed. The Lenten Pastoral of 1960, after outlining the Church's teaching and condemnation of socialism, referred to the attempts being made to diffuse socialist ideas in Malta and, in conclusion, repudiated the attacks being made against the Church and its representatives by the Labour Pary leaders and newspapers.[138]

By that time, it was clear that the Labour Party was becoming increasingly imbued with socialist ideas, which, it was feared, would pave the way for Communist infiltration. This train of thinking was confirmed when it became known that the Labour Party had been affiliated to AAPSO – the Afro-Asian Peoples' Solidarity Organization – considered a Communist-front organization. This, coupled with Mintoff's socialist beliefs and anticlerical mentality, precipitated the situation further.

In the midst of this crisis, Malta and Gozo celebrated the nineteenth centenary of their conversion to Christianity by St Paul. The Church and the colonial administration, headed by Governor Sir Guy Grantham, worked hand in hand to extend a warm welcome to the large number of distinguished guests and for the success of the celebrations which were held in July

1960. The people, fed up with the political crisis and the religious conflict, vented their emotions and expressed their faith in one mammoth demonstration after another to the Papal Legate, Cardinal Muench, to the Archbishop, and to the visiting prelates.[139]

Soon after the Pauline parenthesis, the confrontation continued. On 15 February 1961 the Lenten Pastoral Letter condemned the Communist leanings of the Labour Party.[140] On 17 March, in a statement of policy, the Party's Executive retorted to these 'most serious calumnies' and accused the Archbishop of lack of co-operation in Malta's demand for self-determination.[141] The Church demanded an apology for this outrage. When this was not proffered, on 8 April it placed the whole Executive under an interdict – a canonical sanction that severed its recipients from the Church.[142] The Labour newspapers were also condemned.

On 14 April 1961, the Colonial Office approved the formation of the Gozo Civic Council, a statutory local Government in which several priests were initially elected.[143]

On 24 October Malta attained once again a degree of self-government. The two major political groupings, the Nationalist Party and the Labour Party, but especially the former, made it clear that they would seek independence from Britain. The electoral campaign proved to be a partly Church-led crusade against the forces of socialism and, it must be admitted, it was not free from several forms of exaggeration.[144] The Election Pastoral of 4 February 1962 further emphasized this matter at stake and invited the people to defend their religious heritage through the use of their vote.[145] As expected, the Nationalist Party, led by George Borg Olivier, won the election and immediately sought independence.

The confrontation continued and soon became concentrated on the codification of Church-State relations in independent Malta. Mintoff's proposals, after being listed by Bishop Emmanuel Galea, the Vicar-General and one of the closest observers of the situation, became known as the 'six points'.[146] They proposed:

1. Separation of Church and State
2. The State to be secularist with equal treatment of all religions
3. Recognition of Civil Marriage
4. *Privilegium fori* (by which bishops could not be taken to Court) to

be limited
5. Censorship of films and books to be carried out exclusively by the Government without Church intervention
6. Violence, in certain cases, to be admissible.

These proposals proved to be one of the stumbling blocks in the Malta Independence Conference held in London in July 1963. A referendum on whether the people wanted or not the Independence Constitution as drafted by the Government was transformed by the Nationalists into an expression of support for the Church against the six points.[147]

A relative majority favoured the Constitution, but the British were still unwilling to grant their approval without sufficient safeguards for human rights; they considered certain privileges that the Church wanted enshrined in the Constitution *vis-à-vis* the six points as infringements upon these rights. The British sought the intervention of Mgr. Igino Cardinale, the Apostolic Delegate to Britain. The Second Vatican Council, then in session, had just begun to discuss its declaration on religious freedom and, in view of this, the Apostolic Delegate succeeded in moderating the Maltese Church's stand. He even succeeded in gaining Pope Paul VI's approval for the necessary amendments.[148] The Constitution, as amended, has already been described.

Malta and Gozo became an independent State within the Commonwealth on 21 September 1964. The complicated Church-Labour Party dispute, of which the salient points only have been touched upon, prolonged itself up to 4 April 1969, when a vague agreement was concluded between Dom Mintoff and Emmanuel Gerada, the Auxiliary Bishop.[149] After the Labour Party was returned to power in June 1971, the six points were gradually incorporated in the Constitution and the Laws of Malta.[150]

IX CONCLUSION

The British took Malta under circumstances bearing no analogy in the history of the Empire. They likewise discovered that few, if any, of their colonies had a strategic value in the expansion of the Empire as this mid-Mediterranean island. It was of the utmost importance for them to maintain a good feeling among the inhabitants and this necessarily meant gentleness and benevolence towards their religion and Church. They succeeded. Church-State relations during direct colony rule were on the whole satisfactory and the British reaped the desired reward.

With self-government, the responsibility for the continuation of these good relations shifted to the local political leaders. The motives that had urged the previous co-operation now came lacking and relations soon became strained: but commonsense and the common good of the body politic led to their eventual healthy restoration. Other problems cropped up by the passage of time. Church-State relations definitely played a more prominent role and this, together with the increasing international influence, effectively contributed to the declaration of their respective autonomy in the Independence Constitution. Admittedly, the preservation of this autonomy and mutual respect has not been easy. Yet it is difficult, perhaps impossible, to project national identity without one of the basic components of our cultural heritage — Roman Catholicism.

NOTES

1 *Hansard*, 3rd ser., cxxix, 15 August 1853.
2 The standard works relevant to this survey include: H.I. Lee, 'British Policy towards Religion, Ancient Laws and Customs in Malta', 1-14; A. Koster, *Prelates and Politicians in Malta;* J. Bezzina, *Religion and Politics in a Crown Colony.* For primary sources, see especially those cited in Lee, *passim,* and Bezzina, 394-54.
3 Ralph Abercromby to Henry Pigot, 10 December 1800, quoted in A.V. Laferla, *British Malta,* i, 7-8.
4 *Hansard*, 3rd ser., cxxix, 15 August 1853.
5 Laferla, 27-8.
6 Ibid., 28, Articles 6, 7, 8.
7 CO 159/3, Hobart to Cameron, General Instructions, 14 May 1801.
8 CO 158/19, 120, Royal Commissioners' Report of 1812.
9 PAV, *Gov.* 5 (1813-14), 41, Bathurst to Maitland, General Instructions (Prince Regent's Commission).
10 Ibid., Bathurst to Maitland, 28 July 1813.
11 CO 158/64, 51, Ponsonby to Murray, 18 August 1829.
12 V. Harlow, 'The New Imperial System', 129.
13 Lee, 1.
14 E.W. Evans, *The British Yoke. Reflections on the Colonial Empire,* 181.
15 AAM, *Correspondence* 43 (1826), 615-16, Mattei to Della Somaglia, 6 October 1825.

[16] PAV, *Gov.* 12 (1815), 186, Bathurst to Hastings, 4 May 1825.
[17] See A. Bonnici, 'Thirty Years to build a Protestant Church', 183-91.
[18] On matters concerning the Anglican Bishop, PP, 1852-xxxii-355.
[19] See G. Grima, 'The Constitution and Religion in Malta between 1921 and 1974', 20-40.
[20] Ibid., 22, Malta Constitution (1921), § 56, 1.2.
[21] Ibid.
[22] See Act I (1922) in *Ordinances enacted by the Governor, Laws made by the Legislature, and other official Acts.*
[23] Grima, 29, Malta Constitution (1964), § 2, 1.2.
[24] Ibid.,§ 41, 1.2; § 46, 1.2.3.
[25] Ibid., 30 and *passim.*
[26] Laferla, 99.
[27] MGG, 28 June 1822, Proclamation XXII (1822), 121-2.
[28] Bathurst to Hastings, 3 August 1825, quoted in Laferla, 113.
[29] MGG, 16 April 1828, Proclamation V (1828), 125-6.
[30] Ibid., Proclamation VI (1828), 126; H.W. Harding, *Maltese Legal History under British Rule*, 201-20; A. Bonnici, 'Abolition of personal and local immunities', 323-33.
[31] CO 158/58, 36, Ponsonby to Huskisson, 17 April 1828, written simultaneously with the publication of the laws.
[32] MGG, 7 September 1831, Proclamation VII (1831), 275.
[33] PP, 1838-xxix-141, Royal Commissioners' Report on 'Liberty of Printing and Publishing', 6.
[34] Laferla, 169-70.
[35] ASV, SS, rubric 283, f.10, Le Marchant to Pace Forno, 11 January 1859.
[36] MGG, 10 May 1869, Ordinance II (1859), 97-107.
[37] See the voluminous correspondence in AES, M III, 123/48.
[38] MGG, 18 October 1974, Act XLII (1974), A 385-9.
[39] NAM, Acts of Notary Matteo Briffa, xci, 23 November 1577.
[40] AAM, *Correspondence*, 25 (1796-1801), f.639ʳ.
[41] *Gazzetta del Governo di Malta*, 9 February 1814, Proclamation (4 February 1814).
[42] A. Bonnici, 'The Oath Question', 14-26.
[43] MGG, 9 January 1839, minute (2 January 1839), 13.
[44] NLM, *Despatches* (1847-8), ff.195ʳ–207ᵛ, O'Ferrall to Grey, 13 January 1848.
[45] PP, 1838-xxix-141, Royal Commissioners' Report on 'Liberty of Printing and Publishing', 16-17.
[46] CO 159/13, Glenelg to Ludolf, 15 April 1836 (draft).
[47] MGG, 14 February 1845, Ordinance (draft), 7-11.
[48] CO 158/131, Stephen to Stuart, 7 June 1845 (draft).
[49] A. Bonnici, *History of the Church in Malta*, iii, 234-5.
[50] *Hansard*, 3rd ser., cxxix (1853), House of Commons Debate, 15 August 1853; PP, 1852-1xii-924; ibid., 1854-x1iii-290.
[51] MGG, 10 March 1854, 41-5.
[52] MGG, 2 October 1857, 289-90; PP, 1870-x1ix-251.
[53] Laferla, 217; Bezzina, 233-4.
[54] See G. Piatti, *I cento giorni di Garibaldi in Sicilia nel giornalismo Maltese, passim.*
[55] See J. Bezzina, 'Asylum in Malta: A British offer to Pope Pius IX', 1-12.
[56] See AES, M III, 127/49-51; P.P. Borg, *La Questione Matrimoniale in Malta.*
[57] Ibid.; also P. Debono, *Sommario della storia della legislazione in Malta*, 420-1.

[58] Bonnici, *History of the Church*, iii, 251-2.
[59] AAM, *Correspondence* (1896), f.35, Freemantle to Pace, 6 March 1896.
[60] MGG, 5 August 1975, Act XXXVII (1975), A 345-61.
[61] For a bibliography on the subject, Bezzina, *Religion and Politics in a Crown Colony*, 167-7, and fn. 63.
[62] J. Shebbeare, *Letters of an English Nation*, 144.
[63] ASV, SCC, *Consistoria* (1807-08), f.46^r.
[64] PP, 1813-xi-227, 3.
[65] CO 158/19, Royal Commissioners' Report (1812), 128-33.
[66] CO 158/64, Ponsonby to Della Somaglia, 14 July 1829 (copy).
[67] CO 159/14, Glenelg to Bouverie, 17 January 1837 (copy).
[68] MGG, 17 January 1838, Proclamation I (1838), 17.
[69] CO 158/106, Bouverie to Normanby, 11 May 1839.
[70] See AES, M III, 27/16-24.
[71] CO 158/136, O'Ferrall to Grey, 7 August 1846.
[72] Ibid.
[73] FO 43/66, Lyons to Normanby, 1 June 1857; J. Bezzina 'British diplomacy and the election of Bishop Gaetano Pace Forno', 89-102.
[74] F. Azzopardi, 'The appointment of Bishop A.M. Buhagiar as Apostolic Administrator of Malta', 94-107.
[75] This emerges from Pace's correspondence. See 'Private Papers of Bishop Pietro Pace' in AAM and AEG.
[76] See AES, M III, 120/47.
[77] Koster, 74. The question was discussed in Session 668 (24 February 1890) of the Sacred Congregation of Extraordinary Ecclesiastical Affairs. The concluding resolution, denying the existence of the right of veto, was communicated to Simmons on 20 March 1890. See AES, M III, 122/47.
[78] See D. Fenech, *The Making of Archbishop Gonzi.*
[79] Ibid., 1-26, and *passim*; Koster, 122-8.
[80] See Andrew Vella's interview with Gonzi, in *Storja (1978)*, 129-30; J.R. Colville, *Man of Valour*, 249; G. Pisani, *Il-Ġabra tal-Qamħ*. Contemporary local sources agree that the incident was of no major significance. The election of Gonzi was the result of Vatican diplomacy. See Koster, 127-8.
[81] The story forms the central theme of my *Religion and Politics.*
[82] CO 158/191, Bouverie to Caruana, 17 January 1837, (encl. A, after 25 October 1860).
[83] PAV, *Gov.* 57, f.258^r, Elliot to Le Marchant, 26 September 1860.
[84] PAV, *Letters* (1852-60), f.2^r, Le Merchant to Newcastle, 26 October 1860 (draft).
[85] FO 43/75, John Russell to Odo Russell, 21 November 1860 (draft).
[86] FO 43/83A, Odo Russell to John Russell, 3 May 1861.
[87] See Pope Pius IX's bull *Singulari amore*, 16 September 1864, ASV, SB 5723, 1797.
[88] Laferla, 221-2.
[89] H.I. Lee, *Malta 1813-1914*, 10-12.
[90] W. Eton, *Authentic Materials for a History of the People of Malta*, 178.
[91] MGG, 6 May 1835, Proclamation V (1835), 153.
[92] G.C. Lewis, *Letters ... to various friends*, quoted in H. Sedall, *Malta: Past and Present*, 233.
[93] MGG, 23 August 1849, 109-10.
[94] CO 158/202, Le Marchant to Newcastle, 30 January 1864.
[95] MGG, 10 May 1870, Government Notice, 75-6.
[96] H. Frendo, *Party Politics in a Fortress Colony*, 23.

[97] The leading role played by Panzavecchia in local politics remains to be studied; for a general idea of his career, Frendo, *passim*.
[98] Koster, 69-72; for a deeper study, H. Frendo, *Birth Pangs of a Nation*.
[99] H. Ganado, *Rajt Malta Tinbidel*, i, 198-207, and *passim*.
[100] Ibid., 238-54; Frendo, *Party Politics*, 183-96.
[101] *Exposition of the Malta Question*, 25, 45.
[102] *Report of the Royal Commission of 1931*, 160-3.
[103] Koster, 72-5; Frendo, *Party Politics*, 201-15.
[104] Ganado, 404-22; Koster, 93-119.
[105] CO 158/536, Gonzi to St John Jackson, 23 October 1941, quoted in Koster, 85.
[106] A former secretary to Mgr. Gonzi and a close friend to several parish priests at the time confirmed to me that such an affirmation was baseless.
[107] See especially *Progress*, 21 October 1921, 1; *Times of Malta, passim*.
[108] Strickland to Caruana, 19 July 1928, quoted in Koster, 95.
[109] AAM, *Pastorali/Editti*, Caruana's Pastoral Letter, 15 August 1928.
[110] Ganado, 404; Koster, 99-101.
[111] Ganado, 405; Koster, 99.
[112] Koster, 98.
[113] Gasparri to Chilton, 23 February 1929, in *Exposition of the Malta Question*, 67-7.
[114] A. Rhodes, *The Vatican in the Age of the Dictators*, 58.
[115] *Exposition of the Malta Question*, 58.
[116] Koster, 103.
[117] *Exposition of the Malta Question*, 103-8; Ganado, 415-6.
[118] MGG, 16 May 1930, 371-4.
[119] *Exposition of the Malta Question*, 91.
[120] AAM, *Pastorali/Editti*, Caruana/Gonzi's Pastoral Letter, 1 May 1930; Ganado, 417-8.
[121] *Hansard*, 3rd ser., ccxl, 968, House of Commons Debate, 24 June 1930.
[122] Koster, 111.
[123] Ibid., 111-2; Ganado, 455-6.
[124] Ganado, 462-5.
[125] MGG, 2 November 1933, Official Announcement/Proclamation, 927/9.
[126] E. Brockman, *Last Bastion*, 13.
[127] *Hansard*, 3rd ser., lxxxviii, 320, House of Commons Debate, 3 August 1846.
[128] Ganado, *passim*; Bonnici, *History of the Church*, iii, 114-27, 136-70, and *passim*.
[129] Koster, 144-6.
[130] Ganado, iii, 459-62; ibid., iv, 5-8; Koster, 151-64.
[131] *Times of Malta*, 15 April 1943; Ganado, iv, 5-8.
[132] AAM, *Pastorali/Editti*, Gonzi/Pace's Pastoral Letter, 21 January 1956.
[133] A. Eden, *Memoirs*, 388.
[134] *Times of Malta*, 8 February 1956.
[135] Eden, 387.
[136] House of Commons Debate, 26 March 1956, quoted in Eden, 387-8.
[137] Ganado, iv, 192-3.
[138] AAM, *Pastorali/Editti*, Gonzi/Pace's Pastoral Letter, 21 February 1960.
[139] For an account of the celebrations, Ganado, iv, 278-97.
[140] AAM, *Pastorali/Editti*, Gonzi's Pastoral Letter, 15 February 1961.
[141] Dom Mintoff, *Priests and Politics in Malta*, 19; for the full statement, ibid., 19-29.
[142] For the relative correspondence, Mintoff, 41-4; Ganado, iv, 349-51.

[143]　Bezzina, *Religion and Politics,* 332.
[144]　For a general idea, Ganado, iv, 353-68; Koster, 174-6; Mintoff, 52-7.
[145]　AAM, *Pastorali/Editti,* Gonzi/Pace's Pastoral Letter, 25 January 1952; Ganado, iv, 362.
[146]　Dom Mintoff, *Malta: Church, State, Labour,* 45.
[147]　Ganado, iv, 418-23.
[148]　H.E. Cardinale, *The Holy See and the International Order,* 252.
[149]　Ganado, iv, 549; for the full agreement, Koster, 210.
[150]　Bonnici, *History of the Church,* iii, 284-5; Bezzina, *Religion and Politics,* 328-9.

5

ADRIANUS KOSTER

Regular and Secular Clergy in British Malta

The local Roman Catholic Church was conspicuously present,
both at the beginning and at the end of the British colonial era
in Malta. This can be seen as an indication that the Church
played a very important role throughout the colonial period. It
does not, however, imply that the Church did not undergo
tremendous changes, as did all Maltese society under British
rule.

The Church owed its dominant position on the islands in part
to the British authorities, who granted it important privileges
in exchange for assurances of loyalty and support. But the
privileges, however helpful, were not enough. What made the
Maltese Church into a bastion of power were the protection and
the massive support of a population which in those days clung
to it as the principal symbol of Maltese identity *vis-à-vis* the
colonial power. This gave the Church a chance fully to
monopolize the development of the Maltese population, and only
after the departure of the British was it possible to initiate a
heated debate about Maltese identity and the direction in which
it should develop.

It is impossible to discuss fully the changing position of the
Church and clergy in British Malta in a paper.[1] I have done so
elsewhere[2] and there is no need to repeat or even summarize
myself. But I would like to elaborate in the present paper on
the position of the two types of clergy: the secular or diocesan,
organized on a territorial basis; and the regular clergy, that is
the friars and members of the various religious orders. In doing
so, I am able to make some corrections to the picture I have

previously presented of the Maltese Church, where I tended to neglect the impact of the regular clergy.[3] A brief overview of Church-State relations in the colonial era will precede the actual item. Unfortunately my material contains quite a few gaps as systematic research on this subject still has to be carried out. My arrangement of data will thus be of a preliminary character.

I CHURCH AND STATE

The British overlords on the one hand strengthened the position of Church and Bishop *vis-à-vis* the local population, but on the other hand some measures were taken to establish an efficient colonial administration. The indigenous element within the Church was strengthened at the expense of the traditional ties with Sicily, and useful 'business-like' relations were kept between Great Britain and the Holy See.

The increasing strategic importance of Malta in the second part of the nineteenth century led to a growing British colonial penetration. The emphatic policy of the colonial authorities to replace Italian by English as the official language of Malta is an example of this penetration. This policy led to growing resistance from the local élite, consisting mainly of lawyers and members of the clergy. The Colonial Government deliberately created a pro-British middle class and assured itself of the right of approval whenever new bishops had to be appointed. As a result of the establishment of a naval dockyard by the British, a workers' proletariat emerged, which became increasingly important after the Second World War. This had manifested itself in the riots of 7 June 1919, which probably gave rise to the cession of self-government, at a time when the international situation permitted this. In this period, the Church expanded in many ways.

With the diarchical Constitution of 1921, events accelerated. Party formation occurred mainly on the basis of language preference, with the exception of the Malta Labour Party. The support given to the conservative élite (the Nationalists) by the majority of the clergy led to a growing anticlerical attitude on the part of the middle class and the proletariat. When a combination of the latter two came to power under the half-

British Prime Minister, Lord Strickland, a bitter fight ensued between Church and State, in which the clergy naturally closed ranks. As a consequence of this increasingly escalating struggle, a diplomatic controversy arose between the United Kingdom and the Vatican. When the issue had got out of hand, Britain made use of the growing international tensions in order to suspend the Constitution and restore order in Malta. In the meantime, the Church had managed, by means of spiritual sanctions, to bring Lord Strickland, a sincere practising Catholic, to Canossa.

The Second World War saw Italy settle the Language Question to the detriment of Italian by bombing Malta. This also threw discredit on to the Nationalists, some of whom were interned for alleged security reasons. The war also gave the Bishop of Gozo, Mgr. Michael Gonzi, a chance to rehabilitate himself in the eyes of the British after his alleged anti-British attitude during the Strickland affair. Mgr. Gonzi became the first Archbishop of Malta in 1944.

After the war, diarchy was restored. The workers and middle class united themselves in the Malta Labour Party which was returned to power as a result of strong union support. The middle class, however, soon abandoned the party because of the anti-British policy of Dom Mintoff who had taken over the party leadership in 1949. As a result of the split in the party, Labour found itself in opposition and the Nationalists, who had meanwhile redeemed themselves and developed into a 'normal' conservative party, and having gained the support of the middle class, were returned to power. Some of the latter were lured back by Mintoff's proposal to integrate Malta with the United Kingdom, and this paved the way for another Labour Government in 1955.

Both the Church and the Nationalist Party staunchly opposed the Integration proposals, which they saw as harmful to the Catholic, Latin identity of Malta. As a result of this opposition, and of far-reaching changes in Britain's international defence policy after the Suez Crisis (1956), the hesitant support of the United Kingdom in favour of Integration was withdrawn and Mintoff's extreme financial demands were rejected by London. Mintoff resigned and the Constitution was once more suspended. Archbishop Gonzi's disapproval of riots by Labour supporters, and his 'unpatriotic' behaviour were the cause of a fast-escalating conflict between the clergy and the Labour Party (the *casus belli* was the withholding of support for the Integration proposals by the hierarchy). As a result of ecclesiastical sanctions, the MLP lost the 1962 elections which were held under a new Constitution, and was not in a position to influence developments towards Independence, which was actually gained in 1964 as a consequence of the decreasing strategic importance of Malta. For the hierarchy, Independence meant first and foremost the withdrawal of the British protection which had been vital for the maintenance of its importance during the colonial period.

II CROWN-COLONY RULE (1813-1921): ADJUSTMENTS AND PROSPERITY

New opportunities for the diocesan Church

The leaders of the insurrection against the French had placed Malta under the protection of the British Crown, but expected in exchange

(Clause 6) That His Majesty the King is the protector of our holy Religion and is bound to uphold and protect it as heretofore ...
(Clause 7) The interference in matters spiritual or temporal of no other temporal sovereign shall be permitted in these Islands: and reference in spiritual matters shall only be had to the Pope, and to the respective Generals of the Monastic Orders.[4]

The élite was not in favour of the return of the Order of St John. The nobility and the secular clergy had hardly anything to gain by it.

Like the Knights, the British ruled Malta centrally from Valletta, an administrative consequence of the strategic importance of the islands. The diocesan Church, however, was hierarchically organized with a decentralized apparatus in which the parishes were the most important social and territorial units. The parish priests became the most important spokesmen of their parishes and were as such recognized by the colonial authorities, a peculiar kind of indirect rule which has always been popular in British colonial administration.[5]

The British realized that they owed their presence in Malta

to a great extent to the secular clergy and started out by trying to accomodate them.

Canon law was accepted as valid for all Maltese in respect of marriage, and the activities of Protestant missionaries were often frowned upon and restricted. The head of the diocesan Church, the Bishop, was honoured by the British and recognized as the most important citizen of the new colony, only next in rank to the Governor. He was allowed to settle in Valletta and henceforth he pontificated in the previous conventual church (now St John's Co-Cathedral). Thus the regular regime, which Malta had known under the Order,[6] definitely ceased to exist.

Indigenization of the Church

Although the British were certainly less anticlerical than Napoleon, some of the latter's revolutionary measures were retained. The British too were against foreign interference with the Maltese Church; they only undertook not to undermine the status of the Pope. It should be noted that the large size of the British Empire, with its many Catholic members, often brought about an identity of interests between the Holy See and the British Government. Sometimes the Pope could be motivated to force the Maltese ecclesiastical authorities to accept certain unpopular British measures.

The British saw to it that, after the death of Mgr. Labini in 1807, the bishopric would never again be occupied by a foreigner, and that the right of nomination by the King of Sicily be terminated. The Maltese See was also separated from the Metropolitan of Palermo. All these affairs were negotiated with the Holy See and the results were favourably accepted by the Maltese.[7] All male religious Orders were also separated from their Sicilian superiors, without doubt at the request of the British authorities. Finally, an ordinance of 1838 forbade the appointment of any foreigner who was not a British subject to any benefice or other ecclesiastical office, unless with the consent of the Governor given after the nominee had sworn an oath of loyalty to the British Crown.[8]

The autonomy of the Maltese Church was only relative. It stood under the firm supervision of the Holy See that was not too remote. The religious Orders were also under supervision of their respective 'generals' in Rome. With modern means of communication, 'Rome' came even nearer to Malta. On the other hand, Britain too intervened in clerical affairs, sometimes with the help of the Vatican, as when it abolished some privileges (*privilegium fori* and ecclesiastical asylum). Furthermore, the British sought to obtain influence in certain ecclesiastical appointments such as canonships and the bishopric itself.[9]

An important intervention of the British in ecclesiastical affairs was the enactment of the Mortmain Law in 1822, in order to limit the Church's right to own property; it being laid down that the Church or other pious or religious institution could not acquire immovable property, except under the condition that it should be sold or disposed of within a year; if it were not, the property would be forfeited to the Government *ipso facto*.[10] The law was drawn up because, according to Bonnici, it had been alleged in the beginning of the nineteenth century that the Church owned one-third of the immovable property in Malta and Gozo.[11] It is interesting to note that the Church's property was owned by such scattered units as the cathedral chapter and the various collegiate chapters, parishes, religious Orders, or lay confraternities; in the eyes of the administration, too much immovable 'Church property' would presumably hamper equal taxation of the land.

Expansion of the Church

During the nineteenth century, the diocesan Church expanded rapidly. Many new parishes were created in Malta and Gozo; the latter island even became a separate diocese. The number of collegiate chapters and basilicas increased.

The expansion of the religious orders seemed to be more gradual. It took them some time to recover from the blows Napoleon had dealt them. I do not know if the initial favourable behaviour of the British towards the secular clergy was matched by a similar attitude towards the religious Orders. After all, quite a few civil regimes of the time were more favourably inclined towards the secular clergy, which was more nationally orientated, and less favourably inclined or even hostile towards the religious Orders with their international orientations. But even an initially less favourable attitude of the colonial authorities, if it existed, must soon have been abandoned, as the number of religious Orders and of their members gradually increased. The male and female religious Orders were allowed to expand in the 'quartiary sector' such as education and the running of hospitals, two areas which they almost monopolized. Most probably it would have been cheaper for the British to entrust these tasks to the secular clergy instead. Meanwhile the male religious Orders also took pastoral care of specific groups such as people in hospitals or in prison. Other groups, like orphans and girls in distress, were taken care of by the expanding female religious Orders.

With the penetration of the Church (either secular or regular) in all spheres of social life in Malta, a process of clericalization took place[12] which lasted until after Malta became independent.

An indication of the increasing importance of the religious Orders in the nineteenth century is the elevation of two churches in Valletta, the traditional bulwark of the Orders, to the dignity of basilica. Four religious were even promoted to the (acting) bishopric of Malta and Gozo, though two of them soon had to leave the diocese after a short apostolic administratorship.

In the case of Mgr. Paul Micallef, OSA (Gozo, 1866-67), no troubles occurred. He was promoted because of his qualities to the Sacred Congregation for Bishops and the Religious in Rome and ended his career as Archbishop of Pisa, an important Italian diocese.

Mgr. Antonio Buhagiar, OFM Cap. (Malta, 1885-88) was, however, forced to step down because he was *persona non grata* to the British, who requested the Pope to object to his appointment as Bishop of Malta. This prelate, unfortunately, happened to be a *protegé* of the influential French Capuchin, Cardinal Lavigerie, during a period of tension between France and the United Kingdom. The Governor was against Buhagiar's appointment, and his attitude was stiffened by the fact that the prominent Nationalist, Fortunato Mizzi (supporter of the Italian language in Malta, as against the English language which was officially encouraged) had openly supported Buhagiar.[13] A recent source points to another handicap in Buhagiar: the diocesan clergy did not wish to have a member of a religious Order at the head of the diocese.[14] The Holy See gave in and promoted the Bishop of Gozo instead of Buhagiar.[15]

The appointment of a new Bishop of Malta in 1915 was also a complicated matter. The cathedral chapter had successfully lobbied against the appointment of the able and popular Dominican apostolic administrator, Mgr. Angelo Portelli.[16] The canons must have been furious, however, when unexpectedly Dom Maurus Caruana, OSB, who had been Benedictine abbot in Scotland for some decades, was appointed instead. The British welcomed the appointment, as Caruana had spent most of his life in Britain since there was no Benedictine community in Malta.[17]

Caruana kept Portelli as his Vicar-General and together they were responsible for the creation of four 'regular' parishes. Up till that time, only St Dominic's in Valletta had been taken care of by a religious Order.

Caruana had a rather inauspicious start. His first pastoral letter was, as usual, written in Italian, but a Maltese translation was added. A few weeks later, when the Bishop began his sermon in English, most of the Nationalists present in St John's Co-Cathedral rose in protest and left. The cathedral chapter, highly critical of the regular Bishop and extremely pro-Italian, would never forgive him. The fact that, at the end of the Crown-Colony period, in spite of resistance by the most prominent sectors of the secular clergy, the two most important ecclesiastical offices were held by two religious, and that a start had been made to entrust 'normal' pastoral care to religious Orders, can be seen as an indication of the importance the latter had achieved within the Maltese Church.

The colonial regime was to present another opportunity for the Jesuits to reappear on the Maltese scene. In 1845 members of the British province had been allowed to open a school and had played an important role in the furtherance of the English language. In 1866 the Sicilian province of Loyola's Order was invited by the Bishop of Gozo to set up a seminary and a boarding-school in the recently-created diocese. These Jesuits had been expelled from Palermo by Garibaldi and their guiding principle was to keep Sicilian culture alive. This school was to have a great influence on the intellectual climate of Malta and Gozo because the best families of the islands sent their children to it, while the diocesan clergy in Malta were taught in the

Bishop's seminary by teachers who were themselves educated by the Jesuits in Gozo. The latter had a great responsibility for the pro-Italian cultural climate that was prevalent in Malta until the Second World War among the secular and much of the regular clergy.[18]

Discussion

It is difficult to speak of sharp antagonism between the regulars and the seculars during this period, although some incidents did take place, but these can hardly be compared to the sharp divisions within the secular clergy, which I have dealt with elsewhere, i.e. the division between a small pro-British group at the top and the remaining pro-Italian part.[19] The religious seem to have been less politically inclined; as far as I know the Bishop never appointed a regular priest on an ecclesiastical seat in the Council of Government.[20] The Dominicans had a moderate pro-British reputation, while the Franciscan Orders were near to the working-classes, even in their sympathies. The Jesuits were close to the diocesan clergy and influenced them considerably.

Generally it seems that the Church as a whole profited from the chances offered to them by the British, and continued the process of clericalization which may have already begun under the Order of St John.

III Towards Independence (1921-64): A Church under Challenge

During this period, Malta three times obtained her own Parliament and Self-Government, though with limited competence. Twice the Constitution was suspended by the British after serious conflicts in which the Church had been conspicuous.[21]

In 1930, the faithful were notified by the Bishops that it was mortal sin to vote in the forthcoming election for the pro-British Prime Minister, Lord Strickland, his party, or his allies, the Labour Party. A conflict between Strickland and two secular priests appointed to the Senate by Bishop Caruana, arose because of the support of the Reverend Senators for the pro-

Italian opposition. The conflict escalated and Strickland found
almost the entire secular clergy serried against him. The Bishop
was reluctant to act against Strickland, until the latter protected
two Franciscan supporters of his party against the wrath of a
notorious Fascist Italian Visitor of the Order, Padre Carta.
Strickland's interference in the 'internal matters of a religious
Order' was unforgivable in the eyes of the ex-abbot, who changed
his otherwise pro-British attitude and mobilized all the clergy,
regular and secular, in his battle against the anticlerical Prime
Minister.[22]

A few decades later (1958-69), Archbishop Gonzi again
mobilized all members of the clergy in a hectic fight with the
Labour Party, led by Dom Mintoff. The ranks were closed at the
climax of this fight, but at certain other moments a few members
of the clergy, secular and religious, 'defected'.

In the meantime, the number of secular priests had diminished
from 734 in 1921 to 578 in 1963, while the male religious
increased from 258 to 463, the many religious in Britain and
in the missions not being considered.[23] With the gradual
introduction of the 'welfare state', many new tasks were
assigned to the religious, many more schools and hospitals were
opened, and they were entrusted with the training of elementary
school teachers.

Discussion

It is difficult to explain the increased importance of the regular
versus the secular clergy in Maltese society. The status of the
secular clergy (with the exception of the élite Orders of the
Jesuits and Dominicans) has always been higher than that of
the 'simple friars'. Some explanation might be found in the
latter's preoccupation with the 'quartiary sector', especially
education, in which they were very much engaged. This has been
of course an ideal help to foster vocations. The secular clergy
only had the major and minor seminary at their disposal. But
this can only be part of the explanation.

The potential antagonism of regular and secular not
only did not materialize under the Knights. It is odd that
it also failed to materialize under British rule when regular and
secular were left without any other competing clerical

apparatuses. It is more difficult to link this particular relative absence of antagonism to the process of State formation in Malta. Has cohesion been necessary to confront the British, Strickland, and Mintoff? But why is it that the secular clergy has often been divided in the nineteenth and twentieth centuries?

Maybe the many 'cross-cutting ties' play a role in the intra-clerical pacification.[24] The geographical closeness to Rome may also be a contributory factor.

In other dioceses, the regular priests were relatively more mobile than in Malta, where a sea had always to be crossed before another diocese was reached.

However, I am still looking for a satisfying explanation for the fact that the relationship between the regular and secular clergy in British Malta seemed to be characterized by co-operation rather than infighting. There is ample scope for further research in this field.

NOTES

[1] The present article is a partial report of my research into political and religious leadership in Malta carried out since 1973 with support from the Netherlands Organization for the Advancement of Pure Research (ZWO) and the Free University of Amsterdam. Research was based on field work and the study of written sources. I am grateful to Mart Bax, Mario Buhagiar, Donald Harrison Smith, Matthew Schoffeleers, John Parr, the group 'Religious Regimes' of the Department of Social Anthropology of the Free University, Amsterdam, the 'Study Group Europe', and the participants of two conferences where I presented a Dutch and an English draft ('Paters, broeders, zusters en wereldheren op Malta een orientatie' and 'Regular and secular clergy in Malta: Co-operation or Infighting in a Mediterranean Catholic Regime ?') for their constructive comments. The first part of these drafts was published a few years ago (see 'The Knights' State (1530-1798): A Regular Regime'). This article is the revised edition of the last part.
[2] I did so elaborately in A. Koster, *Prelates and Politicians,* 33-196. See D. Harrison Smith and A. Koster, *Lord Strickland,* and A. Koster, 'The Kappillani'.
[3] I began to correct my views in Koster, 'The Knights' State', under the influence of Mart Bax who, in his studies of the Catholic regime in southern Dutch society and Yugoslavia, has developed a model in which he shows how the dual organizational structure of a territorial diocesan clergy and a non-territorial regular clergy gives the local Catholic Church its own internal dynamics. See M. Bax, 'Wie tegen de kerk piest wordt zelf nat', and *id.,* 'Religious Regimes and State Formation'.
[4] A.V. Laferla, *British Malta,* i, 27-8.
[5] The British Governors adopted the function of the Grand Masters at the Candlemas ceremony and addressed the parish priests on important state affairs,

so that they, as the traditional leaders of the villagers and towns, could inform their parishioners. See Koster, 'The Kappillani'.

[6] See Koster, 'The Knights' State'.

[7] Laferla, i, 58-9, 124-5; A. Bonnici, *History of the Church in Malta*, iii, 5, 6, 10; H.I. Lee, 'British policy towards the religion, ancient laws and customs in Malta', 6-9.

[8] E.P. Vassallo, *Strickland*, 406.

[9] I do not know if they ever tried to interfere with the appointments of Maltese superiors of the religious Orders. If they did, it would be in line with their policy. If not, the religious Orders must have been considered as less important or less potentially militant than the diocesan clergy.

[10] Laferla, i, 99-100; Bonnici, iii, 256-7; Harrison Smith, *Britain in Malta*, i, 73.

[11] Bonnici, iii, 256.

[12] The term has been derived from Bax, 'Wie tegen de kerk piest wordt zelf nat'.

[13] Laferla, ii, 84; H. Frendo, *Party Politics*, 47.

[14] F. Azzopardi, 'The Appointment of Bishop A.M. Buhagiar', 103.

[15] Malta was not only the larger and senior diocese, her bishop also had the rank of archbishop. Mgr. Buhagiar became Apostolic Delegate in Santo Domingo, where he died of fever shortly after his arrival.

[16] F. Mallia, *L-Isqof li ħabbu kulħadd*, 162-3.

[17] It is said that the influential philantropist, Alfons Maria Galea, was behind the appointment. Galea was a well-known friend of the religious Orders.

[18] See Laferla, i, 221-2. Until the end of the Second World War, it was the custom in most Maltese monasteries, and also in the seminaries, to read only from Italian books during meals and to use only this language in conversation. These practices were not abolished until after many complaints that the new novices could not understand what was being said, and as a result of the discrediting of Italian culture after Italy joined the war on the Axis side. Koster, *Prelates and Politicians*, 59.

[19] Ibid., 58-9.

[20] This may also be an indication of contempt for the religious.

[21] See Koster, *Prelates and Politicians*, 79-92, 151-215.

[22] See Harrison Smith and Koster, ii, 382-537.

[23] F. Mizzi, *Priestly Vocations in the Maltese Ecclesiastical Province*.

[24] J. Boissevain, *Saints and Fireworks*, 138-9.

6

CARMEL CASSAR

Everyday Life in Malta
in the Nineteenth and Twentieth Centuries

While describing the Maltese character, Frederick M. Lacroix observed that 'the Maltese are intelligent, hardworking, clever and can surely succeed in all fields of work ... but the English Government looks at the occupation of Malta solely and entirely as an important fortress colony and is indifferent towards the interests of its inhabitants.'[1] Lacroix was writing in 1848, at a time when the French and the British were not exactly on friendly terms but his account seems fairly reasonable if compared to that of Senior Nassau who, in 1882, wrote that 'Maltese incomes are so small that the attempt to keep the appearance which the English think only decent, becomes a ruinous expense.'[2]

The Maltese maintained a cool relationship with the British, mixing very little at least until the 1930s.[3] The Sliema area was the first part of the island to adapt an Anglicized style and sub-culture. This was fostered by the dominant position of the Church. When writing on the matter in the early 1930s, Sir Harry Luke, Lieutenant-Governor of Malta, remarked that 'the Maltese are among the most devoted sons and daughters of the Roman Catholic Church.'[4]

The islanders, notably country folk, depended directly on the local priests, making the church the centre of village life, and the parish priest its first citizen. The priest combined teaching and several other advisory duties with his spiritual role. He was also the main link with the world outside, with the church acting as a meeting place, with the climax being reached during the feast of the patron saint.[5] Likewise, religion was entrenched in the heart of the people, making the parish and the village one and the same thing, a situation that persisted at least up to the late 1930s. The position of the parish priest was therefore dominant. Herbert Ganado related that when, in the 1920s, he was invited by a friend to the Siggiewi village feast, his friend's father asked him whether he had first been to the parish priest.[6] In the village, doctor, lawyer, notary, pharmacist, police inspector, and sergeant all enjoyed an important social status, but the parish priest was the undisputed head.

This state of affairs could also be found, though to a lesser extent, in the harbour area. The British had, early in the nineteenth century, done their best to introduce the Protestant faith amongst the people, but without much success.[7] Protestant clergymen who visited Malta in the nineteenth century could hardly allow such a situation to pass unnoticed. One such pastor, the Revd H. Seddall, wrote in 1870:[8]

Religious fervour is one of the leading features in the character of the Maltese people, and it discovers itself ... in the building of churches and chapels; the erection of images at the corners of the streets, to be devoutly worshipped by the populace.

He further commented on the poor education of the Maltese clergy, and how 'they look with suspicion on everything that is stamped with the religion of England'.[9] Seddall pointed out that the religion of Malta was directed to the senses rather than prayer. Hence, 'it takes the gross form in which we find it in Italy, Spain, in South America, in all countries completely under the ecclesiastical domination of Rome'.[10]

What Seddall wrote, not perhaps without some bias, in 1870, applied also to the 1930s.[11] It was the Second World War which, to some extent, brought about a change in the mentality of the population. The war brought villager and townsman closer together. It also undermined the traditional respect for authority. The younger generation, which came out of the war disillusioned by conscription, had new ideals, including greater freedom. This meant the discarding of old principles and a more general indifference towards the clergy.

I POPULATION, WORK, AND MIGRATION

When the Order of St John left Malta in 1798, the population of the Maltese Islands, which in 1530 had amounted to a mere 20,000, had gone up to 100,000. Although, in the two years that followed, Malta's population decreased slightly, owing to the effect of the uprising against the French, combined with hunger and the spread of disease, there was a gradual increase after 1800. The plague of 1813 once again checked this growth, but by 1828 the population was again on the rise.[12] The histogram below is a clear indication of how the number of inhabitants kept on growing throughout the British period. In fact, from just above 100,000 in the early nineteenth century, it surpassed the quarter of a million after the Second World War and rose to over 300,000 a decade later.

TABLE 1. Population Increase in Thousands
1798-1957

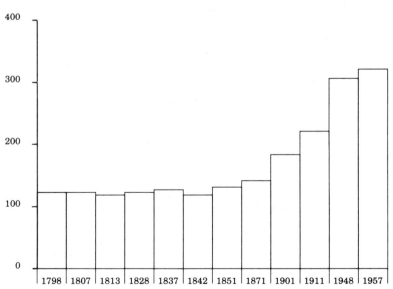

SOURCES: L.H. Dudley Buxton, *Malta*; H. Bowen-Jones et al., *Malta*; E.L. Zammit, *A Colonial Inheritance*; various 'Descriptions' of Malta, and the relevant censuses

At the beginning of the nineteenth century, the population of the harbour area grew slowly. Valletta, for example, had a population increase, reaching the 25,000 mark by 1861. During the 1860s, people were already seeking dwellings in the suburbs. Floriana's population grew steadily in the decade after 1861, but ceased to maintain the same rapid growth after 1871. The dependence of Malta's economy on foreign sources since the time of the Knights, linked with the presence of the British forces, further encouraged the shifting of villagers to the urban and suburban areas. Hamrun grew in importance to such an extent that the need to establish it as a parish was felt in the late 1860s. This new working-class suburb had a population of 1,500 in 1860; it went up to 2,500 by 1870 and to about 6,000 by 1890.[13]

Other suburban areas which had previously been larger villages, like Birkirkara and Qormi, experienced notable increases. Working-class suburbs which, like Hamrun, underwent a more explosive demographic growth, included Paola and Marsa. While in 1871 there were 3,200 persons living in the Hamrun, Marsa, and St Venera areas, by 1948 there were ten times as many. In Paola there had been only 488 inhabitants in 1861, going up to 14,793 in 1948.[14]

A similar demographic growth was taking place on the other side of the Marsamxett harbour. Sliema, which in 1861 had a mere 324 inhabitants, reached the 23,000 mark by 1957, while St Julians, which in 1871 consisted of 600 inhabitants, had 9,122 after the Second World War. By 1945 the suburban area of Sliema, St Julians, Gzira, Msida, and Pietà formed a continuous inhabited belt occupying the northern shore of Marsamxett harbour.[15]

The suburbs had undergone a rapid increase between 1850 and 1900. If taken together, the population of the suburbs, which in 1850 accounted for only 15,000, had by 1900 reached 54,000. Meanwhile, the population of Valletta and the Three Cities remained relatively stable. Population increase in the suburbs does not seem to have taken place at the expense of the old urbanized areas, but was due rather to the migration of people from the countryside to the developing harbour area in search of better jobs.

This phenomenon is explained by Dudley Buxton who asserts that, by 1921, about one-fourth of the population in Malta resided in the towns around the harbour, i.e. Valletta, the Three Cities, and Floriana; one-third lived in the nearby suburban area, while the rest were scattered in the mostly agricultural parts.[16] Therefore, whereas from 1842 to 1901 the rural population comprised 33.6 per cent of the population,[17] it had become proportionately smaller by 1921, and even more so after 1945.

The growth of the suburbs and the strengthening of the non-agricultural element in rural areas, which had developed during the British rule, took root mainly through the modernization of economic life, a highly demanding dockyard and harbour activity, and improved internal systems of transport.[18]

From 1871 onwards, non-agricultural employment became dominant in the Maltese economy. This meant that the local industries tied to the old agricultural pattern had begun to die out, while more people were finding employment with the colonial Government. Malta was so important as a British base that it was felt desirable to provide direct employment for most of the population. This

influenced people's minds as it controlled their fortunes. This applied to civil servants, industrial workers, and especially to those enlisted in the Armed Forces and in ancillary services.[19]

More and more people became dependent on harbour activities. Between 1871 and 1881, the working population increased substantially, from 40,699 to 46,116. Functionally, the largest increase -- 100 per cent -- occurred among porters, carriers, and coalheavers; while the commercial group increased by 27 per cent. The building industry suffered a slight decrease. By 1891 the harbour boom was over, but Government expenditure and imperial military spending continued to grow.[20] The great increase of coalheavers is significant, especially since the majority, about 80 per cent, lived in Luqa, Qormi, and Zejtun. This suggests that, by 1891, the area of harbour activities extended to most of the eastern and central parts of Malta.[21] In the 1920s they were still mainly recruited from the Marsa, Tarxien, Qormi, Luqa, and Zabbar areas. There were about 2,000 who, for a slightly better-than-average pay, had to work under deplorable conditions.[22]

The most important industrial development during the British

period took place in the dockyard which saw a rapid increase
in its working force between the 1890s and the late 1940s. The
total number of dockyard workers at this period is here given
at approximately ten-year intervals:

TABLE 2. Total Number of Dockyard Workers
1896-1969

Year	Number	Year	Number
1896	3 000	1939	10 000
1906	4 000	1949	12 000
1918	13 000	1959	5 940
1928	7 500	1969	5 223

SOURCE: E.L. Zammit, *A Colonial Inheritance*, 42.

This mass employment of the Maltese with the colonial
Government led to a situation where the workers felt committed
to the British cause 'as a result of the fact that thousands of
jobs were secured at a rate of pay... often rather better than that
paid to workers in private enterprise ... or indeed in the lower
ranks of the civil service'.[23] The Armed Forces and the
Admiralty were in constant need of manpower, with the result
that, until the Second World War, unemployment was not a
major problem. This also helped in the urbanization of society
because the sons of peasants, who were abandoning the land,
were getting used to living in the towns around the harbour.

Work connected with the Navy had by the early part of the
twentieth century become so vital to the Maltese economy.
Following the Mediterranean fleet's reduction by six battleships,
it was reported to the Royal Commission in 1911 that
commercial activity was revived as soon as the fleet entered the
harbour.[24] Employment with the Services was to decrease only
after the Second World War. However, in 1957, 27 per cent of
the working force was still gainfully employed in colonial
establishments.[25]

As in other continental European societies, the Maltese family
had traditionally assigned secondary importance to women. This
was further stressed in the Mediterranean region, where they
in fact had a great say in familial and household affairs, but
very little influence otherwise.

In the early part of the nineteenth century, many rural women worked as spinners and weavers in their homes, or as beaters and dyers of cotton at home or in small manufacturing factories. Often they even gave a helping hand in fields or on the farm. In 1861, out of 9,000 workers described as spinners and weavers, together with some other 200 beaters and dyers, 96 per cent were women, whose labour was generally used in the final stages of cloth preparation.[26]

Female work in the first three decades of the twentieth century did not differ much. The main difference was to lie in the number of school teachers. Of these, there were only 22 in 1901 and 50 in 1911, but there were 559 in 1921. The teaching profession was considered to provide both security and status to women. Another seemingly popular job with women was that of shop assistant. In 1891 there were only 20, but by 1901 the total had risen to 212.[27]

The Second World War led to a further increase in the employment of women. By mid-1944 there were 1,038 established and 1,234 temporary female employees in the civil-government list alone.[28] Until the 1960s, the Maltese tended to believe that a married woman should not go to work. Hence, by the late 1950s, 51 per cent of the girls under 25 were in gainful occupations, whereas only 8.2 per cent of women remained in employment after marriage.[29] Female emancipation was gradually achieved in the face of strong male opposition. The clergy were also overtly opposed to the idea of female employment. In the late sixties, the Maltese Church was still insisting that a woman's place was in the home.[30]

The Royal Commission of 1911 described the Maltese as

clever and adaptable; generally speaking, however, they appear to lack confidence in themselves and each other ... They are much attached to their native islands, and seldom migrate to distant countries.[31]

This attitude had already been recorded by many other visitors, whose comments are invariably very similar.[32] The Maltese first became attracted to migration in the early years of the nineteenth century. The migratory flow of Maltese to the Ionian Islands was rendered easier by the latter's annexation by the British during the Napoleonic Wars. In 1826 the first known organized attempt was made to establish a Maltese colony in Corfu.[33]

Other attempts to set up Maltese colonies within the Mediterranean region proved successful. A considerable number of Maltese settled in North Africa, notably after the French conquest of Algiers in 1830. In 1842 there were 20,000 Maltese emigrants in Mediterranean countries, which amounted to 15 per cent of the population of the islands. Of these, the majority settled in North Africa, mainly in Tunisia, Algeria, Tripoli, and Egypt. These Maltese emigrant communities increased rapidly as can be seen in the following table:

TABLE 3. Maltese Emigrants to North Africa 1842-80

Year	Algeria	Tunis	Tripoli	Egypt
1842	5000	3000	1000	2000
1865	10000	7000	?	5000
1880	15000	11000	3000	7000

SOURCE: J. Cassar Pullicino, *Studies in Maltese Folklore*, 47.

British visitors were not always impressed by the Maltese. Seddall comments that 'everyone who has lived among the Maltese ... is aware that they are foolishly attached to the island ... The Maltese will not migrate. Young and old, rich and poor, literate and illiterate cling with wonderful tenacity to their island home.'[34]

Seddall's views were of course biased in favour of a northern way of life which he considered superior to the general Mediterranean mentality. Fernand Braudel points out that a Mediterranean native could travel from port to port, and would feel quite at home in any part of the region but would feel homesick and uneasy when leaving its shores.[35] The Maltese, too, found it hard to travel beyond the Mediterranean. Although the British Government tried to encourage them to settle in other parts of the Empire, all its attempts failed and the majority of the settlers had to return.[36]

According to the 1911 census, the majority of emigrants were still seeking other Mediterranean cities and ports, notably Tunis, Alexandria, Bône, Cairo, Philippeville, Tripoli, Corfu, and Constantinople. Up to the First World War, most Maltese migrants remained in the Mediterranean where they formed relatively large communities till after the Second World War. The type of migration advocated by Seddall began to develop early in the twentieth century when a good number of Maltese left for the USA, Canada, Britain, Australia, and other English-speaking countries. It reached a climax between 1948 and 1966 when it rarely fell below the 5,000 mark annually.[37]

II STANDARD OF LIVING AND EDUCATION

The economic and social pressures of demographic growth after the 1830s came at a time when the general standard of living of the Maltese was deteriorating. Malta, which up to the end of the Order's rule had largely depended on Sicilian grain, enjoyed a temporary prosperity as a result of Napoleon's Continental System. Then, from 1813 onwards, the island began to experience enormous economic difficulties which persisted until the 1850s. The King of Sicily and Naples had prohibited the exportation of grain to Malta at a time when Sicily enjoyed an abundant harvest. Therefore, while in Malta wheat was being sold at 60 shillings a quarter, in nearby Sicily it cost only 28 shillings. Senior Nassau blamed King Ferdinand II for not allowing the continuation of grain exports to Malta. It was very likely the result of the Neapolitan King's displeasure at losing his sovereignty over the islands.[38]

The misery of the Maltese was generally attributed to their lack of initiative and reckless birthrate.[39] Governor Hastings and his secretary blamed the Maltese for their lack of 'enterprise',[40] while G.P. Badger, an early nineteenth-century writer, refers to their 'entire want of spirit of enterprise'.[41] The French consul in Malta in 1840 concurred that the Maltese were more inclined to imitate others than to start things by themselves.[42] However, the official report of the Royal Commission blamed the Government for the poor state of affairs: 'The islanders were in a most miserable condition. Due to official policy, the educated among them were a handful; the Nobles were starving, the rest of the population was even worse!'[43]

On the whole, therefore, the islands in the early part of the nineteenth century had been reduced to indigence. This is best shown by the subdivisions of Maltese society in the late 1840s. Two thousand families belonged to the professional and landowning classes, a substantial number of whom experienced difficulties in maintaining a decent standard of living. The wealthiest persons included a few large landowners, some merchant families, and a number of newcomers who shared trade with several British firms. Established in Valletta, these dealt mainly in cotton and cereals.[44] About 150 merchants, together with a few major industrialists and retailers, were to represent the apex of Malta's trading community. In 1842 this community numbered about 5,000 and included numerous small shopkeepers, dairymen, bakers, and the like. These probably earned little more than their friends and relatives in other occupations.[45] One can observe precious little difference between the conditions and customs of unskilled labourers and those of the numerous artisans on the island. It was a current complaint, for example, that numerous young 'tradesmen' could never rise beyond the level of unskilled labourers as they set up on their own far too soon, and with little training. Likewise, one could hardly distinguish between small farmers and agricultural labourers.[46] Taken as a whole, the profit of the unskilled labourer and the less able artisans in town and country areas is given as 6¾d. for a full day's work in the 1830s. Womenfolk could add to this by spinning or weaving.[47]

In the 1880s Senior Nassau remarked that 'Maltese incomes are so small that the attempt to keep up the appearances which the English think only decent becomes a ruinous expense.'[48]

The sharp lowering of standards can best be seen from an observation made by John Davy in 1842: in 1811, according to Padre Carlo Giacinto, the Maltese worker was receiving 18d. a day; by 1842, he received the equivalent of 6½d.[49] Although the standard of living improved notably during the second half of the century, it was only after 1945 that it began to compare favourably with that of other countries in southern Europe.

The low standard of living of the Maltese was reflected in their food. Visitors to Malta from the 1830s onwards agree that both breakfast and dinner were of the most frugal type. Both consisted mainly of barley bread, cheese, olives, onions, garlic, dried fruit, salt-fish, oil, and similar foods. In season they ate freely of melons, prickly pears, and raw vegetables. They also drank a moderate amount of wine and enjoyed cooked vegetables, or *minestra*, after a day's work. One commentator points out that, in spite of such a diet, the Maltese were a strong and healthy people.[50]

Bread was a staple commodity. More often than not, it was the main import from the urban centres to the countryside since most of the other food was home-produced. Meat was rarely tasted. In 1842, Davy remarked that in Gozo 'only one bullock was killed weekly for the market, and that was sufficient for the whole population, including a detachment of British troops who used a considerable proportion of it'.[51]

In many ways, the standard of living of the 1870s and 1880s remained quite similar to that of forty years previously. The Maltese working class still ate very little meat and not much more vegetables, cheese, oil, pasta, or wine. There was a marked difference, however, in bread consumption. The 1836 Royal Commissioners had reported that a field labourer ate 2 pounds of bread a day. Francis Roswell, a British Commissioner investigating the matter forty years later, concluded that in 1877 the same person ate from 4 to 5 pounds a day. Bread was now being made from a good quality wheat, even though the prices were double those of the 1830s.[52]

As bread was the staple food of the masses, the Lieutenant-Governor, William C.F. Robertson, argued in 1919 that a rise in price could easily lead to a riot.[53] The price of bread had in fact gone up from 2½d. to 7½d. per *rotolo* owing to the complete interruption of the Russian grain trade after 1914. This had led to a strike at the dockyard in 1917. The general atmosphere throughout most of the nineteenth and early twentieth centuries deteriorated; social conditions were poor, often verging on starvation. Such a situation was generally attributed to British colonial policy.[54]

Living conditions improved after 1919 and continued to do so up to the advent of the Second World War. The diet of the rural and urban poor only differed in that, while the latter used various forms of pasta, the former made more use of potatoes.[55] A very striking difference existed in the diet of the well-off classes. Ever since the early nineteenth century, these had adopted an Italian diet, distinguished from that of the poor by the inclusion of macaroni, meat, and good wine. The most humiliating aspect was perhaps the queuing up for the *gaxin*, the surplus of army and navy rations, a common practice still in use even in the immediate postwar years, especially in the harbour area where most military activity was centred. The poor and the idle used to do their utmost to get the choice pieces of meat and of the other left-overs.[56]

In the 1950s, Maltese cooking was described as 'sub-Italian, monotonous, and drab'.[57] It included a high amount of starch which adversely affected the figure of the majority of Maltese by their mid-twenties. British-style food, such as fried eggs, bacon, and chips, quickly spread all over the island. Up to the late fifties, Kininmonth could only think of the Hotel Phoenicia as the place where one could eat in style, adding that the Valletta market had a wide variety of food, indicating that there were people who ate well at home.[58]

There was a striking difference between the social life of villagers and that of townsmen. In February 1910, Dr Alfredo Mattei, addressing the Council of Government, observed that

the men of the casals get up at four in the morning, go to hear mass of the *Parroco* and after that they go to Valletta or anywhere else where their work may happen to call them and spend the whole day laboriously at work. Then at the *Ave Maria* at 6.00 p.m., the poor labourer ... rejoins his family, says his prayers, his *Rosario*, and goes to bed.

The same pattern was followed at Rabat and the old capital, Mdina:

even at the *Città Vecchia* where you have a few learned gentlemen and a few *Canonici* ... they get up very early and the few who study and keep late hours prefer candles to olive oil.[59]

Life in the harbour area was more varied, but the lowest stratum of rural and urban societies suffered great hardships. The harbour area was intimately dependent on the Armed Forces. There were times when between 25,000 and 30,000 soldiers were stationed in the island.[60] The impact of British influence was probably greatest in this area where the troops were concentrated.

The general slump in the standard of living from the second decade of the nineteenth century was registered by the Maltese not only in their poor diet, but also in all other aspects of everyday life. The lower classes, which in the nineteenth century amounted to over 90 per cent of the total population, had very bad housing conditions. According to MacGill, writing in 1839, the dwellings of the peasants seemed 'comfortable',[61] but other visitors gave different accounts of these conditions.[62] A typical rural habitation usually had two floors, the first consisting of one or two rooms where the family frequently slept on straw, covering themselves with rags and sacks.[63] The ground floor was usually occupied by quarters for animals with a dung room receiving all human and animal excreta, which were removed twice a year to be spread as manure.[64] Sewers were non-existent and there was no piped water supply. In the towns, the situation was not much better. Some sort of water drainage was only available in middle-class houses which had troughs of porous stone; poor homes had open sinks. Both in town and country, ventilation was poor, and ordinary houses possessed few windows.[65] The 1851 census gives a fair impression of Maltese households. It is in fact reported that only 17 per cent of dwellings were found to be filthy.[66] It appears that the population of both town and country did their best to keep their places of habitation clean. The people themselves were dirty in habit, displaying a marked reluctance to wash. In such conditions, it is no wonder that many diseases spread and frequently claimed numerous victims.[67] This had other repercussions on Maltese society, such as the death of nearly 50 per cent of the infants born every year.

A very interesting report drawn up by Attilio Critien in 1913, describing the *Manderaggio* in Valletta, which is known to have contained the poorest people living in the capital, gives an idea of the habitat of lower-class townspeople. The population of the *Manderaggio*, he says, was 1,200 but, by the end of the Second World War, it had fallen to 1,000. At that time, 5 per cent of the total population of Valletta is estimated to have lived in the *Manderaggio*.[68] This overcrowded area of the city was the most afflicted by disease, yet during the cholera outbreak of 1887, only 20 out of 282 victims came from the *Manderaggio*.[69] That year the Health Department closed down 99 rooms in the area. Only a few enjoyed the luxury of a toilet. It is hardly surprising that the majority of people never reached old age.[70]

Poor housing conditions were to a large extent the result of overpopulation. The worst cases of overcrowding were found in urban and suburban areas. In 1891 the greatest overcrowding was registered in Floriana, where 1,249 persons lived in 241 rooms, an average of 5.18 persons per room. Valletta came second; in that year 4,571 persons lived in 885 rooms, an average of 5.17 persons per room.[71]

The spread of poverty is best reflected in the hordes of beggars, male and female, roaming the streets of towns, particularly Valletta, where one particular locality was named after them.[72] Beggars were an unpopular sight with the British authorities and there were various attempts to control them. Commissioners, such as Sir Penrose Julyan in 1880, noted that there was 'too much charity' in Malta.[73] In the 1850s, Valletta was described as 'a nest of beggars'.[74] In the 1851 census, 1,452 persons were classed as aged and infirm while 12,483 families, or 49 per cent of the population, were classified as poor.[75] By 1854, 2,018 persons received relief from public funds while 1,524 were kept in charitable institutions at public expense.[76] The situation does not seem to have changed much in the latter part of the century. Sir Penrose argued that anyone who lived by daily labour in 1880 was considered to have a claim to gratuitous medical assistance and medicines.[77] The situation remained pretty much the same in the early twentieth century.

Poverty was reflected not only in the quality of food and housing conditions but also in clothing. In the early nineteenth century, clothing was cheap and generally made from coarse local cotton. Later, when the cotton industry ceased to exist, the Maltese had to make use of cheap imported cotton. Shoes were hardly ever used: up to the late 1930s, it was still common to see town and country people walking barefooted. Badger says that country people had the habit of putting on shoes before entering Valletta and taking them off on leaving. Nineteenth-century visitors often mention the popular story of one country woman who asked her companion who was going to Valletta how long she had been using her pair of shoes. The answer was that she had worn them since the time of the plague (1813). 'Oh!', replied the other, 'mine are much older, for I have had them since the blockade of the French (1798).'[78]

Entertainment and medical care were almost non-existent and leisure time was a luxury the poor could not afford. This was in sharp contrast to the upper classes of society. Apart from a healthier diet, these enjoyed a wide variety of clothes made of fine material, comfortable housing conditions, and a wide range of entertainments. Countryfolk dressed differently from townsmen, and one could recognize a person's class from the way he dressed. After the war, differences became less marked.

Sanitary conditions in nineteenth-century Malta were quite deplorable. Some progress was registered by the end of the century when, in 1885, a system of drains was installed throughout the harbour area. This was carried out just in time. Two years later, an outbreak of cholera killed 435 persons and would probably have caused the death of thousands more in the overcrowded parts of the island had these sewers not been installed.[79] Only after the beginning of the twentieth century was the drainage system extended to most of the villages.

There were also attempts to improve hygiene by conducting the main water supply to all parts of Malta. During Bouverie's governorship,[80] an aqueduct was built to bring water from Fawwara to Mqabba, Luqa, Tarxien, Paola, the Three Cities, Gudja, Għaxaq, Żejtun, and Żabbar. It started functioning in 1845. Sliema, the fast-growing town in the northern shore of Marsamxett, was supplied with water in 1881. In 1856 the first borehole, as proposed earlier by Dr Nicola Zammit, was dug to meet the demands of an ever-growing population.

A domestic water supply was introduced in 1890; until then many people had to make use of public water-pumps and private wells. The Chadwick project, meant to ease the water problem, led to better hygenic conditions in most parts of the island. Personal cleanliness was still generally rare until the introduction of bathrooms and it was only in the second and third decades of this century that newly-built houses began to include bathrooms.[81] Houses with bathrooms were, however, still few in number, although they were to be found scattered all over Malta. The drainage system was not extended to the homes of the poor. In remote villages, like Safi, a domestic water supply was available but drainage was not introduced before 1945.[82]

A perennial health problem in British Malta was the heavy incidence of trachoma and undulant fever. Trachoma, an eye disease transmitted by flies, was endemic before the Second World War. Flies were to be found everywhere, particularly in the popular Valletta market, shops, and other such places. In

Gozo, where hygenic conditions remained backward, the population was more liable to infection. It was mainly due to the work of Prof. Bernard between the wars that trachoma was gradually controlled.[83] Undulant fever was also common in Malta. It was customary for milk vendors, even in towns, to milk goats outside their customer's front door. Some coffee shops in Valletta and elsewhere even had a goat tethered outside to show that fresh milk was available.[84] The setting up of the Milk Marketing Undertaking and the abolition of ambulant milk vendors in 1938 considerably reduced the incidence of this disease. It was only in the postwar period, however, that the older practices disappeared completely.

Education was described by the 1838 Royal Commission as 'small in quantity and bad in quality'.[85] Illiteracy was widespread. The skola tan-nuna (nursery school) taught children folktales, nursery rhymes, and prayers, but hardly anything else. A Government department for primary schools was set up in 1840, but progress was so slow that by 1861, out of a population of 134,055, less than 8,000 males could read Italian and less than 4,000 could read English.[86]

The low standard of living discouraged parents from sending their boys to school. Boys were made to work at a very early age in order to earn some money. The higher the cost of living, the more was this liable to happen.[87] Girls fared even worse. The 1891 census reported that while 80 per cent of males between the ages of 45 and 50 could not read, 85 per cent of females in the same age-group were illiterate.[88] By the turn of the century, about 30 elementary schools had been set up in Malta and Gozo, together with some 20 infant schools, a few night schools, and one Sunday school.[89] The situation was not much different in most other European countries, including Britain. There were also four main secondary schools and a few small private ones. The Lyceum, which had 415 students in 1900, was by far the largest; the Girls' Grammar School had 120; the Technical and Manual School had a mere 15; while the Gozo Secondary School had 23.[90] Technical education was not encouraged by parents as it was considered lowly. The University, which catered almost exclusively for the well-to-do, had only 86 male students.[91] Only this class of people could afford private libraries. Up to the early twentieth century, such libraries included mostly books of Italian literature, law, philosophy, and theology. Culture only began to extend to the lower classes towards the end of the nineteenth century and the study of English was gradually introduced then.[92] It was in the 1920s and 1930s, however, that the knowledge of English started to spread so consistently that eventually it even supplanted Italian.

By 1914, accomodation available in schools amounted to 29,000 places: 25,000 in Government schools and 4,000 in private ones. Even so, pupils rarely completed elementary education. Between 1908 and 1916, 43,000 children were withdrawn from elementary schools.[93] Of these, 17,000 left before reaching grade II. Only 3,000 followed a complete course of elementary education up to grade VII.[94] To make matters worse, teachers were insufficiently trained and badly paid, making the teaching profession unattractive for the more qualified people, many of whom resorted to it only when no alternative existed.

Primary education began to spread after the Second World War. The war itself had wrought havoc with Maltese education; some school buildings were destroyed while most of the others had been requisitioned by the Armed Forces, the Medical and Health Department, or the ARP. Furthermore, many teachers had been conscripted. As a result, compulsory education was completely disrupted and only a section of the population bothered to send their children to school, especially if they were girls.[95] Meanwhile, secondary education was accessible only to those children whose parents could afford to keep them at home or to pay their school fees, while tertiary education was practically limited to the well-off.[96] Elementary education was only enforced by law in 1947. There were still very few who attended school beyond that level. It was only in the late 1960s that secondary and tertiary education came within the reach of the masses.

III Leisure and Popular Culture

There existed sharp contrasts in the modes of recreation of town and country up to the Second World War. In the countryside, during the early part of the nineteenth century, where clubs did not exist, feastdays were given great importance. It was also the time when traditionally the young of the two sexes could mingle more freely than usual.

The main pastime of young men appears to have been that of shooting birds during the migratory season.[97] In the evenings of working days, men met in the wine shops, the only meeting places in the villages. For this reason, feastdays were socially paramount, for they provided an opportunity for people to meet, sell, and exchange products and farm animals, and for labourers to discuss work contracts with their employers. Most marriages were contracted on such occasions — a common enough phenomenon in Mediterranean villages.[98] On feastdays, women used to wear their Sunday best and all their gold. Gold was considered to be respectable, apart from being a form of investment.[99]

Every village was, as it still is, placed under the patronage of a particular saint. Festivities in his or her honour commenced on the eve of the feastday with fireworks.[100] Horse and donkey races were sometimes held while, on the feastday, young and old attended Mass in the morning and abstained from all manual labour. Time was spent in wholesome amusement, singing, and dancing to guitars. Food was of better quality on feastdays.[101] Girls stipulated in their marriage contracts that their husbands must take them to the *Boschetto* on the feast of Saints Peter and Paul, and to Marsaxlokk on that of St Gregory.[102]

Very little had changed by 1913. A popular pamphlet, published that year by Giovanni Battista Mamo from Luqa, relates how the Maltese enjoyed themselves on feastdays.[103] They preferred to pass their time near the sea, especially at Birżebbuġia, Marsaxlokk, Għar Lapsi (off Siġġiewi), St Paul's Bay, and Mellieħa, and at other places where, among other enjoyments, they sang popular tunes (*għana*). A most popular form of *għana* consisted of a flyting contest between two men. This usually ended up with a brawl, with people pelting each other.[104]

On important festivities, people from various areas would congregate at the village that was celebrating its feast. Mamo cites as an example the feast of Mellieħa, the northernmost village in Malta, yet he mentions people from Valletta, Qormi,

Zejtun, and other places. The majority, however, came from the last two villages, which were noted for their love of *għana* as were those of the Valletta *Manderaggio* and of Cospicua.[105] One can best appreciate how keen the people were to visit such places if one keeps the rudimentary transport system in mind. Mamo recalls that, on this occasion, his uncle came with the mule-cart at two in the morning to wake him up. From Luqa to Mellieħa it was a long journey, and they arrived at dawn. He also mentions the food they carried with them: two three-*rotolo* loaves of bread, made of mixed grain (wheat and barley); a kerchief full of cheeses; half a dozen turnips; a *qolla* (jar) of home-made wine; dried figs; and other items.[106]

Apart from the feasts of saints, there was yet another social occasion − carnival − where people could meet and enjoy themselves. Up to the Second World War, carnival, although not so spectacular as the village feast, was a popular occasion which drew enormous crowds. Merry-making was mainly confined to Valletta, but villagers from all over the island came to watch and enjoy themselves.

Until 1860, villagers only had wine shops to while away their spare time. That year, however, the first band club appeared in Rabat. Band clubs soon became popular, and by the end of the century they had become a major social feature in both town and village. In Gozo, the phenomenon was limited to Victoria and its surroundings.[107] Originally, bands were non-religious organizations but they soon became identified with parish rivalries, even within Valletta itself. The bands' musical repertoires included excerpts from popular operas. Opera was very popular then; the young enjoyed its music and its theatrical scenes. The theatre was appreciated by all classes.[108] Even sacred music and oratorios played in the churches were much esteemed by all classes of Maltese society.[109]

The counterparts of the village wine shops in the towns, and in particular Valletta, were the coffee shops. Coffee shops, like the band clubs, were places where males could meet. High-society women would never dream of being seen in a coffee shop, and commoners even less so.[110] In coffee shops one met all types of characters, as in other European countries. They were centres for political discussions and all types of entertainment, including music. A cup of coffee cost 1d. during the earlier part of the twentieth century and had been even cheaper before that.

Kingsway, or *Strada Reale,* in Valletta was, and still is, a popular street for strollers to look at window shops. There the theatre, a number of coffee shops, and all major places of entertainment were to be found. As the principal street of the city, it was popular with all classes of the population, townsmen and villagers alike. One of the most popular sights in this street, during British rule, was that of the military parades which formed an essential part of Maltese social life.[111]

The military regiments left their mark on Malta, mainly through the introduction of various sports. The most important of these was football. Football matches used to be held in the early years of this century at the Mile End ground at Blata l-Bajda, or at Corradino, where the Navy used to play most of its games. The Maltese took an active part, especially when the regiments played against local teams. By the 1920s, Sliema and Floriana had become the foremost of the Maltese teams and there was a great rivalry between them. By then, the Maltese had begun to participate fully in this sport.

Football was a popular winter sport but it had to stop during the dry hot summer season. The most popular recreation in summer was swimming. Waterpolo was later to develop into a popular summer sport. Badger, writing in 1838, points out that 'recreation was also provided by swimming in summer.'[112] Other activities included fishing and rowing. Swimming had become a popular summer activity by the end of the First World War when changing cabins were set up by the shore in Valletta and Sliema.[113]

Lacroix described the Maltese as a people with oriental habits who preferred the intimate pleasures and the *far niente* of their homes to mixing with foreigners. In the evenings, the women enjoyed staying on the terraces or verandahs of their homes with their children, or chatting with the neighbours, often in the presence of their husbands[114] – a custom which still persists in the villages.

After lunch, the Maltese, rich and poor alike, had the habit of indulging in a *siesta*. This was so common up to the 1930s that the then Lieutenant-Governor of Malta, Sir Harry Luke, observed that 'during this time the shops are shut, and to judge by the stillness which reigns in town and country from twelve to three o'clock, one would suppose that the island was deserted.'[115]

The little pleasures of the well-to-do were a shade more sophisticated. These led an easier life and sometimes gave elegant parties. Travel for leisure was then considered a privilege of theirs. Some even took a yearly trip. A typical tour in the first quarter of the century would include travelling by ship to Sicily, from where one would proceed to visit other parts of Italy, France, Austria, Switzerland and, less frequently, Spain.[116] Aeroplanes were not used extensively before the 1960s, when it was still far more popular to travel by ship via Sicily.

The Second World War was responsible for many changes. Feast celebrations were suspended during the war years and there were general fears that such activities would lose their popularity with the postwar generations. Furthermore, there was a considerable internal migration that upset earlier living patterns permanently. But by the 1950s feasts had regained much of the pre-war prestige.[117] The former popularity of feasts was usurped, in the war years, by the cinema and the dancing hall. Such places of entertainment were to multiply fast after the war. Football, too, was to play a vital role in amusement with the end of air raids.[118] Popular outings (xalati) were also organized. The day trippers used to embellish 'trucks' (lorries) or buses with palm branches, coloured papers, and rags, and drive shouting all the way to and from the beaches – those in the north of the island being preferred. Up to the mid-fifties, these xalati were held every Sunday or the day following the village feast and were extremely popular.[119] Opera lost most of its popularity after the war. The bombing of the Royal Opera House in 1942 had much to do with this. After the war, operas were staged in two theatres, the Radio City at Hamrun and the Gaiety at Sliema, creating two audiences which often overlapped.[120]

Cinema became by far the most popular entertainment, especially after the introduction of 'cinemascope'. The Church itself used to show films in parish halls and at the Catholic Institute. The influx of films coming from America and the continent gradually decreased the Church's hold on the habits of the people. As a consequence, it became somewhat rigid and even set up a decency campaign. In addition to the band clubs, the larger villages had at least one cinema while more families installed Rediffusion receivers (the local cable radio network) at home. *Għana* gave way to radio transmissions, followed in 1957 by Italian television. Bars and coffee shops replaced the old wine shops.[121]

IV INFRASTRUCTURE

The British period saw the appearance of the railway, the steamship, telegraphy, and the telephone. Nonetheless, early in the nineteenth century, the communication system was poor and the condition of roads bad. In fact, roads then consisted of numerous uneven and dusty paths and lanes that turned to mud with the first rain, making them almost impossible to use in winter.[122] The internal communication system developed gradually under the British. Some roads were improved for military purposes, while others were constructed to serve new settlements, but by and large the system of tracks, which the island had acquired over the centuries, was adapted to modern needs.[123]

Poor lighting had a negative social influence. All roads were deserted after sunset as everywhere would be enveloped in darkness. In 1853, a foreigner complained in a local newspaper about the inadequacy of oil lamps for street lighting. It seems that up to then this system was limited to certain places, or else some of the villages had only a few ineffective lamps.[124] Gas lighting was introduced in the harbour cities in 1857,[125] but the remaining villages had insufficient lighting. The Government increased the number of oil lamps in such places, since it was not possible to introduce gas light in all parts of the island.[126] This short-term solution, however, proved inadequate. Sums of money were voted regularly for street-lighting projects but, although such novelties were introduced relatively early compared to the rest of Europe, they were greatly restricted. Between 1882 and 1883 there were attempts to set up an electric power-station that actually began to function by 1896. Even so, the majority of village streets were still only lit by oil lamps well into the twentieth century. In Luqa, electricity was introduced in 1929, water in 1930, but the sewage system was not completed until after the war.[127] Smaller villages fared even worse. Although the Government had decided to light up the streets of Safi, in 1899 there was only one paraffin lamp. The number of such lamps was increased to 16 by 1910 and to 18 by 1927. Electricity was only introduced in 1927.[128] Generally speaking, the problem of street lighting was quite widespread even in the towns, at least up to the outbreak of the First World War, when such streets were still lit by paraffin even in Valletta and Floriana.[129]

By 1910, the Melita Telephone Exchange Company had set up a telephone system as a public service. At first only a few families enjoyed the luxury of a domestic set as the service was restricted to Government departments, the Armed Forces, banks, professional men, clubs, and businessmen.[130] In 1933 there were still only 939 telephones and it was only in 1957, when there were 5,159 private telephones, that an automatic system was set up. That year five exchanges were established. By then the telephone had become a social requirement; hence, while in 1958 there were 7,823 telephones, in 1962 the number had reached 13,200.[131]

In the early years of British rule, internal transport consisted mainly of *kalessi* — horse-drawn carriages which seated two passengers, increased to four by 1831.[132] In 1853 there were 278 *kalessi*, 14 of them in Gozo.[133] The *kaless* (calêche) remained in use up to the 1870s, although by then it had evolved into a slightly-improved and more comfortable model.[134] The *kaless* was an expensive means of transport which only a few could afford.[135]

The introduction of the horse-drawn omnibus in 1856 was beneficial to most of the population. Originally it was to run on a fixed timetable from Lija to Valletta, taking approximately 45 minutes for each trip. It carried 16 passengers and proved very profitable. But, although it was much cheaper than the *kaless*, the common worker could not afford it still.[136] Nevertheless the omnibus service did well and it was extended to other villages in March 1857, when further vehicles with a capacity of 24 passengers were ordered. The new destinations included Mdina, Żebbuġ, and St Julians via Sliema.[137] The omnibus company was even entrusted to carry mail from 1859 onwards, which marked a general improvement in the postal service.[138] The omnibus continued to render this service continuously up to 1875 and during the 1880s.[139] Its popularity then began to wane to such an extent that by the 1890s, owing to competition from other means of transport, it had stopped functioning.[140]

In the last decade of the nineteenth century, a more popular form of transport came into being. This was the *karozzin* (cab), a modern version of the *kaless*, with the coachman having his own seat and not obliged to walk beside his carriage. The *karozzin* was ideal for those who wanted to go to places not reached by the omnibus.[141]

The bicycle, at first mostly restricted to British officers, was also introduced around 1870. By the 1890s its use had spread and had become common among civilians.[142]

A novel means of transport was the railway, with fares everybody could afford. Introduced in 1883, it ran between Valletta and Mdina and at first it was thought that the Railway Company would create much work on the island. Although originally planned to fan out into most of the inhabited parts of Malta, only the original line was actually laid. On the whole, the railway was an extravagance, especially since distances were already being reduced thanks to the construction of new roads.[143] In 1892, the railway became Government property owing to financial losses and for a time it prospered.[144]

In 1903, the Electric Tram Company was established, which secured a more practical means of transport than the railway. Originally the tram was planned to provide a U-shaped route around the southern end of the Grand Harbour, but changes were made even before track-laying had begun. Services were run on three lines connecting Valletta with B'Kara, the Three Cities, and Żebbuġ. Although the Valletta-B'Kara line was functioning in direct competition with the railway, commuters actually preferred it.

The tram proved popular, to such an extent that it was strongly opposed by cab drivers[145] whose livelihood depended on the number of passengers they carried. They even severed the overhead wires on the eve of its inauguration.[146] Like the railway, the tram soon found itself in financial straits. By 1929, the tram too was taken over by the State but the Company was allowed to continue operate the Upper Baracca lifts, which were installed at the beginning of the century and which remained popular until the 1960s.[147]

By the 1930s, both tram and railway companies were doing badly and the Government had to close them down. Meanwhile the harbour area had a system of dgħajjes (passage boats) operating from Valletta to the Three Cities and to Sliema. Boat transport was of vital importance to both the Three Cities and the naval base of Tigne' (Sliema). Boatmen had a monopoly of transport in the harbour and in 1856 there were already 42 licensed boats.[148] These boatmen were to face strong competition with the setting up of the Motor Ferry Service in 1881. At first the ferries operated from Valletta (Marsamxett) to Sliema and, although harassed by protests from boatmen, it proved to be the best and cheapest means of transport on the island. A trip to or from Valletta cost only ½d. The ferry boats continued to function until August 1959.[149]

Though the ferry service proved to be of great convenience to the growing urban centre around Marsamxett, the need was felt for an even more efficient system of transport. By 1905, this was partly solved with the introduction of the Scheduled Bus Service[150] which relieved the Sliema people from their complete dependence on the ferries. Other scheduled bus services came into being to serve other parts of the island – particularly B'Kara and Cospicua. Transport facilities were to develop further after 1918 when the British Services sold their lorries and trucks to private individuals, who immediately adapted them for civilian use. By the 1920s the bodies of such vehicles started being built locally.[151] Up to this time, goods were still transported by karettun (cart) even if they belonged to the Services; lorries came into use for the first time in the 1920s.[152]

During the early thirties the bus service was extended even to remote parts of the island like Żurrieq.[153] Later on, secondary routes, like the one from Luqa to Paola and another to B'Bugia, began to operate during the summer months.[154]

At first, buses could carry only 20 persons who had to sit on

two long wooden benches. Later, greater passenger capacity and
more comfortable seats were introduced. The fare was originally
6d. for any trip, but by 1922 fares were regulated, making the
bus the favourite form of transport.[155] Fares were again
regulated in 1941 and were to remain unchanged until the early
1960s. On the Mosta route, for example, the ordinary fare was
4d., and 5d. on feastdays and weekends. Workers paid 2½d.,
while apprentices and schoolchildren paid 2d.[156] In 1974, routes
were amalgamated and the number of companies reduced,
making the system easier to operate.

A major transformation in the transport system was brought
about by the introduction of private cars early this century. The
car replaced the *karozella* or the *parilja* – horse-drawn carriages
used by the better-off classes. In 1906 there was only one
registered car in Malta, but the number increased steadily. At
first, only the Governor and the Archbishop owned cars but by
the 1920s there must have been a reasonable number. In 1926
a foreigner exclaimed that Malta was 'full of motor cars, chiefly
of American and Italian makes'.[157] Nevertheless it was only in
the postwar period that private ownership increased
dramatically.

V INDUSTRY

As early as 1839, the industry of the Maltese had been
recognized by MacGill, who admitted that the local shipwrights
'are by all esteemed excellent workmen and build good ships
of fine model'.[158] MacGill had in fact already suggested the
extension of this industry, predicting that by the building of a
drydock, 'this branch would become one of the most extensive
and important of the island'.[159]

The drydocks, inaugurated in 1848,[160] continued to expand
until the Second World War and immediately proved to be the
island's main source of employment, together with the
opportunities provided by the British Services. The dockyard
catered mainly for the Royal Navy, which had its Mediterranean
fleet based in Malta, and proved, at least at certain times, an
excellent source of employment.

Steamships were to help in the growth of this major industry.

The first steamship called at Malta in July 1825.[161] Up to the 1850s merchant vessels were still mainly sail-powered; however, the introduction of steamships had by then raised Malta 'as a commercial depot from comparative insignificance to one of the utmost importance'.[162] The overall tonnage of shipping calling on the island had increased from 500,000 tons in 1850 to 5.2 million by 1880, decreasing sharply after 1890 to 3.5 million tons. This shows that non-agricultural employment was becoming increasingly more important in the second part of the century.[163]

Meanwhile, small business-links with the North African ports, where many Maltese emigrants had settled, were established in the first half of the nineteenth century. These Maltese businessmen trafficking in cloth, tobacco, wine, oil, skins, and beasts made good profits which the arrival of British regiments increased further as they started to supply provisions to the Armed Forces.[164]

There was so much work in Malta at the start of this century that when, in 1903, the breakwater project was commenced, skilled workers from Sicily and Spain had to be employed. Even so, there were still individuals who lived like tramps owing to their extreme poverty.[165]

The manufacturing industries had, however, done badly in the nineteenth century. The growing of cotton, which had served as a cash crop since the Middle Ages, had lost its importance as an industry owing to the Egyptian economic boom and the importation of vast amounts of cheap cotton from Egypt, America, and the British industrial towns. By the 1840s the manufacture of cotton had ceased.[166]

Other industries included that of cigars, which in 1839 was considered 'a most profitable branch of trade here and gives employment to many thousands of poor families'.[167] By 1856, it provided work for 1,500 workers and exported cigars to all parts of the Mediterranean.[168] But the industry was doing very badly by the end of the century.[169]

In the latter part of the century, Malta had such a weak commercial performance that even the island's highly-valued oranges were being exported only on a small scale. In 1890, 127,000 dozen oranges were shipped, but by 1899 the figure went down to a mere 9,000 dozen.[170]

A very profitable business for the Maltese was that of ship-chandling. Certain families like the Mizzis, the Tabonas, the Bordas, and the Borg Costanzis were well established in the supply of provisions to the British Forces by the end of the First World War. Spiro Mizzi, the pioneer of modern industrialization in Malta, worked originally as a ship's chandler together with his father. In an interesting and stimulating interview, Mizzi relates how his family had to shift from ship-chandling to other enterprises with the coming of the NAAFI in 1919.[171] Mizzi started off with a scheduled bus service which, he admitted, was not profitable enough. This in turn led to the opening of a 'car hire' garage to cater mainly for British naval officers. Meanwhile the scheduled bus service was kept going. In 1924 the Mizzis started to import a new type of car — the Morris. In the early part of the century there were only two agents for cars, one importing Fiat and the other Ford cars. The importation of the Morris proved to be highly successful.[172]

VI THE AFTERMATH OF THE SECOND WORLD WAR

The war contributed towards the thinning out of the number of men who depended on agriculture for their livelihood, partly owing to the war conditions which had brought about a shortage of fodder for animals and subsequently a lack of fertilizer.[173] The war had also helped to change the attitude of the younger villagers. While the old farmer was content to spend the greater part of his time with his animals and in his fields, the young men had come to consider recreation in much the same way as the townsmen did. Furthermore, the young generation attached great importance to dress and personal appearance, making its members look very much like the town dwellers.[174]

Increased spending power, a more varied diet now including a variety of non-local foods, plus the replacement of home-produced cotton have all contributed to the extension of shopping facilities in the village ... specialized shops have also made their appearance ... The 1939-45 war brought flour and bread rationing and the end of home-baking.[175]

Buildings had suffered greatly during the war years. Besides churches, convents, hospitals, auberges, and other buildings, 5,524 private dwellings were totally destroyed; 5,077 were extensively damaged and needed reconstruction; while 19,073 were damaged but reparable.[176] The worst-hit locations were the harbour cities, notably Cottonera, and the villages near the airfields. Housing problems were only partially solved in the immediate postwar years. Meanwhile, by 1947, the Maltese had gained self-government, which facilitated town-planning and helped to resolve some problems, notably in the harbour cities. The majority of slums in Valletta, Floriana, Vittoriosa, Senglea, and Cospicua gave way to better housing facilities. Streets were widened and hygiene was given prime importance. The Government had to provide residential areas with the essential services and could not yet build new housing estates.[177] It was only in the late 1950s that a new residential area was built – Santa Lucija. By then Governments could tackle the housing problem seriously.

The problem of housing was greatly eased thanks to migration. In fact, between 1949 and 1966, 105,146 left for Australia, Britain, Canada, and the USA.[178]

Elementary education played a significant role in reducing the number of illiterates. In the countryside the literate younger generation could now depend less on the more learned people of the village than their parents. They were also able to keep in contact with their migrant relatives while bus transport, the press, Rediffusion, cinemas, and television, put most of Malta, and the wide world, within easy reach of all. At the same time it was becoming easier to travel by sea and air. A further change was the spread of lay religious movements which had been rather few in number before the war but grew noticeably in the postwar period.[179]

Public health, completely disrupted by the war, improved considerably by previous standards, especially with the transference of the main hospital from Floriana to St Luke's at G'Mangia. But it took at least up to the early 1950s for the health system to reach an acceptable level.

All in all, the war helped to change the mentality of the Maltese. The new generation had developed new tastes and a different outlook on life. The standard of living improved for the great mass of the population. From the forties to the sixties, more and more families shared a better standard of living – a condition which before the war had been limited to the privileged few.[180]

VII BRITISH OUTLOOK AND POLICY

Conditions in Malta generally changed for the better in the course of the last twenty years of British rule. Nevertheless, the British still considered the island first and foremost as a fortress.[181] This was the main and constant theme of British occupation from the dawn of the nineteenth century down to the late 1950s.

It is often said that, Britain was slow at first, to appreciate Malta's strategic value. Nelson is reported to have considered it as 'a useless and enormous expense'.[182] In fact, Britain later considered Malta the first line of defence of its grand Indian Empire and did her best to consolidate its position in the Mediterranean by stationing troops and a fleet there. During the early years of occupation, Britain strengthened its legal claims on Malta which were indispensable to secure a greater stability for Britain's position and to establish herself securely on the island.[183] Malta was therefore to prove of the utmost importance as a fortress in the imperial defence system.

In the course of the nineteenth century, Malta's utility as a naval base grew constantly, especially during the Crimean War (1854-56).[184] This in part explains why it did not suit the British to allow much liberty to the Maltese; in fact the natives were excluded 'from all but the lowest offices' in Government, making them feel like 'strangers in their own country'.[185] The Maltese were excluded from high positions even in the Armed Forces and the Dockyard, causing constant friction and resentment amongst the more ambitious.[186] British outlook is nowhere better expressed than in Joseph Chamberlain's speech to the House of Commons in 1902:

We hold Malta solely and entirely as a fortress essential to our position in the Mediterranean. Not as an ordinary colony but as a fortress ... In a fortress anything like open agitation against the Government is a thing that cannot be tolerated on the face of it.[187]

The British were in Malta for its strategic value and they

adapted a 'mild apartheid' in their dealings with the Maltese.[188] Therefore, when Sir Adrian Dingli, perhaps the most influential of Maltese of the time, was excluded from membership of the Union Club, it was felt as a national insult by all Maltese; it even irritated King Edward VII himself and his brother, the Duke of Connaught, Admiral of the Mediterranean Fleet. In fact, both resigned from the Club at the announcement.[189]

Gradually, however, a new middle-class of educated Maltese, acclimatized to the British style, came to accept British rule and developed pronounced pro-British loyalties. These were relied upon to carry out 'acceptable policies' and most administrative posts in the civil service were entrusted to them.[190]

British influence took popular root among the populace in the early part of the twentieth century partly thanks to the stationing of troops in all parts of Malta. British families took to coming to Malta to enjoy the good weather. Meanwhile more Maltese were becoming dependent on the British in various ways. The Armed Forces employed a large force, not only as sailors, but on all sorts of odd jobs such as waiters, cooks, nurses, barbers, clerks, businessmen, coalheavers, washer-women, servants, and even fishermen and farmers. All classes of Maltese were involved in the maintenance of the Island Fortress.[191]

As a British possession and fortress, Malta did not have the characteristics of a nation-state in the full political sense, but socially Malta had the typical features required for nationhood. The islands, unlike several other British colonies, divided by race, religion, tribe, or cultural factions, were homogeneous and the inhabitants felt Maltese.[192] In the nineteenth century,

For a Maltese to be educated and for him to know Italian was one and the same thing: for countless generations Italian had been the language of town and gown, of court and cloister.[193]

Therefore one could not call the Language Question 'a struggle in which a privileged group in Maltese society attempted to maintain its position'.[194]

The prime motive behind the Language Question was defensive, the retention of those recognized cultural traits that historically distinguished Malta. This could be summed up in the motto *Religio et Patria*; that is the Catholic faith, as against

the Protestant rulers; and the Italian language – the official
language of the island since medieval times – against the
forcible imposition of English as an act of imperial *force-majeure*.
It kept alive in the Maltese a separate awareness and ultimately
led to a full and separate Maltese nationhood with all the rights
of a distinct people.

NOTES

[1] F.M. Lacroix, 'Malte e le Goze', 11.
[2] W. Senior Nassau, *Conversations and Journals in Egypt and Malta*, ii, 261.
[3] H. Ganado, *Rajt Malta Tinbidel*, i, 323.
[4] H. Luke, *Malta: An Account and Appreciation*, 221.
[5] H. Bowen-Jones et al., *Malta: Background for Development*, 345.
[6] Ganado, ii, 19.
[7] B. Fiorentini, *Malta rifugio di esuli e focolare ardente di cospirazione durante il Risorgimento Italiano*, ch.vii.
[8] H. Seddall, *Malta: Past and Present*, 296.
[9] Ibid., 297.
[10] Ibid., 309.
[11] A. Bartolo, 'History of the Maltese Islands', 155, where he criticizes the bigotry and partiality of Revd Seddall against the Maltese.
[12] L.H. Dudley Buxton, 'Malta: An anthropogeographical study', 85.
[13] W. Vella, 'Transport in the Maltese Islands, 1850-1890', 20.
[14] B. Blouet, *The Story of Malta*, 177.
[15] Ibid.
[16] Dudley Buxton, 85.
[17] Vella, 15.
[18] Bowen-Jones et al. 123.
[19] E.L. Zammit, *A Colonial Inheritance, Maltese Perceptions of Work, Power and Class Structure with reference to the Labour Movement*, 11.
[20] Bowen-Jones et al., 123.
[21] Ibid.
[22] Ganado, i, 329.
[23] H. Frendo, *En route from Europe to Africa: Malta, her People and her History*.
[24] Ganado, i, 324-325.
[25] Zammit, 18.
[26] Bowen-Jones et al., 124.
[27] Ibid.
[28] J.M. Pirotta, *Fortress Colony: The Final Act*, i, 12.
[29] J. Nicolas, 'The Position of Women in the Maltese Economy 1900-1974', 40.
[30] Pirotta, 12.
[31] H. Frendo, *Party Politics in a Fortress Colony*, 1.
[32] Among others, see J. Quintin d'Autun, *Insulae Melitae Descriptio*; C.A. Vianello, 'Una relazione inedita di Malta del 1582'; Giacomo Capello's account in V. Mallia-Milanes (ed.), *Descrittione di Malta, Anno 1716*; and the more

recent ones, like J. Quintana, *Guida dell'isola di Malta e sue dipendenze;* G.P.
Badger, *Description of Malta and Gozo;* T. MacGill, *A Guide for Strangers
Visiting Malta;* and Lacroix, *supra,* note 1.

[33] D. Cutajar, 'The Lure of the Orient: The Schranzes, the Brockdorffs, Preziosi and other artists', 132-4.
[34] Seddall, 291.
[35] F. Braudel, *The Mediterranean and the Mediterranean World in the Age of Philip II,* 237.
[36] C.A. Price, *Malta and the Maltese,* 8; Cutajar, 133.
[37] L.E. Attard, *Early Maltese Migration;* Zammit, 19.
[38] Senior Nassau, 29.
[39] Price, 29.
[40] J. Bezzina, *Religion and Politics in a Crown Colony,* 74.
[41] Badger, 75.
[42] D. Miége, *Histoire de Malte,* i, 168.
[43] S. Busuttil, *Malta's Economy in the Nineteenth Century,* 1.
[44] Price, 15.
[45] Ibid.
[46] Ibid.
[47] Ibid.
[48] Senior Nassau, 261.
[49] J. Davy, *Notes and Observations on the Ionian Islands and Malta,* i, 416-7.
[50] MacGill, 34-5.
[51] Davy, i, 431.
[52] Price, 131.
[53] P. Bartolo, *X'kien ġara sew fis-Sette Giugno,* 41.
[54] H.I. Lee, *Malta 1813-1914,* 22.
[55] Bowen-Jones et al., 347.
[56] Ganado, i, 328.
[57] C. Kininmonth, *The Brass Dolphins,* 119.
[58] Ibid.
[59] Frendo, *Party Politics,* 3.
[60] Ganado, i, 320.
[61] MacGill, 142.
[62] Badger, 300; Davy, 435.
[63] G.F. Angas, *A Ramble in Malta and Sicily,* 38, 70.
[64] Bezzina, 76; Price, 30.
[65] Price, 30.
[66] Bezzina, 76.
[67] Price, 30.
[68] A. Critien, *The Manderaggio,* 27.
[69] Ibid., 34.
[70] Ibid., 28.
[71] H. Frendo, 'Dimechianism', 43.
[72] *Nix Mangiaris* steps outside Victoria Gate, Valletta.
[73] Frendo, *Party Politics,* 9.
[74] R. Grima, 'Malta and the Crimean War', 120.
[75] Ibid.
[76] Ibid.
[77] Frendo, *Party Politics,* 9.
[78] Badger, 97; Angas, 36.
[79] Ganado, i, 22-3.
[80] See *infra,* Appendix I.

[81] Ganado, iv, 319.
[82] J. Micallef, *L-istorja ta' Ħal Safi*, 66.
[83] Ganado, i, 348.
[84] Ibid., ii, 21.
[85] Frendo, 'Dimechianism', 39.
[86] Ibid.
[87] Ibid., 42.
[88] Ibid., 39.
[89] Ibid.
[90] Ibid., 40.
[91] Ibid.
[92] Ganado, ii, 65.
[93] D. Fenech, 'A Social and Economic Review of Malta during the First World War', 176.
[94] Ibid., 177.
[95] Pirotta, 5.
[96] Ibid.
[97] Badger, 306.
[98] Giovanni Verga, who lived in late nineteenth-century Sicily, gives vivid accounts of everyday life in his *novelle*. An example of life in the countryside is given in *Jeli il Pastore* (see *Vita dei Campi*). Here Verga tells the story of a boy who went to the nearest large village for the feast of the patron saint with the intention of selling his master's horses. A horse is injured on the way, and the boy loses his job allegedly for his negligence, and seeks a new one while hoping to marry a girl, once his childhood playmate.
[99] Ganado, ii, 21.
[100] MacGill, 33.
[101] Ibid.
[102] Ibid., 108.
[103] G.B. Mamo (ta Hal Luka), *Il-Għannej Kormi u il-Għannej Zejtuni*. This pamphlet has been kindly brought to my notice by Mr Nathaniel Cutajar.
[104] Ibid., 7-8.
[105] Ibid., 10.
[106] Ibid., 11.
[107] Bowen-Jones et al., 345.
[108] Ganado, i, 399.
[109] Ibid., 92
[110] Ganado, iv, 29.
[111] Ganado, i, 11.
[112] Badger, 306.
[113] Ganado, i, 344.
[114] Lacroix, 35.
[115] Luke, 173.
[116] Ganado, i, 150.
[117] Ibid., iii, 263.
[118] Ibid., 279.
[119] Ibid., 301-2.
[120] Ibid., 280.
[121] Bowen-Jones et al., 347-8.
[122] J. Micallef, *Ħal-Luqa, Niesha u Ġrajjietha*, 238.
[123] Blouet, 180.
[124] See R.M. Grech, 'The Development of Land Transport in the Maltese Islands', 20.

[125] J. Bezzina, *Servizzi Publiċi f'Malta*, 21.
[126] Ibid., 21-2.
[127] Micallef, *Ħal Luqa*, 287.
[128] Id., *Ħal Safi*, 66.
[129] Ganado, i, 58.
[130] Ibid., iv, 323.
[131] Ibid.
[132] Bezzina, *Servizzi Publiċi*, 31.
[133] Grech, 23.
[134] G. Dimech Debono, *Il-Malti*, 37.
[135] Vella, 11.
[136] Ibid., 10.
[137] Ibid., 13.
[138] Grech, 29.
[139] Vella, 15.
[140] Grech, 29.
[141] Ibid., 30.
[142] Bezzina, *Servizzi Publiċi*, 38.
[143] For a detailed account on the railway, B.L. Rigby, *The Malta Railway*; J. Bonnici and M. Cassar, *Il-Vapur ta' l-Art – The Malta Railway*.
[144] Rigby, 13.
[145] A detailed account on the Tram Service is given in J.H. Price, 'The Malta Tramways'.
[146] Ibid., 271.
[147] Ibid., 277.
[148] Vella, 17.
[149] Grech, 71-2.
[150] For detailed information on the Scheduled Bus Service, Grech, 'The Development of Land Transport'.
[151] Price, 276.
[152] Ganado, i, 62.
[153] Grech, 53.
[154] Micallef, *Ħal Luqa*, 27.
[155] Grech, 52-3.
[156] Ibid., 55.
[157] G. Peto, *Malta and Cyprus*, 101.
[158] MacGill, 24.
[159] Ibid.
[160] A.V. Laferla, *British Malta*, i, 198.
[161] Ibid., 160.
[162] *Malta Mail*, 13 January 1854.
[163] Vella, 16.
[164] Ganado, i, 60.
[165] Ibid., 12.
[166] Fiorentini, 115; Price, 2-5.
[167] MacGill, 25.
[168] Grima, 77.
[169] Ganado, i, 13.
[170] Ibid.
[171] See 'Spiro Mizzi: Il-Karriera twila ta' l-Industrijalista Numru Wieħed ta' Malta', 134-6.
[172] Ibid.
[173] Pirotta, 4.

[174] Bowen-Jones et al., 346-7.
[175] Ibid., 348.
[176] Ph. Vella, *Malta: Blitzed but not Beaten*, 238.
[177] Ganado, iv, 247.
[178] Ibid., 248.
[179] Bowen-Jones et al., 346.
[180] Ganado, iv, 305.
[181] Pirotta, 7.
[182] Lee, 4.
[183] Fiorentini, 1, 10.
[184] Grima, 135.
[185] Lee, 19.
[186] Zammit, 11.
[187] H. Frendo, 'The Maltese Colonial Experience'.
[188] Ganado, i, 329.
[189] Ibid.
[190] Zammit, 12.
[191] Ganado, i, 323.
[192] Frendo, *Party Politics*, 1.
[193] Ibid., 2.
[194] Blouet, 196.

7

ARTHUR G. CLARE

Features of an Island Economy

The economic history of Malta in the nineteenth century,
particularly in the first half of the century, is a case-study in
economic backwardness. Industrial activity was low; the main
form of employment was agricultural, and external commerce
fared badly except in times of war. In addition, the monetary
system lacked uniformity, and fiscal measures were regressive
in that they proved to be inimical to economic welfare. But the
first decades of the century also represented an era of transition
in Maltese affairs and, like every other transitional period in
a nation's history, it was perforce difficult and uncertain. The
very first years were politically unsettling: towards the end of
the eighteenth century there had been a short-lived French
occupation of the island, an event that had begun by raising
Maltese expectations, but which had ended disastrously for the
invaders. Then there was a time when the return of the old rule
of the Knights was not merely possible but also very probable.
However, the years following the failure of the Peace of Amiens
in 1802 heralded the dawn of a new era for the Maltese. Then
came the fruition of a new political permanence: a defensive
arrangement between Malta and the British Crown. In return
for protection of Maltese territory, Britain had control of Malta's
harbours and sea lanes in the cause of imperial defence. British
protection, however, soon took the form of direct rule, and this
caused Malta to lose her former status: once the 'Capital of
Christian Piracy', now a mere colony. But Malta of the Knights
was an anachronism in the nineteenth century, and new
conditions prescribed a new form of government which was
unlike that of the old regime. In fact, what the British brought

to the island was a totally new political and economic relationship between the rulers and the ruled. And this the Maltese had to learn anew.

A characteristic feature of British economic thought at the time was its undue emphasis on individual enterprise. The system contemplated a wide framework within which the individual could operate, but it left little room for state economic action. Indeed, as time passed, the policies of the local British administration moved more and more in faithful accord with the economic tenets of *laissez-faire*. And this in a Maltese context meant three things: first, that the Maltese individual had to seek out his own economic salvation; second, that the Maltese nation as a whole should not expect heavy financial commitments from British sources except by way of defence spending; third, that the island had to survive on its own taxes. While this state of affairs might have had some measure of success in a country endowed with rich resources in terms of both men and materials, in Malta's case it retarded economic growth.

Malta's rather primitive economy was 'open' in that it depended almost exclusively on foreign trade as the main determinant of non-agricultural employment. But foreign trade in the Mediterranean was unstable and subject to a variety of influences many of which lay outside the economic system. Moreover, competition in the transit and carrying trade was intense. This, coupled with Malta's inability to widen its industrial structure due to a dire lack of essential raw materials and to an inadequate capitalist development, proclaimed a bleak economic future. There was no industrial revolution in Malta and there was an unhealthy disregard for the benefits of a secure economic base. In times of economic difficulties, therefore, welfare depended on piecemeal administrative measures designed merely to alleviate the conditions of none but the very poor. The presence of British military establishments necessitated a direct flow of funds from Britain, but these fluctuated according to defence needs: rising in times of tension and falling in times of peace. There was thus a fortuitous element in direct British expenditure, and as such it did not generate sufficient income in the long run. It was no accident that pauperism became one of the chief preoccupations of the Government in the first decades of the century. But very few funds from the revenue system could be transferred to relief projects. There was a limit to the amount of revenue that could be raised for this purpose − a limit imposed by the very need to sustain trade which was the island's life-blood − and when this limit was exceeded the repercussions were wide.[1]

Judged by European standards, Malta in the first half of the nineteenth century exhibited all the symptoms of economic retardation for which no remedy appeared to be forthcoming. The situation was aggravated by the reluctance of local capitalists to explore new avenues of business. The leading industrial sector, cotton, was inefficient, but it was at least a foundation on which more ambitious native enterprise could be built. That this was not grasped at the outset is evidenced by the blind faith that the Maltese placed on commercial capital. And it took some time for them to realize the paucity of the dividends it paid in the long run. The outcry for industrial protection took second place to tariff reform and free trade and, in their search for short-term benefits, Maltese capitalists overlooked the undoubted virtues of industrial development. Of course, the lack of coal and iron constituted a major obstacle to industrial advancement, and seaborne raw materials would have introduced a high-cost element in local production. But there were compensatory factors. Labour was very cheap, for instance, and British capital and know-how were available. Moreover, other Mediterranean cotton producers, notably in Spain, had not yet advanced far enough to overwhelm competitors in overseas markets. British competition and foreign tariffs were a much more serious threat, but, notwithstanding these, Maltese cotton goods had gained a foothold in Europe, the eastern Mediterranean, and North Africa.[2] In short, the local industry had a potential for expanding on modern lines, even perhaps for initiating an industrial revolution, but the extent of this potential rests with future researchers to uncover.

In the first fifty years of the period, most of the lower ranks of society tried to make a living from agriculture. But land was saturated with labour and, inevitably, rural earnings were very low. Conditions in towns were only slightly better and times of prosperity were interspersed with times of gloom. Overpopulation characterized the economy, and when employment opportunities did present themselves they were transitory. At this time, perhaps more than at any other time in Malta's history, the lack of resources began to bear heavily on the population, and it was now that the most venturesome began to look beyond Malta's shores for their livelihood. To contemporaries it became clear that the old, glorious Malta of the Knights, when privateering and Mediterranean trade had served Maltese interests well, had vanished. But with this realization came the belief that good government embraced all the aspects of social and economic life of the subjects. For this reason, the aloofness of the administration perplexed contemporaries. Moreover, the two-tier Government, at Valletta and London, was less intelligible to the Maltese, and definitely more remote, than the home-based administration of the Order. Decisions affecting an entire nation were seen to be taken by a narrow clique cut off from the mainstream of Maltese life. And many times these decisions meant the subordination of local interests to the expediency of the British Crown.

Although the Maltese were left out of all important political issues affecting their land, the discontent that flourished in the first decades of British rule sprang from economic causes rather than political ones. These years saw Malta in the throes of a prolonged economic depression occasioned by the abrupt ending of a commercial boom which had endured, for reasons that will be discussed later, from about 1807 to 1813. An uplift appears to have come only in the late twenties but even then permanent prosperity was still a long way off. Thus, in the intervening period, the Maltese faced severe hardships, having had their first taste perhaps of what it was like to be poor in an individualistic age.

Our main interest in the economic fluctuations of the time stems from the question of whether it lay in Britain's power to alter the course of events. Contemporaries seemed to believe so. In fact, they alleged that the Knights had done much to stabilize economic conditions and to bring about economic welfare, implying that the government of the Order had intervened directly to stimulate the economic life of the subjects. Of course, in times of economic difficulties it was easy to gloss over the shortcomings of the Order's rule in order to emphasize current British deficiencies, but there is evidence to suggest that Malta had experienced a degree of prosperity under the Knights. It seems that the island had reached a peak of affluence as a transit depot for French goods in the heart of the Mediterranean in the late eighteenth century.[3] Although quantitative material relating to incomes and the distribution of wealth is limited, impressionistic evidence points towards a rising prosperity even before this time. The Knights, it seems, had paved the way for economic expansion, having provided employment in the war industries, attracted an entrepôt trade to the island's harbours, and developed agriculture.[4] They also encouraged local manufactures by protective measures, and stimulated maritime activities by indulging in both privateering and legitimate trade. In addition, they brought to the island, via their property abroad, additional foreign income which could be used for basic imports. Of course, occasional food shortages, wars, and plague did play havoc with Maltese economic life at times, but there were many compensations. More important there seems to have been a responsible government, mercantilist in outlook and expansionist. In these circumstances, population grew but living standards were maintained, so that the Maltese on the whole fared better than some of their Mediterranean neighbours. It is understandable, therefore, that the picture which contemporaries drew of the old Malta was one of economic advancement, and this contrasted sharply with their view of conditions in the first decades of British rule.

Historians agree that the first thirteen years of British rule were prosperous ones for Malta. Defence requirements in the very first years provided employment to a section of the labour force which had previously served in the naval workshops of the Order. Thus, the first to benefit directly from the British connection were the skilled craftsmen: shipwrights, caulkers, coopers, painters, sailmakers, and smiths. In the naval yards there was also a demand for ropemakers, masons, labourers, bakers, and clerks. In addition, local personnel enlisted in the army and served on British ships. The arrival of troops on the island meant more mouths to feed and this acted to the advantage of the local agricultural community. Furthermore, the spending of the Services on the island encouraged both internal and external commerce so that gradually all sectors began to partake of this newly-found wealth. But real prosperity began sometime after 1806. The foundation of this prosperity stemmed from the imposition by Napoleon of the Continental System which involved the transfer of British commerce from Italian ports to Malta, thereby making the Malta route the main artery of supply of British contraband goods into Europe. The strategic position of the island soon became vital to the British attempt to maintain their important commercial links with the Italian States during the war years, and this invested Malta with a great commercial significance. Davy claims that Malta 'had become not only the entrepôt of British commerce in the Mediterranean, but also for the greater part of Europe'.[5]

The commercial boom which this situation produced appears to have been marked by considerable commercial investment,[6] though there appears to have been little investment in industry other than perhaps shipbuilding. The way to wealth, it seems, was only through trade in re-exports, carrying, and contraband traffic. But there were other opportunities: in 1809 the *Banco Anglo-Maltese* was set up and three years later the *Banco di Malta*. The growth of traffic and invisible earnings necessarily contributed substantially to the wealth of Malta's commercial community and had a direct influence on the development of commercial services, including marine insurance, in general. Traffic also extended the range of foreign commercial contacts. Vessels plying the Mediterranean were calling daily at Valletta harbour. In 1801 the number of British ships stopping in Malta was 291; ten years later the figure doubled, while the total number of arrivals in 1812 rose to around 3,000 ships. In the meantime, the number of Malta-registered ships swelled from 165 in 1803 to 840 in 1811.[7] All this indicates the extent of commercial activity in and around ports, a situation which benefitted all classes of society. Indeed, such was the demand for labour that wages were rising faster than food prices at this time. Moreover, the increased demand for food, which the influx of foreign merchants and troops engendered, ensured the livelihood of the farming community by raising farm incomes. There was also a land boom, for rents went up in both rural and urban areas. Land, it seems, was earning a high premium everywhere.

Until 1813, the favourable conditions in commerce had guaranteed the incomes of a large part of the labour force in civilian occupations. The only sour note was sounded by the industrial sector, cotton, whose chief foreign market, Catalonia, had been closed by order of the Spanish authorities in 1800. Furthermore, it was during this time that British cottons were beginning to threaten local products. Booming conditions in agriculture, from which cotton outworkers were drawn, were then providing the sector with supplementary earnings, and so the damage being done to local cotton production was temporarily obscured. Cotton growers got round the difficulty by devoting less acreage to cotton and more to wheat. Nevertheless, the real problems of the industry – lack of capital and technological improvements – were neglected. Cotton, being a major growth commodity, could perhaps have contributed substantially to Malta's external balance by way of visible earnings had production been intensified and carried out in mills during this phase of capital accumulation. The fact that the industry continued to linger on well into the second half of the century, despite its technical shortcomings, seems to indicate the feasibility of factory production. Certainly, overseas markets were still providing an outlet for local goods, even though many of these were protected. As for the lack of coal and the cost of imported fuel, Maltese producers would have been in no worse position than textile manufacturers in, for example, Catalonia, where a cotton industry had grown despite the lack of essential raw materials. The greatest economic drawback of the boom was that it diverted funds away from industrial development. It was thus a retarding factor which blinded men from the real need to diversify an economy which had remained virtually unchanged.

But the boom could not last for ever. In 1813 a plague hit the island with such severity that its commercial life came to a standstill. Henceforth all ships leaving the island were suspected of harbouring infection. Merchants were scared away, many would never return. The final blow came when, at the end of the war, British merchants re-established their old bases on the continent. From then onwards the precariousness of the economic situation in Malta came to the fore. As commercial activity took a downward trend, unemployment rose and pauperism spread. The illusory basis of the commercial boom and the fact that Malta was a transit depot of wartime convenience only became painfully clear. The idea that the

island could not really compete as a peacetime European
entrepôt died hard. This was to bedevil relations between the
mercantile community and the administrators for a long time.
With a foreign capital much diminished, incomes fell. The
worst years, it would appear, were those between 1813 and the
mid-twenties. There were some gains in that real wages of the
working classes rose after 1817, but gains in this direction were
offset by the fall in employment. The figures available for food
prices and money wages in this period are far from satisfactory,
but one can discern a clear trend. For instance, money wages
paid to artisans employed by the public works departments
during 1815 to 1825 show a continuous downward trend,
reflecting the falling demand for labour at the time.[8] Figures
in other sources also tell the same story. They show a rise in
wages from 1806 to 1813, a slight fall in 1815, and a drop in
the early twenties. The most to suffer were the unskilled. A farm
labourer's wage, for instance, was 1s.6d. per day in the booming
war years; in the ensuing years it fell to about one-third of that
figure.[9] Skilled workers were more fortunate. Their services
were in demand at the naval yards and their earnings were thus
safeguarded. A table of money wages for certain classes of
workers is given below.

TABLE 1. Representative Daily Wages of Maltese Workers 1800-40

Category	1800-05	1806-13	1815	1820	1822-40
Farm labourer	6¾d.	9d.-18d.	12d.	8¾d.	6½d.-8¾d.
Town labourer	6¾d.	9d.-10d.	12d.	8¾d.	6½d.-8¾d.
Skilled worker	2s-3s.4d.	-	-	-	4s.3d.
Semi-skilled Worker	1s.8d.	-	-	-	2s.1d.

SOURCES: *Malta Blue Books* and figures in Price, Davy, and Chesney. Figures
approximate.

In the meantime, however, food prices fell and this mitigated
the hardship caused by the fall in wages. According to one
source, prices of essential foodstuffs, such as fruit and vegetables,
fell by 60 per cent between 1818 and 1824, while meat in the
early twenties fetched one-third of its price in 1810.[10]

Unfortunately, this source fails to give exact figures and so an allowance has to be made for possible error or exaggeration. Moreover, a fall in the price of an item such as meat would only show the gains accruing to the middle classes, the real consumers of the good. A more satisfactory insight is given by prices of grain, which was a staple food item of the labouring class. Evidence suggests that grain prices fell from 1817 to the early twenties, after having been at a high level between 1810 and 1817.

TABLE 2. Average Cost and Sale Prices per Salme of Grain
sold to the Public 1781-1821

Period	Av. Cost Price	Av. Sale Price
1781-90	£2.00s.0d.	£2.08s.0d.
1791-98	£2.06s.0d.	£2.18s.0d.
1801-13	£2.13s.4d.	£3.03s.8d.
1814-21	£2.05s.0d.	£3.00s.0d.

SOURCE: Statement on Grain Prices, CO 158/113. Prices have been approximately converted into £stg. calculated at 2s. per scudo between 1781 and 1798, and at 20d. between 1801 and 1821. 1 salme = 98.5%; imperial quarter.

The period also witnessed offsetting movements in real wages. From a peak in 1808 they fell to a low in 1817; thereafter money wages stabilized, while food prices in general fell. This trend was reversed from the fifties onwards.

Despite these developments, the overall picture from 1815 to the mid-twenties remained gloomy. The carrying and transit trades were in decline and this affected the employment of a large section of the labour force. It must also have created balance-of-payments problems, for Maltese entrepôt was a major foreign-income earner. Another large sector which experienced difficulties was agriculture. Having expanded the acreage necessary for more wheat production during the boom, farmers after 1815 were faced with imports of foreign grain which interfered with their earnings. Until 1821, grain imports were purchased by the Government, so that the internal trade in grain was a Government monopoly. In 1822 this trade was opened to private dealers with the result that competition forced down the price of the commodity, even though a tax was imposed upon it. In these circumstances, depressed wheat farmers turned to cotton growing to gain some relief, but even here imports of the foreign commodity, this time from Egypt, created further difficulties.

A contributing factor to the decline of Malta's external trade seems to have been the quarantine regulations in force after the plague of 1813. Many vessels by-passed Maltese harbours because health regulations involved too many delays and restrictions. In addition, dues were high and this rendered Malta less attractive than other Mediterranean ports. But, perhaps, the greatest drawback was that goods coming from Malta were kept in quarantine in foreign ports. This acted to the disadvantage of both the carrying and transit trade; restrictions were raised only after the mid-twenties but great damage was done in the meantime.

There were many in Malta at this time who regarded the Government's policies as being too passive. They expected official intervention in matters of trade. But such a step on the part of the Government would have meant the negation of individualism, the antithesis of a cherished principle to which many of the British administrators subscribed. It is significant that even such matters as the supply of water to the cities were still in 1814 regarded as items of private enterprise rather than of public expense.[11] The doctrine of self-help was as yet unassailable. Nevertheless, there were Englishmen who felt that the island deserved better attention. In the words of one such Englishman: 'Malta has been too much considered as a garrison or naval station instead of a central depot for our merchandise'.[12]

But the truth is that the local administration could do little to attract trade. Admittedly, had dues been abolished and free trade tried, the situation might have improved, albeit at the expense of revenue. But the crux of the problem was not free trade but the fact that continental ports enjoyed greater advantages over Malta. In other words, Malta had formidable competitors. In the rich Mediterranean trade, cheapness mattered little; what did matter a great deal were direct linkages with principal European trade routes. And this is what other ports had to offer. Traders, operating from such ports as Leghorn,

Naples, Trieste, Marseilles, and Barcelona, among others, had a whole hinterland to supply. Markets were closer at hand and trade was more direct. In the relatively untroubled times of the nineteenth century, when privateers were no longer a common menace and when ships were faster and safer, direct trade began to be preferred to indirect trade. It was less time-consuming and promised a more rapid turnover. These developments, more than anything else, rendered false the idea that Malta could become a great peacetime entrepôt centre.

In times of falling incomes, British parsimony appeared all the more vexing. Stringent policies on the part of the British Treasury tied the hand of the local administrators with the result that public works spending was kept down until the late forties. But the low level of expenditure also reflected the inability of the Government to increase its revenue yield owing to reduced trade. Trade was further handicapped by the reluctance of Britain to extend to Maltese shippers privileges which other colonies enjoyed under the Navigation Acts. These Acts gave preference to ships carrying the British flag and also confined the trade of the colonies to the mother country. Maltese shipping, before the mid-twenties, was excluded from this preferential system and was prevented from engaging in direct trade with other colonies. That Malta might have benefitted through direct trade was realized as early as 1814 when local merchants petitioned the Government for the opening of colonial trade, particularly that with the West Indies, which would have involved the export of local goods and the re-export of European products from Valletta.

But this alarmed merchants in England who had a monopoly over West Indian trade, and the local petition could not be met in so far as it involved the re-export of European goods.[13] Free trade was further suppressed when both imports and exports were burdened with duties of one per cent and half of one per cent respectively. Five years later, in 1819, the export duty was abolished, but the duty on imports was retained, though drawbacks were allowed on re-exported articles in 1824. That same year goods were admitted in bond, but the charges were adjudged to be

high by local merchants. The latter also voiced the complaint
that government warehouses were unsuitable for displaying
goods.[14] Their demand for the removal of all obstacles to
trade was a clear manifestation that all was not well with
Maltese trade.

In the absence of trade figures, it is impossible to ascertain
the extent of the decline. We can only surmise that for
a time after the end of the Napoleonic War trading activity
dropped to a low level. The transit trade was perhaps
more buoyant than the carrying trade, especially that of
grain. However, compared to what their fortunes must have
been in the booming war years, when Maltese shipping
plied the Mediterranean alongside British shipping, the
two activities suffered a dramatic downturn. From the mid-
twenties onwards, however, the situation seems to have
changed for the better. This coincided with the lifting of
certain quarantine restrictions on Maltese shipping and
with the granting of the long-awaited privileges to Maltese
shippers under the Navigation Acts. Judged by the number
of incoming ships to the island, it would appear that commercial
activity in ports began to increase from about 1827. Although
the change was not spectacular – charges for depuration
and other port dues were still higher in Malta than at
other ports[15] – the transit trade seemed to have picked up
after a long period of stagnation. With regards to the
carrying trade of Maltese-owned vessels, it seems that Maltese
owners were losing much of this traffic to competitors.
Duties paid by Maltese ship-owners on the transfer of vessels
had fallen from about £5,000 as a total in 1815 to a
mere £100 in 1823. Because of adverse conditions, it seems,
fewer vessels were changing hands. The services of locally-
owned vessels were less in demand, and this was also
true, as far as the grain carrying trade was concerned, of a later
period.

Part of the trouble can be traced to the commercial treaties
which Britain compacted with other States. For instance, the
Sicilians were allowed to engage in the grain-carrying trade of
the Maltese as a result of a treaty which Britain and Naples
had signed in 1816. Twelve years later, of the 500 or so ships
engaged in this activity, only about 48 were Maltese-owned.[16]

This same treaty has also allowed the Neapolitans to extract heavy port dues from Maltese ship-owners with the result that the latter found themselves at a disadvantage in Neapolitan territories from which grain was supplied. Reciprocity treaties, as they were known, aimed at the exchange of privileges between countries in the interest of trade. In Malta's case, however, they represented a total disregard for local commercial aspirations. Others were to follow. In the early thirties, treaties with France, Austria, and Greece allowed signatories to operate directly from Maltese ports.[17] These treaties, however, were not without compensations. First of all, they promoted freer trade; secondly, while they interfered with the local carrying trade, they aided entrepôt besides giving local mariners the opportunity of employment on foreign ships. By the end of the 1830s, mariners formed a large part of the island's mercantile community. There were some 16,880 individuals, representing about 3,370 families, depending on the mercantile marine for their livelihood.[18] How many of these actually served on locally-owned ships is difficult to measure, but the number of mariners and their families is an indication of the importance of this sector to the economy. Anything which affected their earnings was bound to have many side-effects.

Godechot claims that there were other circumstances aggravating Malta's economy. From 1817 to the 1840s, he says, the purchasing power of many potential customers in the Mediterranean area itself was still rather weak. Further, the introduction of more efficient vessels made it unnecessary for certain types of ships to call at Malta for supplies and shelter.[19] But perhaps there was a more convincing economic reason for by-passing Malta. As ships became larger and, therefore, more expensive, shippers found it more profitable to carry larger cargoes to and from any one place, and it is possible that bigger ships coming to Malta found both outward and inward cargoes insufficient for their needs. This also explains why local tonnage remained for the major part small. In fact, Maltese vessels rarely exceeded 400 tons, and there were many small coasting craft. These small ships had their own problems, especially when it came to the question of security at sea. When, in the twenties,

Greek privateers interfered with Maltese traders in North African waters, the latter could not defend themselves.

To afford some relief to the population in general, the Government undertook to reform the tariffs in the 1830s. Ships of a certain size were given preferential treatment in the payment of port dues. The latter, which had comprised six different charges before 1832 – anchorage and lighthouse, water, pilotage, hospital, ballast, and health – were consolidated, and a single rate was applied to tonnage ranging from 6d. a day for vessels of 250 tons and under to 3s. for vessels of 251 tons and over. Furthermore, ships built locally were relieved of all port dues for two years. In addition, duties on transfer of shipping and on marine insurance were repealed as was the notorious transit charge. Import duties were also modified so that by the mid-thirties over seventy articles destined for local consumption entered duty-free. The quarantine charges, however, were retained as were the duties on imported grain. The latter, which had been based on a sliding scale in 1824, averaged about 10s.3½d. For the rest of the period, this rate did not vary much.

The reforms had a threefold aim: to lower the cost of living, to encourage the local carrying trade, and to stimulate the transit trade. Traffic did increase, presumably as a result of these measures, but the gains were not large.[20] In years to come, in the fifties and sixties especially, Malta's prosperity was to depend once more on the circumstances of war. Before that time, her trading situation did not change much. In one respect, trade even suffered a setback for, with the repeal of the Navigation Acts, Malta had less to offer by way of preferential shipping. According to Blow-Williams, by the 1850s the older British firms declined and business went to the 'native shopkeepers and little traders of all nations'.[21] The next half-century was to see little change in the organization of local trade; it remained confined for the most part to these 'little traders', though the opening of Suez did bring the island to the attention of the larger firms once more.

According to Montgomery-Martin, direct British expenditure in Malta, excluding military and naval expenses, amounted to £668,666 between 1800 and 1829.[22] Price put the figure for naval and military expenditure alone at £125,000 per annum between 1820 and 1825, rising to over £200,000 by 1851.[23] The influx of sterling was at first too small to have an appreciable effect on the monetary system. In fact, the island's currency in the first two decades of British rule consisted of non-British coins. From the 1820s onward, however, sterling began to assume a greater importance in local currency, so that by 1857 it became the sole legal tender. But for a long time foreign coins continued to be used in local trading circles. The use of foreign currency in nineteenth-century Malta was one way of overcoming the shortage of local circulating media; it also facilitated the payment for foreign goods. Nevertheless, it acted against uniformity in the currency system and must have introduced an element of uncertainty at the exchanges. Here further research is needed to establish the real effect of this system on Malta's internal and external trade.

At this stage it is worth investigating the responses of Malta's other sectors – industry and agriculture – to the conditions prevailing in the first half-century. The little that is known about industry seems to suggest that the leading sector, cotton, was already past its prime by the time the British arrived. According to Eton, the value of Malta's cotton exports in the late eighteenth century amounted to £500,000 yearly.[24] We cannot say whether this figure is anywhere near the truth, but there is a strong indication that the industry occupied a very prominent place in the economy.[25] Eton suggests that it employed 35,000 men, women, and children, although this figure is almost certainly an exaggeration. Nevertheless, it does appear to have kept a good part of the rural community occupied for most of the year. In the nineteenth century, however, conditions changed. Because of the war, Malta's chief foreign market, Catalonia, was closed in 1800 and this signalled the beginning of a gradual decline. The industry's greatest drawback in the following years was that it remained a domestically-based pursuit, dependent on outdated machinery, at a time when new conditions of demand and supply were tipping the scale in favour of steam-power and factory production. Then came competition from abroad. Like other textile industries on the continent, the local industry was faced with severe competition from British mills, where technology, capital, and know-how combined to produce cotton goods of exceptional quality and at the most competitive price. The Maltese produced both yarn and cloth, but they were inferior to machine-made goods and exporters began to find it difficult to sell in markets which had already been penetrated by the Lancashire producers. At the same time, local growers were suffering through the importation of cheap Egyptian raw cotton which local spinners mixed with the home produce. In the 1820s, spun cotton from Malta was allowed into Britain free of duty, while that coming from Britain's own cotton districts was taxed locally at the rate of one per cent. These measures, however, did not arrest the decline, and matters were not helped when the tax on cotton was abolished in the late 1830s. By then the value of Maltese cotton had fallen to perhaps less than £90,000, a figure which is only 18 per cent of Eton's estimate.

A foreboding of the difficult times ahead for cotton had appeared in 1816 in the form of an Anglo-Neapolitan treaty which forbade the importation of Maltese yarn into Neapolitan territories. This had the effect of lessening the demand for local supplies of cotton, for by that time Neapolitan markets had been absorbing large quantities of the Maltese product. But all was not yet lost. In the twenties and thirties, domestic and foreign demand for local cotton goods, albeit much reduced, kept the industry going. Maltese coarse cotton, for instance, found a market in the eastern Mediterranean where it was made into sail-cloth and uniforms. Then there were exports to the German States, Tuscany, Venice, the Papal States, Spain, the Ionian Islands, and North Africa, which included such articles as coverlets, nankeens, towels, and blankets. But behind the apparent resilience of the cotton industry lay a more sinister aspect: long hours of work and starvation wages. This, it seems, was the price it had to pay for survival. In the late thirties, as many as 7,600 female spinners laboured at their wheel for the meagre wage of a penny a day each, a penny less than their male counterparts. A more fortunate male weaver might earn something like 3¼d. per day,[26] but even this was low by contemporary standards. By then the industry was employing around 15,000 persons – beaters, spinners, weavers, dyers, and weighters – drawn almost entirely from rural areas, and evidence suggests that the working day for, say, a spinner began at 4 a.m. and continued till midnight. Children were employed in great numbers, especially when seasonal factors drove them off the fields. The industry lingered on, but by the late nineteenth century it had become insignificant. Very little cotton was manufactured then and most of the labour force formerly engaged in cotton had long retired or turned to some other pursuit.

At one time the local administration set out to establish an embryonic silk industry on the island. Production of silk was not new to Malta, but it was domestically-based with the raw material being grown and spun in the homes of the workers themselves. In the mid-twenties an ill-fated firm was set up, backed by British capital, to initiate production on a large scale. It was promised Government support and in fact received a large tract of land on free lease for a stipulated period. Mulberry trees were then brought over from Naples and the project got under way. By 1827, production reached some 40 lbs. per year, and in the next four years the figure increased tenfold. The future of the whole enterprise did not look too poor by local standards, even though production methods were outdated, and had it not been for some initial setbacks, it might have enjoyed a greater success. By the late thirties, the fortunes of the industry were low and interest in silk-production on a large scale evaporated.

One of the reasons why silk failed in Malta was that the basis of the industry was unsound. In an age when capital and technology were paving the way for greater factory-production, the local scheme was technically weak. Whether silk-throwing factories would have made much headway is difficult to say; they would certainly have produced a much better-finished product. But capital for this type of venture was not forthcoming. True, the absence of coal was a major stumbling block, and silk was heavily protected abroad. But British markets would have absorbed the product; in fact, colonial silk-production was one way of undermining the continental dominance, particularly French, over the product. Duties on imported silk in Britain had at the time been lowered in favour of the colonies.

The concept of factory production was not altogether new to the local scene. Houses of industry and cotton workshops, intended for the relief of the poor, were based on the factory principle — the housing of workers under one roof. The superiority of factory-production over other types of production was also realized then. But the reluctance of local capitalists to tie their wealth to industrial projects, which could only pay their way in the future, set many difficulties in the way of factory production. Maltese capitalists financed trade, aspired as bankers — the Sciclunas in the thirties, for instance — invested in property and foreign debentures, and engaged in commerce; but they lacked the drive to diversify their economy. Perhaps, the risk element was too high in the circumstances, higher than can be possibly imagined at this stage of research.

There were shipbuilding and ship-repairing activities, however, on the island, and also a pool of able shipwrights. But again the industry was small-scale, confined, for the major part, to the naval shipyards. The latter increased their output in the thirties and by 1840, or so, the shipyard in the Grand Harbour had about eight slips for laying down vessels of any size. In 1842 alone, a total of nine ships, with an aggregate tonnage of 990 tons, was built locally.[27] In that year also, Maltese owners had a total of 101 vessels of 400 tons and under, besides a number of smaller coasting vessels. Many of these were built on the island, but the advent of the steamer was destined to thwart local production.

The only other pursuit of note at this time was cigar-manufacturing. This appears to have been viable and, by the 1830s, it was employing some 600 workers. Although nothing is known about their earnings, about 50 million cigars were being manufactured annually with exports contributing around £10,000 to foreign earnings. This sum surpassed the export value of other manufactures, namely, wrought stone and precious metals taken together, by £3,000. Other crafts were insignificant.

The composition of Malta's exports for a good part of the period was as follows: cotton goods, cigars, precious ornaments, wrought stone, soap, leather, macaroni, some furniture, oranges, and salt. These were purely local products. There were also several imported goods entering the re-export trade, such as coffee, cocoa, indigo, spices, flax, hemp, silk, tobacco leaf, wax, wood, foreign cottons, and wool. In the latter part of the period, total value of exports, including re-exports, is estimated to have been about £300,000 per annum, while imports, which included goods meant for re-export, averaged about £550,000. The chief import item for local consumption was, of course, food, but there were also manufactures and raw materials, including colonial products, both for home consumption and for re-export. As time passed, exports of local products were to form an increasingly small part of total foreign trade, and in the latter decades of the century local consumption of foreign manufactures increased appreciably. The vulnerability of Malta's economy, its increased dependence on commercial pursuits for the payment of basic imports, became even more glaringly obvious in the second half of the period under survey.

One of the main employers of labour during the first half of the nineteenth century was agriculture. In the 1830s alone, it sustained about 5,200 families, or a total of about 26,000 persons.[28] This number is in addition to the 400 or so families who were returned as landed proprietors in 1837.[29]

The main crops grown on the island were wheat and cotton. The type of farming adopted was intensive and essentially a form of spade-husbandry. There was little scope for mechanization on Maltese fields, and local agriculture was very laborious; its returns hardly justified the effort exerted. In these circumstances, yields were low, and all the food grown was never enough to feed the entire population for more than a few months in the year, hence the need to import large quantities of food to the island. But cheap foreign corn depressed farm incomes to the extent that both petty farmers and labourers, who overcrowded the land, were generally poor, and this was true for most of the century. The falling fortunes of cotton pushed earnings further downwards and the distress in the rural districts was acute and widespread. Overcrowding produced low output per head and many farmers were nothing more than subsistence farmers. In a much worse condition were the landless labourers who had to support their families, when employment was available, after the bleak winter months, on as little as 8d. a day. Cotton-spinning and weaving augmented their earnings while the going was good but, when cotton declined, charity was the only alternative. Farmers made regular use of members of their families, and it was only on the larger farms that outside labour was demanded. The large farms rarely exceeded 30 acres, while the smallest of farms were only about one acre large.

References to the skill of the local farmers abound in nineteenth-century literature. Indeed, Maltese husbandry required great care and patience. The occasional visitor was struck by the strange appearance of the fields. Many of these formed, as they still do today, a succession of terraces, giving the impression of steps. The manner of forming them involved much skill on the part of the cultivator. When a piece of land was to be reclaimed, the rugged surface had first to be broken up and furrowed. Pieces of rock were then inserted in the furrows and soil was laid over the whole surface at a depth of about three feet. A rubble wall was then erected around the whole field.

This type of land reclamation was heavily engaged in during the French wars. Then Maltese farmers were called upon to produce food not only for the local population but also for the thousands of foreigners – perhaps as many as 30,000, including the entire British contingent – who came to Malta at this time. In common with other sectors, agriculture was prosperous between 1800 and 1813, farm incomes having increased substantially over the years. During this period, the Government bought a total of 807,429 *salme* of wheat, 446,063 of which were locally grown. This was in contrast to later years when, between 1815 and 1822, the local produce totalled only 74,665 *salme*. In the 1820s and 1830s, wheat grown on the island rarely averaged more than 15,000 *salme* per annum. During this same period, imports rose to an average of 55,000 *salme* per year.[30]

The fall in local produce reflected the depressed state of agriculture in the years following the end of the wars. According to one official in the grain department, rents on government property in both urban and rural areas – some 14,000 acres of cultivated land in the countryside alone – were in arrears by the early twenties. From 1814 to 1824, 'the circumstances of the island and the value of property have been gradually falling, thereby creating difficulties in the collection of rents... During the last two years I have taken upwards of 1,000 warrants of seizure of property'.[31] The same source claims that farmers on government land were subjected to 1,200 seizures of crops.

Foreign imports of grain and cotton were clearly bearing heavily on local agriculture, once the booming conditions of the war years had disappeared. In the twenties and thirties, the situation was worse. The value of cotton exports, which stood at about £118,000 in 1830, fell to about £86,270 in 1842.[32] This fall in the value of exports also affected farm profits. In the 1830s, these were ridiculously low. According to Davy, the difference in favour of an average cotton farmer, after deducting the costs involved in the cultivation of a cotton field from the value of its produce, was only the small sum of 8s. 10¾d.[33] Of course, returns varied with the size of the field, its rent, and the amount of crop grown. High rents and falling farm prices, however, did not lead to any spectacular gains even in the larger farms. Rent was sometimes as high as £4.10s. per acre on good soil and this diminished profits even further.

Notwithstanding the fact that Maltese farms were not mechanized, farmers did require some sort of capital occasionally to pay off their labour force before the gathering of crops. For this purpose, credit was usually available from the landlords themselves. But the interest was high, at times rising to 10 per cent and few farmers must have borrowed out of pure enterprise. Farm tools were not even provided on this basis. In fact, labourers not only had to provide their own strength, they also had to furnish their own goods. This was one of the conditions of employment. In some cases, the wage they received was in kind, so precarious was the situation in agriculture.

Agriculture completes our picture of the first half of the nineteenth century and, as has been shown, the credits on the economic balance sheet were few. The next half-century, however, saw some changes in the material well-being of the nation, sometimes for the better, but the need for a secure economic base remained. From the mid-century onwards, British parsimony subsided and, by the 1860s, Malta received about £450,000 per annum direct from Britain. This, together with increased expenditure on local public works, acted as a stimulant on the economy and labour was afforded some relief. Wages rose but only a little; in fact, while earnings of 1s. or more a day were now common for unskilled work, this rate was to remain more or less unchanged right up to the First World War. In the meantime, however, food prices resumed an upward trend, and the gains in wages were offset by the rise in the cost of living. Already in 1846-7 the price of food had suddenly shot up in consequence of a European shortage, and although prices fell in the next two or three years, they rose again in the early fifties and remained high for a long time. This gave a fillip to local agriculture, but the gain was small and was reflected mainly in farm wages which rose to about 10d. per day at this time. It was during this time also that the increase in steamer traffic in the Malta route was enabling the local population to tap new sources of grain supplies in the eastern Mediterranean.

The 1850s were years of war and increased defence spending. Traffic to the island rose rapidly in the years 1854 to 1856, and once again Malta went through the stages of commercial boom, comparable in its intensity with that of the Napoleonic era. But even during this phase of capital growth, the economy remained basically the same, and this meant that, with the return of peace, the weaknesses of the economic system would be exposed once more. Nevertheless, during the short period of the boom, conditions were very prosperous, at least around the ports. Shipping tonnage averaged more than 15,000 *salme* per annum. Imports rose to over 1 million tons in 1855. Navy ships brought supplies and military personnel in their thousands, and in their wake followed the traders. As a result, dockyard and victualling work increased,[34] and the demand for labour soared. In these circumstances, incomes took a sharp turn upwards, especially in the harbour trades, and the whole economy benefitted. Malta became the supply centre of the Mediterranean, a replica of what it had been forty years before. Food prices rose rapidly during this time but their full effect was not felt, owing to the general prosperity.

The end of hostilities inevitably reversed the situation. Economic activity in 1856 and 1857 took a downward trend and pulled down wages and profits in the process. Indeed, survival now depended more and more on expenditure by the local Government and by the garrison. The late fifties also witnessed the increase in the popularity of the steam-driven ships and the beginning of the decline of the wooden vessel. The Steel Age was coming in and with it the demand for steel hulls. This signalled the end of Maltese aspirations as shipbuilders but it opened new avenues of employment for the local population. The new ships were easy to service and repair and, more important, they needed bunkering. The growing size of ships and their coaling requirements led to an extension of the harbour area, and this meant increased employment. Indeed, the enlargement of the dockyard and the construction of a new drydock and a coaling station served the harbour community well in the early sixties.

Then out of the blue came another brief period of prosperity to the island, agriculture being the main beneficiary. Owing to the outbreak of the American Civil War the supply of cotton from the south dried up, and this forced buyers to tap other sources of supply. The price of cotton trebled and Maltese farmers, quick to grasp the situation, doubled their cotton acreage to meet the new demand. Throughout the war, foreign ships called at Malta for cotton bales and departed fully-laden for Europe and the USA. Needless to say, this activity had an important side-effect in increasing the demand for coaling facilities and other port services. During this time, however, the Maltese were taking less and less part in the carrying trade, and the number of local mariners engaged in this activity began to fall. One great source of foreign income was slipping away. Nevertheless, Maltese vessels still had regular communication with Southampton, Marseilles, Constantinople, Sicily, Tunis, Egypt, and the Levant. The transit trade too appears to have been fairly buoyant.[35]

The war in America soon came to an end and the cotton boom was over in the second half of the sixties, rural areas became depressed once more, for now the demand for raw cotton was not justifying the supply. Moreover, there were three years of drought in this period and cholera struck.[36] The result was great distress among the farming community. And, although food prices were high, overcrowding on farms depressed earnings. Labourers were compelled to accept less for their efforts and petty farmers could not make ends meet. With cotton in decline, the problem of underemployment came to the fore. The cotton dearth had put local manufacturers at a disadvantage but, when supply became more flexible, the local produce was not absorbed fully by the local market.

The sixties witnessed the introduction of a steam-driven factory for the production of biscuits, but industrial development on these lines still lay outside local interests. Commerce was still taking the lion's share of capital on the island, and commercial pursuits were further enhanced when, in 1869, the Suez Canal placed Malta in the centre of an increased traffic between the primary producers of the east and the manufacturers of Europe. The economic uplift which this event engendered was of a longer duration than previous booms and it was destined to effect a structural change in the economy. In the seventies and eighties there was a definite movement of rural labourers from traditional agricultural employment into port occupations. This was caused by the opportunities which the bunkering activities began to offer. The Suez traffic invested Mediterranean ports, like Malta and Aden, with a new vitality. They became convenient stopping places for all ships plying the Mediterranean route to the east. According to Bowen-Jones, 'not only from the Mediterranean littoral, Australia, and the Orient, but also from the Russian and Danubian Black Sea ports came the ships which converged on the Malta Straits'.[37] Malta, in fact, secured a snug position within a widening framework of the international economy. The number of port arrivals increased considerably, so that total tonnage grew from about 1½ million in 1879 to over 5 million in the late 1880s. An important development was the increase of the Black Sea grain trade which, combined with the need of steamers to load with coal, meant that inward and outward cargoes of vessels stopping at Malta paid their way. Thus, steamers from northern Europe and beyond called at Malta to unload coal and to take up Russian grain and raw materials from the east for their return journey, and so side by side with the bunkering trade there developed an important transit trade on the island. This state of affairs was to produce new invisible wealth and was mainly responsible for attracting men away from the fields. It is significant that coalmen were among the highest paid of all unskilled workers at the time.

During this period, however, food prices began to rise, particularly in the seventies, and real wages took a downward slide, but the buoyant conditons created by the new entrepôt activity raised the level of local consumption.[38] This mirrored perhaps a rise in the living standards of at least that section of the population engaged in commerce. Those of fixed incomes, the civil servants for instance, were not so well-off in consequence of the reduced purchasing power of the money. There was, though, an improvement in the earnings of those who chose to remain on the fields; the shift of a part of the rural labour force to non-agricultural occupations brought about a new adjustment in the supply and demand conditions in the labour market. Food prices fell a little in the late 1880s and this, given the stability of money wages at the time, pushed up real wages, so that the Maltese in general were prosperous. This development also coincided with increased official spending.

Prosperity was short-lived. The 1890s brought a reversal of former trends, as both the grain trade and bunkering activities began to decline. The economy had already felt a jolt in 1887 when cholera visited the island once more and dislocated trade for a time. But the real trouble came in the mid-1890s when international demand for grain slowly turned away from the Black Sea produce. Moreover, steam-shipping was becoming more and more efficient and fuel requirements did not necessitate frequent stops for bunkering. As a result, Mediterranean traffic became more direct, and this development enabled other Mediterranean ports, which were not so strategically positioned as Malta had been, to re-establish themselves. The late nineteenth century saw Malta once more struggling for a trade which only exceptional circumstances had brought within its reach. Competition from southern European and North African ports set the clock back for Malta and she was faced once more with the prospects of having to rely solely on British defence spending for her income. By then her transit trade was becoming increasingly confined to goods destined to the Middle East, North Africa, and Britain; her cotton industry had become almost solely a lace-making trade, and population pressure was adding its weight on the employment problem. It is significant that the first decade or so of the twentieth century was to direct the attention of a great number of Maltese to the safety-valve of emigration to places outside the Mediterranean.

Maltese emigration in the nineteenth century has attracted a great deal of interest among historians, not so much for its success in decreasing population pressure as for its failure to present itself as a lasting solution to the problem of over-population. The Maltese, it seems, were reluctant to seek permanent settlement abroad. Those that did emigrate had a definite preference for the Mediterranean littoral, and few went further afield. Moreover, there was a high rate of returning migrants, so that inward and outward movements sometimes cancelled each other out. There were several attempts at organized settlements abroad, but these had little success. One of the very few successful settlements was in North Africa where a large Maltese community was to be found, but ventures to places such as Cyprus, the West Indies, and Australia, despite greater economic attractions, met with little success in the nineteenth century. There was a host of economic and non-economic reasons for this phenomenon which lies outside the scope of this paper, but what is striking is the fact that the majority of those Maltese who suffered much economic hardships throughout the period declined to take the advantage of the better living standards which the Americas and Australia had to offer.

The opening of the twentieth century, however, saw the Maltese in the clutches of a dilemma. Population had been increasing fairly rapidly since the eighties, but since economic opportunities from the nineties onwards were not rising in step, unemployment at the turn of the century was high. This, coupled with the absence of a developing industrial sector which would have offered eventually an alternative form of employment, meant that the choice for many lay between starving or migrating. For most of the nineteenth century, rural labour had something to fall back on − cotton − even though the returns were low, and the problem was one of underemployment rather than unemployment. The seventies and eighties had then presented new opportunities in the ports and induced a rural exodus, but when conditions in the early twentieth century were unfavourable there was a number of unemployed for whom employment abroad was the only alternative. For a time in the late nineties and early twentieth century, increased Government spending and imperial requirements guaranteed work in the harbour area and in public works in general, but from 1905 onwards activity in the naval base slowed down and this meant unemployment for more than 4,000 men who went on to fill the already growing army of unemployed. Tension and war in the Mediterranean in the second half of the nineteenth century − Crimea, the Eastern Question, Fashoda, the South African War − had made necessary the presence of a large British fleet in that area and had enhanced the strategic value of Malta. But, in the first decade of the twentieth century, Anglo-German rivalry shifted attention to defence requirements much further north, and this detracted from Malta's naval importance. From 1906 to 1914, the problem of what to do with the unemployed was a constant source of worry to the local administration. Increased expenditure on public works, it seems, was having only a limited effect. And it was in these years that significant numbers of Maltese were beginning to leave Malta's shores for permanent settlement abroad. The twentieth century had indeed arrived.

From the foregoing, one vital fact stands out: that the basic realities of Malta's commercial significance in the beginning of the twentieth century were much the same as they had been a hundred years before. Except in times of crisis, or during economic developments which lay outside Malta's own system, the island's dependence on commercial activities and defence spending signified a weak economic structure; one with no industrial base ready to fortify the weaker parts. Had something been done to diversify the economy at an earlier time, then, perhaps, a different story would today have been written.

NOTES

[1] H.I. Lee, *Malta 1813-1914*, 20.
[2] R. Montgomery-Martin, *History of the British Colonies*, v, 217.
[3] J. Godechot, *Histoire de Malte*, 57.
[4] B. Blouet, *The Story of Malta*, 145.
[5] J. Davy, *Notes and Observations on the Ionian Islands and Malta*, i, 42.
[6] H. Bowen-Jones et al., *Malta: Background for Development*, 117.
[7] CO 158/19, Memo on Maltese Commerce.
[8] CO 156/36, Wages Paid to Artificers in Land Revenue Department.
[9] Davy, 416.
[10] CO 158/36, Greig to Thornton, 24 April 1824.
[11] CO 158/119, Minute on Despatches, 19 February 1841.
[12] Montgomery-Martin, 292.
[13] J. Blow-Williams, *British Commercial Policy and Trade Expansion*, 87.
[14] Ibid., 88.
[15] CO 158/64, Ponsonby to Murray, 16 September 1829.
[16] Lee, 44.
[17] CO 158/52, Convention on Commerce.
[18] CO 158/115, Classification of Population, 1837.
[19] Godechot, 92.
[20] Blow-Williams, 89.
[21] Ibid.
[22] Montgomery-Martin, 280.
[23] C.A. Price, *Malta and the Maltese*, 208-9.
[24] W. Eton, *Authentic Materials for a History of the People of Malta*, 215.

[25] Price, 2-5.
[26] CO 158/115, Commission of Inquiry, Austin and Lewis, 1837.
[27] NLM, *Lib.* 388.
[28] CO 158/115, Classification of Population, 1837.
[29] Ibid.
[30] CO 158/113, Consumption of Foreign Wheat.
[31] CO 158/36, Greig to Thornton, 24 April 1824.
[32] Montgomery-Martin, 219. See also NLM, *Lib.* 388.
[33] Davy, 407.
[34] Price, 107.
[35] W. Tallack, *Malta under the Phoenicians, Knights and the English*, 86.
[36] See *The Malta Observer*, 13 February 1868.
[37] Bowen-Jones et al., 120.
[38] Ibid.

8

SALVINO BUSUTTIL

An Overview of Malta's Economic Development

The Maltese economy under Britain was characterized by the syndrome, albeit one that was not by any means new to the country, whereby the islands generally prospered in times of war and were pauperized in times of peace. Under the Knights, economic behaviour had broadly followed the maritime fortunes of the Order, with periods of relative freedom from pirate and Ottoman incursion being dedicated to the creation of fortifications or, when magistral grace and chevalier generosity allowed, to the erection of temples.

In its decline, the Order of St John paid scarce attention to the social and economic needs of the Maltese; and what the French found in taking over the island in 1798 was a poor economy labouring under the constraints imposed by lack of resources for a growing population.

The ephemeral presence of Napoleon and his countrymen hardly had any impact on the Maltese economy except that, once more, it gave the Maltese a furtive savouring of warmongering pleasures. With the constitutional uncertainty that followed the forced departure of France and the uneasy arrival of Britain, the Maltese Islands were ushered into an economic turpor that lasted for several decades. For even after the Treaty of Amiens, the British were not at all sure that they should retain a colony which had fallen into their none-too-waiting lap. They evidently preferred having an imperial lion, rather than an imperial eagle, 'guarding' Malta; but they were not overtly enthusiastic at having the country under their Crown except to avoid unfriendly hands having it under theirs.

It was, then, for Britain, a holding operation, a transitory phase in expectation that somehow, in some vague but not distant future, they would pass on Malta to some power which would have an interest in retaining the island while not causing any nuisance to British interests. Neither politically nor psychologically committed to Malta, the British, initially at least, regarded the island as a fortress which belligerent exigencies stipulated should be theirs.

If, therefore, there is one principal feature running through the economic denouement of Malta since the advent of Britain till Independence one hundred and sixty-four years later, it is that of the island-fortress economy. As in antiquity, so in the nineteenth and the first half of the twentieth century, the national income of the Maltese was principally derived from the geo-political nature of their country as a strategic island with which, and by which placated, the gods of war awarded the fortitude of the fortunate and the strong. In this politico-military ritual, it was hardly noticed that the sacrificial lamb was the economy of the islanders.

Indeed, relative peace in the Mediterranean after 1815 brought about a second decline for the Maltese economy hard on the heels of the one that had marked the last days of the Order in that traditional demand for the island's services — repair and construction of galleys, building of fortifications, and the general engagement of Maltese on military or naval-related activities — fell spectacularly. As the years of the British presence wore on, there were undertaken, of course, works connected with the maintenance of fortifications and the occasional construction of amorphous barracks.

Moreover, Maltese merchants were able to develop a lucrative import/export business through sales of imported wares to merchantmen calling at Valletta, thus preparing the ground for that entrepôt trade which was to flourish after the opening of the Suez Canal. Favouring this business were the rules introduced by Civil Commissioner Alexander Ball, whereby British ships or ships which had a crew made up of at least one-third British sailors, and calling at Malta, were privileged and protected in the Mediterranean by the British Crown. Import/export licences issued by Malta for this purpose were a boon to local trading.

Yet these activities were essentially commercial, their impact on the economy resting on the ability of the Maltese to buy and sell overseas products through the foreign exchange earned by providing services to Britain. This characteristic was to mark the economic performance of Malta right up to Independence and, indeed, even thereafter. Over the years, this phenomenon came to condition Maltese economic and political attitudes in taking for granted that Malta and its people could buy foreign goods with no limitations and with impunity to the value of 'local' currency.

Foreign exchange elasticities of demand had practically no orthodox relevance in a context where a growing supply of local services to Britain implied an increase in foreign exchange earnings and where the 'local' currency was *de facto* sterling. In essence, of course, this process was a carry-over from the days of the Order which, dealing in monies largely derived legitimately from the princely purses of Europe and, less legitimately, from quasi-piratical adventures, had no foreign exchange problems. In regarding such economic behaviour as entirely normal, the Maltese came to feel that as long as they were able to afford foreign goods, the matter of paying for them in overseas currency did not arise. Hence it was very late in the day, and mainly in post-1964 Malta, that the foreign exchange problems were tackled seriously.

An important first corollary to this situation is that, till the run down of the British base in the late 1950s and early 1960s with the attendant need to diversify the economy, the prevailing economic attitude of Maltese politicians and businessmen was in no way export- or, indeed, production-oriented. Business came to mean merchandising principally through retail outlets, through ship-chandling, and through supply and servicing contracts with the army and navy. In these ventures, which became quite lucrative for the more entrepreneurial, the Maltese businessman was quickly joined by British and, to a lesser extent, Italian (mainly Sicilian) fellow journeymen.

There were, in this overall pattern, some important industries, such as the local production of sails and textiles, in which Maltese craftsmen excelled. But such sporadic exceptions apart, it was through providing services rather than goods that Malta earned its living over the period as a whole.

A second corollary, as far-reaching as the previous one in its impact on the Maltese political and economic philosophy, emerges from this foregoing. Another type of expectation which was to ingrain itself in the natural psyche was the eventual dependence of the Maltese economy on the military budget annually voted at Westminster. With the growth of Maltese employment in navy and army activities, the relationship between the domestic economy and the British Services became closer. As Britain began to create work for Maltese at the Dockyard, and as more British men-of-war called at Malta for bunkering and repairs, a very considerable proportion of the economy became a function of what the United Kingdom Parliament would vote for the upkeep of the fleet and its garrison in Malta and for the maintenance and occasional new construction of barracks and military facilities on the island. It therefore became crucial for Malta to seek an increase in the budget which London provided each year. On its amount would hinge the behaviour of the Maltese economy for the coming year. This dependence, too, was to mark Maltese economic thinking right up to Independence.

Concomitant with this occurrence was the evolving feeling that a career with Government offered the best employment, relatively well remunerated and secure. Modelled on the British Civil Service, the local Service came to attract some of the better minds on the island. It also brought about a situation where the public sector, in terms of jobs and of their multipliers, became the most important segment of the economy.

One had then, for the period as a whole, a pattern where blue-collar workers were largely Service employees and white-collar ones were principally Government ones. It was symptomatic that new entrants on the labour market should seek to pass the apprenticeship examinations for the Dockyard if they were tool-oriented and the Civil Service examination if they preferred to be desk-bound. The private sector would be generally sought only if the above avenues were blocked or in the somewhat rare case where one could join a family business.

The upshot of these circumstances was an overall web of Maltese economic dependence and of Maltese expectations on the patronage and whims of Westminster, itself conditioned by political considerations in London and by naval and military requirements in the Mediterranean. For Malta and its people, the web covered national life and aspirations in identifying 'Government' – the British till 1921, and partly British and partly Maltese thereafter – as the main provider of livelihood, as the paterfamilias to attend to every need, as the stimulus for the economy, and as the *deus ex machina* when problems arose. It was really *Government for the people.*

The fact that for most of the period under study it was not Government *by* the people seemed hardly to distress the average citizen who came to regard the British connection as salutary for his immediate well-being. It is indeed significant that moves for constitutional improvement were often mooted in periods of relative peace in the Mediterranean; and it was usually during such periods that Britain went through the motions of appearing, however superciliously, conciliatory in this respect.

But it was to take one hundred and twenty years into the British colonial presence before the Maltese convinced themselves that they could no longer forge their future on the anvil of war, and that they had to seek some form of direct say in the economic affairs of their homeland through constitutional advancement.

For all nascent self-governing aspirations which Malta may have harboured up to the mid-nineteenth century were swept away in the frenzy for enrichment which, first the Crimean War and, then, the opening of the Suez Canal ushered in. While the former circumstance confirmed once more the syndrome of wartime prosperity, the latter event offered, for the first time in recent Maltese history, the possibility of peacetime success. The Golden Age of Malta, which was to last till the eve of the twentieth century, indicated that the island's strategic position could be exploited not just for wartime activities but that, properly planned and managed, it could allow the country to thrive without strife.

However, the problem with this unexpected windfall in Malta's fortunes was precisely that it was neither planned nor properly managed. It was taken for granted that the Golden Age would last for ever, and that Malta could rely on entrepôt trade, bunkering, and repair of vessels as its main resource for the foreseeable future. No attempt was made to introduce effective management of the economy, and *laissez-faire* became the hallmark of policy or, rather, of its absence: one that, like other features mentioned above, acquired a chronic dimension in the domestic affairs of Malta.

When, as all good things, the Golden Age came to an end, and when hands were wrung in despair at the turn of the century, as no warmongering appeared on the horizons of the island, the British rulers introduced a factor in the economy which was destined to become a leitmotif of successive Governments: embarking, that is, on a large programme of public capital expenditure. With massive unemployment threatening to wreck the social fabric of Malta, Britain undertook the building of a breakwater at the mouth of the Grand Harbour, a massive project which created jobs not just for the Maltese but called for additional labour which was mainly provided from Sicily and other neighbouring areas. A measure of Government intervention through important public works at times of economic distress was to endear itself to several administrations, even after Independence. As a short-term palliative in situations of serious unemployment, this approach had undoubted merits. Negatively, it accentuated reliance on Government to offer solutions, softening the need for the emergence of real private entrepreneurship. It also institutionalized an *ad hoc* and, therefore, unstructured economic policy. On its own, it laid no basis for the future, providing an admittedly necessary physical infrastructure with no lasting productive structure to follow.

Economic behaviour in the first half of this century did not belie the syndrome with which this essay opens. When the breakwater was terminated, unemployment, now augmented by some foreign workers who stayed on, came to haunt the island once again. At the same time, new attempts at a constitutional advancement were launched. And as Malta struggled to make ends meet through a decade of near misery, the First World War once more placed the country on the Mediterranean strategic pedestal, bringing the dubious advantages of armed conflict to the economic scene. With the end of hostilities and with what promised to be a long period of Mediterranean tranquillity, Britain felt it could be generous enough to grant a measure of self-government to Malta.

True to form, 1921, when Malta started to govern itself, marked the accentuation of serious unemployment problems leading to economic upheavals. But, in a sense, the 1921 letters patent acted as a *deus ex machina* to distract the legislature from economic considerations and to indulge in the luxury, practically right up to the Constitution's abrogation in 1936, of the Language Question. It was, in fact, the relative merits of English, Italian, and Maltese in local usage and, particularly, in education, that provided the Legislative Assembly with learned, and not so learned, debates. In the heat and passion of discussion, cultural priorities obfuscated economic realities. Remaining unaddressed, the basic issues of economic life were very much left to the gods of tomorrow.

The rites and rituals of the Language Question wore on, wearing out politicians in the process. Indeed, between the introduction of self-government and the breakout of the Second World War, the Maltese economy ran its monotonous cause of increasing dependence on a 'benevolent' Britain for its daily sustenance, nourishing itself on a Dockyard idling away and on a skeletal garrison and fleet to which only the spectre of conflict could add body, the economic soul endured by dint of perseverance, hard work, and lowered expectations.

Nonetheless, the impression one forms of the interwar years is not, in human terms, entirely negative. The cohesive solidarity of the Maltese among themselves, and the lived conservation of their traditions, allowed them to derive an enjoyment of life well beyond what seemed to be possible through their meagre lot. There was no great wealth, and no great poverty. Income gaps existed in a climate of passive class distinction rather than of active class struggle. Social differences were perceived more in their traditional and historical context than in their economic causality and significance. The legislators were not unaware of social issues, and were certainly not ignorant of the educational poverty to which, by and large, British design had condemned successive generations.

It is, therefore, all the more a tribute to the tenacity and the far-sightedness of the interwar Maltese legislator that important studies were made in the educational system. That similar progress was not made on the economic front is largely due to the infamous Section 41 of the 1921 letters patent, whereby the Legislative Assembly could not enact any measures affecting the public safety and defence of the Empire, including such matters as the control of naval, military, and air forces, the defence of the island, navigation, coinage, immigration, naturalization, and foreign relations. Clearly, all the external factors having a determining bearing on Malta's economy were *ultra vires* the local Parliament; and this in an economic situation characterized by overbearing and overwhelming external dependence. It is true that the Language Question was a distraction but, objectively, there was little else of moment on which the Maltese side of the diarchy, ushered in the letters patent, could act.

The Second World War gave the islands the usual economic respite that war reserved for Malta. Full employment and a heavy British military presence took care of economic fortunes, even as somebody else's made victims of thousands of Maltese. Peace then brought unemployment and mass migration, coinciding once more with the return in 1947 of self-government, again with basic matters reserved to the British Crown.

The vicissitudes of the Maltese economy between 1947 and 1964 showed for the first time the need to plan the economy and to steer it away from one based on defence to a modern industrial and tourism structure. Successive Governments drew up successive plans with varying degrees of success. But it was clear, by the late fifties, that the economic future of Malta could no longer lie at the mercy of British demand for Malta's strategic services.

With constitutions suspended, withdrawn, and revoked at the whim of Westminster, Malta realized in the early sixties that it had to bid farewell to its Romantic association with Britain and to seek its economic destiny as a new State, identifying its resilience on the self-reliance of the resources and resourcefulness of its people. Malta had to have a planned economy, if only to endow it with that infrastructure required by a modern industrial State. As independence was attained in 1964, the haphazardness of the past was abandoned, and a scientific approach to economic management was introduced. For the first time in its milleniar epic, Malta was free to determine its fortunes. Independence was a political aspiration, but an economic necessity.

9

EDWARD L. ZAMMIT

Aspects of British Colonial Policies and Maltese Patterns of Behaviour

In this essay an attempt is made to relate some aspects of Maltese social life to the policies implemented by the British colonial administration. The emphasis is on economic, political, and religious institutions. The aim is to provide a sociological interpretation of certain processes and patterns of behaviour as these may relate to certain historical events, the evidence for which is drawn from published historical studies. This account does not present a comprehensive assessment of the extent of British colonial impact on Malta's socio-economic life. Important areas which were deeply influenced by the exercise of colonial power structure like education, health, and sanitation are barely touched upon or simply mentioned in passing. Certain concepts like that of 'élites' or 'culture' which are widely used in this essay are intended as usually understood by sociologists. Thus the former refers to a political, economic, or status minority which may be entrenched at the top of a society, group, or other social category whether this is openly democratic or not. The latter refers to the ideas, values, and norms influencing social behaviour and defining inter-relations rather than simply to an artistic or literary heritage.

The period of British rule over Malta, stretching for a century and a half, is highly significant because during this time many characteristic aspects of Maltese social, political, and economic life became firmly established. Undoubtedly the island experienced many upheavals during that period. Yet, in some important respects, the British simply continued filling a role which had been left vacant after the Knights' departure. And, ironically, the Maltese leaders themselves, who had protested strongly against the Order's return, expected Britain to play that role. True they also expected Britain to safeguard their interests, to revive the economy, and to grant some form of representative rights.[1] But essentially they expected Britain to act as *il più paterno dei governi* and in this sense recognized the British King as their sovereign. For this reason British colonial administrators found little difficulty in suppressing any ideas of self-government and civil liberties which may have been nourished by a few 'political agitators'.[2] As a result the important changes which had been taking place in Europe, inspired by the French Revolution and the nationalistic movements of the period, did not gain ground within Maltese society – apart from a few of its urban and intellectual élites – until many decades later. Although the Order had been swept away precisely by these changes and ideologies, the new colonial administration which replaced it succeeded in establishing itself into the 'old role' because it rallied the support of the main traditional social institution – the Maltese Church.

Towards the end of the Knights' rule, some ideas of revolt had actually found their way into Malta – following the usual route for novel ideas – from abroad. These ideas had been an unmistaken by-product of the French Revolution. In fact, when Napoleon threatened to take over the island, hardly a shot was fired in defence of the Order's 'rights'. A Maltese delegation made it quite clear to the Order that they had no intention of resisting the French.[3] However, as the French had disregarded their initial promises to safeguard the Maltese religion and 'priviliges' so soon after their take-over in 1798, the Maltese naturally felt that they had merely exchanged one form of despotism for an even worse one. Indeed, the Order's rule, though absolutist, seemed paternalistic by comparison for, after all, the Knights had brought prosperity and security into the island and they had been generous with their employees and protégés.

When the French authorities in Malta started imposing heavy taxes and despoiling the churches so as to make up for revenue lost after the Order's departure, some reaction from the local leaders was inevitable.[4] With the help of British, Portuguese, and Neapolitan vessels, a blockade was organized on the French garrison who had locked themselves up in Valletta and the Three Cities. They eventually surrendered and some Maltese leaders promptly asked for 'British protection'. It seems, in retrospect, that the Maltese leaders had naively nourished unrealistic expectations from the British. Malta became officially a British 'protectorate' through the Treaty of Paris in 1814 though Britain had really retained full control over the island since 1800. The British initially hesitated as they were not sure of the value Malta had for them. Soon, however, they changed their minds and established on the island an important defence base for their Mediterranean fleet and a centre for entrepôt trade with Europe and the eastern parts of their expanding empire. Therefore, while it is generally true that the many changes which took place during the nineteenth century were mainly of a 'quantitative' rather than a 'qualitative' nature, it is also true to state that in many aspects of life the amount of 'quantitative' changes was such as to bring about, in sum, a radical or 'qualitative' break with the past.

They generally followed a pattern which had been established under the Knights – but at a much more accelerated pace. This was because the British, on their part, had very narrowly-defined interests in Malta, namely that of exploiting its strategic values.[5] They sought to interfere with local affairs as little as possible – except, of course, when their strategic interests required such interference. Where it suited them, on 'internal' matters, they very conveniently professed their liberal philosophy of *laissez-faire.* Yet, as military efficiency often depended upon civilian compliance and co-operation, the colonial administration could not escape getting heavily involved in managing local affairs. In so doing they introduced various social and material reforms often against the opposition of the local 'élites' and other sections of the population. Other innovations, particularly of an ideological and political kind, generally entered Malta later as a result of informal associations between the Maltese and the British and continental individuals they came into contact with, or as a reaction to colonial policies, rather than by the conscious design of the colonial administrators. These ranged from the demand for political autonomy to the setting up of trade unions and reformist political movements.

Under the British, the Maltese population trebled in size — from about 100,000 in 1820 to about 330,000 in 1960.[6] The geographical spread of the population shifted from the countryside to the urban and suburban areas around the harbours where about half of the population are now concentrated. The heavy dependence of the economy upon foreign sources continued to keep pace with the increase in population. The ability of the Government to provide direct and indirect employment became the determining factor in the living standard of the population as a whole. In fact, this became another important tool at the disposal of the colonial administration through which it influenced the people's minds as it controlled their fortunes. This applied to civil servants, to industrial workers, and especially to those enlisted in the Armed Forces and in ancilliary services. The enlargement of the dockyard around Cottonera to cater for British naval repairs on a large scale was a case in point. This establishment provided the largest, and until recent times a unique, concentration of industrial workers in Malta. For that reason it also provided the 'cradle of the Maltese workers' movement' — as it is popularly known. Frendo points out:

This fact is highly important in the country's social history during the colonial era, because the proletariat, on the whole, was favourably disposed towards the colonial regime, not so much because it agreed with its politics, but as a result of the fact that thousands of jobs were secured at a rate of pay which was not any worse, often rather better, than that paid to workers in private enterprise, on the farms, or indeed in the lower ranks of the Civil Service.[7]

The pattern of the British colonial policy in Malta was clearly indicated in the Royal Commission Report of 1812. The Commissioners decided that 'The Maltese temperament was incompatible with an ordered system of representative government'. Such a 'conclusion' provided a convenient justification for colonial policy. Admittedly it was partly prompted by the Commissioners' first-hand experience of fundamental disagreements, intrigues, and personal rivalries among the Maltese élites. But the memory of the effective, national resistance organized by them against the French was still vivid as to belie that conclusion. In any case, 'complete authority' was to be vested in the Governor aided by a small advisory council made up of Maltese and Englishmen selected by him. The Commissioners also recommended that 'The Roman Catholic faith was to be maintained and protected.' In these respects the pattern applied in other British Crown colonies was to be followed here.[8] The man appointed to establish this policy in Malta, Sir Thomas Maitland, had been singled out for the success of his 'benevolent despotism' in Ceylon a few years previously. As Lee points out:

His governorship was ... a continuation of the benevolent despotism of the Grand Masters, but far superior to it as a system by reason of its efficiency and even less popular than it because of its essential lack of any real sympathy with the Maltese people.[9]

He reorganized the civil administration and placed Englishmen at the head of every department. The Maltese were excluded 'from all but the lowest offices'. As a result of such measures the latter 'began to feel like strangers in their own country'.[10] On their part the English officials were often accused of 'arrogance', 'contempt', 'insolence', and of being 'ambitious of showing their authority [towards] all classes of persons'.[11] The exclusion of Maltese from high positions in the military service and in the dockyard continued throughout the period of British rule and this provided a constant source of friction and resentment among some aspiring Maltese individuals,[12] though the majority were generally complacent and submissive.[13] In the Civil Service, however, as a new 'middle class' of educated Maltese gradually emerged, who had been socialized in the British style of government, who had developed pro-British loyalties, and who could thus be relied upon to carry out acceptable policies, most of the administrative posts were handed over to them. It was, in fact, the development of such a 'new middle class' − as distinct from the traditional 'élite class' − which contributed to the emergence of rival political interests and parties in the latter half of the nineteenth century and which continued to dominate Maltese political life throughout the greater part of the twentieth century.

Maltese political and economic developments have never been so intricately bound together as under the British colonial administration.[14] This resulted from their policy of retaining absolute control over the reins of Government − ignoring the constant pleas for autonomy from any aspiring local political leader. And this was made possible by the increasing dependence of the economy upon military expenditure. Such measures offered no stable and secure means of livelihood but fluctuated according to the political situation which prevailed internationally and the strategic decisions taken by the Colonial and War Offices in London. As Busuttil has pointed out:

The economy of the Maltese Islands under Britain took the form of an artificial cycle determined not by vicissitudes of the market, but by the exigencies of military security. War marked the upswing of the Maltese economic cycle; the return of peace was always the harbinger of a downswing.[15]

Throughout most of the nineteenth and the early part of the twentieth centuries the social condition of the population was very bad. It often verged on starvation. This was partly the result of a policy which, like Maitland's,

did not aim at securing the best interests of the Maltese, but of Britain in the fortress of Malta. Not primarily concerned with the effects of [such] policy on the people but with the results of it in maintaining a secure strategic base in the Mediterranean.[16]

This situation was officially acknowledged in the report of the 1836 Royal Commission who blamed the Government for the poor state of affairs.

The islanders [the Commissioners reported] were in a most miserable condition. Due to official policy, the educated among them were a handful. The nobles, formerly the backbone of Malta, were starving. The rest of the population fared even worse.[17]

The Commissioners strongly condemned the manner used by many of the Englishmen who ran the island, whom they depicted as 'vulgar, offensive types'. Reforms, however, were not easy to implement. Not only was it difficult to raise any money through local taxation, but the Maltese élites often instinctively suspected that any reforms would hit them adversely by diminishing their incomes, power, or prestige among the population. They thus fomented popular discontent and raised a public outcry against any reforms whether of a badly-needed drainage system or of the equally-ailing educational set-up. Such an opposition was generally aimed at extorting from the British Government a measure of local autonomy by making Malta appear as ungovernable without their participation. In reality, however, the vast majority of the population was subservient and compliant. This often puzzled the British administrators and made potential leaders appear as isolated 'agitators'. In 1878, for instance, the Secretary of State, Sir M. Hicks-Beach, could only attribute 'the absence of any complaint of oppressive taxation from the Maltese to their ignorance, when the burden of taxation did fall in undue proportion on the lower classes'.[18]

Therefore, the most common Maltese response to their powerlessness in the colonial situation was their 'quiescence and fatalism, the sense of inferiority and dependence arising out of the paternal tradition' which has impressed several foreign observers.[19] Among the most deep-rooted Maltese values governing their daily lives are those of sobriety and thrift. The successive periods of relative prosperity and extreme depression, which have characterized Malta's economic fortunes for centuries, have brought home the importance of 'saving for a rainy day'.[20] In adopting these attitudes they were certainly influenced by Church teachings. Yet, as Price observes, 'when it came to a question of the Eighth Commandment, poverty often defeated Canon Law in the struggle which took place in the minds of Maltese faced with complete destitution'.[21] Thefts became so common that police protection and legal redress became practically useless. Offenders often threatened litigants and prosecutors with even worse retributions. Price concludes:

The Maltese may have been quiescent vis-à-vis his Government and social order; he was certainly not quiescent as regards his neighbour's property.[22]

During the present century the police have become better-equipped and organized so that their control over criminal activities is effective. Besides, the widespread prosperity and social services have reduced the need for widespread thefts. Public begging, which was also widely practised in the nineteenth century, has almost completely disappeared.[23]

Another characteristic Maltese response to their powerlessness, however, is still very much in evidence. This refers to the constant grumbling and other informal expressions of discontent which one hears in daily conversations on almost any topic of public interest. The Maltese have retained an unrealistic image of what to expect from Government, partly as a relic of their past experiences under colonial rule. These expectations have been further fostered by the attitudes of local politicians in their electioneering practices since the setting up of self-government in 1921. In order to win votes, they must liberally bestow favours. As a result, the concept of *il-Gvern* (the Government) is often 'vaguely referred to by many Maltese — particularly those living in rural areas — as a high centre of authority which is endowed with every conceivable power and which is held responsible for many economic and social problems'.[24] In the context of such unrealistic expectations, coupled with the absence of any formal channels of protest or representation, informal grumbling takes an added significance. The British colonial administrators taking a sarcastic, superior view had labelled it *Maltese gemgem* and their successors, the Maltese politicians in Government, are equally ironic about it.[25]

The Maltese language itself was obviously an excellent medium for grumbling against the foreign colonizers unable to speak it. This way it has served as a safe outlet and a defence against foreign intrusions. More recently it has also served as a positive national rallying symbol, through which what is typically Maltese can find its true expression.[26] And, although the Maltese language which is now spoken abounds with English or Italian imports, the language continues to provide a clear dividing line between the locals and the thousands who visit the country.

In times of distress, particularly during times of war, outbreaks of cholera in the nineteenth century, and other national disasters, the Church usually came to the rescue, as 'the ultimate protector of the population'.[27] Parish priests, in particular, were the undisputed leaders on the village level and anyone who aspired to local leadership needed their support. On its part, the Church, like the other traditional élites, tended to suspect that any reforms introduced by the British administrators would, either intentionally or as a by-product, threaten its place in Maltese society. Accordingly it was easier for Britain to come to terms with the situation by maintaining good relations with the Church as the only powerful organization which could offer any effective opposition to their rule.[28] They also chose to ignore, as best they could, any political agitation from other quarters and to appeal directly to the people's material interests. Any changes which they felt were necessary were usually presented in the name of 'progress'. This is particularly evidenced by the long political struggle stretching for half-a-century to introduce certain changes in the educational medium of instruction – particularly in supplanting Italian, the traditional language of the Church, the Law Courts, and the local élites, with English and Maltese. As Britain was a Protestant country, the Maltese Roman Catholic hierarchy was always on the alert against any hidden attempts at Anglicizing Malta. The other local élites had enough evidence to prompt their resistance to any attempt to supplant their traditional privileges by a new, pro-English middle-class which they saw emerging.

Eventually two camps were set against each other in a long-drawn-out battle which went far deeper than the original issues warranted. The Language Question symbolized what Frendo has typified an opposition between the 'colonial dynamics' and the 'patriotic consensus'. The former comprises the (a) domination of one society by another; (b) modernization of techniques and living styles; and (c) the gradual assimilation of the colonized social, political, and economic structures into those of the colonial country. The latter comprises (a) a demand for political and social autonomy; (b) the assertion of traditional values and structures; and (c) organized resistance often passive, through all means available including alignment with other foreign powers and symbols as a means of leverage, to the overriding weight of the colonizer.[29]

The type of 'resistance' which was commonly adopted by the average Maltese, as already stated, generally avoided a direct confrontation with the overriding powers of the colonizer. It was only on those rare occasions, when a convergence of various issues was evident, that some mass protests, or even riots, could be organized.[30]

For the most part, the British administration managed to keep issues apart and usually to manipulate or exploit situations where the interests of one section of the population were opposed to those of another. A case in point is the 'language controversy'[31] in which the country became polarized into two opposed camps engaged in a political confrontation over issues which, on the face of it, appear as having a relatively minor importance. It is not necessary here to enter into the detailed ramification of this prolonged dispute. [32]

What matters is that the real though latent issues overshadowed by this controversy developed into a bitter politico-religious crisis in the thirties, and again in the sixties, and again in the eighties[33] when different political and religious leaders were on the scene. These crisis followed the entrance into the political arena and the temporary coalition between two representative parties, one with its roots in the 'working class' and the other among the 'new middle class'. Both of these classes had come into existence as a direct result of colonial policies in Malta.[34] Frendo has shown how this 'party' had its foundations laid in the nineteenth century, beginning with Sigismondo Savona's 'Reform Party' in 1891 and has evolved through various splits and new foundations into the present-day Malta Labour Party.[35] Likewise the present-day Nationalist Party has its roots in the *Partito Anti-Riformista*, founded in 1884 by Fortunato Mizzi − having also passed through various permutations.

In fact, this polarization between two political camps had occurred as early as the 1830s and the issue concerned the best way of dealing with the British colonial masters.[36] The 'anti-reformist' side opposed any social and economic reforms introduced by the British administration until constitutional liberties had been granted in advance. The 'reformist' side was ready to compromise autonomy on humanitarian and utilitarian grounds. The 'Anti-reformist' or 'Nationalist' movement was constituted of the traditional, professional élites, often in alliance with the Church hierarchy, both of whom feared that any 'reforms' would eventually remove their privileged status in Maltese society. They rallied behind them the majority of the local population who held them in high esteem. Thus, apart from combating the professional élites, whose priviliges it sought to curtail, the 'reformist' movement became successively involved in a bitter clash with the Maltese Church authorities. Such a clash was inevitable in view of the powerful, central position which the Church enjoyed in Maltese society and the new aspirants to local power had to re-define its jurisdiction and limit its influence over men's lives. Eventually the 'reformist' movement was also bound to conflict with its previous ally, protector, and source of its inspiration – the British colonial overlords.[37]

The role played by the Church in Maltese politics is a consequence of the central part it plays in social life as a whole. As such it merits further consideration. Dench maintains that under the British, the Maltese 'national Church became projected into a new and more significant position as defender of the faithful population against an alien system of government.'[38] It can also be said that this role had essentially been played by the Maltese Church for several centuries under the Knights, long before the arrival of the British.[39] Yet, the replacement of the Catholic Knights by the Protestant British added a new dimension. It created a precarious situation with the local Church becoming relatively isolated from the dominant colonial administration. It has been shown that the British interest in Malta was limited to its strategic values. Once this had been safeguarded, Britain was quite uninterested in Maltese domestic affairs. It even offered the local Church a measure of protection in exchange for its promotion of the people's loyalties towards their earthly sovereign.

In other areas of social and economic life, however, British strategic interests inhibited local initiatives. These might have tampered with the centralized efficiency of a 'fortress' administration. As most other areas of Maltese life – vital areas like economic and political activities – were beyond the control of the local population, 'the energy and interest of the Maltese seem to have become displaced, as so often happens among powerless minorities, into religious activity and contemplation.'[40] Accordingly the people's interests were concentrated on religious symbols which became the object of personal and collective pride and satisfaction.

Not only was it important to save one's soul through leading a good life according to established moral principles and participation in religious ritual as presented by the Catholic Church anywhere, it also became important to contribute one's share to the parish church's physical aspect and its cult of patron saints which are celebrated everywhere with great pomp annually to this day. Class conflicts and political rivalries were likewise sublimated under an unending competition between *partiti tal-festa* often in the same village, each celebrating its own patron saint in the best way it could.[41] Boissevain has also demonstrated how local rivalries over the cult of saints are often intermingled with national political contests. This is because a number of political and economic functions have been developed by the Church in the absence of secular structures which could not emerge due to the colonial situation.[42] Moreover, parish priests and other priests often acted as their parishioners' patrons and intermediated for them with civil authorities and other influential persons.[43] Thus the Maltese Church, even more than it did during the Knights' rule, assumed the role of national protector of the local population, represented their interests, provided leisure and other expressive pursuits, ordered people's lives, and commanded their loyalties. As Dench has concluded,

Much of the passionate interest in religion displayed in Malta has therefore been escapist, and the alleged fatalism of the islanders simply a pursuit of spiritual goals rather than material — over which the Maltese individually and collectively enjoyed so little control ... The central position of the church has for generations channelled political debate into essentially symbolic and unrealistic issues.[44]

It is in this context that the language dispute and the politico-religious controversies of the thirties and the sixties need to be interpreted. For the emergence of a new 'reformist' movement, initially implicitly and later explicitly, challenged the traditional place occupied by the Church in Maltese social life. Ultimately, however, the Church was led into assuming this role by the circumstances of colonialism which imposed strict controls in certain vital areas of social life and adopted an indulgent, permissive attitude in others. The Maltese had been effectively reduced to a minority status in their own country. In such a situation, 'a mixture of petulant irresponsibility and fatalism was a perfectly rational response to British paternalism'.[45]

Thus, paradoxically, there was, under British rule, a parallel development of both centralization and localism. Such opposite tendencies are still evident today in many spheres of Maltese social life. The 1973-80 Development Plan, for instance, stresses that 'Malta has a greater degree of social cohesion and solidarity' than other countries but also acknowledges the existence of deep internal divisions.[46] Such contrasting statements about the Maltese social structure are commonly made and manifest dual normative standards of reference. The 'ideal' and the 'real' are worlds apart.[47]

It can be argued that Maltese culture offers a typical example of what Parkin has called the 'subordinate value system' in relation to the 'dominant value system' implanted by successive generations of colonial domination. 'The subordinate class tends to have two levels of normative reference, the abstract and the situational ... The generation milieu of these values is the local underclass community.'[48] Not only were the Maltese powerless in tackling their own problems but they often lacked any alternative solutions of their own other than those imposed upon them 'from above'. They thus felt compelled by sheer necessity and the general circumstances of colonial presence to adapt themselves, even if this implied the transgression of traditional norms. Whenever this happened, however, it was accompanied by strong public condemnations from local religious sources – as a means of safeguarding the 'well-being of society' in general and of traditional institutions in particular. The incidence of prostitution which is a common form of Maltese criminality at home and abroad is a typical example of the types of dual constraints confronted by many Maltese individuals.[49] Dench has attributed this notorious form of Maltese criminal behaviour in London to a

central dilemma in colonial Maltese society, revolving around the discrepancy between an extremely strict set of moral principles on sexual matters, and a practical reality of extensive prostitution in the Island, meeting the needs of the large garrision.[50]

He argues that this situation particularly manifested to the Maltese 'their dependent status and inability to control their own lives'.[51]

A less noticeable yet more important response to British colonialism on the part of Maltese individuals was the widespread resort to patronage. This practice has deep roots in Maltese society colouring social interactions at every level. Thus, in spite of its widespread condemnation as a corrupt practice – giving some citizens an unfair advantage over others – everyone admits that it is arguably the most effective way to secure scarce resources, ranging from a house to a telephone.[52]

In the colonial context, Malta itself was in the situation of a 'client-state'. Its economic and political dependence upon the 'mother country' was well known. Internally it still incorporates a highly paternalistic set of social and religious institutions with a self-conscious system of patron-client relations challenged by a monopolistic and centralizing political bureaucracy.[53] In the situation which developed under British rule where most economic activities — including employment opportunities — were under their direct control,[54] the colonial administrators had at their disposal an unlimited supply of patronage potential. Unlike some other colonies, the local administration of the Civil Service has long been entrusted to Maltese personnel who readily followed the patronage pattern which had been firmly established since the times of the Knights. These bureaucrats/patrons therefore joined the ranks of the traditional professional, clerical, and other influential persons whose clientele resided in the villages or their immediate localities.

With the advent of representative government most of their power passed on to the elected deputies who needed the support of electors and had rather more to offer in return. To the clients, of course, patronage presents a possible way of coping with a generally difficult situation through a personal intervention with power-holders. Patronage, of course, depends upon the inadequacy of formal institutional arrangement to provide for the needs of the powerless. From the colonial viewpoint, the availability of widespread resort to patronage — though offending their declared principles and official policies — served an important divisive function.[55] Thus, it provided an important concomitant to a nominally 'paternalist' policy.[56] The latter is basically 'a collective form of social organization' in which 'all subordinates basically stand in the same relation to the paternalist'.[57] The ideological basis which justifies paternalism as a manner of administration rests upon the care and relationships of parents towards their children in an ideal-type family and ultimately of God, the Divine Father of all men. This implies that

people tend to be treated as members of a group who share a similar position rather than as individuals who have unique relationships with the paternalist ... Benefits become common to the whole group rather than varying from person to person, and the customary regulation of relationships develops for all.[58]

Though in the Maltese situation paternalism and patronage were both essential tools for the colonial system, they ultimately militated against each other.

In recent years there have been various attempts by colonial and local Governments at reducing, and possibly eliminating, Malta's dependence upon paternalism or its 'client status' once and for all. Ambitious investment and industrialization programmes, aimed at transforming the Maltese economy, were promulgated. This was the declared objective of a series of official reports and development plans since the Second World War.[59] These suggested ways of diversifying the economy in view of a succession of anticipated rundowns of British service establishments in Malta. The rundowns brought about a heavy loss of foreign exchange, unemployment, and other economic setbacks. For these reasons there was a general consternation and an antagonistic reaction in Malta each time such plans were effected. The development plans also aimed at raising the social living levels of the population to that of accepted western standards through education and the establishment of statal agencies to act as official brokers and cater for people's needs without recourse to personal favours.[60] This had been viewed by some observers as representing a progressive trend in Malta towards 'a modern, rational, bureaucratic, and industrial world' in which there is no need or even room for traditional patrons and clients.[61] It is, of course, highly debatable whether these efforts are effectively promoting a lasting form of economic and social 'development' or only a 'modernized' form of neo-colonial dependence.[62] 'Modernization' refers to a diversification of the economic base and the consequent changes in living styles, consumption, and employment patterns for those directly or indirectly affected by such a transformation. A standard criterion to measure the extent of 'modernization' in a particular country is that of economic growth. Such a process can certainly take place within a neo-colonial context where economic, social, and political activities in one 'client state' remain on the periphery and the State continues to depend upon its 'mother country' as the source of its growth. On the other hand, in the case of true 'development' the dependent country itself generates its own wealth. This is achieved through the contribution of the mass of its people who are rallied behind local leadership and inspired by a local ideology. Some scholars have attempted to attribute the failure of 'underdeveloped' countries to 'develop' to a persistence of 'traditional' thinking and to a failure of a strong, central Government in such countries.[63] Indeed, what happens in many 'underdeveloped' former colonies is that their available political and intellectual leadership, their economic élites, and their dominant ideologies are more likely to be conducive to 'modernization'. Economic activities, particularly in satellite firms owned by large, international companies which provide employment, higher incomes, and consumption levels, depend not on local sources but mainly on activities generated at the 'centre'.[64] Nevertheless, as Black has argued, one needs to specify the historical conditions which produce the available leadership and ideologies in particular former colonies. This involves 'a clear specification of the particular, historically-determined, class structures and struggles through which the system is actually worked out.'[65] Only then can one explain the contrasting development paths followed by the undeveloped neighbouring countries like Malta and Sicily.

A quick glance at the changing patterns of employment in Malta in recent decades reveals that, in this respect, planned development has had a remarkable degree of success. The hand-over of Government controls to local politicians proceeded apace with decisions to reduce British military spending on the island.[66] The constant threats of large-scale redundancies provided an ideal incentive for workers to rally behind their leaders in the Labour Movement.[67] The need to create alternative employment for those who were losing their jobs with the Services also presented a constant challenge to successive local Governments to restructure the local economy.

In retrospect, it appears that as the Maltese politicians battled endlessly among themselves – as a by-product of the divisive policies pursued by the British colonialists – both sides unwittingly ended by having very similar beliefs and fears. Thus, for instance, both the goal of some prominent Nationalists of a political unification of Malta to Italy in prewar years and that of the Malta Labour Party plan to 'integrate' Malta with

Britain in the fifties had two basic things in common. They both stemmed from a profound disenchantment with the Maltese citizens' imposed inferior status to that of their colonial masters and an equally deep conviction that Malta was powerless to stand on its own feet in a hazardous world. In this context, the achievement of political independence in 1964, along with the decision to abandon Malta's 'fortress role' after the complete departure of the British Services in 1979, are indeed important milestones in Malta's socio-economic history. Yet, it would be unrealistic to expect these events to signal the actual termination of the influences of former colonial policies on Malta's social life. These are likely to persist, even if imperceptibly, for some time to come.[68]

NOTES

[1] *Dichiarazione dei Diritti degli Abitanti di Malta e Gozo.*

[2] As the Maltese leader Portelli submitted to the Austin and Lewis Commission (1836): 'The Maltese under the government of the Order of St John of Jerusalem were accustomed to repress the sentiments of liberty... and were restricted by the general system of absolute governments.' Quoted in H.I. Lee, *Malta 1813-1914.* As Canon Don Francesco Saverio Caruana, one of the Maltese generals during the French blockade, informed the gathering of the Assembly in Mdina on 4 September 1798, 'the ancient flag of Malta was nothing more than an historical reminiscence while what Malta then needed was the protection and aid of an existing power.' Anon, 'Why Malta Chose Britain', *Times of Malta,* 25, 26 June 1976. Such an attitude dominated the pattern of fatalistic dependence to British paternalistic colonialism for many decades afterwards.

[3] B. Blouet, *The Story of Malta,* 156.

[4] The Church, whose interests were directly threatened by the French, played an important role in this revolt. As a result, probably for the first time since the Monroy uprising, the Maltese of all social classes were united for a common, national cause. During this short period, all social divisions which had emerged under the Knights were bridged. However, they re-appeared soon after – only to be exploited to the full by the British imperial administrations.

[5] Actually, Britain was initially slow in recognizing Malta's strategic value. Even Nelson, who was mainly instrumental in securing British dominion over it, wrote in 1799: 'To say the truth, the possession of Malta by England would be a useless and enormous expense: yet, any expense should be incurred rather than let it remain in the hands of the French.' Lee, 14. Subsequently, however, Britain's decision to retain Malta was based upon a reappraisal of the island as a fortress in imperial defence. 'Such a role necessitated government by one who, unfettered by local obligations, was responsible to the Secretary of State alone'. Lee, 16. The 1811 Royal Commission stated that 'the military authority should be free from all restraint in superseding the civil power whenever the

security of the Island appeared to demand it'. Ibid. In the same vein, a century later, Joseph Chamberlain stated in 1902 in the House of Commons, Britain's interest in Malta in this way: 'We hold Malta solely and entirely as a fortress essential to our position in the Mediterranean. Not as an ordinary colony but as a fortress ... In a fortress anything like open agitation against the Government is a thing that cannot be tolerated on the face of it.' Quoted in H. Frendo, 'The Maltese Colonial Experience'. See also Lee, 217.

[6] Since then it has remained roughly at the same level due to the general acceptance of family limitation and emigration.

[7] H. Frendo, 'En Route from Europe to Africa', 4.

[8] Lee, 17.

[9] Ibid., 18.

[10] Ibid, 19, 237. In a recent article, A.D. Smith has argued that the emergence of 'nationalism' as a movement for autonomy in colonial territories 'has been preceded by attempts to make the relevant ruling bureaucracy more scientific and effective.' As a result of the exclusion of local élites from these centralizing forces, they 'furnish the chief recruits of the nationalist movement'. Smith, 'The Diffusion of Nationalism: some Historical and Sociological Perspectives', 231-48. In Malta's case this happened in the nineteenth century with the emergence of the Nationalist Party and after the failure of the Malta Labour Party's integration proposals and the threat of Dockyard closure in 1958.

[11] Lee, 19, 26.

[12] Ibid., 75. British recruits were officially considered to be 'men of a superior class' to the Maltese. Even after a 'Royal Fencible Regiment' was set up for Maltese recruits in 1825, it had an inferior establishment, pay, rations, and barrack accommodation to British forces stationed in Malta. Ibid., 76.

[13] Maitland actually disliked the 'cowed servility' of the Maltese which was, ironically, provoked by the type of government he exercised over them.

[14] As Salvino Busuttil observes: 'Malta's economic history makes little sense unless incorporated into the history of her political life'. Busuttil, *Malta's Economy in the Nineteenth Century*. Yet Price fails to realize this and maintains that Maltese politicians were generally involved in purely political and cultural issues.

[15] Busuttil, 1. This pattern was established from the very start of British rule. 'Great prosperity had been experienced during the Napoleonic Wars, and with a period of peace the Island was faced inevitably with an economic depression.' Lee, 39, 244. See also, C.A. Price, *Malta and the Maltese*, 109-112, 208-9; G. Mangion, 'Per una storia di Malta nel Secolo XIX'.

[16] Lee, 22.

[17] Reported in Busuttil, 9.

[18] Ibid.

[19] M. Miège, *Histoire de Malte*, i, 168. H. Bowen-Jones et al., 112, 334. Price, 19.

[20] The results of a survey conducted by the author in 1976 show that even nowadays the traditional Maltese virtues of *għaqal* and *bżulija* are still widely held by Maltese workers.

[21] Price, 19.

[22] Ibid. A detailed account of the way bands of thieves were organized was described by the Royal Commission of 1836. Thefts continue to remain widespread even in contemporary Malta – particularly where Government property is concerned – in spite of relatively high living standards and the availability of social services. I have argued elsewhere that this is another manifestation of 'individual manipulation' of rules resulting from a condition

of 'national powerlessness'. See E.L. Zammit, *A Colonial Inheritance,* 35-60.
[23] The official numbers of 'professional' mendicants were listed in the early censuses published in the nineteenth century. Price reports that in the mid-1830s there were as many as 2,500 beggars reported in the villages alone. See also Lee, 45-6.
[24] Bowen-Jones et al., 158, 344.
[25] For example: Reno Calleja MP: 'Undoubtedly the rule of the present [MLP] Government has confirmed that the Maltese people are professional grumblers.' 'Maltese Gemgem' See also E. Mifsud, 'Who are the Grumblers?'; A. Darmanin, 'Grumbling', 79-83. Boissevain, 'Social Trends in Malta', 7: Lee, 21.
[26] C.J.M.R. Gullick, 'Language and Sentiment in Malta', 10; see also id., 'Issue in the Relationship Between Minority and National Language: Maltese reaction to Non-Maltese Speakers of Maltese'; E.L. Zammit, 'Adult Education: The Role of R.U.M.', 40-5, and especially 43.
[27] Busuttil, 9.
[28] As the maintainance or cordial relations rested on mutual consultations which to a large extent depended on the personality of the local bishop, the British were keenly interested whenever the succession of a new bishop had to be decided. The various complications which this choice involved are illustrated by D. Fenech, *The Making of Archbishop Gonzi.*
[29] H. Frendo, *Party Politics.*
[30] The most spectacular riots occurred in 1919 when several sections of the population, each of which had its own particular grudge, joined forces in spontaneous demonstrations in the streets of Valletta. Some Maltese were killed and many wounded when the British soldiers opened fire on the crowd. These riots are generally credited with constraining Britain to grant a more liberal Constitution to Maltese representatives democratically elected in 1921. See Frendo, *Ir-Rivuluzzjoni Maltija tal-1919.*
[31] *Vide supra.*
[32] See *Esposizione della Questione Maltese;* Dobie, *Malta's Road to Independence,* 38-107. A brief account is in D. Austin, *Malta and the End of Empire,* 7-20, and in Boissevain, *Saints and Fireworks,* 9-12.
[33] A bitter politico-religious dispute flared up again between the Labour Government and the Church authorities during 1984 about the administration of Church schools and its considerable property. The Church saw this as a direct intrusion into its internal affairs while the Labour Government depicted the Church as a 'medieval' conservative force which was obstructing the social and economic reforms it wanted to introduce.
[34] The 'new middle class' was composed of pro-British importers, contractors, and traders who flourished on the presence of the large garrison stationed in Malta and also of the civil servants and other employees in the civil administration. The 'working class' was mainly composed of drydocks and other Admiralty employees who constituted the bulk of the industrial working force around the Grand Harbour.
[35] Frendo, *Party Politics.*
[36] Lee, 8-109.
[37] After the failure of the MLP proposal to integrate Malta with the UK in the 1950s, the Party has adopted an anti-British policy. Cf. Mintoff, 'Isolation is no answer'.
[38] G. Dench, *Maltese in London,* 11.
[39] As David Martin has observed, 'a nation denied self-determination by another dominating society will either seek sources of religious differentiation or use the pre-existing religious difference as a rallying point.' quoted in

M. Vassallo, (ed.) 'Religious Symbolism in a Changing Malta', 244, fn. 9.
[40] Dench, 11
[41] J. Boissevain, *Hal Farruġ: A Village in Malta*, ch.7.
[42] Boissevain, *Saints and Fireworks*.
[43] Patronage, in fact, is one of the basic institutions in Maltese society — as it is in other Mediterranean societies — and usually expresses an image of society in religious terminology with God on top as the Supreme Patron, followed by interrelated strata of patrons and clients in a hierarchy. M. Kenn, *A Spanish Tapestry*. Boissevain has elaborated a model of Maltese social interaction based upon friendship networks of patrons and clients. See his *Friends of Friends*.
[44] Dench, 12-13.
[45] Ibid., 13.
[46] *Development Plan for Malta 1973-80*, 205.
[47] See E.L. Zammit, 'Some Social Aspects of Maltese Developments'.
[48] Parkin, 94-5.
[49] Zammit, 'Adult Education'.
[50] Dench, 107.
[51] Ibid.
[52] 'Patronage' or 'clientelism' is, of course, a typical asymmetrical form of social relationship which often develops in situation of unequal access to scarce resources. Those who dispose of such resources put their dependants under a personal obligation and expect their esteem and services in return. While such relationships tend to predominate in Mediterranean and other 'traditional' societies, they are by no means confined to these. Recent reviews of such studies are found in: E. Gellner and I. Waterbury (eds.), *Patrons and Clients;* J. Davies, *People of the Mediterranean: An Essay in Comparative Social Anthropology*. Weingrod and Boissevain have shown the extension of patron-client relationships into the system of political parties. A. Weingrod, 'Patrons, Patronage and Political Parties', 377, 400; Boissevain, *Friends of Friends*.
[53] D. Boswell, 'Patron-client Relations in the Mediterranean', 1-2.
[54] Busuttil, *Malta's Economy*.
[55] As Catanzaro and Reyneri have pointed out: 'Polarization can generate conflicts only when a social group is in contact with another, the members of which have similar occupational income and social status. Where class conflicts do not occur, we have a ruthless individualist struggle to enter the employment benefit and security system.' R. Catanzaro and E. Reyneri, *Multiple Job Holding and Class Structure in a Southern Italian Town*, 8.
[56] 'The principle of benefits shows clearly one of the most important aspects of clientelistic associations: paternalism.' M. Caciagli and F. Belloni, *A Contribution to the Study of Clientelism: The New Clientelism of Southern Italy*, 2.
[57] N. Abercrombie and S. Hill, *Paternalism and Patronage*, 414.
[58] Ibid.
[59] In addition to five Development Plans covering from 1959 to 1971, the most important reports were: W. Woods, *Report on the Finances of the Government of Malta;* G.E. Schuster, *Interim Report on the Financial and Economic Structure of the Maltese Islands;* T. Balogh and D. Seers, *The Economic Problems of Malta;* W.F. Stolper et al., *United Nations' Economic Mission to Malta;* Lord Robens et al., *Joint Mission for Malta Report*. After its return to power in 1971, the Labour Government announced its determination to revise the Financial and Defence Agreement with Britain of 1964. A new treaty was signed with the intention of accounting for 'the financial requirements needed to enable Malta

to achieve economic independence in the shortest possible time'. Subsequently a new development plan was published with the aim of realizing this goal. *Development Plan for Malta* 1973-80. Subsequent Development Plans (1981-5 and 1986-8) sought to grapple with problems of continuing industrialization and heavy unemployment during a period of economic recession.

[60] Boissevain has argued that these 'social and political' goals were explicitly formulated by Labour Party development plans whereas the previous Nationalist Party plans were merely interested in promoting economic growth. He sees in this change a logical sequence in Maltese perceptions of progress and development. Boissevain, *A Causeway with a Gate: the Progress of Development in Malta*, 14.

[61] Boissevain has expressed such a view in 'When the Saints go marching out', 81-96. This view has been challenged by Boswell, 7.

[62] P. Schneider, J.Schneider, and E. Hansen, 'Modernization and Development – the Role of Regional Élites and non-corporate Groups in the European Mediterranean', 328-50.

[63] N.J. Smelser, 'Mechanisms of Change and Adjustment to Change', 43-68. Similarly, the 'end of ideology', theorists have sought to explain the persistence of widespread industrial and class conflicts in Italy and France despite a developed industrial base to 'extra industrial elements of society' such as 'issues concerning the place of religion and the traditional status structure'. Mann, 11.

[64] As argued by P. Schneider and J. Schneider, *Culture and Political Economy*. If an economy remains externally dependent, the local 'westernized' bourgeoisie are likely to exert pressures towards modernization, against any available political and intellectual leadership.

[65] A. Black, 'Tourism and Migration – Causes and Effects in Social Change', 4. For instance the Maltese tendency to hoard savings rather than indulge in conspicuous consumption makes sense when considered in the historical context of a siege economy and traditional insecurity.

[66] One of the most important decisions was that stated in the Defence White Paper of 1957. The threat to close down HM Dockyard and other Service establishments in Malta led to the downfall of the proposal to 'integrate' Malta with Britain, and subsequently to the Labour Government's resignation. L.E. Davis, *Defence Outline of Future Policy*.

[67] The Malta 'Labour Movement' here refers to action co-ordinated by the leadership of both the Labour Party and the General Workers Union. Since 1979, the long-standing relationship has been placed on a statutory basis.

[68] The recent resurgence of political patronage, the elevation of political party leadership to that of traditional community 'patron-saints', and, above all, the intensity of political campaigns underscore these persistent trends.

10

HENRY FRENDO

Maltese Colonial Identity:
Latin Mediterranean or British Empire?

Influenced by history as much as by geography, identity changes, or develops, both as a cultural phenomenon and in relation to economic factors. Behaviouristic traits, of which one may not be conscious, assume a different reality in cross-cultural interaction and with the passing of time.

The Maltese identity became, and is, more pronounced than that of other Mediterranean islanders from the Balearic to the Aegean. These latter spoke varieties of Spanish and Greek in much the same way as the inhabitants of the smaller islands of Pantalleria, Lampedusa, or Elba spoke Italian dialects and were absorbed by the neighbouring larger mainlands. The inhabitants of modern Malta, however, spoke a language derived from Arabic at the same time as they practised the Roman Catholic faith and were exposed, indeed subjected, to European influences for six or seven centuries, without becoming integrated with their closest *terra firma,* Italy.[1] This was largely because of Malta's strategic location between southern Europe and North Africa. An identifiable Maltese nationality was thus moulded by history, geography, and ethnic admixture – the Arabic of the Moors, corsairs, and slaves, together with accretions from several northern and southern European races – from Normans to Aragonese. Malta then passed under the Knights of St John, the French, and much more importantly, the British. All this time, however, many Maltese were seafarers, sailing to the four winds. Migration, first to the Mediterranean littoral and then to the English-speaking world, and, later, return migration became extremely important.[2]

The two outstanding dates in the evolution of a Maltese 'colonial' identity are 1798 and 1964. In September 1798 the Maltese, as Catholics perhaps more than as 'nationals', joined forces in a popular uprising against the French. Courageous and successful against superior odds, they had for the first time an inkling of what nationhood (if not statehood) would mean. The second date, 21 September 1964, one hundred and sixty-six years later, marked the attainment of political independence and sovereignty, after a long struggle. In between these two most significant episodes, a Maltese identity gradually took shape and form. I have described it as a 'colonial' identity because it was much influenced by nationalism and imperialism.[3]

As a British possession, and a fortress, Malta was clearly not a nation-state in the sense of a political entity wherein those who govern share the outlook and aspirations of the governed; but socially, Malta had the characteristics of nationhood. Isolation, homogeneity, and a common historical experience, aided the feeling of being Maltese; the islands were not, like the other British colonies, divided by race, religion, tribe, or culture.[4] The British experience, without which Malta might have become one more fragment of a united Italy, acted as a stimulus for the Maltese to come to terms with themselves, and set them on the path leading to full and separate nationhood: they matured in the course of outlining their rights and expectations as a people.

The Maltese had, before the nineteenth century, a unity of language — Maltese — and of religion — Roman Catholicism: the islands were 'a melting-pot where an original race and language were formed'.[5] The Maltese type is 'South European', the 1911 Royal Commission reported:

but the people are fairer in colour, in the towns at any rate, and have a better appearance than south Italians and Sicilians. They are a strong, hardy race, and have a reputation of being temperate, thrifty, and industrious. They are clever and adaptable; generally speaking, however, they appear to lack confidence in themselves and each other, and have little power of co-operation. They are much attached to their native lands, and seldom migrate to distant countries.[6]

The ideas of the Maltese about themselves were much influenced by the Order of St John. The Turkish siege of 1565 symbolizes their legend: the Knights and the Maltese, then under Grand Master La Valette, repelled Suleiman the Magnificent's invading force, an event which came to be seen not only as a defeat of the Muslims by the Catholics, but also as a European victory over the Ottoman Empire, and even, in the nineteenth century, as a symbol of Maltese fortitude in the face of a foreign enemy.[7]

Sicilian Italian was the language used for all official purposes in medieval times,[8] but the Order consolidated Malta's Catholic European identity and considerably Latinized the culture of the people. Their building of fortifications, towns (including Valletta), palaces, hospitals, aqueducts, and naval facilities provided wide-ranging employment; Malta coined her own money, had a printing press and university, and standards of conduct and modes of thinking were established with which at least the educated sectors of the native population could associate themselves.[9]

By the nineteenth century Malta had, in appearance, a thoroughly Italianate culture. Practically everybody, educated or not, spoke Maltese in daily life, and there were also a few publications in the vernacular.[10] Maltese, however, had not been made an official language, and had neither a standard orthography nor a literature. For a Maltese to be educated and for him to know Italian was one and the same thing: for countless generations, Italian had been the language of town and gown, of court and cloister.[11]

Still there was no general national identity for the Maltese. There were several 'identities': a rural peasant one, an urbane cosmopolitan one, even a Gozitan one, and even more parochial ones, centred around the parish square and the family. Religiosity and secularization featured differently in these lifestyles, and perceptions of Malteseness, to the extent that these existed, would have differed accordingly. Though occupations influenced dispositions, indeed allegiances, still there were other elements in common, native-life feelings that transcended the attachments to opposed cultural and/or political pulls.

Malta had a numerous middle class: in the 1870s, the 141,775 inhabitants were mostly artificers and labourers or employed in agriculture. Nearly 10,000 were engaged in commerce, 2,290 belonged to the professions, and 1,210 to the clergy. Of the 2,133 listed as nobles and landowners, the *titolati* (those entitled to precedence as nobles) were relatively few.[12] In 1877 the 'working' or 'poorer' classes were estimated at 112,360, about three-fourths of the population, the remaining one-fourth (36,910) being the 'non-manual' classes.[13]

The parochial structure was intact: religion was at the heart of Maltese life just as the church was physically in the centre of the village, and formed part of the strong social nexus by which the common people looked up deferentially to the 'respectable' members of the community. The parish priest was always at hand with advice not just in his capacity as clergyman but also on a personal level. Similarly, the notary, lawyer, architect, or doctor was close by — one went to his office, he came to one's house — and such people would be presidents of the local band clubs or secretaries of the religious confraternities. Practically everybody went to church — people therefore met in church on feast days, if not daily. 'The principal recreations of the Maltese have, in general, some connection with their religious ceremonies', observed G.P. Badger in 1838; the numerous processions afforded the stranger many opportunities of seeing 'every rank and class of the people, in their best attire, congregated together in crowds' witnessing such scenes.[14]

Malta was a closely-knit community partly because the small archipelago (122 square miles in all) could not but give its inhabitants a feeling of being Maltese (*Maltin*), besides being *Sengleani* (from Senglea city), *Żebbuġin* (from Żebbuġ village), *Furjaniżi* (from Floriana suburb), and so on. From the Sceberras peninsula, on which Valletta was built in the sixteenth century, one could look across both sides of the majestic harbour to the 'Three Cities' of Senglea, Vittoriosa, and Cospicua, on one side, and to Msida, Sliema, and Gżira on the other, comprising between them one-third of the entire population. Peasants never strayed far from the village squares; farmers, petty vendors, and middlemen travelled by horse-cart from the country to the city to sell their produce or wares; the employees at the dockyard were mostly recruited from the surrounding areas. Before the railway was inaugurated in 1883 a journey by horse carriage from the former capital Notabile to Valletta took three hours.[15] 'As a rule', explained Dr Alfredo Mattei, the men in the casals get up at four in the morning, go to hear the mass of the *Parroco* and after that they go to Valletta or anywhere else where their work may happen to call them and spend the whole day laboriously at work. Then at the *Ave Maria* at 6 p.m., the poor labourer... rejoins his family, says his prayers, his *Rosario*, and goes to bed ... even at Città Vecchia where you have a few learned gentlemen and a few *Canonici* and *Abatini*, even they get up very early and few study and keep late hours.[16]

The mobilization of political opinion within a closely interconnected area of such small dimensions, where gossip and rumour were necessarily rife, was a relatively easy task. Newspapers in Italian and Maltese were 'taken to the cafés where the people congregate and read them'.[17] 'A stranger reading the partisan newspapers', noted a visitor in 1927, 'is liable to be rather staggered at the strength of feeling which seems to exist over politics'.[18]

Imperialist strategic considerations sometimes led British colonial policy to be assimilationist rather than, as was more usual, *laissez faire* or 'informal'. Governors were almost all military men, not particularly versed in the art of 'indirect rule'. English colonialism in Mediterranean Europe, especially in Malta, shows how profound cultural clashes motivated collaboration and resistance for well over a century.

Cultural rather than economic, Maltese nationalism, inspiring itself from the native intelligentsia's traditional *italianità*, heightened throughout the Risorgimento, posited Europeanity against the Anglicization policies in public life. It was Dante against Shakespeare, Pope against Queen, the Southern against the Nordic. Political parties came into being to uphold Italian and English values and vice versa, as new alignments, interests, classes, and perceptions slowly evolved. Out of the conflicting loyalties and social engineering, awareness of a body politic developed and the Maltese vernacular gradually emerged as a measure of national identity. Party divisions, however, remained intense.[19]

Language battles may well be said to account for the origin of Maltese political parties. Anglicization could be accomplished only at great cost to human relations inside the colony. But in de-Italianizing Malta, the British forced the birth of a more home-grown product. In resisting assimilation and colonialism, pro-Italians and others engendered a national political conscious- ness upon which a body politic could feed. Paradoxically, the Maltese language emerged as a synthesis of the pro-English and pro-Italian rivalry.[20]

Cultural allegiances also came to embody an economic or
financial component, however, and were increasingly influenced
by this. 'English' or 'Italian' became, to quote Joe Chamberlain,
'a question of bread and butter'.[21] It was the British
occupation, and British colonial policy, that made it so. In the
long term, it appeared more profitable for rising generations to
adopt and conform to the obvious preferences, or dictates, of the
ruling class — the British. The element of *italianità* in Maltese
nationalism suffered as a result. But two different visions of
what Malta ought to be, of whom the Maltese were and should
be, lay at the bottom of the conflict. Influenced by their own
education and professions, but also by tradition and a sense of
history and continuity, even by religion, pro-Italians saw Malta
belonging to a Latin Mediterranean world. By contrast,
'Britishers' saw it as an outpost of empire in the central
Mediterranean on the route to India and the Pacific, a harbour,
naval station, and garrison town whose economy and survival
were tied to its place in the British Empire. These two visions,
or interests, also belied different attitudes to government,
nationhood, and right — the former being the more *independent,*
the latter the more *dependent.*[22] There was agreement on some
basic tenets where national self-pride was concerned in a general
way, but otherwise they saw and sought different directions for
the island, especially after 1870.

The British allowed the Maltese the free practice of their
religion but denied them, at first, any political rights: critics
were persecuted.[23] Although Malta was ceded to and not conquered by Britain, the Maltese came to see little difference between cession and conquest considering the way they were treated;[24] it was not until half a century after the occupation that
the elective principle was introduced.[25] This greatly disappoint-
ed the elected leaders of the national *Congresso,* who had taken
charge of the anti-French insurrection and now expected to lay
down the rules. According to their charter of 1802, the British
monarch would have 'no right' to cede Malta to any other power:
should he withdraw his protection, sovereign rights would
devolve upon the Maltese. The *Congresso,* representing all the
cities, towns, and villages, expected a *Consiglio Popolare* to
administer the constitution that would be agreed upon,
particularly with regard to legislation and taxation, subject to

the King's assent. Finally, the King was to protect the religion of the country, allowing religious freedom, and to ensure the rule of law, safeguarding the rights of life and property.[26] The Royal Commissioners of 1812, however, felt 'persuaded of the mischievous effects that would result from entrusting any portion of political power to a people so singularly unfitted to enjoy it.'[27]

'Was it for this', protested the nobles, 'that we took up arms and made our brave stand against the tyranny of France?'[28] 'The Maltese gave themselves up spontaneously to the English and in return freedom was promised to them', complained Giorgio Mitrovich, once described as 'the Maltese O'Connell',[29] who, at the head of a *Comitato Generale Maltese,* campaigned successfully for a free press (granted in 1839) and the franchise (granted in 1849).[30]

Apart from newspapers and elections, public opinion was influenced throughout the Risorgimento by the activities of exiles who found refuge in Malta (among them Francesco Crispi, who later became Prime Minister of Italy);[31] Mazzinian pamphlets were printed in Malta for distribution abroad;[32] the Bishop warned on 'the incalculable damage' which the presence of Italian nationalists was causing 'in this small island whose language they speak'.[33] When Garibaldi visited Malta, he was both cheered and jeered.[34] Small, rather crowded, lacking mineral wealth of any kind, and even water, with much of the land barren, 'plain, bare, naked Malta', said Charles James Fox in 1803, should have been placed 'in the hands of the Emperor of Russia';[35] but the violation of the Treaty of Amiens was rendered necessary, as Canning noted, by the retention of Malta 'not for its own intrinisic value and importance only', but in view of imperial interests in Egypt and India, and as 'that point upon which the honour of this country was committed'.[36] Napoleon's advisers were in no doubt as to Britain's intentions: 'On se demande, Malte vaut-it la guerre?'[37] One of the reason why Malta was governed by a succession of generals who were at the same time Commanders-in-Chief of the armed forces, was that, as James Lowther told the Commons, Malta was 'not only a colony of some importance' but 'also an important fortress'.[38] 'Did not the Duke of Wellington say', wrote Joe Chamberlain, 'that you might as well give a Constitution to a man-of-war as

give it to Malta?'[39] The use of the word 'fortress' with regard
to Malta was, as in Aden after 1880, 'a statement of policy'.[40]

The conflict between civil rights and military needs was at
the heart of Maltese politics. Every time the Maltese petitioners
invoked the *Melitensium Amor* argument – the idea that Malta
had been freely ceded by the Maltese – the British reiterated
the fortress formula, the strategic value of Malta made it
unlikely that it could be treated like an ordinary colony.
Mistrust was fomented on both sides because of this
preoccupation. Misgovernment was inevitable because generals
usually had little knowledge of representative institutions and
civil affairs: the Head of Government was often not the man in
charge of running the country. Sir Alexander Ball's prophetic
advice to the Secretary for War as early as 1801 went by
unheeded:

> The inhabitants conceive their liberty insecure until the military and
> civil power be divided. They observe that a Military Governor cannot
> spare sufficient time from his garrison occupations to direct the Civil
> Administration of the Island without giving too much power to
> secretaries, who seek their own interest and not the happiness of the
> people ... I speak from a thorough knowledge of the character and
> sentiments of the inhabitants, and I now write under the fullest
> conviction of the necessity of this being attended to, otherwise we shall
> lose the affection and attachment of these brave Islanders and risk
> serious consequences.[41]

To Maltese politicians, imperialism usually meant thinking
of Britain in Malta rather than of Malta, with the Maltese being
treated not as a people but as the native inhabitants of a fortress.
As Britain did not care for local interests, Dr Fortunato Mizzi
once declared he did not care for imperial interests.[42] British
rule in Malta, said Sigismondo Savona, was 'government on
garrison principles'.[43] 'We are not sheep! We are not soldiers!'
shouted F. S. De Cesare at the Governor.[44] These three
journalists and politicians were rivals but, at heart, they all
tended to subscribe to a patriotic consensus – that *cumulus* of
shared experiences and instinctive attachments, embodying
common grievances and expressing similar expectations.
Particularly, it expressed the desire, indeed the belief, that a
Maltese should not be treated or considered as the Englishman's
inferior. To assert publicly that Malta belonged to the Maltese,

as Dr Zaccaria Roncali did in 1885, could be tantamount to sedition.[45]

As Britain was a great industrial and naval power, the Maltese could benefit materially from the application of British technology and financial resources, as well as from the indirect export of capital through the presence of thousands of servicemen; but in all this Malta generally played the role of a pawn.

Subjected to strategic priorities, Maltese constitutional history lacked an evolutionary development: Malta's 'special' position in the Empire was eloquently summed up in 1931 in the observation that it was almost possible 'to plot a graph' of Constitutions 'modelled alternatively on the principle of benevolent autocracy and that of representative government'.[46]

The turning point in Maltese history came at the time of the opening of the Suez Canal, the unifications of Italy and Germany, and the subsequent expansionist or precautionary policies in the big-power rivalry over the Mediterranean and elsewhere. In response to a new calling after 1870, there emerged a different breed of men destined to persevere in national politics and to stamp their marks on Malta's development.

As 'the most advanced post on the European part of the road to India', Malta's value since the Crimean War had grown enormously, wrote the Director of Navy Contracts at the Admiralty, F.W. Rowsell: nowhere else along the route could ships be coaled 'so well, so quickly, or so cheaply as at Malta'.[47] Gradually colonial government changed from a relatively stable, easy-going routine into a businesslike, intrusive, and more authoritarian rule.

This heightened, indeed provoked, the clash between Anglicization and *italianità*. Preferment for those learning English, or supporting anti-Italian policies, was raised to a method of government, bitterly dividing the local parties, and forcing the issue of identity in 'British' Malta.

The principle was crudely enough enunciated in 1883 by Lieut.-Governor Sir Walter Hely-Hutchinson, whose advice was:

Insist on a knowledge of English in all public appointments. Appoint no one and promote no one who does not thoroughly understand it. Pay your public service well and make the public officers as comfortable as possible. And let those who oppose English understand that their

opposition shuts them out from all hope of employment or favour from
the Government. Appeal, in a word, to their personal interests. I do
not care so much about the Lyceum and universities. Look well after
your primary schools, see that the boys and girls are taught Maltese
and English, and in twenty years there won't be a chance for the
propagation of Italianist ideas.[48]

An early British-trained Maltese campaigner for Anglicization
was a former army sergeant and schoolmaster who later became
Director of Education and Rector of the University, Sigismondo
Savona. He was an assimilationist, a utilitarian liberal and
prone to serve, clearly, as a collaborator. He was not alone in
this, so his views and attitudes deserve attention.

After leaving the army, Savona set up his own school
in Valletta specializing in the teaching of English. In 1867
he started a paper called *Public Opinion,* of which he
served as editor until he successfully contested election
to the Council of Government in 1875. After a few years
he crossed the floor from the elected to the official side – just
as at least one other distinguished member of the same House
(the Crown Advocate Sir Adrian Dingli) had done before him
many years earlier.[49]

At that time education was directly concerned with re-
arranging priorities and curricula in the question of the
languages and so, for a very long time, this was by far
the most controversial and problematical department to
manage. Savona, however, was well qualified for the tasks
at hand. In a public lecture to the Maltese Scientific and
Literary Society some years after returning from his London
training course (where he had been placed first), Savona
had favourably quoted Thomas Babington Macaulay that
'the history of England is emphatically the history of progress',
and that the English were 'the greatest and most highly
civilized people that ever the world saw' who had 'spread
their domination on every quarter of the globe' and 'created
a maritime power which would annihilate in a quarter
of an hour the navies of Tyre, Athens, Carthage, Venice, and
Genoa together'. Savona's lecture was called 'The Necessity of
Educating the People'. A second edition of it was printed in
1870.[50]

In a strictly utilitarian vein, the Maltese Anglophile leader spoke convincingly in favour of Anglicization especially for the benefit of the working classes who sought employment, as he noted, 'on the shores of the harbours, as sailors, firemen, coalheavers, boatmen, or porters; as policemen, artillery men, domestic servants, messengers in government offices; as labourers or artisans under the Royal Engineers or Commissariat Department, in the Royal Dockyard or the Hydraulic Dock'.[51]

Savona went further than this, apologizing for Anglicization by implying that Britain was more lenient than other great powers with regards to her assimilation policy. Stating his belief that all parts of the British Empire should be 'knit together resolved to do or die for the fatherland', he declared:

If the French had not been driven from Malta by the Maltese, before they had been two years on the Island, it is certain that French would long ago have been the official language of the island. If the Russians had made themselves masters of it, as at one time it seemed likely that they would, I am sure that before this we should have been thoroughly Russianized.[52]

This mentality was carried forward in time and in emphasis by Count Gerald Strickland who was eventually knighted and raised to the peerage. Strickland was a wealthy man, the son of an English naval captain and an aristocratic Maltese mother. He received a Maltese education, went to Cambridge, twice married English ladies, and his children could barely speak Maltese. After being elected to the Council of Government as a candidate of Dr F. Mizzi's *Partito Nazionale* in 1889, Strickland soon crossed the floor to the official side to become Chief Secretary to Government, which was practically the most powerful job in the island. He was subsequently made a governor in the colonial service overseas (from 1902 to 1917, serving in the Leeward Islands, Tasmania, Western Australia, New South Wales, and Norfolk Island).

More markedly than Savona, Strickland was a clever administrator and an expert dispenser of patronage. When he eventually re-entered the Maltese political arena in the 1920s, after the grant of self-government, he attracted enough support to become Prime Minister of the same colony where in the heyday of imperialism he had been the Chief Secretary to Government — a case without parallel in the history of the

Empire. A true-blue Tory in British politics, but in Maltese
politics daubed as a 'reformer' and as a 'progressive', if not also
as a 'radical' figure, Strickland saw Malta in an imperial
framework, arguing that imperial and Maltese interests were
one and the same thing. The closer Malta was to Britain,
therefore, the more she stood to gain from it. The least signs
of dissidence, particularly as expressed by *cultural nationalism*
in the form of *italianità*, were to be ruthlessly suppressed —
albeit always with a semblance of democracy in the name of
progress, freedom, and the will of the majority. Colonial
administrators did not believe in the consensual ethic, and
Strickland certainly belonged with them. Indeed he repeatedly
irritated the Colonial Office by his insistence on Orders-in-
Council as an easy means for imposing laws whenever he met
opposition. At one point he even suggested a startling
constitutional provision to enable the governor to legislate 'by
proclamation'. This would have been a course rather similar to
the one proposed by Savona in 1886 when the latter had secretly
proposed the abolition of representative government.[53] In a
closed gubernatorial autocracy, those belonging to the regime's
inner circle and having the ear of the governor, would stand to
benefit — since such collaborators and advisers would find it
much easier to have their way, whether right or wrong.
Strickland's method of dealing, raised to a method of
government, was inspired partly by his desire to make the
Maltese 'as English as possible' and partly by his ambitious,
intolerant, vindictive zeal.

As for the first characteristic, Strickland declared for example
that 'We should henceforth be as thoroughly British as possible
in speech and in thought as well as in fact.'[54] Or, again: 'I
certainly would strain every effort in my power towards
rendering the Maltese as English as possible.'[55] Strickland
actually held that the Maltese race was more akin to some
important sections of the English race than to the Latin or
Italian race, or to the Semites. He wanted to show, basically,
that the Maltese were Aryans not Semites nor Latins. He wrote:

The Maltese are a good-looking, agile race with rounded limbs and well
set up; blue and brown eyes are usual and they have a tendency to be
stout; the Arabs are thin, lanky, angular, and sallow. The Arabs are
nomads by land, and adverse to the sea, and dwell in tents; on the

contrary the Maltese like their Phoenician ancestors delight in buildings of solid cut stone. No close observer could confuse the two races ...
Let it be hoped that a true spirit of unity with the British Empire shall henceforth be based on the fact that Malta is a European portion of His Majesty's Dominions, peopled principally by men of a kindred race to that which is characteristic of the eastern coasts of the Irish Sea, the Isle of Man, and the Islands of Scotland.'[56]

As for Strickland's second characteristic, that regarding the methods of government, suffice it to state that he adhered fully to the Hely-Hutchinson principle of appealing to personal interests to obtain Anglicization through systematic discrimination. Strickland actually twisted this further to read in biblical terms: rewarding 'the good' and punishing 'the wicked' – or else, he said, Government will soon come to the end of 'available resources for maintaining discipline and order'.[57] He upheld the view of 'only giving appointments to those whose loyalty could be relied upon', evidently using the degree of assimilation or at least the servile disposition of the individual as a criterion for determining loyalty and believing that such a policy achieved a marked effect by being followed consistently for a period of years.[58] 'The law of the survival of the fittest is not of my making', he wrote.[59]

Like Joe Chamberlain and Admiral Sir John Fisher, Strickland upheld the *fin de siècle* imperialism's philosophy of 'thorough' and indeed carried this forward well into the twentieth century. In a letter to the Minister for the Colonies in 1908, Strickland asked, 'Why do we hold Malta?' and continued to answer as follows:

(a) because it is the key of our Eastern trade, and emblem of sea power held by the strongest from time immemorial;
(b) because, under present conditions, no European navy can fight us East of Malta and retain enough coal to get home;
(c) because when the German Emperor gets Trieste, Salonica, or other Mediterranean possessions, his conquests can be made value-less by whoever holds Malta with the sword. No servant of the Crown in Malta should be allowed to forget that, in the interest of the liberty and the prosperity of the Maltese, defence is the principal justification for his existence.[60]

This tallied perfectly with Chamberlain's view. 'In a fortress', he had told the House of Commons, 'anything like open agitation against the Government is a thing that *cannot be tolerated on the face of it* ... you cannot allow sedition to prevail within it.'[61] And Sir John Fisher had seen no difference between Malta and Gibraltar, or indeed Metz and Cronstadt. Malta existed solely for the Navy, he wrote in a memorandum at the turn on the century:

For imperial purposes it has no other value whatever. It produces nothing. It has no manufactures. The Algerian ports have filched the larger portion of its coal trade. Algiers now offers such temptations that it is preferred as a port of call. Malta possesses no military value whatever; it exists *for* the Navy; and it exists *by* the Navy. Without the British fleet in the Mediterranean it could not hold out more than a few weeks against the 87,000 troops available in Algeria.
Malta is a fortress, pure and simple, and should be governed as a fortress. Fancy Metz or Cronstadt, with a local parliament, cutting down the governor's electric light or water supply for his official residence, and vilifying the Authorities in language almost too disgusting to repeat! ... It is quite impossible to suppose that either through a seditious press, or priestly pressure, the splendid and loyal feeling of the Maltese for the English (which are heartily reciprocated) should be permitted to be sapped.[62]

After the Second World War the Malta Labour Party (MLP) attracted many of the pro-Britishers. This was partly because Strickland's Constitutional Party – to which the MLP under Sir Paul Boffa had allied itself in 1927 – had largely died with him; but it was also because the MLP was itself pro-British. Under the leadership of one time Rhodes Scholar Dominic Mintoff, like Strickland married to an Englishwoman, the MLP until 1958 strove for Malta's integration with Britain. Only after that failed did it turn anti-British.[63]

By contrast, many Nationalist Party (PN) leading figures and ordinary supporters had been interned and deported, without any charge in 1940.[64] The Nationalists rather successfully opposed the plan and the idea of integration, advocating instead greater internal autonomy. Once again, however, the question of identity, of belonging, of loyalty and affiliation, culturally no less than politically, was at the fore.

At an earlier time, before the First World War, a Nationalist leader Enrico Mizzi had suggested an Italo-Maltese

Federation.[65] Nothing came of this either – except, indirectly, a court martial,[66] and later on the deportation of Mizzi – but the proposal was an extension of the deeply-embedded Maltese philosophy of *italianità*, expounded by, among others, Enrico's father and founder of the PN, Fortunato Mizzi, whose wife was Italian.

This philosophy was as much linguistic, culturally, as it was political, constitutionally and juridically.

Feelings of belonging, of national pride, were strongly voiced by the elder Mizzi. In one of his addresses to 'the Patriots' shortly before the grant of representative government in 1887, Mizzi vouched that the 'sacred national cause' would triumph over the colonial regime 'which instead of considering us as men having secular rights to govern ourselves, depicts us as slaves to be treated like merchandise'. His opponents thought, he added, that 'they could suffocate the heart-rending cry in many a thousand breast inveighing against the absolute power which tears apart our soul and which wants to struggle our very thoughts'.[67]

In another strident appeal at this time Mizzi condemned 'the bureaucracy that misgoverns us' and he urged his followers: 'Break your chains, because your life will signify their death.' Mizzi's beliefs in representative government are complemented by his views of Malta as an Italian-like island in a Latin Mediterranean context, as opposed to the rival view of Malta in a British imperial context as a bustling garrison centre. When representative government was revoked in 1903, Mizzi gave vent to his party's feelings:

How can an enlightened people who crave for political liberty and are conscious of their dignity as a civilized nation accept such a Constitution? And for what purpose? And what citizens could ever be induced to abandon their own affairs and accept the popular mandate to study and discuss the affairs of Malta, to sweat and create bad blood, to have their nerves continually harassed, to sicken and age prematurely in pursuit of the arduous task of persuading a Government whose interest it is not to listen to reason, to see themselves continually voted down by the official puppets, in a crushing majority, and to have to submit to all decisions, even the most odious ones, passed under the formula 'with the advice and consent of the Council of Government', and in return for all this, to find themselves insulted and maligned in the Government dispatches? No! A people, such as the Maltese, who have a secular name to cherish, and the sympathies of Europe to sustain them, will never accept such a Constitution.[68]

When the Government sought to de-Italianize the sinews of
Maltese education, Mizzi expounded the philosophy of *italianità*:

How can we, in the central Mediterannean, surrounded by Latin
peoples, how can we, us 160,000 souls, adopt as our language the Anglo-
Saxon tongue? How can we, through it, express our sentiments? How
on earth could we, caressed by this sun, we who are poetic and a music-
loving people, adopt the language of a people who inhabit the Nordic
snows? How can we adapt our way of thinking and of feeling to the
way of thinking and of feeling of the English people? And if we cannot
strip away the soul from the word, that is the thought, how can we ever
dress this thought in any other form but that which suits our
sentiments, that is the Italian form?[69]

He held that the English language was necessary because 'we
are under British rule', but, he added, it should likewise be
considered that 'we live in the midst of many nations: Italy,
France, Spain, Morocco, Algeria, Tunisia, Tripolitania, Egypt,
etc. As we have relations with all these countries, Italian is
necessary for us.'[70]

Had it not been for the fact that Maltese was spoken in the
island, Mizzi's ideology would have conformed to accepted
contemporary theories about self-realization that relate thought
processes to language and environment. A mixture of Renan and
Herder, influenced generally by Italian and European secular
thought and, to a lesser extent, by British liberalism, Mizzian
nationalism was the result of circumstances rather than a
doctrinaire commitment arising from acquired knowledge
through familiarity with writers such as the Neapolitan
Gianbattista Vico (popularized in the nineteenth century by
Michelet) or the German Romantic school, although Professor
Ramiro Barbaro did mention Heinrich Heine, and the *Diritto*
had been clearly inspired by Terenzio Mamiani. The equation
of *italianità* with self-realization, consonant with nationalist
theories about government and regeneration, was reaffirmed by
Mizzi and Salvatore Cachia Zammit in their case for retaining
Italian in the Courts. (Maltese laws were based on Roman Law,
codified and encapsulated in Italian for ages, with all the legal
jargon, even that in common parlance, being Italian or derived
from Italian.) This is what they believed:

The Maltese will never speak English in the same way as the English
people for the reason that there are profound differences in thought

and sentiments between the two peoples. They will speak Italian with English words, but their thoughts must be Italian, however correct the phrases may sound. Obliged to use a language that is not their own and that does not correspond to or naturally express their feelings, the people will lose the native dignity which today is so conspicuous in our courts of law.[71]

Such beliefs are good examples of the twofold character of Maltese nationalism — *liberal* in the quest for representative institutions, and *cultural* in the identification of traditional education with the qualities of nationality. These views also underline the fact that Malta was a European colony.

The younger Mizzi's quest for a union with Italy becomes in this context more readily explainable, but Enrico's disposition towards Italy may be compared to Strickland's disposition towards Britain. The maternal influence on Enrico — the language commonly spoken at his home was Italian[72] — may have, in a way comparable to the paternal influence on Strickland, unduly influenced the son's disposition; although Enrico, unlike Strickland, married a Maltese lady and spoke Maltese. As Britain was the dominating power in Malta, Mizzi was the one who suffered for his ideas, Strickland the one who was promoted. But did not Enrico, like Strickland, conceive of Malta as a separate nation, yet not as potentially an independent state — as a country that would be better off, politically or economically, as part of a larger, sovereign whole? This recurring 'apron-string' theory — that Malta was small enough to cohere as a nation but not strong enough to subsist as an independent state and that the island had a unique nationality but, equally, a strategic importance and a military impotence that so required to be defended from a position of strength — could lead to a comparison between Enrico Mizzi's proposal for federation with Italy to Mintoff's proposal for integration with Britain nearly half-a-century later. How far, if at all, was Mizzi's federation plan what Dennis Austin wonders that Mintoff's integration plan may have been — 'that like Mrs Todgers' embracing of the Miss Pecksniffs "there was affection beaming in one eye and calculation shining out of the other"?'[73]

In Enrico Mizzi, *italianità*, nationalism, and irredentism were moulded together and almost indistinguishable as separate

aspects of his thinking. Following in his father's footsteps, he
was enthusiastic about celebrating the *otto settembre* (the date
marking the 1565 siege) as Malta's national day.[74] He held the
Maltese race to be superior to the English, as well as — it would
seem — to the Italian (unless the two were the same).[75] Not
unlike his father, Enrico Mizzi apparently viewed the
Mediterranean as one ethnico-cultural entity, inhabited by
peoples sharing a common affinity. *Italianità*, in this sense, could
be seen to include — 'in the classic island of the Knights' where
'every persecution of the Nordic stranger' would always be
resisted — all that which seemed un-English or non-British. It
would extend to such qualities of Latinity as were usually
identified, in Malta, with Italy or the Mediterranean region:
'that serene melancholy of the Orient, such as could not be
hidden in the passionate looks of the Spaniards, the Greeks, and
the Sicilians'; the traditional women's costume — the *faldetta* —
which 'those who had travelled in the Mediterranean, in the
Barbary Coast, in the Orient' so liked, and which could be seen
'in a street in Tunis or Tripoli or by the pier in a Sicilian village';
the dark complexion reflecting 'the great sun and the great sea';
the sea breeze; the moonlight; 'the characteristic life of the
mezzogiorno, in the open air and communally (*in comune*)'.[76]
But Italy was more to Enrico than it had ever been to Fortunato
— Italy to him was not only the fountain of culture in Maltese
civil life, nor just a political lever with which to win concessions
from Britain, but a spiritual mother, perhaps like his own
mother, a magnetic caress without which, he felt, the Maltese
people could not move towards their natural destination. Malta
was 'the furthermost fringe of Italy' (*l'ultimo lembo d'Italia*),[77]
the Maltese were by 'natural attachment' linked *alla gran
madre Italia*. 'The soul of a people' was not transformed in a
year, wrote Mizzi:

Centuries of tradition are not cancelled. A mother language is not
abandoned for another, like a change of clothes. Certain mental habits,
certain social customs, are the outcome of a long and slow elaboration.

The patriotic principles and sentiments of the Maltese, he wrote,
should serve as an example to many of 'our brothers across the
sea and beyond the frontiers' (*nostri fratelli d'oltremare e d'oltre
confine*).[78]

Italianità ceased to be a dominant motif in Maltese national life after the Second World War and after Dr Borg Olivier replaced Enrico Mizzi as Prime Minister and leader of the Nationalist Party in 1950, when Malta again had responsible government.[79]

The other significant cultural development during the colonial period was the emergence of Maltese as a national and literary language. Maltese has had a standard orthography since 1931 and it was entrenched as the official language of Malta in the 1964 Independence Constitution.[80] English became a second language, but Italian influence continued mainly through the Italian TV channels which came to have a strong following among the better-educated sections of the community. For various reasons, the emancipation of Maltese was controversial, at least until the Second World War.

Paradoxically, it was the British who mainly pushed Maltese, mainly as a medium for the easier and faster spread of English; and that was one reason why the Nationalists themselves opposed it.

It is clear that no instant or static correlation exists between native languages and national cultures, or between ethnic groups and nation-states. While it seems natural that a people sharing common experiences and using the same medium of communication should constitute a nation, the relationship of nationality to nationhood may be complicated by a multiplicity of factors – sectarian, social, ideological. More fundamentally, a sense of common nationality may be hindered by different religions or ethnic origins of the inhabitants of a defined area, resulting for example in conflicting language loyalties, as in Canada. The situation appears even more perplexing when linguistic differences do not stem from perceptibly diverse racial origins, yet serve to polarize opinion in a society having common attributes. Nineteenth-century Maltese society is probably a unique example of the case in which trilingualism became a battleground in the successful quest for a national identity. Maltese nationalism rotated in time on this triple paradox: the championing of Italian as a non-Maltese national language; the active promotion of the Maltese vernacular by the British Imperial power as a means of expunging Italian; and the gradual emergence of Maltese as a national tongue and as the prime expression of anti-British sentiments.[81]

Savona, for one, had agreed with British advisers that English and other subjects should be taught through Maltese, which was to be studied by means of a newly-composed 'phonetic alphabet', during the first years at school, according to Franz Ahn's method.[82] Dr Ahn's method of learning foreign languages through the local vernacular, first launched in 1848, had become popular in Britain at the time when Savona was following a schoolmaster's course at the Royal Military Asylum.[83] Savona also knew from his teaching experience how the use of Maltese could facilitate instruction, strengthening the motivation to learn. 'At a word of Maltese', observed the Chief Secretary Hely-Hutchinson, 'the child's countenance brightens − intelligence leaps into the eyes, the mind is awakened and prepares itself to receive and to develop the ideas which are conveyed to it from the mind of the teacher.'[84]

The pro-British party regarded Italian as the 'great impediment to education', holding 'without the possibility of cavil' that the language of the Maltese was 'Arabic and not Italian'; instruction in Maltese and English was necessary for the 'humbler classes', but Italian was unnecessary. They advocated reforms which would benefit 'the community in general, although prejudicial to the interests of a class': unless the language which promised to be 'the prevailing tongue of civilization' was rendered general, and the people educated, Malta would remain backward. Moreover, the authorities 'at home' would never confer upon the Maltese the exercise of political liberty and the benefits of free institutions, until they would have been so educated.[85] They said that the interests of the professional classes and landed proprietors were at stake and they had naturally 'bandied together to oppose all the measures of reform proposed and to keep the people in ignorance and darkness':

They are actuated by the very same narrow-minded motives which impelled the English Conservatives of 1830 to oppose the abolition of the corn tax and the extension of popular education.[86]

As it is normally the more educated or imperilled section of any community − that section which is sufficiently self-conscious and free to seek to protect itself against threats to its cultural or economic existence − which assumes the leading role in the anticolonial movement, and thus in the moulding of national consciousness, it was mostly established middle-class families in cities, especially Valletta and Senglea, who were the vanguard of the PN:

Leaders are actuated by the desire to benefit their fellows, as well as by the desire to place themselves in a position of dominance; possessiveness and self-sacrifice are combined.[87]

Politicians have made good use of arrogating to language 'the function of the "badge" or "uniform" of a nation';[88] but language lays a kind of foundation for the more complex structures which correspond to the different aspects of culture.[89] Language loyalty, like nationalism, can be an *idée forcée*

which fills man's brain and heart with new thoughts and sentiments and drives him to translate his consciousness into deeds of organized action. In response to an impending language shift, it produces an attempt at preserving the threatened language; as a reaction to interference, it makes the standardized version of the language a symbol and cause.[90]

Government, retorted the pro-Italians, was for the benefit of those being governed not for that of those governing them. If Britain governed Malta, she did so 'for ourselves, not for herself'; therefore it was incorrect to say English was 'the language of our Government'. 'If those who administer our Government are unable to communicate with us, the worse for them. They should learn our language; we do not have to learn theirs.'[91] The Maltese preferred to be left free to see for themselves what was or was not to their greater advantage; they did not like being spoiled by those who so incessantly strove to promote their welfare: 'We are a free people who have not been conquered.'[92] Such statements were a claim to self-government, if not a thinly-veiled presumption of independence: Hely-Hutchinson described this speech by Zaccaria Roncali as 'a plea for self-government in its widest sense'.[93]

A similarly nationalist reasoning was applied, under a more liberal guise, but with less justification, with regard to the suggested elevation of Maltese into a 'purified' language of study. The local patois was considered only an accident of birth, the mark of insularity, if not of inferiority, and anyway useless for educational purposes; it had always been used informally to make meanings intelligible to schoolchildren. But it was held that to invent a grammar and alphabet, thus introducing a third language of study, was motivated by the principle, as enunciated by Mizzi, *inclusio unius est exclusio alterius*.[94] Maltese was

being made into a language, said Dr Agostino Naudi, 'out of
hatred of the Italian language'.[95] What would children, who
learned Maltese as they were nursed, read in it except some
recipe on how to cook pumpkins and egg-plants, observed
Roncali. In Wales, although Welsh had a literature by means
of which children could improve themselves and develop their
intelligence, English was taught orally through Welsh, without
Welsh itself being studied.[96] The same English Government
that had done so much to eradicate Gaelic from Ireland, noted
Mizzi, now wanted the Maltese to study their native dialect.[97]
The idea of having the euphonistic system in England (as
intended by George Bernard Shaw) had failed, argued Capt.
Kirton; it involved 'the destruction' of English.[98] Comparing
the study of Maltese to that of Latin and Greek, [99] Mizzi said
there was nothing wrong in cultivating Maltese for philosophical
purposes; this could serve as a key to other ancient
languages.[100] But 'to put Arabic words instead of the Italian
words we use', he said, 'is not to purify Maltese but to create
a new language'; the aim of this purification was to destroy or
banish Italian 'which has been amongst us since its birth'.[101]
And besides, even if Maltese were 'the most beautiful of all
languages, it would still be a mishap for us not to be able to
communicate with any other people'.[102]

The 'Arabization' of Maltese was also opposed because the
Arabic heritage had no place in the nationalist Christian-
European prototype: the Maltese saw themselves as south
Europeans not as North Africans; even those who settled in
North African countries, such as Tunisia, held steadfastly to
their language and still more to their religion as characteristics
of Maltese nationality and hence of separateness from the Arab
Muslim native.[103] Even Savona's party, while holding rightly
that Maltese was derived from Arabic, maintained that the
Maltese people were Phoenician in origin. Invoking Napoleon's
saying that if you scratched a Russian you found the Cossack,
the author of a pro-Government *Xirka Xemia* (Semitic Society)
pamphlet in 1885 affirmed that if you scratched a Maltese you
found the Phoenician.[104] The period of Arab rule over Malta
from the ninth to the twelfth century was commonly held to have
been oppressive; in deriding the use of Arabic sources the 'pro-
Italians' could rely on popular feelings about religion and race.

Maltese, said Enrico Mizzi, 'received its last form from the Saracen domination, so that Maltese is the monument of our infamy and slavery'; it was 'for the sake of patriotism' that the study of Maltese should be confined to the libraries.[105] Mizzi went so far as to describe Maltese as 'the curse of the country'.[106]

Although the attempt to 'Arabize' on Keenan's instructions was a linguistic fallacy when it exceeded certain limits – a rich Romance superstructure could not be discarded – the philological structuring of Maltese necessitated a recourse of the Arabic roots. Maltese was not to Italian what Afrikaans was to Dutch; nor was it possible, out of an admixture of Italo-Maltese elements to create a 'new' language in a way similar to the creation of a 'Common Norwegian' (*Samnorsk*) out of the mutually comprehensible Danish (*Bokmal*) and old Norse (*Nynorsk*).[107] Sir Ferdinando Inglott, the Collector of Customs, argued that there was nothing strange when a word or root be found wanting

if instead of borrowing it from a *foreign* language, we should take it from the language which has the greatest affinity with our own ... It strikes me as being far from patriotic to hear Maltese persons uttering so contemptuous an opinion of their own language.

Malta's university, added Savona, could not gain distinction in any other branch of knowledge except in oriental languages 'of which we have the basis in our own language'.[108] 'I believe the Maltese language is the greatest blessing the Maltese have inherited from their forefathers; and the Governments are doing their duty in promoting the cultivation of that language', he said.[109] It was hardly convincing to see even the filibustering Hely-Hutchinson almost turn into a *de rigueur* nationalist by singing the praises of Maltese as Malta's language.[110]

The irony was that the colonial regime and its supporters seemed to be intent on being purely nationalistic, though in fact their chief concern was utilitarian; the Nationalists themselves, allegedly on liberal and patriotic grounds, could never abjure the outstanding ingredient of the standard version of Maltese nationality they upheld – that was Italian. To identify not Maltese but Italian with nationhood was rather a misapplication of the classic nationalist view expressed by Herder, that the nation remained intact provided it maintained its distinctive linguistic traditions; yet *italianità* expressed the average educated man's feelings, and political leanings, better than the vernacular itself. On the other hand, Savona and Inglott were not exactly the Douglas Hyde and Eoin MacNeill of the Gaelic League. Perhaps the best clue to this persistent pseudo-linguistic tangle may be found in the exchange of insults between Mizzi and Savona with regard to examples of words having an Arabic or Italian derivation. When once Mizzi was explaining how similar Maltese was to Italian he gave as an example, presumably looking at Savona, the words *inti traditur* (you are a traitor), whereupon Savona, in a repartee, gave, as his example, the Arabic words *inti ħmar* (you are a fool); Mizzi insisted that the better example was *traditur*.[111] Indeed, it appears that Savona and Mizzi conceived a nation differently: Savona pointed to the message 'to the Maltese nation' by the pro-Maltese language scholar M.A. Vassalli, who had regarded native speakers of Maltese as *veri nazionali;*[112] Mizzi referred to the proclamation 'to the Maltese nation' made by the Civil Commissioner Sir Charles Cameron in 1801 wherein the Maltese had been promised 'full protection, and the enjoyment of all [their] dearest rights'.[113]

The slow acceptance of Maltese as a language worthy of cultivation was an induced process of growing self-awareness as well as a direct consequence of the wish to impart knowledge through the vernacular; in these respects the *Riformisti* were using the right arguments from the wrong side of the fence. The Nationalists, being mostly the products of a special class, construed the nation largely in their own image; they were also the prisoners of a system: they saw the light through iron bars. The laws of sympathy and antipathy were applied to politics: the *Riformisti* were rather like 'the Afrikaners with "English hearts" ', the *Antiriformisti* more like 'the Afrikaners with "Dutch hearts" '; with some notable exceptions, the 'Afrikaners with "Afrikaans hearts" ' were still in the making.[114]

Apart from a handful of scholars, few public figures had upheld the value and the need of Maltese for its own sake in a national context. One of the first publicists to do so – a classic nationalist, in this respect – was Manwel Dimech. A self-made individual and a convert from crime, for half-a-century after his death

Dimech was the unsung victim of clericalism, colonialism, and the surreptitious censures of the closed community. He had begun to muster a working-class following before the First World War, but his social, religious, and political views were, like his outlook on language, considered revolutionary or undesirable. The Church excommunicated him, the faithful stoned him, and the British exiled him to Egypt, where he died. Dimech wrote:

A nation and a language are one and the same thing; if one is lost so will the other be lost. Let us therefore cultivate our language, let us not insult it by using some other language instead of it, because when we insult the language we insult the nation, and when we insult the nation, we insult ourselves.[115]

Opposed to Strickland, the pro-British leader, Dimech respected the elder Mizzi but distanced himself from any irredentist leaning.[116] Ironically, a bitter rival of his was Ġużè Muscat Azzopardi, onetime editor of the Church's paper *Il-Ħabib*.[117] But Muscat Azzopardi was a supporter and active promoter of Maltese – he has been described as the father of Maltese literature.[118] Thus, to be a pro-Italian nationalist did not necessarily imply any opposition to the Maltese language *per se*. Gradually it became quite acceptable for authors to publish in Maltese and Italian, or in Maltese and English. The belief in *Malta Maltija* (Maltese Malta) was taking root.

The British presence both restrained and assisted the slow crystalization of a national identity and of a consciousness of it. In terms of nationality, Malta was in a position somewhat comparable in the Empire to Quebec, Ireland, or South Africa and, in Europe, to Poland, Belgium, or other smaller nationalities struggling to survive against superior odds. Economically and strategically, Malta's colonial identity was that of an outpost of Empire: it could be seen alongside Gibraltar and Cyprus in the Mediterranean, Singapore and Hong Kong in the Far East.

In 1964 Malta obtained its independence, retaining initially a constitutional monarchy on the Westminster model: there was pluralism in a parliamentary democracy, an independent judiciary, the right to strike, free elections, and protection under the law.[119]

It was with independence, and the experimental years of freedom that followed on it, that Malta and the Maltese truly came to life. This realization becomes more telling when one sees the difference in mentality between 'pre-' and 'post-' independence Maltese, between those who lived through the transition and those who, being overseas, were passed by. I have expressed it thus:

In the history of Maltese culture, Independence is a watershed. Malteseness came of age. Artistic endeavour flourished: subjects and styles changed. Composers orchestrated melody complementing the traditional singing. Painters experimented with collages of native flora and fauna. Architects designed modernized versions of rustic dwellings and farmhouses. Literary criticism developed as new poets suddenly emerged. There was a flair of soul-searching, a rediscovering and questioning of past and present — without the need to present a common front against anyone. Malta assumed its place in the international community of nations *sur le pied de l'égalité* (proposing, for example, a Law of the Sea). Union Jacks were no longer stamped on Maltese history books ... Maltese gradually assumed more importance than English as a medium of instruction, as educational institutions increased and improved, with secondary and tertiary education becoming free by 1971. Maltese Theatre (as opposed to farce) started to be taken seriously, as were original TV documentaries and discussion groups. Tourism boomed: hotels, such as Hilton and Sheraton, sprang up; British settlers came; Maltese tourist guides abounded, talking about archaeological remains, bastions, tapestries, acqueducts, auberges, paintings, and the Blue Grotto, in a babble of tongues from German to Russian, with English and Italian the most popular. Traditional Maltese dishes started to be served in restaurants. Incentive schemes saw the opening of many light-industry factories, causing a radical change in the occupational status of women, especially young women. It was an emancipation. So this cultural revolution, spontaneously influencing Maltese nationality and self-pride, transforming identity or at least the appreciation of it, made little or no practical impact on Maltese overseas who simply could not experience it, except perhaps remotely. Colonial Malta's habits of mind, impressions, and norms persisted untouched by the revitalized air of self-discovery and autocriticism, of challenge and opportunity, except in so far as these were influenced one way or the other by the host society itself.
Emigration from Malta reached a bottom low by 1969.

Naturally there could be no sudden or fundamental break with the past. The new state was, after all, an old nation. Moreover, this challenging self-assessment phase, after centuries of subjection to foreign rule, could turn out to have been just a euphoria. It could be nipped in the bud by neo-colonialism, by statism. A democratic political culture was a fragile reed in Malta, in spite of all make-believe to the contrary. And the overseer could be worse than the master. Monolithic sanction could be restored by a rather more familiar breed, if not by a new invader as before.

But the soul was stirred. Conscientization became possible. Subjection and alienation could not be quite the same again.[120]

NOTES

[1] See H. Frendo, 'Religion and Ethnic Identity in the Maltese Australian Community'.

[2] See id., 'Cultural Interaction and National Identity: The Maltese Case'.

[3] On this and part of what follows, id., *Party Politics in a Fortress Colony* and other related works published by the same author. In this paper, wherever possible, reference will be made to the original sources.

[4] See *Problems of Parliamentary Government in Colonies*, 41-4.

[5] R. Pinon, *L'Empire de la Méditerranée*, 413.

[6] 'Report of the Royal Commission on the Finances, Economic Position and Judicial Procedure of Malta', 5, 22.

[7] F. Balbi di Correggio, *Diario dell'Assedio di Malta*.

[8] A.T. Luttrell (ed.), *Medieval Malta*.

[9] C.E. Engel, *L'Ordre de Malte en la Méditerranée; Q.* Hughes, *The Building of Malta*.

[10] 'It is mainly Arabic with a groundwork of Punic', the folklorist Manwel Magri told G.M. Hopkins in 1874. 'Newspapers are published in it in European script ...': *The Journals and Papers of Gerard Manley Hopkins*, 259.

[11] For example, 'Statement showing Language in which judgements in the Courts were delivered between 1530 and 1814', CO 158/341, enc. Grenfell to Chamberlain 24 March 1902.

[12] *Census of Malta, Gozo and Comino; PP*, (1878-9), li, 387.

[13] PP, 1878-lv-12.

[14] G.P. Badger, *Description of Malta and Gozo*, 98.

[15] B.L. Rigby, *The Malta Railway*, 6.

[16] CG, 23 February 1910, col. 306.

[17] CO 158/264/8247, enc. Borton to Derby, 10 May 1883.

[18] G. Peto, *Malta and Cyprus*, 99. On Strickland's pro-British party and his compact with the Malta Labour Party in 1927, when he became prime minister, *infra*.

[19] On all this, Frendo, *Party Politics, passim*.

[20] Id., 'Language and Nationality in an Island Colony: Malta', 31.

[21] Id., 'Language of a Colony: A Study of the Maltese Language Question', 42, and *passim*.

[22] For an elaboration and evaluation of such traits and their repercussions in post-colonial Malta, id., 'Messages from Mintoff's Malta: The Grenada of the Mediterranean', 18-33; id., 'Freedom After Independence: A Western European or a Third World Model for the Maltese Islands?'.

[23] See *Mr. W. Eton's Vindication of his Public Conduct in Malta*.

[24] A. Mifsud, *L'Origine della Sovranità Inglese su Malta*.

[25] J.J. Cremona, *An Outline of the Constitutional Development of Malta*.

[26] 'Dichiarazione dei Diritti degli Abitanti delle Isole Malta e Gozo', 15 June 1802, 6-7.

[27] 'Report of the Commissioners of Inquiry (August 1812)', 130.

[28] *Appeals of the Nobility and People of Malta,* 79-80.

[29] Cornwall-Lewis to his father, 25 October 1836, in G. F. Lewis (ed.), *Letters of the Rt. Hon. G. Cornwall-Lewis Bart. to Various Friends.* According to Cornwall-Lewis, Mitrovich was 'Malta agent' mainly because he knew English (Cornwall-Lewis to Glenelg, 14 September 1838).

[30] Mitrovich to Stanley, 22 May 1859; G. Mitrovich, *Council of Government in Malta.*

[31] B. Fiorentini, *Malta rifugio di esuli.*

[32] For example, *Lettera di Giuseppe Mazzini Ai Signori Tocqueville e Falloux.*

[33] G. Mangion, *Governo inglese, risorgimento italiano ed opinione pubblica a Malta 1848-51,* 51.

[34] V. Laurenza, 'Garibaldi a Malta', 143-61.

[35] *Hansard,* 1st ser., xxxvi, 1803, 1484.

[36] *Hansard,* 1st ser., xxxvi, 1803, 1427.

[37] *Rapport fai par Daru,* 23-4.

[38] *Hansard,* 3rd ser., ccxxxii, 1877, 388.

[39] Chamberlain to Fremantle, 10 January 1896; H.I. Lee, *Malta 1813-1914,* 218. See also H. Frendo, 'Self Identity in the "British" Mediterranean: Gibraltar, Malta, Cyprus'.

[40] R.J. Gavin, *Aden under British Rule, 177.*

[41] Ball to Dundas, 6 March 1801; F. Mizzi and S. Cachia Zammit, *A Statement of Claims and Grievances of the Maltese,* appendix II.

[42] CG, 13 May 1885, cols. 941-2.

[43] H. V. Wiseman, *The Cabinet in the Commonwealth,* 122.

[44] CG, 14 December 1881, col. 61.

[45] CO 158/249/9674, Wingfield minute on Borton to Hicks-Beach, 24 July 1878.

[46] Report of the Malta Royal Commission 1931, 5-6, 9.

[47] F.W. Rowsell, 'Malta', 262.

[48] CO 158/265, Hely-Hutchinson to Anderson, 27 October 1883.

[49] See Frendo, *Party Politics,* 19.

[50] S. Savona, *The Necessity of Educating the People.*

[51] Id., *Report on the Educational Institutions of Malta and Gozo,* 6, 22.

[52] CG, 21 May 1877, xl, col. 418.

[53] See Frendo, *Party Politics,* esp. 48, 98-9, 167.

[54] CG, 6 April 1899, ii, col. 24-5.

[55] Ibid., 4 December 1895, viii, col. 460.

[56] G. Strickland, *Malta and the Phoenicians.*

[57] CO 158/338/45108, Strickland's comment on F. Mizzi's speech, enc. Grenfell to Chamberlain, 16 December 1902.

[58] CO 159/338/43061, Strickland's letter to Colonial Office, 30 November 1901.

[59] See *supra,* n. 57.

[60] CO 158/359/27300, Strickland to Crewe, 23 July 1908.

[61] *Hansard,* 4th ser., ci, 1902, cols. 1187-8, 1196, 1205.

[62] CO 883/5.6125, enc. 3, 109A.

[63] See D. Austin, *Malta and the End of Empire.*

[64] See R. Bondin, *Deportation, 1942.*

[65] *Infra.*

[66] On this, Frendo, *Party Politics,* 163-5.

[67] See 'Appello agli Elettori', 18 January 1887.

[68] CO 158/345//35170, enc. 1, Kelly to Chamberlain, 15 September 1903.

[69] CG, 19 April 1899, v, col. 207. 212

[70] CO 158/336/18207, enc. 21 May 1901.
[71] Mizzi and Cachia Zammit, *A Statement of Claims and Grievances.*
[72] CO 158/398, enc. 2, Methuen to Long, 3 September 1917.
[73] Austin, 31.
[74] E. Mizzi, *Per il VIII Settembre, 1565.*
[75] Id., *Malta Italiana*, 8.
[76] Ibid., 4, 6, 8.
[77] Ibid., 6, col. ii.
[78] Ibid., 8, col. ii.
[79] See H. Frendo, 'Borg Olivier's Legacy', 59-65.
[80] See D. Marshall, *History of the Maltese Language in Local Education.*
[81] H. Frendo, 'Language and Nationality', 22.
[82] Savona, *Report on the Educational Institutions, 8*, para. 30.
[83] See F. Ahn, *Handbuch de englischen Umgangs-sprache, mit deutscher und franzosischer Vebersetzung*, and subsequent multilingual writings.
[84] CG, 9 January 1884, 8.229.
[85] *Malta Standard*, 21 August 1880.
[86] Ibid., 6 October 1880. The Corn Laws were repealed by the Conservatives under Sir Robert Peel in 1846.
[87] *Nationalism. A Report by a Study Group of the Royal Institute of International Affairs*, xvii.
[88] S. Rundle, *Language as a Social and Political Factor in Europe*, 56.
[89] C. Lévi-Strauss, *Structural Anthropology*, 68-9.
[90] H. Kohn, *The idea of Nationalism*, 19; U. Wenreich, *Languages in Contact*, 99.
[91] CG, 11 January 1884, 9.248-249.
[92] Ibid., cols. 252-3.
[93] CO 158/267, enc. Borton to Derby, 21 January 1884.
[94] CG., 11 January 1884, 9.285, 278.
[95] Ibid., col. 260.
[96] Ibid., 18 March 1885, 21.651-652. Since the Act of Union made English the official language in Wales, Welshmen were debarred from taking office unless they were bilingual; only in 1943 did Welsh become admissible in the courts. E.G. Bowen (ed.), *Wales*, 250.
[97] CG, 30 March 1885, 23.746. Gaelic, spoken generally in 1600, subsequently declined through Anglicization; the famine killed it in the 1840s as many Gaels emigrated or died.
[98] Ibid., 26 March 1885, 22.673.
[99] Ibid., 21 November 1883, 4.140.
[100] Ibid., 11 January 1884, 9.289.
[101] Ibid., 30 March 1881, 11.345-359.
[102] Ibid., 13 May 1885, 29.958-959.
[103] C. Sammut, 'La Minorité Maltaise de Tunisie: Ethnie Arab ou Européenne?'
[104] Anon, *Qari għall-Maltin, mahruġ mix-Xirka Xemia*, 13.
[105] CG, 11 January 1884, 9.289.
[106] Ibid., 13 May 1885, 29.958-959.
[107] See R.G. Popperwell, *Norway*, ch. 3.
[108] CG, 30 March 1881, 11.345-359.
[109] Ibid., 13 May 1885, 29.964, 967.
[110] Ibid., 9 January 1884, 9.228.
[111] Ibid., 27 January 1886, 45.190.
[112] Ibid., 21 November 1883, 4.137.
[113] Ibid., 30 March 1885, 23.748.

[114] F.A. van Jaarsveld, *The Awakening of Afrikaner Nationalism*, 112.

[115] H. Frendo, 'Language and Nationality', 26; but id., *Lejn Tnissil ta' Nazzjon;* id., *Birth Pangs of a Nation;* and id., *Story of a Book.*

[116] Id., 'Il-"Ktajjen" tal- Kolonjaliżmu', 7; id., *Ir-Rieda għall-Ħelsien*, 159; id., *The Popular Movement for a New Beginning;* id., *Party Politics*, 149-151.

[117] Ibid., 151; id., *Birth Pangs of a Nation*, 183, showing Dimech's flysheet 'A Cui Mi Rivolgerò? Cui Chiamerò in mio Soccorso?'.

[118] Id., *Party Politics*, 191, 202-4.

[119] See, however, id., *The Popular Movement; supra*, n. 22; and Frendo, *Party Politics*, 211-215.

[120] Id., 'Maltese Settlement', part 3. See also Frendo's series of articles 'Lejn Storjografija Post-Kolonjali'.

11

JEREMY BOISSEVAIN

Festa Partiti and the British: Exploding a Myth

My fascination with Maltese *festa partiti* goes back thirty years.* Over the years I frequently asked informants why so many villages have two bands and often celebrate two feasts. Then, as now, a frequent answer was: 'The British introduced the *partiti* to divide us. They encouraged feasts to keep us occupied and to divert our attention from political issues and social problems.' In short, they maintained that the British introduced band-club and *festa* rivalry as a conscious instrument of colonial government, a combination of *divide et impera* and *panem et circenses*.

The evidence they provided for this theory was that 'most band clubs are named after British imperial figures, such as "Queen Victoria", the "Prince of Wales", the "Duke of Connaught", and so on.' And they contended that 'the British founded and sponsored clubs to have support among the people. All clubs were either for the British or against them.' These are not apocryphal comments. They were again put forward seriously to me by an educated public figure as recently as April 1987.

I contend this theory is pure myth. This is borne out by a closer examination of the background to the *festa partiti*.

I THE *FESTA* BEFORE 1850

By all accounts *festa* celebrations in the late eighteenth and early nineteenth centuries were very modest events, at least by today's standards. Although one foreign observer, writing on

Maltese holiday customs in 1835, noted 'that the principal recreations of the Maltese have in general some connection with their religious ceremonies,'[1] he and the other two leading recorders of Maltese customs of the period[2] ignored the parish *festa*. The reason for this lack of attention to what today are among the most striking events of popular culture is quite simply that 'the Maltese *festa* in its present form emerged in the course of the nineteenth century'.[3] During much of the eighteenth century, *festa* celebrations were limited to some minor illumination, often a bonfire, and the occasional firing of small mortars. The chief events were the internal liturgical celebrations, while the day of the *festa* was a day of welcome rest from the normal heavy daily labour. Strolling musicians playing pipes and tambourines gradually appeared, as did processions. But the custom of including the statue of the patron saint in the procession on the day of the *festa* was a late development, for example, at Luqa in 1781 and Tarxien in 1829.[4] In Gozo this did not occur until 1840, when the statue of St George at Rabat was the first to be paraded around in the procession on his feast day.[5]

Parishes apparently also celebrated other saints with almost equal pomp. For example, during 1846 and 1847 at Cospicua the feasts of Santa Kruz, St Theresa, and St Agatha, as well as that of the parish patron the Immaculate Conception, were all celebrated with music, illumination, fireworks, a statue, and with various confraternities taking part in the procession.[6] From the comments in *Ġiaħan,* the satirical newspaper of the day, it is also clear that something called a *banda* had joined, or replaced, the fife and tambourine players during the *festa* of St Theresa at Cospicua in May 1847. By the middle of the nineteenth century, all the *festa* ingredients with which we are familiar were present. The only exception was the band club.

II BAND CLUBS

Pietro Paolo Castagna records that the first band club was established in Żebbuġ in 1860 by Indri Borg.[7] Six months later Borg helped found Malta's second band club at Rabat, and the third one, in Żebbuġ. After that, band clubs multiplied rapidly.

By 1890, two military bands and thirty four civilian bands had been established in twenty two towns and villages in Malta and Gozo. In view of the argument we are developing, it is significant that, of the thirty four bands Castagna lists in 1890, only two have 'imperial' names: the 'Prince of Wales' of Valletta (which had started life in 1874 as 'La Stella' and later would become the 'King's Own' band) and the 'Duke of Edinburgh' at Vittoriosa. (See Table below)

TABLE   Maltese Bands 1890
          (La Società Filarmonica Nazionale)

Valletta	1	Royal Malta Artillery – Dir. Eman. Bartoli.
	2	Royal Malta Militia – Dir. Fil. Galea.
	3	Prince of Wales Band – Dir. Alf. P. Hare.
	4	La Valletta – Dir. Cav. V. Carabot.
Floriana	5	Vilhena Band – Dir. Gius. Borg.
Senglea	6	La Vincitrice – Dir. Gius. Portelli.
	7	La Croce di Malta – Dir. Bern. Costa.
Cospicua	8	San Giorgio – Dir. Carmelo Abela.
Vittoriosa	9	Duke of Edinburgh – Dir. Gaet. Grech.
	10	La Vittoriosa – Dir. Gius. Micallef.
Sliema	11	I Cavalieri di Malta – Dir. Ferd. Camilleri.
Notabile	12	L'Isle Adam – Dir. Carm. Camilleri.
	13	Conte Ruggiero – Dir. Fran. Xuereb.
Luqa	14	Sant'Andrea – Dir. Salv. Spiteri.
	15	L'Unione – Dir. Gaet. Grech.
Żabbar	16	Santa Maria – Dir. Gius. Micallef.
	17	San Michele – Dir. C. Abela Scolaro.
Żejtun	18	Beland – Dir. Ang. Mifsud.
	19	Santa Caterina – Dir. P. Caruana Dingli.
Żebbuġ	20	San Filippo – Dir. Gioac. Galea.
	21	Rohan – Dir. Lor. Gatt.
Birkirkara	22	La Stella – Dir. Gavino Camilleri.
	23	L'Alleanza – Dir. Constant. Fenech.
Qormi	24	Pinto – Dir. Ant. Agius.
	25	San Giorgio – Dir. Gius. Portelli.

Żurrieq	26	Il Cavaliere − Dir. Carm. Zammit.
Hamrun	27	San Giuseppe − Dir. Carm. Doneo.
	28	San Gaetano − Dir. Edwardo Farina.
Naxxar	29	La Pace − Dir. Gav. Camilleri.
Siġġiewi	30	La Nicolina − Dir. Ruggiero Carabott.
Tarxien	31	San Giuseppe − Dir. P. Caruana Dingli.
Mosta	32	Nicolò Isouard − Dir. Eman. Camilleri.
Kirkop	33	L'Unione − Dir. Ignazio Catania.
Victoria	34	Il Leone − Dir. Cav. V. Carabott.
	35	La Stella − Dir. Ant. Agius.
Nadur	36	Calypso − Dir. Fran. Decesare.

SOURCE: P.P. Castagna, *Lis-Storia ta' Malta. Bil Gżejjer Taħħa.*

It is clear that rivalry between bands was present almost from the beginning. The two Żebbuġ bands were established within six months of each other, as were those in Valletta in 1874. By 1890, twelve of the twenty two villages and towns in which band clubs were established were divided by rival bands. Most of this rivalry is related to the cult of saints, for most of the villages that are divided celebrate two saints − the titular or patron, and a secondary saint who has come to assume almost equal social importance. Each saint is celebrated by a faction, or *partit*, of which the band club forms the social and political centre. *Festa partiti* compete over almost every aspect of the feast, including the decoration of the streets, the adornment of the statue, the number of communicants, the number of lights on the façade of the church, the size and number of candles, the number of guest bands and, above all, fireworks. Rival band clubs were both the product of, and contributed to, this competition.

By the 1920s this rivalry had escalated to such an extraordinary degree that the celebration of many secondary saints eclipsed that of their titular rivals. Finally, in 1935 the Church, long alarmed by the extreme forms that this rivalry had assumed, took steps to reduce the celebration of secondary saints. It promulgated a series of regulations designed to reduce the scale on which secondary feasts could be celebrated. These stipulated that for secondary feasts there was to be no Translation of Holy Relics on the eve of the feast, that only the church and the area immediately adjacent to it could be illuminated, and that only one band on the eve and one on the day of the feast would be allowed. The regulations also placed limits on the variety and quantity of the fireworks and the duration of the displays. Finally, they drew attention to existing regulations that church decorations and new works of art introduced for secondary saints and feasts should be less costly and beautiful than those for titular saints.[8]

Parish priests insisted on the observance of the 1935 regulations. In this they were supported by the police, who refused the necessary permissions and licences for street decorations, band marches, and firework displays that were not approved of by the parish priest. A number of secondary feasts that had had widespread support were consequently reduced to minor celebrations (St Valentine in Balzan; St Joseph in Għargħur, Mosta, and Siġġiewi; St Aloycius in Lija; Our Lady of the Rosary in Safi). Moreover, the rivalry between *partiti* in Żabbar and Qrendi was so violent that the secondary feasts there, respectively St Michael and Our Lady of Lourdes, were suppressed completely. Not surprisingly, intense rivalry persisted between the bands in these villages in spite of the church's measures.

During the Second World War band-club and *festa* rivalry was dormant. It flared up again in the postwar years, but then abated. Massive emigration during the 1950s and just before independence in 1964, together with the vicious political confrontation between the Church and the Malta Labour Party during the 1960s, drained off manpower required to keep the *festa* rivalry at high pitch.[9]

By 1961, on the eve of independence, there were fifty six band clubs located in some thirty seven towns and villages, nineteen of which housed pairs of competing band clubs. Twelve paired rivals were linked to existing *festa partiti* (Għaxaq, Gudja, Kirkop, Luqa, Mqabba, Qrendi, Rabat, Vittoriosa, Żebbuġ, and Żurrieq) or past rivalry (Ħamrun, Żabbar), while four were tied to rival parishes in the same town (Qormi, Victoria, Sliema, and Valletta). In only three towns was band-club rivalry apparently unrelated to *festa partiti* (Birkirkara, Mellieħa, and Żejtun).[10] Band-club rivalry during the period of British Malta was thus clearly linked to rivalry between *festa partiti* in virtually every case.

The rivalry began to flare up again in independent Malta in the early 1970s, and especially following 1975. That year, probably as part of the run-up to the 1976 elections, the Socialist Government instructed police to cease consulting parish priests before issuing or denying permits regarding street decorations, band marches, and fireworks for the village feasts. This effectively removed the Church's control over the external celebration of secondary feasts. Needless to say, the measure was popular among supporters of secondary saints, most of which are celebrated in the southern electoral districts, which are also very heavily Labour. With the removal of the Church's lid on secondary feasts, rivalry flourished. The result was a tremendous escalation of *festa* celebrations in the divided villages. This enthusiasm rapidly spilled over into undivided villages.[11] Today the Maltese *festa* is booming as never before and violent rivalry has kept pace: in 1986 police had to intervene in Żurrieq and Żabbar to separate scores of fighting *festa* partisans.

III WHY *FESTA PARTITI* AFTER 1850?

Two important questions must now be answered. Why did *festa partiti* arise in the fifty or so years following 1850, and what reasons prompted people to join one *partit* rather than its rival?

To begin with, factionalism is not unique to Malta. It occurs in all societies. The chief characteristics of factionalism are its black and white polarization, the bitterness it engenders among rivals, the absurd lengths members go to in order to score points off each other, and the shame they feel towards outsiders for such pettiness. Factions are particularly prevalent in small-scale societies where people live in face to face contact with each other.[12]

Chronologically, *festa* factionalism developed at the same time as *festa* celebrations were expanding and band clubs were being established. Obviously the territorial cleavage between parishes in the same town – such as Rabat, Victoria, Valletta, and later, Qormi – forms a natural basis for rivalry. But besides these divisions, I found no pre-existing cleavages onto which rivalry between *festa partiti* was grafted, though this is an area which demands further research. The establishment of formal band clubs is a logical outgrowth of the growing scale of the external celebration of saints and the consequent demand for band music.

The interest in band music was no doubt stimulated by the presence in Malta of British military bands. The two Maltese military bands, the 'Royal Malta Artillery' band and the 'Royal Malta Military' band, trained bandsmen and generated enthusiasm. More important, however, was the cultural link with Sicily, which was at the time close. Sicilian influences were furthered by the influx of Italian refugees in Malta during the Risorgimento, especially after 1850. They promoted Italian and Sicilian culture especially in the urban areas. It had long been a custom in Sicily to celebrate saints with brass-bands. In fact, many of the Sicilian villages in the province of Syracuse, the province nearest Malta, were divided by factions supporting rival saints.[13] Verga has given a dramatic description of this rivalry in his famous short story *'Guerra di Santi'*. Much of the vocabulary associated with the Maltese *festa* is of Italian origin (*banda, mortaletti, kaxxa nfernali, trikki-trakki)* if not Sicilian (*bradella, vara)*.

Band clubs were also a manifestation of a conception of social organization new to Malta that was gaining currency, namely, the idea of voluntary associations for laymen, and in particular social clubs for 'gentlemen'. Following the establishment of the exclusive British Union Club in 1826, clubs of various kinds began to spring up throughout the island. They multiplied so rapidly that Castagna could write in 1890: 'Today you do not find a village without one or two, nor a city without three or five.'[14]

The second half of the nineteenth century was also a period of relative prosperity for Malta. This was a consequence of

increased military and naval activity as a result of the outbreak
of the Crimean War (1853-56); the expansion of Government
public-work projects from 1859 to 1865; and the renewed
demand for Maltese cotton as a consequence of the shortage
caused by the American Civil War.[15] This prosperity facilitated
the not inconsiderable expenses associated with expanding
festa celebrations (decorations, illuminations, fireworks),
and the cost of equipping a band and furnishing a club-
house. This economic boom also increased the demand for wage
labour from the villages. This in turn helped to disseminate
urban Italianate ideas. They were also disseminated by
city-born schoolteachers who began moving into the rural
communities about this time to staff the newly established
Government schools. In Għaxaq, for example, I found that
a Valletta-born teacher introduced the custom of decorating
streets for the *festa*. There were therefore a number of
factors which facilitated and contributed to the establishment
of band clubs after 1850.

Various reasons have been put forward to explain why
particular clubs, once founded, divided. For example, Robert
Mifsud Bonnici suggests that *festa partiti* developed out
of a dispute between persons who wanted to play sacred
music composed by Vincenzo Bugeja and those who preferred
the music of his rival, Paolo Nani.[16] As far as I was able
to determine, however, the only *partiti* which arose directly
out of this dispute were those in Żebbuġ. However, many
partiti, once established, played the music of either Bugeja
or Nani during their feasts. The former chose a star as
their symbol, the latter an eagle. On the other hand, bands
in three towns (Valletta, Birkirkara, Victoria) were officially
named 'La Stella' when they were established, apparently
lending further support to Mifsud Bonnici's thesis. The
composers and their music and their respective symbols
thus became banners of faction. Today many *partiti* are
still nicknamed either *tal-istilla* or *tal-ajkla*, reflecting this
once-important division.

Sometimes persons, often priests vigorously promoting the
devotion of a secondary saint, provoked a schism in the parish
that led to the establishment of *partiti*. At Kirkop, for example,
the secondary *partit* of St Joseph was the result of the efforts

of a new parish priest, Dun Ġużepp Barbara from Għaxaq, to establish the cult to his personal patron. In 1877, a year after his arrival, he founded a confraternity dedicated to St Joseph. In October 1878 the new confraternity celebrated its first feast. Although the new secondary feast at first was a simple affair, it and the feast of St Leonard, the titular, grew rapidly. The measures of the new confraternity also increased and, in 1880, it established an altar in the church dedicated to its patron. By 1886 people in this poor rural village were beginning to grumble at having to contribute to two feasts. In 1888 there was an encounter between those who organized the St Leonard feast and the parish priest which brought matters to a head. Several persons complained to the Archbishop that Dun Ġużepp was buying street decorations for the feast of St Joseph with funds collected for other purposes and, moreover, that he was raising the rents of local parish property for the same purpose. Following an investigation, the Archbishop sided with the parish priest's accusers and took away the administration of the church property from him. From that day onward, I was told, Dun Ġużepp threw his full support openly behind the feast of St Joseph. This divided the village into opposing factions. The village's 'Unione' band club divided and new clubs arose. The 'St Leonard' club played the music of Bugeja and adopted the star symbol. Its rival, of course, favoured Nani and the eagle. Both clubs still exist and are very active. The rivalry between the *partiti* today appears as vigorous as ever.[17]

Disputes over details of the celebration of the *festa* and the related cult of saints thus loom large in the explanation of why clubs split and *festa partiti* arose. But there are also other ingredients that entered into the factional mixture.

The later half of the nineteenth century, which saw the establishment of most of the band clubs and *festa partiti*, was also a period of intense political ferment. With the guarantee of Crown Colony status, and the introduction of limited franchise for the election for the Legislative Council in 1849, the way was open for the emergence of national political parties. The run-up to council elections was hotly contested. In 1878 riots took place to protest against new tax measures. The year 1879 saw the first mass rally in Floriana to protest against Government plans to force through an ill-conceived drainage scheme for the Three Cities.

Political polarization became more pronounced following the acceptance in 1880 of the Keenan Report aimed at the rapid Anglicization of Maltese education. This was a radical problem. Italian until then had been the language of Church, courts, university, and Government. Consequently, the period from 1880 to 1888 saw the rise of Maltese nationalism, and the polarization of Maltese politics into pro-Italian and pro-English factions.[18]

This division at the national level provided new symbols for band-club and *festa-partit* factional allegiance. The 'La Vallette' band club in Valletta became a national focal point for pro-Italian supporters. Its rival, quite naturally, performed a similar function for the pro-English faction, and consequently changed its name from 'La Stella' to 'Prince of Wales' and then to 'King's Own'. Other bands followed suit. In 1903 Senglea's 'La Vincitrice' became the 'Queen's Own' band.[19] In Vittoriosa, 'La Vittoriosa' became the 'Prince of Wales' band. In 1899 the 'St Elena' band of Birkirkara was granted permission to call itself the 'Duke of Connaught's Own Band'.[20] The *festa partit* of Our Lady of Mount Carmel in Żurrieq, nicknamed *del Cavaliere*, in 1908 bought the uniforms and the name of the 'Queen Victoria' band of Sliema.[21] In 1910 the 'Santa Marija' social club of Mqabba's titular *partit* changed its name to 'King George V' to commemorate his coronation.[22]

It is therefore evident that the introduction of English 'imperial' names occured after clubs and *partiti* were already well established. The change reflected a mixture of pro-English sentiment and the competition for markers to signal excellence to rival clubs. National politics thus became one of the issues on which established *partiti* and clubs took up positions after 1888, just as a preceding generation had done regarding the second music of Bugeja and Nani. There is no evidence that national political issues played a role in the establishment of band clubs. There is only one exception: the 'Imperial Band' club in Mellieħa, founded in the 1920s to promote Strickland's interests. Local issues and sentiments related to the celebration of parish feasts and rituals seem to have been the root of the foundation of band clubs and *partiti*.

This principle was again illustrated recently. In 1985 a second band club was established in Mosta, the 'Santa Maria Philharmonic Society'. This was the first new rival band club to be founded since the Mellieħa 'Imperial Club' was. established more than half a century earlier. It was founded by ex-members of the 'Nicolò Isouard' band club who had disagreed with the club committee. Even though Malta at the time was fiercely divided politically and caught up in the fanatic run-up to the 1987 elections, the disagreement was not about politics. The divisive issue concerned a new demonstrative band march on the morning of the feast of the parish patron, Santa Marija which took place at the same time as the festive high mass was being celebrated. Some members had organized it against the wishes of the archpriest. When the band club committee, not wishing to alienate the archpriest, refused to sponsor the march, the march activists hived off and, together with others, established a new, rival band club.[23] Once again, parochial rather than national political issues brought about factional conflict that led to the division of an existing club, and the establishment of a rival club.

IV   *PARTITI* AND CLASS

It is altogether more difficult to establish the personal motives that prompted people to join a particular *festa partit* at the time it was founded. One possible clue is the present day correlation between occupational class and *partit* affiliation. In general, the supporters of the titular saint, in parish political terms 'the establishment' *partit*, have more prestigeful occupations than their rivals in the secondary, or 'opposition', *partit*. The latter tend to be less well-educated and more solidly working class (and more generally Labour supporters).[24] In Kirkop, for example, I found in 1960 that 83 per cent of the village's professional and white-collar workers belonged to the *partit* of 'St Leonard', the parish titular saint. The corresponding figure for 'St Joseph' members was 17 per cent. Conversely, of the village's farmers, 62 per cent supported 'St Joseph' and 38 per cent 'St Leonard'.[25]

In view of the way that membership of a *partit* is inherited rather than chosen,[26] the position the founding generation occupied in the village's class structure in some way influenced their choice of *partit*. Frequent marriages to outsiders, emigration, and the changing employment structure of the country during the past century have blurred this picture. But the underlying pattern is pronounced, and is repeated in almost every town divided by this type of rivalry.

In Kirkop I was also told that many young people joined the secondary *partit* when it was founded. The new secondary *partiti* must have appealed more to those who, for whatever reason, held no offices in the older confraternities or band clubs and/or did not form part of the circle who surrounded the parish priest and organized village affairs. Through the new cult and band club they could gain office and perform organizational activities which gave them greater prominence and a resultant higher status. In short, the secondary *partiti* appealed to the poor, the marginal, the young, and those seeking higher status.

I believe these *partiti* were a form of opposition to established authority, an expression of protest against the monopoly of power by the establishment cliques focused on the parish priests. The second half of the nineteenth century was a period of great social upheaval. In Malta, as elsewhere in Europe, there was a surge of nationalism. There was also an active, though diffuse working-class movement that propagated an egalitarian ideology of the brotherhood of all men. This new ideology questioned established authority. It reached the Maltese urban area first. It seeped into the villages through the industrial areas around the Grand Harbour, where ex-agriculturists worked together as wage labourers with workers from the Three Cities. It was expressed at the national level by means of the support that the working classes gave to the pro-English language reforms. These reforms were opposed by their rivals, in class terms, the ecclesiastical, legal, and university establishments that supported Italian.[27] The radical teaching of Manwel Dimech was another expression of this stirring of the working classes.[28]

I suggest a third manifestation of the same movement can be found in the establishment of secondary *partiti*. Besides the class-biased composition of the secondary *partiti* and their occasional political alignment, I think there is further evidence for my contention that they reflected this pro-working class sentiment. I have already noted that a number of the *partiti* were dedicated to St Joseph. He is the patron saint of the working classes, and was declared patron of the Catholic Church in 1870. There are many signs that the devotion to the saint was very strong in nineteenth-century Malta. There were many new confraternities dedicated to him after 1850 (among others in Naxxar, Għargħur, Kirkop, and Xagħra) and he was chosen as patron of the new parishes of Kalkara, Qala, and Msida — all towns located on or near harbours. Moreover, four parishes have secondary feasts dedicated to him (Rabat, Għaxaq, Kirkop, and Żebbuġ). Besides these, Għargħur, Siġġiewi, and Mosta had St Joseph *partiti* which succumbed to the 1935 Church regulations.

V CONCLUSION

To sum up my argument then, I find no evidence that the British introduced or stimulated *festa partiti*. *Festa partiti* arose as part of the expansion of *festa* activities and the establishment of Italianate band clubs during the second half of the last century. Intense participation in *festa* activities stimulated factional division over details of the celebration of various saints. In a few cases bands changed to show their pro-British political allegiance. But this change occurred long after the clubs themselves were established. Britain did not stimulate this division, or in other ways foment rivalry between clubs and *partiti* for political purposes. Rather, it is obvious that Britain supported the Church's efforts to limit the rivalry between *partiti* by providing police assistance to the parish priests' attempts to enforce the 1935 regulations designed to reduce secondary feasts. Yet, as noted, these secondary *partiti* were generally more pro-British than their rivals. Nevertheless, their activities were curtailed and several were suppressed.

If there is no evidence for the widely-held belief that Britain introduced *festa* and band-club rivalry for political reasons, why does this belief persist? To begin with, it is an attempt to explain this intriguing polarity that even to insiders often seems illogical. Secondly, British colonialism provides a convenient scapegoat to explain to outsiders the petty factionalism of the *partiti*. The blame for the often excessive and absurd actions of the *partiti*, of which many are ashamed, can conveniently be placed on an outsider. Thirdly, I suggest that the *divide et impera* conspiracy explanation reflects the degree to which current thinking in Malta about society has become politicized by the bitter political antagonism which has corroded social life for the past decades. It is a projection on the past of current models of conceptualizing social action. Malta's two political parties now resemble *festa partiti* in their pettiness and the absurdity of their excesses, and politicians manipulate parochial divisions for electoral ends.

This brings me to the final reason why it is most unlikely that British administrators manipulated parochial issues to further colonial policy. To manipulate parochial rivalry demands insight into local values and culture. I suggest that British colonial officers in Malta did not have this knowledge. They, unlike their counterparts in India, Africa, and South East Asia, never learned the vernacular language. They relied upon information and advice on local affairs provided by Maltese employees. These were recruited from the urbanized, upper-class élite who, even today, are astoundingly ignorant of the culture of those who engage in *festa partiti* rivalry. The way in which information on local affairs was selected, fed to, or withheld from British administrators in colonial Malta might be well worth examining systematically.[29]

NOTES

* The argument in this paper was first presented to evening BA students in History and Mediterranean Studies at the University of Malta in June 1987 and to the Malta Rotary Club a month later. I am grateful for their helpful comments. The Faculty of Education of the University of Malta kindly provided the hospitality during sabbatical leave from my own university which enabled me to prepare this discussion. Nettie Westerhuis transcribed the dictated manuscript.

[1] G.P. Badger, *Description of Malta and Gozo*, 98.
[2] L. de Boisgelin, *Ancient and Modern Malta;* M. Miège, *Histoire de Malte.*
[3] J. Cassar Pullicino, *Studies in Maltese Folklore*, 15.
[4] Ibid., 36.
[5] J. Bezzina, *Religion and Politics in a Crown Colony*, 136.
[6] *Ġiahan* (1846-47).
[7] P.P. Castagna, *Lis Storia ta Malta. Bil Gzejjer Tahha*, 248-9.
[8] Concilium Regionale Melitense (1935), *Decreta*, 91.
[9] J. Boissevain, *Saints and Fireworks*, 149 *et seq.*
[10] Ibid., 78, 79, 149 *et seq.*
[11] J. Boissevain, 'Ritual Escalation in Malta', 165-184.
[12] M. Silverman, R.F. Salisbury (eds.), *A House Divided?.*
[13] G. Pitrè, *Feste Patronali in Sicilia*, xlviii *et seq.*, 273 *et seq.*
[14] Castagna, 128.
[15] C.A. Price, *Malta and the Maltese*, 105 *et seq.*
[16] R. Mifsud Bonnici, *Ġrajja ta' Baned f'Malta u Għawdex*, i, 38 *et seq.*
[17] Boissevain, *Saints and Fireworks*, 75-96; id., *Friends of Friends*, 192-4, 210-12; id., *A Village in Malta*, 82-6.
[18] H. Frendo, *Party Politics in a Fortress Colony*, 15 *et seq.*
[19] Ibid., 125.
[20] E.B. Vella, *Storja ta' Birkirkara Bil-Kolleġġata Tagħha*, 498 *et seq.*
[21] Mifsud Bonnici, 79.
[22] Ibid., 97.
[23] My thanks to J. Agius for providing valuable introductions.
[24] Boissevain, *Saints and Fireworks*, 83.
[25] Ibid., 84, 94.
[26] Ibid., 82 *et seq.*
[27] Frendo, *passim.*
[28] H. Frendo, *Birth Pangs of a Nation.*
[29] My own experience with Colonial Malta is interesting in this respect. In 1960 I received a grant from the British Colonial Social Science Research Council to explore village culture and politics in Malta. In November 1961 I presented a 40-page report in triplicate on my research to the Colonial Office. I, naïvely as it turned out, supposed that this expensive report would be read with interest by those in Malta and the Colonial Office charged with administering the islands. To the best of my knowledge all three copies of the report disappeared without trace into the great maw of the Colonial Office. They apparently did not find their way to Malta. Well over a year after submitting my report, Governor Sir Maurice Dorman, who knew I had been carrying out research in Malta for the CSSRC, asked me if I had ever written a report. If so, he would like to read it, for he wanted to understand more about the country of which he was soon to become Governor-General. I loaned him my personal copy.

12

DOMINIC CUTAJAR / EMMANUEL FIORENTINO

Trends and Influences in Maltese Art 1800-1964

Part One: 1800-60

Artistic Crisis and New Ideals

The eviction from Malta of the Order of St John brought to an abrupt end an epoch of Maltese history. Significantly, it coincided with an irresistible movement of social renewal that was then sweeping across Europe. One may argue that, to a large extent, the misfortunes of nineteenth-century Malta were the result of its exclusion from the socio-cultural life of the continent as a result of its new colonial status. The blockade of 1798-1800 had shaken the country's social structure, while its economy was eventually ruined by the termination of Napoleon's Continental System in 1812 and the outbreak of plague the following year.

Still, the British colonial administration succeeded in entrenching itself through a tacit accomodation with the Church, the landed gentry, and the commercial class. In effect, a cultural *status quo* was reached, in which the prestige and authority of the hierarchy and of a decorous 'notability' became the paramount features of a frozen social establishment. Feeble ripples of discontent, largely roused by the 1830 and 1848 revolutions in Europe, led to the grant of the first elected representation of 1849. But throughout the first half-century of British rule, the aspirations of the nascent nationalism of the Maltese were thwarted by local British officialdom.

The general stagnation of Maltese art throughout the nineteenth century was conditioned by general cultural considerations and socio-political developments. Isolated from the increasingly emancipated culture of Europe, local efforts were confined within traditional and insular limits – for the great part, condemned to a sickly, stunted growth. Taken all together, nineteenth-century Maltese art leaves one with the disturbed sensation of a narrow, ecclesiastical art; by and large, a provincial exercise. The best of it is marked by features of intense introspection, a kind of inner migration, that often tends towards a barren rarefaction, and practically always a form of escapism. It also hints at a morbid fear of contamination with matter, particularly in the art of the first half of the nineteenth century, later lapsing into an effete avowal of a romanticized idealism recoiling from reality.

The phenomenon is not rare in the history of art. One senses a subconscious drive to avoid contact with commonplace reality, an attempt to purge one's mind of a flood of harsher images. In such circumstances, art becomes a palliative, nourishing a private vision of a remote world that, like Plato's Republic, is ordained by immanent fatalistic norms and moderated by an austere aestheticism. The situation was further aggravated by the instinct of Maltese artists to look no further than Rome, and which persevered in imbibing the artistic culture of the equally paralysed provinces of southern Italy, to which for centuries they had constantly turned for guidance. In the decades under consideration, the art of these very provinces became increasingly detached from the mainstream of development, becoming in effect backwaters under the equally reactionary rule of Papal and Bourbon administrations.

I DEVELOPMENTS IN ROME AND NAPLES

It is necessary to take a cursory look at the nature of Romanticism as an artistic movement, noting the frustrated course of its development within the Italian peninsula; for although it would be a grave error to infer that the crisis of Maltese nineteenth-century art was an imported phenomenon, yet it is immediately obvious that Maltese nineteenth-century artists continued to receive influential justification for their artistic stand from the aesthetic tendencies in contemporary Italy.

Neo-classicism, the intellectual and aesthetic trend which dealt a death-blow to the baroque and rococo, was itself a complex ideology. On one hand it set out – in Johann Joachim Winckelmann's own words – 'to imitate antiquity', to acquire through the disciplined study of antiquity the right aesthetic approach to attain 'the true style'. The emphasis on study led to the proliferation of academies where 'new' canonical rules were taught, so that artists were expected 'to dip their brush in intellect' – another pregnant phrase of Winckelmann.

In so doing neo-classicism inevitably nurtured the cult of heroic endeavour as a means of self-liberation. As early as 1754, La Font de Saint Yenne encouraged the study of Plutarch's *Lives* because it could provide a whole gallery 'of virtuous and heroic actions of great men, examples of ... passionate zeal for the honour and safety of their country.' Even Rousseau, Europe's first great Romantic, decried these 'perverted' tastes of the eighteenth century. In his famous Dijon essay, he condemned rococo art because it did not represent 'the men who defended their country, or those still greater who enriched it by their genius.'

The seed of the Romantic movement lies precisely in this repressed yearning for heroic fulfilment, opening up new vistas of spiritual and political liberation, and of personal emancipation. Precisely for this reason, it was to prove such a potent and explosive mixture, a heady philosophy that ended one phase of European civilization.

Its most earth-shaking consequence was of course the French Revolution that had stirred up in Italy great hopes of a national awakening, dashed largely by Napoleon's self-aggrandizing mania. With the Vienna Settlement of 1815, the Italian territory was parcelled out mainly among a number of principalities dominated by a massive Austrian military presence. As a result, Italian intellectuals found themselves compelled to wage a rearguard fight to revive Italian nationalism.

The latter struggle was to last the better part of the century, with negative effects on the development of much of Italian culture, particularly in artistic achievement. For, owing to the concentration of efforts to achieve national liberation, the loyalty of Italian artists to the Romantic sensibility could never be whole-hearted or sufficiently profound. The theme of liberation, as a fundamental experience of self-consciousness, lies at the very core of the Romantic experience. It is this self-appraisal that failed to become the object of contemplation among Italian artists of the first half of the nineteenth century.

As a result, Italian nineteenth-century art found itself side-tracked in the general evolutionary pattern of European art, continuing to fall further behind as time progressed. One necessary corollary of this situation was the inadequacy of Italian art in exerting a corrective influence on the numerous Maltese artists who, during the entire course of the century, had proceeded to the mainland seeking artistic guidance.

Nevertheless, within the limits of this discouraging picture, there always was an element of individual choice offered by the dichotomy of religious and lay accentuations. So, by noting the personal choice affected by individual Maltese artists, one can also arrive at the basic disposition assimilated from the native artistic environment.

The main centres of Italian artistic endeavours were Rome, Naples, Florence, and northern Italy. Rome had ceased to be the great centre which it had been during the sixteenth century; yet it remained an obligatory stage for German, French, and English artists, as well as for provincial Italians. By comparison, neither the developments in Lombardy nor those in Florence appear to have impinged visibly on the artistic formation of Maltese painters, while events in Rome and, to a lesser extent, in Naples determined the entire aesthetic orientation of Maltese nineteenth-century art by overlaying a native disposition that was already emotionally and temperamentally akin.

Although Rome had ceased to dictate the artistic taste of the times, it provided an artistic forum during the first quarter of the nineteenth century. Antonio Canova had returned to Rome in 1799, remaining there practically up to his death which took place in Venice on 13 October 1822. Ingres won his *Prix de Rome* in 1801, moving to that metropolis in October 1806 and only leaving it in 1820. Among the host of lesser artists, Francesco Hayez studied and worked in Rome from 1809 to 1817. The German Nazarener group, headed by Fredrick Overbeck, settled in Via Gregoriana – practically next door to Ingres's studio – in the autumn of 1810.

The *Accademia di San Luca* was so dominated by Canova's

personality that in 1814 it altered its own rules to nominate him as its *Principe perpetuo.* He had founded the *Concorso dell'Anonimo,* a prize for pupils at the *Accademia,* the 1813 edition of which was won by Hayez in face of stiff competition from thirteen other candidates, including Ingres, Schnechts, Pielli, and Tommaso Minardi. Nearly all these artists were to come into some form of contact with the Maltese students then studying in Rome, exerting a great formative influence on their art.

The group that most fascinated these young and impressionable Maltese artists were not, however, the *Accademia* neo-classicists, but a number of German expatriates, known as the Nazareners. Originally founded as the *Lucasbund* in Vienna (1809), they moved in Rome late in 1810 where, after some years of peregrination, they made the former convent of St Isidoro the community's headquarters.[1] Their ideal was to live in a brotherhood of Christian artists (most of the original German nucleus were converts from Protestantism or Judaism) and to restore the ideal of a truly religious and Christian art, taking as their model the Italian art of the quattrocento, especially the Umbrian school.

The heart of the movement was Fredrick Overbeck (1789-1869), who was flanked by Peter von Cornelius, Philipp Weit, Schnorr von Carolsfeld, Wilhelm Schadow, L. Vogel, and F. Pforr. Their reforming zeal soon took on the character of a crusade, arousing considerable lay opposition. Hegel was to charge them with concentrating far more on saving their souls than on their art. Such was the dearth of novel ideas among neo-classicists, that Nazarener influence penetrated the *Accademia* itself, up to then the ultimate bastion of neo-classicism. In a short time they recruited a considerable following of Italian artists who diluted their classicism accordingly. These included Pietro Tenerani, Tommaso Minardi, and Luigi Mussini, while other sympathizers included the Neapolitans Domenico Morelli and Giuseppe Mancinelli. These were to be the direct mentors of practically all Maltese artists of the nineteenth century, from Giuseppe Hyzler (d.1858) to Giuseppe Cali (d.1930).

The importance of the Nazarener movement for the development of Maltese art can hardly be overrated. Yet, in terms of real accomplishment, the contribution of the

Nazareners to art in general must be counted infinitesimal. In conjunction with the kindred artistic school known as puristi, headed by Tommaso Minardi, they attempted a futile and irrelevant compromise between neo-classical academism and that obscure mysticism innate to Romantic sentiment. What they really accomplished was an 'exorcism' of those pagan elements inherent in neo-classicism, an operation they consciously saw as an act of purification — whence their general denomination, puristi.

In essence, both Goethe and Hegel were not far from the truth in indicating their artistic irrelevance. Yet the Nazareners did perform one important service to art, even if perhaps unconsciously. They succeeded in arousing interest in 'primitive' manifestations of art, destined to become one of the great artistic rages at the turn of the century. It is curious that of all the Maltese followers of the Nazareners, none ever exhibited the slightest interest in the latter development.

The Roman school of the nineteenth century was therefore characterized by three artistic tendencies: the rigid neo-classicism of the *Accademia* descended from Mengs via Canova; the purismo of Tommaso Minardi and Pietro Tenerani that accepted the exorcism of the neo-classical tradition affected by the Nazarener 'ideology'; and the Nazareners themselves, an out-and-out revivalist movement heavily impregnated with Christian mysticism. All three currents won the adherence of individual Maltese artists studying in Rome, although it did not take long for Nazarener influence to predominate in Maltese art.

The Neapolitan artistic scene had a very different evolution from that of the Roman school, owing mainly to the deeply ingrained interest in naturalism among Neapolitan artists. The latter trait had its root in the Caravaggism of the early years of the seventeenth century, reinforced by a strong Spanish influence, becoming a veritable form of realism because of the activities of several Dutch genre painters. On this account, the Neapolitan realistic tradition flourished notably in genre and landscape painting, contrasting with the celebrative mood of Neapolitan baroque.

French and northern European landscape painters found Naples and its hinterland an irresistible attraction, largely owing to Salvator Rosa's reputation as a master of the picturesque, suggested by his various *paesaggi con banditi*. Further refined by Claude-Joseph Vernet (1714-89) who frequently achieved a 'sublime' interpretation, the tradition reached a full Romantic transfiguration with Jacob Philipp Hackert (1737-1807). William Turner visited Naples at least twice, in 1823 and in 1828,[2] while the Dutch Antonius Pitloo spent years teaching in the city, where he died in 1837. Both had liberated the art of landscape painting and made it a genuine vehicle of Romantic transfiguration.

A more explicit Romantic key characterizes the landscapes of Gabriele Smargassi (1798-1882), a pupil of Pitloo, and, even more, those of Giacinto Gigante (1806-76) in whose art the *macchia* is creatively used for poetic purposes, contrary to the intents of the *Macchiaioli* school of Florence of the 1860s, where interest was purely realistic. The naturalism of the Neapolitan painters reaches its peak in the veristic animal painting of Filippo Palizzi (1813-99), as well as in the works of Giuseppe de Nittis (1846-84) and his Pertici circle.

In sharp contrast, Domenico Morelli (1826-1901) and Giuseppe Mancinelli (1812-75), both former sympathizers of the Nazareners, predictably moved in an anti-realist direction, lending a warm grandiloquence, clothed in a theatrical Romantic envelope, to their religious-historical work. They exactly complemented Hayez, with his glacial, but otherwise parallel, romantically florid *mise-en-scène*.

The four foreign-born Schranz artists were touched at more than one point in their development by the Neapolitan landscape tradition, particularly at the moment it was achieving its Romantic transformation through Hackart. The romanticized vision of nature, typical of Smargassi and Gigante, is the basic influence in the art of Girolamo Gianni (1837-95) as well as in that of Vincenzo D'Esposito (1886-1946), the latter receiving it from his father Giacomo.[3]

The Neapolitan tradition encountered another artist with a Maltese background in Giuseppe Cali (1846-1930), who studied in Naples under Mancinelli and assimilated heavily the influence of Morelli, so that his art never ceased to reflect the sweet Romantic theatricality of their manner.

This brief survey indicates that practically all artists – both native and foreign-born – who were active in Malta during the nineteenth century were solely attracted by the schools that developed in Rome and Naples, showing an instinctive preference for the more involuted art developments in these two centres.

The air of crisis, implicit in the development of Italian nineteenth-century art, was not guilelessly imported into the more modest Maltese environment. A definite choice was made, one that can be read to assert a congenital aversion to all contacts with realism whenever a choice seemed available. In the case of the Roman schools, it was increasingly the Nazarener ideology that was overwhelmingly embraced. A similar relation obtained in Malta's artistic contacts with Naples, except for the foreign-born Schranzes, all four of whom were already adults by the time they settled in Malta;[4] all contacts with the Neapolitan naturalistic tradition were carefully shunned, and in fact never succeeded in filtering into Maltese art.

II THE MALTESE AESTHETIC IDEAL

At this stage it is advisable to examine the aesthetic notions that inspired Maltese art of the nineteenth century. A fair amount of critical comment had begun to be published − a feature distinguishing nineteenth-century art from that of previous centuries, although in matters of historiography, the information they preserve of the past is generally suspect and often notoriously unreliable.

Two extensive historical accounts presume to cover Maltese art history, in part containing a comment on the contemporary scene. The first, the *Discorso sulla storia artistica di Malta*, published in 1850, was written by Stefano Zerafa, Professor of Medicine at the University.[5] Written in the inflated oratorical manner of the time − it was in fact delivered as a 'panegyric' at the University − the work is of little worth. However considerable Zerafa's merits as a botanist may have been, as a historian he cuts a modest figure, lacking altogether a critical acumen. Not only does he misrepresent his (generally secondary) sources; he also contributes not a few prejudices of his own. When it comes to the contemporary scene, he suddenly turns niggard, alleging his reluctance to offend the artists' modesty.

So his value as a contemporary art historian is practically self-nullified.

The second published text, the *Malta Artistica Illustrata* by Canon Vincenzo Caruana dei Conti Gatto, appeared in 1906. Although sharing the same uncritical approach, it is a safer historical record and has preserved a substantial, even if rather dry, account of nineteenth-century Maltese art, bringing the story down to the time to Giuseppe Calì and Lazzaro Pisani, both of whom were competing with Attilio Palombi (1860-1912) for local Church commissions. In common with the trend of the time, Caruana Gatto exhibits interest in this type of art and in portraiture only, except for a brief dry paragraph on Giovanni Schranz, a passing reference to the *quadri di fiori in acquarello* by Giorgio Giuseppe Bonavia, and a bare five lines on Amodeo Preziosi's work in Constantinople – erroneously giving his name as Roberto. The rest of the account deals exclusively with Church art.

A third source, in manuscript form, has survived. Around 1850, there appears to have been a project afoot to reform the art classes in the Lyceum as an extension of the University which, in theory, was still obliged to impart also the principles of architecture. With this notion in mind, an unidentified but well-informed individual drafted a report for the Government's consideration.[6] Nothing appears to have materialized from these manoeuvres. The report not only provides a striking insight into the frustrations of teaching art in a country where cultural activities had been squeezed to suffocation by narrow considerations, but also throws a flood of light on those principles of aesthetics idealized by Malta's prevailing culture.

The writer traces back the new impulses that were to sweep away baroque art to the very dawn of the nineteenth century, attributing this change, rather surprisingly, to the presence of some volumes on classical art received by the National Library:

It is true that the publications on the Antiquities of Herculaneum and of the Pio-Clementine Museum, received by the Bibliotheca as gifts from the Pontiff and the King of Naples, had impressed with better ideas on the forms of decoration, so that from that time such admirers of the Ancients found among the Knights and the Maltese could easily anticipate a general and imminent change. Fortunately for us, they also inspired Mgr Caruana (University Rector from 1800) who, reasoning step by step, arrived at the main conclusion that a School was needed which would shed a strong guiding light on Art and Industry.

The anonymous writer goes on to explain the school's original curriculum and how it gradually fell away from the expected standard, a theme we shall presently return to. In the preamble, he volunteers to give a brief outline of contemporary developments in art as a frame for the aesthetic ideas held in nineteenth-century Malta:

For a broader understanding of our subject, I believe it is proper to give in a brief form some ideas of the contemporary progress in the Continent as regards the pursuit of the Fine Arts. The Christian arts have established the first movement, having turned their back on all forms of baroque (*barocchismo*) which has ruined not only the arts, but even those norms with which to restore them. Young artists from Germany travelled to Rome to meditate mutely and thoughtfully on the Vatican frescoes; spending whole hours of the day in this intellectual contemplation, they were able to draw a comparison with the methods of the modern academies, of modern artists and their teachings. In this way they discerned an infinite difference between the high works of their meditation and modern works of art.[7]

The writer then explains how 'constancy and brave German patience' were blended with Italian vivacity 'to return to the system of studies of their forefathers'. The craze for the Antique at the heart of neo-classicism that had become 'the ruling fashion of the Republican and Consular' establishments was outrightly condemned as a return to paganism. Emphasis was instead made on 'severe drawing, great attention and faithfulness in copying from nature, and on the discrediting of the Academy's pretensions' in correcting figure drawing, presumably an oblique condemnation of classical idealism.

Next, the author outlines briefly the rise of purismo among members of the *Accademia,* betraying an intimate knowledge of developments in Rome between 1810 and 1820. He then observes:

With the premise of the foregoing short and detailed note, it is proper to add that the Movement as such, intended to bring about a general revolution of ideas regarding the pursuit of the arts, was as yet unknown here among our people.[8]

He further charges that the inadequate preparation imparted

by the University class of Drawing served little purpose, so that
Maltese students sent to Rome received adverse comments and
were able to make headway solely thanks to the wise guidance
of their Roman mentors, thus producing excellent works of art:
'Freed from baroque-ism and from the stench of Voltairianism
that had infected people with a hatred of religion, these works
spread instead a joyful tide.'[9]

The report — which the present writer believes to have been
drawn up by Giuseppe Hyzler, particularly because of the
identity of aesthetic ideas — accurately reflects the intellectual
climate of nineteenth-century Maltese society. The cordial
relations between the colonial administration and the Church
authorities produced an inward-looking culture compounded of
obscurantism and reactionary political attitudes that
intellectually insulated Maltese society from the dynamic
growth of European culture. The report also delineates, with an
incisive eloquence of its own, the artistic horizon of at least four
generations of Maltese artists, defining the aesthetic programme
they were to follow faithfully. This included the following
relevant points:

1. An anathemizing of baroque exuberance, as well as a deeply-
felt condemnation of the pagan aspects (i.e. the sensuality) of
neo-classicism.

2. An insistence on 'severe' drawing, at times described as
'chaste', seemingly implying a very restricted use of chiaroscuro,
evidently to diminish the level of allure.

3. A declared aim to 'revive' a truly religious ideal in art; art
lacking a religious sentiment was deemed either useless or
irrelevant.

4. In spite of the stated aim to copy faithfully from nature, in
effect they disdained naturalism. Nature to the Purist circle had
a polemical connotation, and was used merely as a foil to the
idealism of the neo-classicists.

These views were being constantly asserted and re-asserted
in Malta throughout the nineteenth century until they became
idées fixes, to the great harm of Maltese art, especially Church
art. There is a plethora of such declarations to choose from,
starting with Giorgio Grognet (1774-1862) who, in his erratic
way, was a truer classicist than most of his Maltese

contemporaries and very likely out of sympathy with Nazarener ideology; yet he was vehement and insistent in decrying *il cattivo gusto Borrominesco*.[10] Another practising artist, Giuseppe Calleja − one of Hyzler's protégés as well as a sententious dilettante − never missed a chance to hit out at baroque taste. In his biographical sketch of Rocco Buhagiar (where, as usual, his imagination embroiders the facts), he apologizes for the early training Buhagiar received from Arnau 'who had instilled in him the first notions of drawing according to the miserable method of the time'.[11]

Similarly, in a report carried by *L'Ordine* of 17 February 1854 concerning the uncovering of the vault-paintings in the church of St Paul Shipwrecked − at first carried out by Antonio Falson under the direction of Giuseppe Hyzler, but finished by Letterio Subba − the reporter could not help drawing a comparison with Preti's vault-paintings in St John's, adding insensitively 'in spite of this unfavourable circumstance'.

The same crude dogmatism was even applied to drawing techniques, with sometimes ridiculous effects, as in one of Giuseppe Calleja's interminable harangues on aspects of art. He expounds on the use of the chiaroscuro: 'The chiaroscuro of one colour, varied only for the purpose of creating the effect of chiaroscuro, is not painting ... The use of chiaroscuro is necessary for theatrical scenarios and feast-decorations.'[12]

The artist's religious commitment was rated at least as highly as his artistic merits: his brush was expected to exude spirituality with each stroke. In this sphere, Giuseppe Hyzler was held up as a veritable paragon. His brother Vincenzo, a retiring figure about whose art little is factually known, is reputed to have had spectacular spiritual qualities: 'his life was one of total unworldliness, devoid of passions and spent in meditation and thinking.'[13] But in spite of his insignificant contribution to art, the same text confirms that he had *il genio d'un ristauratore profondo*.

Giuseppe Hyzler's obituary makes a useful point when it explains that he was 'respectful ... particularly towards the ministers of the church'.[14] But he was also

the friend and colleague of the most celebrated artists of the time ... the friend of Viet, Cornelius, Overbeck, Tenerani, Thorwaldsen, Minardi, and Canova ... Hence derives the superiority of our Hyzler to the common brethren, and it accounts for his aesthetic genius, for his excellence in philosophy and in the history of art. [15]

According to a contemporary source, 'Hyzler has already given us the first models of a *gusto* that is truly Christian, transmitting onto his canvases a profound religious sentiment.[16] In point of fact, Hyzler was an artist who possessed solid and considerable artistic merits as well as an apparently spiritual life of his own. One has, however, to clear the ground of the rank undergrowth that has grown around his figure before reaching the flowering bush.

The same craze to emphasize a palpable religious appeal marks the contemporary comments on works of other lesser artists, as Tommaso Madiona, Antonio Falson, Salvatore Barbara, Carlo Darmanin, Ignazio Cortis, and of the ubiquitous Giuseppe Calleja. Even as serious an artist as Michele Bellanti was not above this prejudice. A comment on a work of his, solemnly asserted that 'in the painting there dominates through all its composition and through its colours a serene religiosity, the chief specialization of the artist's own studies.'[17]

Yet this chorus of voices, with its hysterical insistence on the Christian renewal of the arts, did not go uncontested, although the number of dissidents were few and always sounded like shrill voices in the wilderness. A commentator in *The Malta Times*, writing in 1840, took a long hard look at the state of the arts in Malta, and then came out with a harsh, unambiguous judgement: 'The arts in Malta are nearly stagnant or wholly so'; he reviews in particular the progress of architecture and discovers that 'in fact it has degenerated from that of the Order'.[18]

The most persistent, the most intelligent and dogged opponent of this opaque system of aesthetics was Dr Nicola Zammit (1815-99), a neo-classical architect of considerable repute and real merit, apart from being a discerning and articulate critic. He had married a daughter of Giovanni Schranz's (1794-1882), thereby aligning himself with a group that included the Schranzes, Preziosi, the Brockdorffs, and a few others who felt temperamentally ill-at-ease in the suffocating world of Nazarener aesthetics. Zammit tried hard, using lucid arguments, to stem the tide of the 'restoration' zeal unleashed by Nazarener sympathizers, although his efforts appear to have left no visible effect. Tolerant, urbane, gifted with sensitive and acute critical faculties, he figures as the clearest-headed, as well as the unhappiest, intellectual of the Maltese nineteenth-century milieu.

In 1864 Dr Zammit contributed to *L'Arte* a strange kind of biography of Francesco Zahra, a rococo artist of the previous century and probably Malta's greatest painter of the past. Zahra has been particularly badly served by the inept historiography and art criticism of the eighteenth and nineteenth centuries, a lamentable situation that threatens to become a tradition for it has proceeded on the same confused course down to our days. Dr Zammit, faced with the dearth of reliable biographical information, grasped the occasion to defend the integrity of baroque aesthetics which, as a neo-classicist, he recognized as a thing of the past, and launched a withering attack, laden with irony, on the disembodied aesthetic pretensions of his Maltese contemporaries.

[Zahra's] method [writes Nicola Zammit] would today be termed baroque, and perhaps it is, in the accepted meaning of the word. But is it on this account further from the truth, less impressive and artistic? Art has been frozen dead ever since the use of the compass and the slide-rule was imported into art. An interpretative zeal that rests upon metaphysical subtleties has proclaimed the rule of the spirit in religious art, decrying the sensualism of the form. In the present craze for mummies, for rods dressed in clothes with vertical pleats, and in the taste for sickly figures afflicted with consumption, in fact in the negation of all that is wholesome and attractive, it is thought to have discovered the origin of the sublime, terming as divine that which good sense reveals as deformed. If this kind of hieroglyphic painting assists contemplation, it cannot leave any impression, nor represent anything fine even when it hints at it. In the poverty and harshness of the style, in the abstinence of the senses, in its aversion to the finite, it claims to reveal an infinity. Francesco Zahra did not belong to this sect that came into being after his time, inspired not so much by an ascetic refinement, as by a sterile imagination compelled to interpret silence as eloquence, renunciation as sublime, and poverty of art as divine.[19]

Sensible and forthright as it is, Dr Zammit's earnest appeal fell on deaf ears. As late as 1910, Giuseppe Calleja, writing in the *Malta Letteraria,* the most important cultural publication of the time, gave voice to the hardened aesthetic consensus still widely embraced in Malta. He condemned the rivals of the

Nazarener restoration ('restorers of good taste') in these terms:

So that subsequent to the malicious manoeuvres of these adversaries, the defences repeatedly built by these new restorers of good taste availed naught: in consequence, art fell into the lowest level of materialism, beginning with — if you will excuse me the expression — the stupid Verismo whose sole merit is its enormous distance from all that is true (vero), beautiful, and good.

Throughout the nineteenth century, Nazarener influence in Malta prevailed in one guise or another; even the main Italian artists who were brought to work in Malta, or whose works were imported, were followers of the Nazareners. The two principal Maltese painters of the later nineteenth century, Giuseppe Cali and Lazzaro Pisani (1854-1932), had both studied under former pupils of Minardi — Cali under Giuseppe Mancinelli, Pisani under Luigi Fontana, both Maltese painters then falling respectively under the spell of Domenico Morelli and Domenico Bruschi — two more artists of Nazarener extraction who had been mellowed by Romanticism.

In the last decade of the nineteenth century and the early ones of the twentieth, the vapid fervour of Nazarener-inspired art tended slowly to merge with some of the more miasmal late Romantic formulae, each in turn yearning for a concretization of some vague, indiscernible ideal. These basically mystic yearnings — which Nicola Zammit was right in analysing as metaphysical in character, a definition that can be stretched to later forms of Romanticism — did in fact occasionally produce works of art worthy of serious consideration. For the spirit did genuinely move these tormented souls, and the best and more gifted of them struggled with it valiantly, distilling spiritual messages from the anguish of their hearts. The phenomenon succeeds in telling us something of those hard times; at the same time it is bereft of social relevance, except in a narrow and purely negative sense, since it speaks with rare eloquence of a flight, a desperate attempt at escape, from an unpleasant and discouraging reality.

III THE HISTORICAL DEVELOPMENT

The essential historical account of Malta's artistic development
in the nineteenth century can be told in few enough words as
it was fairly homogeneous in character. Artistic excellence had
been reached in the course of the eighteenth century with the
flowering of the Maltese rococo, particularly with Francesco
Zahra (d.1773) and Gio. Nicola Buhagiar (d.1752). As already
intimated, the growth of neo-classicism had been anticipated in
Malta. The 1850 *relazione* had suggested that neo-classicism in
Malta was introduced with the publications on the Herculaneum
antiquities as well as those of the Pio-Clementine Museum.

Such a view is, however, insufficient. Another important factor
had been the presence on the island of Antoine de Favray
(d.1798), a painter of the French Grand Manner who, like most
French artists, had an innate bent for classicism. Favray had
in fact studied with J.F. de Troy in Rome, to where Ingres moved
in 1806; in fact, some of Favray's later works clearly anticipate
the lucid classical line of Ingres. By way of contrast, Zahra was
unable to assimilate the new tendencies, as classicism with its
emphasis on restraint was so antithetical to the exuberance of
his temperament. Yet some of Zahra's followers transferred
themselves to the 'school' of Favray, among them Giuseppe Pace
(1744- after 1807) and Antonio Xuereb (d.1805). Their older
contemporary, Rocco Buhagiar (d.1805) was able to moderate
somehow the manner of his Maltese rococo mentors, while his
brilliant pupil, Giuseppe Grech (1755-87), moved from the circle
of Favray to the *Accademia di San Luca* in Rome where he was
to die prematurely. With time it is becoming clearer that Grech's
sudden death had robbed Maltese art of the best chance of
effecting a dignified, organic transition into nineteenth-century
art.

That responsibility next fell on the shoulders of Michele
Busuttil (*c.*1762-1831), a painter eminently unsuited for that
particular task owing to his confused eclecticism and to some
grave defect in his eyesight. According to the contradictory
account of Stefano Zerafa, who knew him well, Busuttil *era
eccellente nel disegno ma attesa la debolezza dei suoi occhi,
eseguiva non tanto bene le sue opere in grande.*[20]

Yet it was this very man who, on 1 November 1800, received

the appointment of Professor of Drawing in the newly-opened arts classes at the re-established University under its new rector, Canon F.S. Caruana. Busuttil was able to hold on to his post until 1831, gradually becoming an increasing embarassment as well as a grave liability as the 1850 *relazione* suggests.[21] The writer of that document claimed that Busuttil's method was to set his pupils the task of turning out highly-finished drawings *(disegni leccati)* which only a handful of the more gifted could do well.

In 1803 another Professor of Drawing was added '*con più abilità e migliori idee e disposizione per far meno scontento il pubblico*'.[22] The new personality was Giorgio Pullicino (1779-1852) who, in his first burst of enthusiasm, introduced lessons in sculpture and in architecture, as well as a great innovation, the first class of nude study to be established in Malta. But this innovative urge soon got him into serious trouble: the nude class was closed by the authorities, a measure that did not dampen Pullicino's spirits; in fact, he reopened it as a private class at his own residence. The stratagem brought the poor artist into greater social and official odium so that, throughout his forty years' career as teacher, his salary remained pegged at the 1803 level.

There was another more fundamental cause for the antipathy which Giorgio Pullicino had to put up with, to understand which one needs to examine Pullicino's aesthetic sympathies. Pullicino's family had firm, long-standing ties with the world of art; his uncle, Alberto Pullicino, was a highly appreciated *vedutista* of the eighteenth century,[23] which fact certainly inclined the young Giorgio to favour naturalism; in fact, he was later to enjoy a discreet reputation as a water-colour landscapist and as a miniaturist. From the workshop of the Busuttil family, he was sent in 1792 to the Roman *Accademia di San Luca* to study under Bernardino Nocchi at a time when neo-classicism reigned supreme and contemporaneous with Canova's first stay in Rome. Seven years later he returned to Malta.

Pullicino's professorial appointment held out great hopes for a truly modern turn in the art development of Malta. He had the right background, the necessary exposure to the latest developments, and the enthusiasm needed to carry out such a programme. It was the country's second chance of initiation in nineteenth-century art; yet all these hopes were dashed when the ruling colonial-clerical establishment discarded Pullicino's ideas one by one, leaving him no proper didactic tool except to urge drawing from a number of casts of classical models that he had imported from Rome. Even his attempts to teach architecture were nullified as the students came to his class without the essential preparation. He was left to plod on hopelessly and increasingly embittered, so that in 1830 he requested permission to practise as *agrimensore* in order to supplement his meagre salary. Practically all his attempts to obtain commissions as architect ended in failure, although his intelligent neo-classicism proved to be a cut above that of his rivals.[24]

Together with Giorgio Grognet, Pietro Paolo Caruana, Tommaso Madiona, and Antonio Falson, Pullicino signed with other local fellow-artists the political petition of 10 November 1836 in support of the demands of the *Comitato Generale Maltese* to effect some alleviation of Malta's harsh colonial conditions. It would not be amiss to recall that the Hyzlers and many of their followers did not subscribe to the document. The issue considerably clarifies the political stand and the ideological orientations of the figures concerned.

In effect, Giorgio Pullicino emerges as a victim of the oppressive intellectual atmosphere permeating nineteenth-century Malta. He was snubbed at every turn, cold-shouldered, and practically starved into submission – a manoeuvre that was already under way by 1810 – well before Giuseppe Hyzler had become a force to be reckoned with. His disgrace cannot thus be attributed to artistic jealousies: he suffered primarily for his classicist and progressive ideas that clashed with the 'restoration' policies pursued by the colonial administration and the Church authorities.

When Pietro Paolo Caruana (1793-1852) assumed the post upon the death of Michele Busuttil in 1831, his appointment was defined as 'teacher of Drawing at the Lyceum', a phrasing that indicates the demotion of the art class from the university to the secondary level of education, an arrangement that remained unaltered until after the grant of self-government in 1921. It thus ceased to influence the course of art development in Malta, in spite of the fact that the appointment often went to leading

Maltese artists, more as a sinecure than as a serious measure
to advance the progress of the arts.[25]

The lacuna in Malta's artistic tradition, created by the lack
of an organic continuity with the country's eighteenth-century
art as well as through the loss of the Order's cosmopolitanism,
necessitated some kind of remedial programme. The problem
was rendered even more urgent by the increasing ineffectiveness
of the Univeristy art classes. During the administration of Sir
Thomas Maitland, the Government was induced by Canon F.S.
Caruana to grant bursaries to Maltese art students to enable
them to proceed to Rome for studies at the *Accademia*.

The practice was unaccountably discontinued upon Maitland's
death, to the great detriment of local art, as the four recipients
of the bursaries had built up a solid reputation through the high
quality of their work and through the influence they were to
exert upon the Maltese artistic scene. The four beneficiaries of
the scholarships were Giuseppe Hyzler (1814), Giovanni
Farrugia (1817), Salvatore Busuttil (1818), and Pietro Paolo
Caruana (1819). Tommaso Madiona missed the 1824 bursary
through Maitland's sudden death, although he was able to raise
enough funds to proceed to Rome on his own.

Of these figures, Giuseppe Hyzler was the one who eventually
came to dominate Maltese art; his hegemony lasted nearly 40
years, during which time he successfully imposed his own
aesthetic ideas on the country. Strangely enough, no modern
analysis of Hyzler's personality and influence has so far been
attempted. Yet the impact of Hyzler's personality on Maltese
art was so thorough-going that his development and career have
to be explained in some detail, to note how typical a product he
was of his times and milieu, and how far-reaching his influence
turned out to be.

1. Giuseppe Hyzler (1787—1858)

The Hyzlers were in origin Bavarians from Deggendorff, a small
town on the Donau in Lower Bavaria between Ratisbon and
Fassau. They settled in Valletta in the first quarter of the
eighteenth century; it is thus likely that Giuseppe was aware
of the Bavarian origins of his great-grandfather Johann Fredrick
Risler (the surname was soon transformed to Leizer before

assuming the present form in the early years of the nineteenth century). This consideration might have played some part in Giuseppe's whole-hearted identification with the German nucleus of the Nazarener community. His father, Luigi Leizer, described as *bottegario,* died in 1828 and was long outlived by the wife, Antonia née Borg.

One of Giuseppe's sisters, Vincentia, had married in 1808 a certain Giovanni Galdies, described in the *Muir's Malta Almanack* for 1845 as an artist, who is also known to have been a close friend of Filippo Benucci, a friendship that stretches at least as far back as 1813. It seems likely that Benucci had exerted his considerable influence in persuading the authorities to award the 1813-14 Maitland bursary to Giuseppe Hyzler, by then already 26 years old.[26] If, therefore, the portrait of Sir Hildebrand Oakes, now in the National Library of Malta, was painted in 1811, as one may infer from the inscription, then it must rank amongst the earliest works of Hyzler that we know of. Yet, this is not the present writer's considered view.

At the *Accademia di San Luca,* which he joined in 1814 at the height of his neo-classicist ardour, Hyzler received instruction at the hands of Andrea Pozzo (b.1778) who was soon to be elected *principe* of the same *Accademia.* But, by natural inclination, the Maltese artist gravitated to the newly-formed Nazarener community headed by Fredrick Overbeck, an exposure that had a deep and lasting effect. The religious effervescence of the Nazareners' art, their ascetic idealism, and their retired way of life appeared to have struck an innate chord within Hyzler's heart, satisfying a deeply-felt inner craving for order and serenity, coupled with a burning religious sentiment.

Hyzler seems to have found his vocation and from that moment his art was made. Never again was he to experience the slightest hesitation or a flicker of doubt, following single-mindedly the marked path with all the ardour of a crusader. In those eight years in Rome he had learned a great deal. From the *Accademia* he absorbed a feeling for a clean, neo-classic line that also features in the art of Ingres, who left Rome in 1820. From the Nazareners he assimilated their taut ascetic vision, learning also to give his paintings a flat enamelled finish accomplished with minute, fine brush-work − a technique much favoured by the Nazareners, conscious as they were of the artisan side of art.

Hyzler returned to Malta on 19 August 1822[27] and does not seem to have experienced much difficulty in obtaining commissions. Before he had left for Rome, he had enjoyed a discreet reputation as an artist, since he had designed the relief-sculpture decorations above the main and side doors of the new Birkirkara parish church, finished in 1814. One of the first commissions after his return was the portrait of Pius VII ordered in 1823 by the collegiate canons of Cospicua. His services were sought for the most varied artistic works, including designs for altar-fronts, silver oil-lamps, and even sculptures in the round; the statue of St Gregory, standing in front of the old parish church of Żejtun, was in fact designed by Hyzler in 1838 and executed by Salvatore Dimech (1805-87).

Hyzler readily accepted the collaboration of assistants, a service he frequently resorted to, no doubt pressed by his numerous and varied commissions. At different times he employed as helpers and assistants his brother Vincenzo, Salvatore Micallef, Antonio Falson, and Giuseppe Calleja. The practice seems to have become more frequent after 1832 in part owing to an unknown infirmity – no better defined than as 'a nervous condition' – which forbade prolonged physical endeavour and was soon to play havoc with his painting activity. The practice of using collaborators was, however, widely diffused. The Nazarener community had undertaken, as a team, the fresco-decoration of Villa Massimi, among other works. Minardi, too, often worked in this fashion with his students, including some of the Maltese ones; while Pietro Gagliardi not infrequently made use of the services of his brother Giovanni.[28]

In 1832 Vincenzo Hyzler, Salvatore Micallef, Antonio Falson, and Michele Bellanti, under the direction of Giuseppe Hyzler, tried to work as a team to decorate the sanctuary area of the church of *Santa Maria di Gesù* in Valletta. The group, the hard core of the Maltese Nazareners, attempted the experiment of collective art as familiarized by the original Nazareners at Villa Massimi. Towards 1850 Giuseppe Hyzler was entrusted with a major operation, the vault-decoration of the church of St Paul Shipwrecked in Valletta. The actual execution was left to Antonio Falson, but the whole operation was ill-starred from the beginning. It proved to be so thorny that at one point Hyzler himself practically disowned Falson when the next work was nearing completion. Eventually, the authorities discharged Falson and commissioned instead a painter from Messina, a certain Letterio Subba who undertook to finish off painting the vault independently of Hyzler's original drawings. Nothing of this work, completed in 1854, has survived.[29]

After the 1851 disagreement with Falson, Hyzler (whose brother Vincenzo had died in 1849) took on as his assistant Giuseppe Calleja (1830-1915). Achille Ferris lists no less than nine paintings reportedly carried out by Calleja 'under the direction of Hyzler' who by this time seems to have been in no condition to intervene actively in the paintings which his studio kept turning out. It is the present writer's view that it would be both unfair, as well as an unkindness to Hyzler's artistic reputation, to assign these works to him; it would be even worse to judge his art by their standard when they merely contain his ideas.

In fact Calleja proved to be an unfortunate choice for, among his other ineptitudes, he was a singularly incompetent painter. The portrait of Governor Richard More O'Ferrall, now in the sacristy of the church of St Paul Shipwrecked, was painted by Calleja in 1858, a few months after Hyzler's death when Calleja could no longer rely on his guidance. It shows clearly where Calleja stood in art as soon as he was left to fend for himself, barely succeeding in rising above the level of popular art.

Probably Giuseppe Hyzler's chief claim on our gratitude is his direction of operations to restore St John's, the former conventual church of the Order of St John. This task entailed the renewal of the 400-odd marble memorial slabs covering the pavement,[30] an operation apparently concluded by 1833; it was kept covered with rushes which were removed for three days of each month to permit public viewing.

The general antipathy felt for the *barocchismo* was, however, to have unfortunate effects. A mad plan was put forward to change the baroque interior of St John's, giving it a 'correct' neo-classical dress.[31] The project, subscribed to by other artists such as Giorgio Grognet, intended among other things to widen the Grand Masters' crypt and convert it into a neo-classical pantheon. Some actual damage was incurred in the chapel of the French Langue, where as a result of the introduction of the Pradier neo-classic sculpture − the memorial to the Count of

Beaujolais – the altar and the entire frontispiece, designed in 1606 by Melchiorre Gafà, were completely re-done to accord with neo-classic aesthetics. Luckily the project was halted before the harm proceeded further, consequent on a protest made in July 1840 by Count Alessi Fontani, who had drawn attention to the mutilation inflicted upon the de Rohan monument. *The Malta Times* carried a comment decrying the abuse, while asserting the very important principle that 'the object of a civilized people is to preserve monuments intact'.[32]

The controversy served some good purpose, exerting a salutary effect on the rescue operations of St John's. Giuseppe Hyzler, who appears to have been held responsible, seems to have learned his lesson: as the restoration proceeded, he became much more careful and circumspect in dealing with the baroque heritage in St John's. Under his direction, most of the altar-pieces and other paintings were cleaned and restored carefully, apparently with the exception of Caravaggio's *Beheading of St John the Baptist*, which was deemed to be in too ruinous a state.

A new polemic on Hyzler's restoration methods broke out in a local newspaper in 1853 and 1854.[33] He was charged with negligence as a result of his age and his malady. The competence of his assistant, Giuseppe Calleja, was also called into question. Yet the outburst serves to tranquillize us: Hyzler himself, in his intervention, makes it clear that he took the greatest care not to alter in any way the original character of the paintings. It is well to remember that he had not always thought in this way, especially before the 1840 scandal over the re-structuring of the French chapel. He had not scrupled then to add a section to the two mannerist canvases representing the *Madonna del Divino Amore* and the *San Giovanni,* thereby falsifying the original intent.[34]

When Giuseppe Hyzler died on 19 January 1858, the encomiums were effusive and largely deserved. He was an excellent and dedicated artist, possessed of a generally well-informed and intelligent approach. His shortcomings were largely emotional, tied specifically to the local nineteenth-century environment, with its petty and bigoted cultural horizon which Hyzler either could not, or refused to, rise above. He was the single most important artistic influence in the island, with many of the other rivals, including the equally gifted Pietro

Paolo Caruana; aided also by the voluntary absence from Malta of others, and especially of Salvatore Busuttil, who shrewdly turned his back on the hostile Maltese environment, preferring the opportunities of a large metropolis. With his gifted contemporaries more or less neutralized, Hyzler was able to rear the younger artists under his wings, to confirm them in the spirit of Nazarener aesthetics, predetermining the course of Maltese art for practically another century.

2. Hyzler's Contemporaries and Followers

Hyzler's success would not have been possible without the pre-existing socio-political disposition assured by the colonial situation of nineteenth-century Malta and its dominantly clerical culture. The more liberal spirits among artists who might have injected a balanced lay influence were either progressively disarmed, as had happened with Giorgio Pullicino (1779-1852) and hardly less so with Giorgio Grognet (1774-1862), or they deliberately kept away from Malta, probably conscious of the withering effect of the local intellectual climate.

Among the latter group must be counted Giuseppe Casha (b.c.1745) who settled to a successful career in Rome after winning the first prize in sculpture awarded in 1762 by the *Accademia di San Luca*.[35] There were also two other artists who had won a considerable reputation in Europe and whose beneficent influence Maltese art very badly missed. These were Massimo Gauci and Salvatore Busuttil.

Like Giuseppe Casha and Giuseppe Grech, Massimo Gauci (1776-1852) was sent to study at the *Accademia di San Luca* at the Order's expense, together with Giorgio Pullicino, a kindred spirit. Gauci specialized in miniature art, in which there had been considerable interest in Malta ever since the sixteenth century. While Pullicino returned to Malta, the more forward-looking Gauci migrated to France at the time of Napoleon's ascendancy; after the latter's fall, he moved to London where, apparently, he was among the first artists to practise lithography.[36] Yet his heyday of glory had been under the Napoleonic First Empire, when he was one of the more favoured artists in Court circles. Gauci appears to have lost all contact with his native land after parting with Pullicino; the latter's decision to return to Malta was to have the unfortunate sequel already discussed.

On the other hand, Salvatore Busuttil (1798-1854) continued to maintain both family and artistic contacts with Malta. He was the son of Michele Busuttil (d.1831), the first to be appointed *professore di disegno* by the University of Malta. Salvatore proceeded to Rome on being awarded the Maitland bursary in 1818 at the age of 20. He adhered to the stricter neo-classicist current at the *Accademia*, although adopting a warmer and thicker version than the cold Romanticism of Francesco Hayez.

In spite of a contrary tradition, Salvatore Busuttil seems to have actually paid a visit to Malta soon after his father's death in 1831. This fact agrees well with the presence of a few paintings of his in the country that cannot be accounted for otherwise. He then returned to Rome in February 1833. A local newspaper report communicating news of his death makes unusual and enigmatic allusions to his testamentary arrangements with his wife.[37]

Another artist who returned to settle in Malta after an absence of 20 years was the highly gifted engraver Giovanni Farrugia (c.1795-1861). To his misfortune, he found it almost impossible to accept the country's claustrophobic atmosphere. While he was still a mere youth, Farrugia's drawings enthused many of his contemporaries; the Latinist littérateur abbé Rigord wrote a poem inspired by one of Farrugia's early drawings representing Ajax, a Homeric hero.

Farrugia left for Rome early in 1817, studying at the *Accademia* at first with Minardi, then specializing in engraving with Raffaele Morghen, the most famous engraver active in Rome after Piranesi's death. Farrugia's engraving proved popular, the artist having attained a very admirable level of competence in the medium; he seems though to have lacked inventiveness, preferring to engrave the works of Raphael and Thorwaldsen, apart from repeating some of Morghen's own productions.

Farrugia travelled throughout Italy and for a time settled in Milan, where he engraved a portrait of Gioacchino Rossini that was to have a wide currency. He returned to Malta on 2 February 1837 — an ill-considered decision as the island could not offer sufficient scope for his talents. In fact, he was soon reduced to the extremity of requesting a Government job to survive. He was posted to Gozo, teaching village boys for the last six bitter years of his life.[38]

A more substantial figure, in terms of his influence on Maltese art, was Pietro Paolo Caruana (1794-1852).[39] Another beneficiary of the Maitland bursaries, he left Malta, at the age of 24, on 19 February 1819. As a young man his painting abilities were so highly thought of that the British administration in Malta commissioned him to carry out a copy of the portrait of George IV by Sir Thomas Laurence presented to the Pope. Caruana's copy, now in the Palace, Valletta, was deemed to be only slightly inferior to the original. Like his exact contemporaries and fellow countrymen Busuttil and Farrugia, Caruana at first showed preference for the strict neo-classicist circle in the *Accademia* that had gathered around Canova. Later on, Dr Nicola Zammit, as keen a critic as ever, seized on this peculiarity of his style. In polemic with Hyzler's out-and-out espousal of Nazarener aesthetics, he remarks:

Caruana rejected the severity of the contemporary school and that type of purismo which more often succeeds in producing a stucco-like hardness, which even if it speaks mysteriously to the soul, yet has nothing to communicate to the senses.[40]

Caruana paid a brief visit to Malta in the summer of 1827, probably to prepare a home for his family as he had married Ursula D'Andres in Rome, where some of his children (including Raffaele, the future painter) were born. In fact, on 28 October 1827 he turned up in Malta with his family. He was soon inundated with commissions, especially by the administration, and in 1831 he was appointed Teacher of Drawing as soon as the first vacancy occurred.

The period between 1827 and 1835 witnessed a silent and relentless tussle for the supremacy of the local art-scene between P.P. Caruana and Giuseppe Hyzler. Caruana had the tacit backing of the British administration, while Hyzler enjoyed the support of the Church and its ponderous network. Two beautiful mementoes of this rivalry are two works in the Church of St Dominic in Valletta – the main altarpiece representing *The Visitation* by P.P. Caruana and the altarpiece of *Our Lady of the Rosary* in the north transept by Giuseppe Hyzler. Both works

1 Mdina, the old capital city of Malta

2 The traditional nougat-seller: a common sight in every town or village *festa*

3 A Maltese milk-seller

4 The slow rhythm of commercial activity: a native trader and his donkey at their warehouse

5 Native women wearing the *faldetta*, a traditional (now obsolete) Maltese costume

6 The Malta Railway that linked Valletta to Mtarfa

7 The traditional *Karrozzin*, or horse-driven cab

8 The Strand, Sliema

9 Hotel Phoenicia, Floriana

10 General Vaubois:
Commander-in-Chief in
Malta during the French
occupation of the island
1798-1800

11 Sir Thomas Maitland,
the first British
Governor of Malta,
1813-24

12 Sir Maurice Dorman, the
last British Governor of
Colonial Malta, 1962-4,
and the first Governor-
General of Independent
Malta, 1964-71

13 Dr Fortunato Mizzi,
   1844-1905: Founder of
   the Nationalist Party

14 Sigismondo Savona,
   1835-1908: Director of
   Education, and Leader of
   the Reform Party

15 Dr Enrico Mizzi: Prime
   Minister of Malta, 1950

16 Ignazio Cortis, *Sir
Adrian Dingli*. Cathedral
Museum, Gozo

17 Lord Strickland: Prime
Minister of Malta,
1927-30

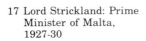

18 Dr George Borg Olivier:
the first Prime Minister
of Independent Malta

19 Mr Dom Mintoff: Prime
Minister of Malta
1955-1958

20 Mgr. Sir Michael Gonzi:
Archbishop of Malta

21 One of the first public meetings held by the Malta Labour
Party in Senglea, 1931

22 A Nationalist Party
demonstration following
a public meeting at
Żabbar, 1932

23 Mr Dom Mintoff (fifth from left): Prime Minister of Malta 1955-8, with Archbishop Sir Michael Gonzi at the height of the Integration controversy

24 A diocesan rally at Blata l-Bajda in the early 1960s

25 Manwel Dimech, 1860-1921:
rebel poet, journalist, novelist,
social reformer, and a ferocious
opponent of the British colonial
administration

26 Dun Karm Psaila,
1871-1961: Malta's
National Poet since 1935

27 An isolated monument to a revered hero, Sir Alexander Ball, at the Lower Barracca, Valletta. Design attributed to Giorgio Pullicino

28 The Naval Hospital at Bighi: a living symbol of English Romanticism adorning the entrance to the Grand Harbour. Designed by Sir George Whitmore. The master mason was Gaetano Xerri

29 The Royal Opera House in Valletta. Designed by E.W. Barry

30 The *Rotunda* or Mosta Dome (1833): a popular expression of Neo-Classicism. Designed by Giorgio Grognet de Vasse

„Grand Harb

31 The Grand Harbour at the turn of the century, before the building of
the breakwater in 1903

THE ROYAL YACHT IN GRAND HARBOUR · MALTA

32 Another view of the Grand Harbour

33 St Paul's Anglican Cathedral in Valletta. Originally designed
by Richard Lankersheer. Later redesigned by William Scamp.
The foundation stone was laid by Queen Adelaide in 1839

34 Valletta, the capital city of Malta

35 The Main Guard in St George's Square, now Palace Square, Valletta:
an early essay in Neo-classical architecture in Malta, possibly designed
by Giorgio Pullicino

36 The Royal Coat-of Arms crowning the portico of the Main Guard. The Latin
inscription, recording the 'compact between Malta and Britain' reads: MAGNAE
ET INVICTAE BRITANNIAE / MELITENSIUM AMOR ET EUROPAE VOX /
HAS INSULAS CONFIRMAT AD 1814 (To the great and unconquered Britain,
the love of the Maltese and the voice of Europe confirm these Islands AD 1814)

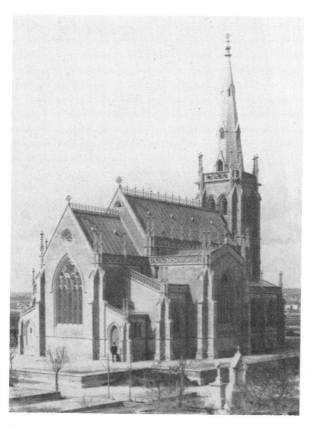

37 Neo-Gothic architecture: the chapel at the Addolorata
Cemetery. Designed by Emanuele Luigi Galizia in 1869

38 Neo-Gothic architecture: the Carmelite Church overlooking Balluta Bay,
St Julians. Designed by Giuseppe Bonavia

39 Giuseppe Cali, *Fra Crispin* . The Capuchin Church, Floriana

40 Edward Caruana Dingli, *Giuseppe Cali*. National Museum of Fine Arts, Valletta

41 Antonio Sciortino, *Les Gavroches*. The Upper Barracca, Valletta

49 A detail from Lazzaro Pisani's decoration of the Parish Church of Nadur, Gozo

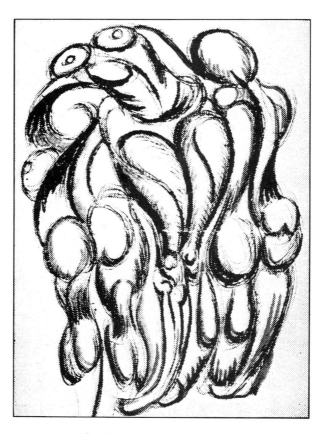

50 Joe Calleja, *Imaginative Drawing*

can be arguably considered as two masterpieces of nineteenth-century Maltese art: they epitomize at one and the same time the excellent qualities of each artist as well as the essential difference between the purist classicism of the Minardi circle and the wistful, rarified religiosity of the Nazareners.

Unfortunately, as time went by, Caruana lost much of the refined sensibility that shines out in *The Visitation*. His drawing ability and his inventiveness seem to have waned too. In fact, he ended up by succumbing to the metaphysical vortex of the Nazareners as borne out by the altarpiece of the *Immaculate Conception* at Cospicua. The painting rests heavily on popular elements, while its composition harks back patently to Favray's altarpiece of *St Barbara* which Caruana follows slavishly — a sad denouement for so brilliant a start.[41]

Caruana's failure to expand the potential of his more classicist art represents perhaps the greatest triumph of the Maltese Nazareners over even his milder form of neo-classicism. The nature of this defeat becomes more decisive when one examines the paintings of Raffaele Caruana (b.1821), the eldest son of Pietro Paolo. In painting he was nowhere as gifted as his father who surely must have coached him in art, apart from arranging his marriage to a daughter of Tommaso Minardi's. Raffaele not only never rose above the level of a mere painter-raconteur — as one can conclude from the two oblong lateral paintings flanking his father's *Visitation* in the choir of St Dominic's — but often his work becomes indistinguishable from that of the lesser-talented Nazareners, such as Antonio Falson.

Of the actual followers of Giuseppe Hyzler, the one whose art was backed by solid qualities was undoubtedly Michele Bellanti (1808-83). Michele was the most talented, as well as the most intelligent and the most independent of the group, with a marked preference for the clinical austerity of quattrocento Umbrian art, which he further tames with his use of mild, soothing, pastel-like colours. In effect, he moderates both the harsh abrasive severity preached by the Nazareners, and also their feverish religious feeling.

Bellanti's family had an intellectual background. His father was librarian at the *Bibliotheca,* while his brother was eventually appointed dean of the Cathedral Chapter. He himself had graduated as a lawyer but almost immediately proceeded

to Rome to study art professionally. Although, like many other
Maltese artists of the time, he travelled to Constantinople, it
seems that he found the exotic Romanticism of the East rather
overpowering.[42] Bellanti's fine lithographic production
approaches the rich qualities of Giovanni Schranz — perhaps
not as detailed, but just as painstaking; their atmosphere is,
however, generally chaster — as becomes a Nazarener
sympathizer.

Tommaso Madiona (1803-64) was Bellanti's exact
contemporary and a comparison between the two could prove
instructive in more than one way. Madiona studied in Rome from
1827 onwards, allegedly under Minardi. According to one
version, Minardi was far from impressed by his drawing abilities
and advised him — not without some irony, one suspects — to
stick to painting *del genere storico*. His adulatory biographer
in *L'Arte* admits that Madiona produced 'an immense amount
of work painted with the sole purpose of earning an honest
livelihood'. Yet even the serious commissions that have survived
the War — for much was destroyed when the Senglea basilica
was hit — reveal an insensitive eye as well as a cluttered,
confused mind that, to all appearances, never quite understood
what art is all about. He did though invent a guitar 'with pedals
and additional strings'.[43]

If quite a lot was made of Madiona in contemporary literature,
even more was made of Vincenzo Hyzler (1813-49) which, in our
days, has become difficult to understand. An air of mystery
surrounds this artist — including his birth, the place of which
so far has not been identified; he might not even be a brother
of Giuseppe Hyzler as has always been assumed.[44]

The scarcity of works produced by Vincenzo Hyzler is
extraordinary in the annals of local art history. All writers refer
only to the same two paintings — as well as to his drawings —
one of which carried out on the instructions of Overbeck and
intended for the Stresa oratory of the religious community
established by the Christian philosopher Rosmini. Strangely,
Vincenzo Hyzler's reputation rests on this single episode and
I believe that none of those who had written on the artist have
ever seen the work — a typical Nazarener piece as one would
expect from a painter working as close to Overbeck as Vincenzo
was. Between 1839 and 1843, he lived in Italy, mostly in Rome.

The *St Andrew* at the parish church of Żejtun, painted in 1846, is his other known painting, a discreet piece of work, midway in temperament between Giuseppe Hyzler and Michele Bellanti, technically closer to the latter. Vincenzo Hyzler the artist appears to be more the product of myth than reality.[45]

Of the other Maltese Nazareners, Antonio Falson (1805-after 1868) features prominently in contemporary literature, being the most in circulation and the closest of Hyzler's collaborators until the 1851 disagreement over the vault-decoration of St Paul Shipwrecked in Valletta. His father, Giuseppe Falson (d.1837), was also a painter, but Antonio, who had been trained under Pullicino, was soon appropriated by Hyzler, thus developing a rich, mystic approach that at times can be suggestive. A small easel-work representing *The Good Shepherd*, in the sacristy of Our Lady of Victories in Valletta, bears his initials and the date 1863, probably one of Falson's last paintings.[46]

Salvatore Micallef, about whom so little is known, was another of Hyzler's assistants, with a collaboration that goes back to the 1830s; he appears, though, to have been employed most of all on work of restoration in which career he specialized after leaving his master's entourage. The works of restoration carried out by Salvatore Micallef include the *La Verdalle* lunettes by Filippo Paladini in Verdala Palace, restored in 1863, according to an inscription. The altarpiece of *Our Lady of Graces* in the Church of St Mary of Jesus in Valletta, is, however, an original work of Salvatore Micallef, signed and dated 1849, revealing him as an intelligent follower of Hyzler's, more florid and certainly less grave in temperament. Unfortunately the scarcity of his works seems to indicate that he produced little that was original and creative.

Both Salvatore Barbara (active in the 1850s and the 1860s) as well as Giuseppe Bonnici (1834-1900) belonged to the younger generation of Maltese Nazarener artists. Bonnici passed from Madiona's care to that of the aging Minardi,[47] developing a rhetorical, statuesque classicism, more decorative than anything else. On the other hand, Barbara was more of a traditionalist; his art looks backwards, attempting a compromise with the baroque tradition, although not always understanding its basic feeling for curvilinearity.

With Henry Casolani (1817-85) and Giorgio Giuseppe Bonavia

(1821-85) a new but kindred phase becomes obvious. Both had started as Nazareners, having both studied in Rome in intimate contact with that community; in fact, Casolani had returned to Malta on 12 July 1843 in the company of Giuseppe and Vincenzo Hyzler. Both Casolani and Bonavia were well-connected and imbibed with Anglicized tendencies that were gradually becoming a sensible feature of Maltese culture. Their Nazarener background conditioned them to establish spiritual links with the Pre-Raphaelite Brotherhood. Casolani settled in London — having apparently left Malta on 26 May 1847 — while Bonavia followed later.[48] He had, in fact, designed the Scottish Presbyterian church in South Street, Valletta, arousing hostility in several local circles.

It cannot be a mere coincidence that about the same time Amodeo Preziosi (b.1816) and Antonio Schranz (b.1801), together with Frederick (b.1811) and Luigi Brockdorff (b.1814) left Malta as well, apparently never to return. The constriction that characterized local nineteenth-century culture left little scope for the more enterprising artists. Their reaction varied greatly. While Antonio Schranz tried hard to maintain a local footing, others, like Preziosi, resolved their dilemma without hesitation, effecting a sudden, clean break, seemingly without regrets.

Artists of earlier generations, as Giuseppe Casha and Massimo Gauci, had likewise been faced with a similar decision, although less dramatically and without those signs of desperation suggested by the nineteenth-century confinement. The crisis was clearly sensed and anticipated by Salvatore Busuttil, soon followed by Giuseppe Schranz (b.1803) and Luigi Taffien (b.1811) who left Malta in 1828 and 1832 respectively.[49] That the art of these painters happens to be more progressively orientated, when compared with that of the artists who chose to stay, is in itself a significant social phenomenon that cannot be overlooked.

Equally revealing is the fascination that the eastern Mediterranean, with its exotic, mysterious charm, exerted on these artists. It acted as a powerful distant magnet that pulled towards it those who had assimilated in a diluted form the Romantic sensibility of the age with its insistence on personal freedom.[50] The total effect was a calamitous drain on Malta's top artistic talent that again deepened the crisis, depressing further the general view of Maltese art. It also created a widening lacuna that, in turn, started a novel, dangerous fashion — the commissioning of works of art from generally *retardateur* Italian painters, beginning with G. Gallucci, who first appeared in 1857, followed, in the next decade, by Pietro Gagliardi[51] and, still later, by such others as Grandi, Coccoli, Conti, Testa, and Palombi, as well as several others active as late as the 1940s. The story of nineteenth-century art in Malta makes rather melancholy reading. The appropriate human material was indeed there, rich in talent and abundant. Yet, when a comparison with the previous century is drawn, one is immediately aware that a number of inhibiting factors had intervened. Globally, these not only hindered the flourishing of Maltese art; they actually stunted its growth and deformed its development. If one is to point an accusing finger, then it is to the political situation that precipitated and worsened the socio-cultural conditions of the Maltese.

Nineteenth-Century Sculpture: A Note

Developments in sculpture have been deliberately side-tracked as there is not much that can be usefully meditated upon. The story of nineteenth-century Maltese sculpture is generally bleaker than that of painting. With Giuseppe Casha a conspicuous absentee, the major sculptor was Mariano Gerada (1766-1823).[52] He had begun as an artisan wood-carver, a field of activity of which in Malta there was an old and respectable tradition. Gerada's art was supposedly fertilized through contact with the realism of Valencian sculpture, in actual fact not very evident in his art, that seems rather to veer towards a timid form of classicism. His followers interpreted it in an increasingly popular form.

Vincenzo Dimech (1768-1831) also worked as an architect-cum-decorator and was employed in this role by Governor Maitland on Corfu. Dimech was a stricter classicist than Gerada. He opened an industrial workshop in Valletta, on the site of Palazzo Ferreria, producing in stone certain items of neo-classical decorative sculpture, mostly for export purposes. Unfortunately, after his death, the production became stiltedly artisan, degenerating into a mere craftsmanlike production.

Vincenzo Bonnici (d.1863) was an oft-mentioned wood-carver whose work was much praised by the sound and reliable Dr Nicola Zammit.[53] Yet the major sculptural activity of the century was in papier-mâché production, which had an old tradition in Malta that went back at least to the mid-seventeenth century. In the nineteenth century, although still practised at the level of popular art, it strove to attain a higher and more satisfying level of art through such dedicated statuaries as Carlo Darmanin (1825-1909),[54] whose iconographic models were apparently sought in baroque works of art.

A sudden revival in sculptural standards took place towards the end of the century, particularly with the appearance of Antonio Sciortino (1879-1947), a phenomenon difficult to comprehend against the background of the meagre sculptural tradition of nineteenth-century Malta.[55]

Dominic Cutajar

Part Two: 1860-1921

Maltese Art Astride Two Centuries

The visual arts in the Maltese Islands during the last few decades of the nineteenth century and the initial twenty years of the present century present a picture which seems to languish in a kind of impotence, condemning most of the artists involved to witness an established perception of 'making art' without any apparent consciousness of new modes of vision being developed abroad. It is enough to point out, for example, that when the eighth and last exhibition of the Impressionist group was held in Paris in 1886 Maltese painting was still very far from that stage where the chromatic and tonal analysis of reality could be tackled with an inherent satisfaction.

Though essentially a French movement, Impressionism had its counterpart practioners in nearby Italy where the *Macchiaioli,* best represented by Federigo Zandomeneghi and Giuseppe de Nittis,[1] made their own substantial mark on this new way of relating the artist to reality. The artistic climate in southern Italy, particularly around Naples, was, however, less congenial to these purely visual developments than towards the traditional meridional love of *bravura* combined with a poetic vein. Among the new giants of the latter vision was Domenico Morelli[2] whose spectacular religious creations were to have a great bearing on Giuseppe Cali (1846-1930). For all his immense ability at recreating the deep explorations of shadows and light which was a direct legacy of the seicento, Morelli was, however, contributing directly towards the relative stagnation which Italian art suffered throughout the nineteenth century. It is no wonder then that Maltese artists, who almost naturally gravitated to the Italian mainland to pursue their training, exhibited related symptoms upon their return to a homeland plagued by a perennial disadvantage of limited human resources.

Giuseppe Cali is the dominant Maltese painter during the period under survey and, practically right up to his death, less than a decade prior to the psychological turmoil of the Second World War. In other words, Cali painted for an audience which cultivated values, both religious and aesthetic, that might not fit exactly postwar viewpoints. Cali's style conditioned artistic tastes; his uncontested dominance of Maltese art made him a figure to be revered.

Born in Valletta of Neapolitan parents on 14 August 1846, Cali showed a precocious talent which was readily noticed by William Eynaud who financed his studies abroad. Eventually the Neapolitan link, which already existed due to his parental origin, was restored in the Campanian capital when he received his artistic training. At the time Naples was not simply basking idly in the afterglow of a glorious baroque past, but it was contributing to the conscience of Italian art, however deficient of significant impulses we can now judge it to have been. It could boast of some really influential masters like Giuseppe Mancinelli with whom Cali was apprenticed. While in Naples the latter also had the opportunity to benefit from the presence of his father's cousins, the sculptors Antonio and Gennaro Cali.[3] It appears, however, that Cali forsook such immediate influences and instead became attracted to Morelli's ostentatious compositions.

Ideally equipped, Cali returned to Malta ready to embark on

a long career that was to see him as the most sought-after decorator of the local baroque churches, apart from receiving a large number of private commissions, especially portraitures. Such a vast output made one art historian note that 'there was hardly a church or moderately affluent home in the island but could boast one of his canvases'.[4]

For the sake of convenience, Cali's work has been classified into three phases, ranging from the brilliant surfaces and the dynamic strength of his draughtsmanship of the initial period, towards a progressive crowding of the compositions of the intermediate phase, and thence to a gradual affectedness which weakens the inner virility and makes the composition suffer.[5] Thus when the entire output of Cali is observed through a perspective of almost a century, there is a tendency to visualize him as an artist whose maturity meant in effect a decline in artistic powers. At the same time there is no doubt that he succeeded in exalting the dominant tastes and religious mores of the age. Such was the extent to which individuals went into raptures in front of his work that he seemed to be projecting an unassailable position in the eyes of his admirers.[6] His overpowering stature pre-empted, even among rival painters, any aspirations towards variant modes of expression and meant in effect that his qualities could hardly be emulated, let alone surpassed. A chilling imposition came to be exerted on official and public audiences who treated with suspicion that which was not fully compatible with the aesthetic precepts expressed in his numerous altarpieces, vault-paintings, and portraits.

Even to this day certain theatrical overlays in his compositions of sacred themes have continued to determine accepted norms among several church decorations. Still there were no real inheritors of his style which can at best be vaguely identified in works by his son Ramiro and, even more vaguely, in those of his relative, Raffaele Bonnici Cali (b.1907),[7] apart from the more obvious case of the Caruana Dinglis.

In the final analysis it is apposite to add that Cali's detractors tend to view his work as an unending choreography of statements largely playing on popular sentimentalities. At the same time they conveniently eschew his intuitive flair to identify the people's needs and relate them to his paintings. Cali, in other words, proved himself to be that rare type of artistic master who made use of his uncommon talents to conform with the spiritually-uplifting sensibilities of contemporary Maltese society. Even after his death, the great esteem which his vast artistic legacy had generated continued unabated – the exhibition held at the Palazzo De La Salle to mark the centenary of the artist's birth attracted crowds of people from all walks of life who flocked to pay homage to the man who provided them with visions of celestial bliss on canvas.[8]

The exclusive popularity of Giuseppe Cali was to prove a formidable barrier to other competent artists intent at securing their fair share of ecclesiastical commissions. Foremost among these was Lazzaro Pisani (1854-1932), born at Żebbuġ (Malta) and who, throughout his life, was forced into viewing from a distance the figure of Cali glowing in the limelight while for him seemed to be reserved only the flickering embers of fame. Still Pisani left a considerable number of works ranging from portraits and still-life subjects to sacred art in several churches in both Malta and Gozo.[9]

Pisani was at first tutored by Ignazio Carlo Cortis (1826-98) but when he was barely sixteen years old he proceeded to the *Accademia di San Luca* in Rome to study under Luigi Fontana and Domenico Bruschi.[10] His return to Malta was at first marked by a close adherence to the style already being established by Cali. Still, he soon started going his own way, churning out religious subjects in an academic manner, definitely more frail than Cali's, but still of popular appeal. However, the unrelenting shadow of his great contemporary never ceased to hold its subtle threat towards the establishment of a proper identity, and it is with some justification that Pisani's foremost apologist notes that the artist 'had the disadvantage of being eight years younger than his contemporary Cali who, during those eight years, had already affirmed himself, creating a halo of glory around his name.'[11]

The figure of Pisani's first tutor is unfortunately associated primarily with his incompetent restoration in 1867-74 of Mattia Preti's unique fresco-cycle on the ceiling of St John's Co-Cathedral.[12] He was one of several Maltese painters who were apprenticed at the studio of Tommaso Minardi[13] in Rome where he acquired a creditable reputation for his work in churches, such as Santa Maria in Trastevere. Several churches in Malta and Gozo were also to acquire their own share of his neo-classical pretensions marked by an over-confident dependence on his draughtsmanship which consequently meant a cold artist-subject relationship. His painterly concepts should, however, also be credited with a kind of monumental gravity that purges his figures of inessentials in order to reach out for a noble simplicity.[14]

The opening years of the twentieth century witnessed the initial stages in the long artistic career of Gianni Vella (1885-1977) who can be stated to have assiduously maintained right up to his death an attitude profoundly attached to an academic vision. In general it can be said that he lacked real depth of feeling which was instead replaced by a sweetened sentimentality that almost became his trademark. Yet to his credit it must be noted that he was among the pioneers in Maltese art to be occasionally attracted towards the representation of landscape with an impressionistic timbre.[15]

Having spent five years at the turn of the century in various academies in Rome, including the British Academy, Gianni Vella returned to his country with the knowledge of the diverging trends of art at the time. And yet it appears that his inclination became directed through the general artistic climate then prevalent towards popular subjects, including portraiture in which he achieved a measure of success. He also received numerous commissions for altarpieces and decorative schemes in churches. His distinctively light palette filters through, betraying a frame of mind compatible with visions of a clean nature, that seeks a general serenity. Even in his later years Vella retained his original precepts with no significant developments in his style. He was, if not oblivious of, at least incapable or temperamentally unsuited to responding to certain awakenings among those local artists who were trying to retrieve some of the huge disadvantages by which Maltese art had fallen behind the rest of Europe. Such attempts at widening our artistic firmament started coming to the fore just after the Second World War but Vella, who had still about thirty years of artistic practice before him, apparently renounced all temptations to redirect his attention.[16]

Though Gianni Vella exhibited an occasional proclivity towards subjects extolling the ethnic core of Malta, the genre was extensively expanded by Edward Caruana Dingli (1876-1950) and his brother Robert (1881-1940). The former, especially, built up a reputation which was enhanced by his standing and influence at the Government School of Art which was established in 1921. During the thirties, in fact, several of the present older generation of artists were tutored by him. Edward himself had been an old pupil of Giuseppe Cali from whom he acquired a penchant for portraiture and rich chromatisms. Contrary to Cali, however, sacred art never seems to have excercised any real calling to the Caruana Dinglis. Their clientele instead was to be found within those strata of society eager to have private salons and public halls decorated by the best talent available. Among many patrons of the arts, a Caruana Dingli painting became a byword for technical excellence.

The era of the Caruana Dinglis (and its attendant glory) were proof that the situation of Maltese painting together with the general demands were not yet ripe for a revision of its principles which looked back to the ottocento. And yet some Maltese artists still pay homage to that era and its crucial role among the more sophisticated Maltese art patrons.

Just as Cali lays down a strong claim to be looked upon as the giant of Maltese painting during this period, so does Antonio Sciortino (1879-1947) in the field of sculpture. The latter in fact spread his practice and reputation far beyond the shores of his native land, thereby making himself a worthy successor, albeit separated by three centuries, of Melchiorre Gafà (1635-67), practically the only Maltese sculptor till Sciortino to make a significant name outside Malta.

Born in Żebbuġ (Malta) on 12 February 1879, Sciortino was for a time apprenticed to Vincenzo Cardona who had been invited in the 1890s to come to Malta from Reggio Calabria to establish a school of modelling and carving.[17] In 1900, however, the young artist left for Rome to commence his studies at the *Istituto di Belle Arti*. This marked the real beginning of a career which was to result in the recognition of his great talents in various corners of the world.[18] In 1911, for instance, he won a prize for a monument to Tsar Alexander II and, three years later, he was placed first in an international competition for a monument to Shevchenko at Kiev. In the twenties his international reputation became enhanced by another monument, this time to Anton Chekov at Rostov-on-Don,[19] and by his winning the second prize for an equestrian monument to Simon Bolivar.

Malta, too, was set to gain from this flair for public monuments by her famous son who in 1907 presented the Government of the island with that much-loved group of *Les Gavroches* in the Upper Barracca Gardens. This work catches the momentary movement of its three figures in a spirit which Sciortino appears to have synthesized from a study of Auguste Rodin, the greatest name in international sculpture at the time.[20] When the monument to Christ the King was erected at Floriana in 1917, it was already apparent that Sciortino was veering towards a more formal language of shapes which led gradually to the elegant blossoming of his *Rhythmi Vitae* (1924) or the balance of internal harmony and manifest strength in the *Great Siege* Monument (1927). Ultimately this tendency became transformed into an impulsive fugitiveness from the restraints of inertia to several representations of speed, like the *Lindbergh on Eagle* of the thirties. True to the nature of a sprinting exercise, this dynamic vision eventually fizzled away to be followed by the frozen immobility of his last public monument, that to Lord Strickland (1945). It was the final renunciation of the mellower sides of the sculptor's past, without impairing the nobility of form which remained, right up to the end, the visible hallmark of his art.[21]

Sciortino proved to be that rare kind of phenomenon in the uneven evolution of Maltese art which, in a way, could hardly make others aspire to any significant emulation unless through mannerisms.[22] He stands poised at the proper point in time when art in Malta was idly toying with the idea of turning on a truly modern course but lacked real conviction to attempt the leap. Sciortino may yet be looked upon as the catalyst that was needed to effect that move which was ultimately to render the path to modernity less stifled by outdated modes of vision. The peaks of fame which he conquered favoured not only his own inalienable position in the wide spectrum of Maltese art but also served to awaken a conscience among fellow Maltese artists.

After Sciortino begins a completely new chapter of aesthetic considerations.

Emmanuel Fiorentino

Part Three: 1921-64

A Travailed Ascent to Modernity

The beginnings of 'modern' art in Malta can be dated to the early 1950s, although in the previous half-century a few individual artists came near to expressing themselves in the modern idiom. At the very dawn of the century, Antonio Sciortino produced his still outstandingly-fresh sculptural group, *Les Gavroches,* a dynamic study in youthful ebullience; but this early happy essay was to remain unmatched as the sculptor increasingly sought refuge in rhetorical devices and stereotyped models of elegance.

In 1921 the Maltese were granted a considerable measure of responsible internal government which, in spite of various inquietitudes, lasted until 1933, and was subsequently resumed in 1947. One of the most foreseeing measures taken by the new Maltese administration in education was the establishment of a School of Art with classes in drawing, painting, and modelling. The Caruana Dingli brothers – Edward (1876-1950) and Robert (1881-1940) – who taught painting and drawing respectively, dominated the Maltese art-scene, particularly Edward who, although a pupil of Giuseppe Calì, manifested in his work strong Pre-Raphaelite leanings.

The revivalist tendencies of British art had already attracted the sympathies of Henry Casolani and Giorgio Bonavia some time after the middle of the nineteenth century; unfortunately the link between these two groups of Anglophile artists is as yet unclear. Still, there is no doubt that the influence of the Caruana Dinglis on the formation of the next generation of artists proved to be both great and constructive. Their pupils were only able to outgrow it through resumed contacts with the academic circles in Rome, facilitated by the Government's awards of bursaries to promising artists, enabling them to study art in that city. Through these strange twists of fate, Maltese art never succumbed to the temptation of becoming a satellite of British artistic development. Contacts with British art were to be resumed in earnest in the 1940s, but by then the cosmopolitanism obtaining in the world of art had come near to obliterating meaningful national traits.

I A New Beginning in Sculpture

The master of the modelling class at the School of Art was Antonio Micallef (1883-1957), a highly-skilled artist who was to leave his mark on modern Maltese sculpture, not at all through the impact of his own works – for he seems to have produced but little – as much as through the successive generations of sculptors reared under his direction and guidance. Academically orientated, he rigorously applied classicist views in his class, a circumstance that, although it often had the effect of insulating his pupils from modern ideas, unconsciously served to wean them away from the muddled rhetorical notions of the aging Sciortino, so that, excepting a couple of weak imitators, the latter never had a real local following.

After settling in the Italian capital, Antonio Sciortino was appointed Professor of Sculpture at the British Academy in Rome. His class was joined in 1927 by Vincent Apap (b.1909), a gifted young sculptor, one of the first products of the School of Art who in that year won the very first Government bursary. In spite of the prestigious example of his new master, Apap decidedly turned his back on the rhetorical and inflated manner of Sciortino, opting instead for classical simplicity as a kind of surrogate for purer natural forms. It proved to be a momentous decision, as it implied that the ferment for renewal which kept pervading Maltese art was to take its cue from a more genuine spirit of enquiry rather than from the nebulous mysticism of the later Sciortino.

Such a turn in the development of Maltese art is probably due to the influence of Antonio Micallef, a conclusion that finds added corroboration from the fact that another of his pupils,

George Borg (1906-85) who had won the Rome bursary in 1930, likewise opted for a classicist expression, although of a drier and more academic mould. The same option was originally made by Samuel Bugeja (b.1920), one of Malta's most inventive wood-carvers. In Bugeja's case, the grim experience of the war years, coupled with a more modern orientation, was to affect his development — as indeed also happened to Apap. During the 1950s Bugeja discovered his congeniality in a kind of expressionism inspired by Romanesque sculpture.

The constant unorthodoxy of Josef Kalleya (b.1898) makes it difficult to fix him into the above scheme of gradual development from classicism through natural forms to a kind of expressionism. With Kalleya, Maltese art enters almost directly into the realm of modern sensibility. While others were gradually edging their way in that direction, Kalleya instinctively reached it thanks to his untrammelled and eclectic training, and to his chance joining an additional course at the *Regia Scuola della Medaglia* in Rome. The latter experience enabled Kalleya to imbibe the *sgraffito* technique which proved particularly adapted to his expressive, religiously-infused temperament. By the time he returned to Malta in 1935, his works were already endowed with an authentic 'modern' feeling.

In the circumstances prevailing in Malta at the time, Kalleya's uniqueness was to prove a severe handicap to his worldly progress, heightened by other misfortunes, particularly from his well-meant attempt to open a private school for nude study, which, although it proved to be immensely popular among the artists themselves, was decried and hounded out of existence. From 1937 Kalleya was forced to seek employment as a drawing teacher with the Education Department, although he doggedly continued his unique artistic search in isolation, undeterred by the air of hostility and neglect that effectively prevented this most religious of Maltese artists from ever being offered any Church commission. Kalleya returned to the limelight in the 1950s when modern art began to gain an audience in Malta.

II PAINTING – PRE-WAR RESTLESSNESS

The atmosphere of modern renewal affected Maltese painting

later, as is to be expected when one remembers that Giuseppe Calì died in 1930 and Lazzaro Pisani in 1932. The sterile, ailing religious-historical tradition in painting was then carried forward by Ganni Vella (1885-1977) and Joseph Briffa (1901-86), followed by others of lesser standard to this very day. Briffa was, though, a better-informed artist, for in his privately-executed work, he shunned the showy virtuosity and aplomb favoured by 'official' commissions, producing works that attest a genuine awareness of artistic truth. Significantly, during this phase of development, a number of other artists were forced to lead a kind of double life, producing commissions to order while privately pursuing their personal artistic search guided solely by their intuition. Giorgio Preca and Emvin Cremona have gone on record as resorting to this stratagem − a sure sign that the cold tradition had lost all its vitality.

As it seems most likely, the change would have come about slowly and gradually except that the 1940 entry of Italy into the war disrupted entirely this orderly development. Luckily, before this sad turn of events, the next generation of artists had been launched on their career, some of whom were to be key protagonists of the overdue transformation of Maltese art, while others were to follow down the same path in due course.

Between 1938 and 1940, a cluster of young and promising Maltese artists had contrived through various means to proceed to Rome, generally to attend painting classes at the *Regia Accademia* supervised by Carlo Siviero, and other courses at the British Academy in Rome then still under the direction of Antonio Sciortino. The group included Giorgio Preca (1909-84) who had finished his main studies in 1935, but had preferred to return to Rome where his services as a portrait-painter were much sought after. The other young contemporaries of Preca included Willie Apap (1918-70), Anton Inglott (1915-45), Emvin Cremona (1919-86), Esprit Barthet (b.1919), as well as the sculptors Victor Diacono (b.1915) and Samuel Bugeja.

These young painters' early training appears to have been of the conventional kind − in Malta at the hands of the indomitable Edward Caruana Dingli and Carmenu Mangion (b.1905). The latter had travelled widely in Europe and the USA, having even spent some time studying in Paris. He might well have intimated a broader approach and a wider appeciation of art in his young charges' minds. Siviero's ideas were altogether orthodox, although he did possess a rare feeling for colour which he managed to communicate. It is, therefore, not an accident that the Maltese group's first forays in art were understandably conventional but also marked by a sensitive chromatic treatment, and a repressed restlessness beneath the surface which betrays a deep-lying psychological uncertainty. Indeed, such a gifted and sensitive group of artists could not remain unaffected by the freedom and seriousness of modern art — anathemized in their native environment.

The war abruptly halted the inevitable denouement although even in these dark years some artistic activity was organized with the greatest of difficulties. Thus an art exhibition was held at the Palace in 1942, two Arts and Craft displays at the British Institute in 1942-3, as well as an Emvin Cremona personal exhibition at the same premises in December 1943. Preca's own first personal show had been organized in 1939. With the end of hostilities and the gradual return to normality, the rhythm of development was almost immediately resumed.

III SHIFTING CULTURAL LOYALTIES

A sign that the phalanx of conventionality was cracking became apparent in 1945 with Anton Inglott's *Death of St Joseph*, commissioned for the apse of the Msida parish church. Inglott's inspired stylization conjures an invisible but yet palpable frozen medium of religiosity — a far cry from the hollow, theatrical sentimentality that had been plaguing Church art in Malta for close to 150 years. As a cruel fate would have it, Inglott's delicate health gave way almost immediately. It was to prove a calamitous loss for Maltese art, particularly for Church art which never recovered from the blow.

In 1946 Giorgio Preca returned to Rome where he always felt more at home. By then, a big change had come over the city where at least the modern artistic movement had come into its own. Preca needed very little prompting to respond accordingly, for his enquiring nature had often been tempted to lean in the same direction — a transformation that was soon to prove providential for Maltese art. Still one of the effects of the war was to drive Italian cultural influence in Malta to the point of extinction. New bursaries and scholarships became available to Maltese art students, but this time the traffic was directed to UK institutes and schools – an opportunity availed of, among others, by Emvin Cremona, Samuel Bugeja, Victor Diacono, and Esprit Barthet.

The shift in cultural loyalties turned out to be more pronounced with the newer generation of Maltese artists, of whom Frank Portelli (b.1922) and J.M. Borg Xuereb (b.1928) studied art in Great Britain, while Antoine Camilleri (b.1922) proceeded first to Paris and then to Bath. The process continued further with the next generation of artists, so that Alfred Chircop (b.1933), Harry Alden (b.1929), Anton Agius (b.1933), and Toni Pace (b.1930) all studied in the UK. Gradually Italy began to regain some of its past appeal, especially the *Accademia Pietro Vanucci* of Perugia which has since claimed a giant share in training Maltese artists.

Other up-and-coming figures have to their credit a more picturesque itinerary, such as Gabriel Caruana (b.1929) who studied first in Perugia, then in Detroit, and subsequently at Faenza. More typical of the pattern is Alfred Chircop's record with his first studies in Perugia, Bath, and ultimately at the *Accademia di Belle Arti* in Rome. The same generation of Maltese artists were still in the initial stages of their career when the country gained its political independence; consequently, this paper will be concerned particularly with the activities of the first postwar generation.

The latter were effectively responsible for achieving that vital breakthrough towards a truly modern artistic expression. Luckily, they were also to prove so successful that in their wake they dragged in the same direction practically all the exponents of the previous generation who had so far held back. The instrument that helped them to turn back the tide and to attain their end turned out to be the foundation of an artists' association.

IV ART ASSOCIATIONS IN MALTA

Malta had already had by then a considerable tradition of art societies, probably the oldest of which was the Malta Art Amateur Association, alternatively known as the *Amatori dell'Arte*, composed of art-lovers, amateurs, and a sprinkling of artists. Its main activity appears to have consisted in organizing a huge yearly exhibition, generally in spring, at the Auberge d'Italie. By April 1931, it was organizing its eighteenth annual event – on which occasion sculptor Vincent Apap and *il giovanissmo Giorgio Preca* (in fact, he was already 22 years old) made their début.

In the previous year, Josef Kalleya had founded the first association of Maltese artists we know of in modern times. Grandiloquently termed *Accademia di Belle Arti* it held its first general meeting at Palazzo De La Salle, which was attended by such figures as Edward Caruana Dingli, Carmenu Mangion, Vincent Apap, V.M. Pellegrini, and others. Although its life appears to have been doomed from the start – it had no less than three honorary presidents – it proved to be the germ-society that lent inspiration to future artist-groups. As a matter of fact, it was soon faced with a rival group, the *Società degli Artisti Maltesi*, organized by sculptor George Borg, although again nothing concrete appears to have been accomplished.

Immediately after returning from Rome, Kalleya refounded his old group with the help of Antonio Caruana, this time on a more private basis, calling it *Studio Artistico Industriale Maltese Arte Sacra*. It represented a significant advance in the development of Maltese artistic ideas, for it offered facilities for nude study by subscription. Artists generally welcomed the idea, especially the younger ones who eagerly patronized the *Studio*; these included Vincent and Willie Apap, Emvin Cremona, Giuseppe Arcidiacono, Anton Inglott, Carmelo Borg Pisani, Esprit Barthet, Emm. Borg Gauci, and Giorgio Preca. Kalleya managed to keep it alive for eleven months between 1935 and 1936.

Both during the war and in the immediate aftermath, the British Institute – then sited in the Auberge D'Aragon – had kept up a lively tempo of artistic activities. It even promoted the organization of an Art Study Circle, founded on 9 May 1947, to which belonged various prominent British personalities stationed in Malta, together with several Maltese. It also organized too a very important exhibition of sculptures by

Antonio Sciortino in July 1947 at the Palace, Valletta, apart from holding other displays in which Antoine Camilleri, Emvin Cremona, Willie Apap, Joe Calleja, Frank Portelli, and others participated. It failed, though, to answer the needs of up-and-coming Maltese artists most of all because of its conservative bias.

Towards the end of 1948, Giorgio Preca, who used to commute between Malta and Rome, held a personal exhibition of his paintings at the Phoenicia Hotel. During the previous two years he had spent in the Italian capital, Preca liberated his art from the trappings of conventionality, entering upon the most exciting phase of his artistic career. He was careful, however, not to exhibit any of his more daring works in Malta. Still, the event presaged the change to come and managed to stir the stagnant waters of Maltese art.

The pace became even more hectic as the younger artists,who had been sent abroad for their studies, returned brimful with new ideas but doubting the reception reserved for all departures from conventionality. The winter of 1950 turned out to be full of promise. No less than four significant exhibitions were held, the first of which at Palazzo De La Salle by Antoine Camilleri. It was followed in the same place by a display (inaugurated by Nerik Mizzi, then Prime Minister) by a trio of artists – Jerry Caruana, J.F. Muscat, and Frank Baldacchino. In essence, the three formed a kind of nucleus prefiguring the later Modern Art Group. The third event was a show of watercolours by Giuseppe Arcidiacono (b.1908), an old-timer whose orderly and logical evolution from tradition-bound art to a genuine modern expression seems an instructive model of the course Maltese art would have followed had not the war disrupted the process. The last artistic event of 1950 was the winter exhibition of paintings and etchings by Frank Portelli that ran from 30 December 1950 to the following 13 January.

That winter witnessed the sowing of the seeds that were to cause a radical change in artistic orientation, bringing Malta on a level with the times, after lagging behind for well over a century. Strange as it may now seem, the situation was precipitated by an innocuous letter signed by S. Casabene carried in the *Times of Malta* of 12 May 1951. The letter drew attention to the lamentable state of art-education in the island

and the concomitant stagnation in the arts. More incisive still was a further contribution signed by J.F. Muscat – one of the inspirers and future founders of the Modern Art Group – which appeared in the same newspaper on 23 May 1951:

But I will be more frank and consequently more outrageous [wrote J.F. Muscat]; though art has passed through Impressionism, Dadaism, Nabism, Surrealism, Fauvism, and I do not know how many other movements, we have remained at a standstill, and we can still fondle any picture that is old and greasy and brown, irrespective of its value as a work of art.

The reaction was immediate and electrifying. It brought in its wake a shower of adverse and indignant comments, although the arguments put forward by the opponents of modern art were threadbare and confused. Wilfrid Flores, the most vociferous of the lot, remarked cryptically : 'But I do disagree with the fox or his publicity agent who, having lost his tail, returns to Malta and tries desperately to persuade the other foxes that it is much nicer to have no tails' – ostensibly a reference to Preca's role in rousing among his fellow artists a solid interest in modern artistic expression.

Apart from the strenuous efforts of J.F. Muscat, there were also powerful contributions from Hugo Carbonaro and Francis Ebejer; letters from Ebejer appeared in the same newspaper on 11 June and 2 July the same year.

It is all very well [he pleaded] to talk about the lessons and inspiration of tradition. But tradition may become a rut through long use. At the same time tradition has to start somewhere. It is based on experiment; it cannot live without experiment. Giotto was an experiment away from the stiff, formal art of his time.

In effect, the partisans for modern art kept scoring all the time, using one persuasive argument after another, although that was not to be the end of the matter. With the temperature still rising, the British Institute decided to hold a public debate on the specific motion that 'Modern art is no art at all'. As one can expect, a hot debate ensued with the younger artists pressing home their advantage so that, in spite of the prestigious opposition ranged against them, they carried the day by rejecting the motion with 36 votes to 14. Looking at the sequence of these events with the benefit of hindsight, it was a historic victory for Maltese culture.

V   THE MODERN ART GROUP

Flushed with their triumph, still the younger artists knew that they needed next to translate it into concrete action which they promptly proceeded to do by organizing the Modern Art Group, on the suggestion of J.F. Muscat, J.M. Borg Xuereb, and Frank Portelli. Months were spent in discussions during which the members often met in various Valletta cafés. Apart from these three artists, the Group's membership came to embrace Oliver Agius, Antoine Camilleri, Giorgio Preca, Jos. A. Caruana, Hugo Carbonaro, and Samuel Bugeja. For wider moral support, as well as to secure an adequate measure of publicity, the Group decided to affiliate as a component body of the Malta Cultural Institute (MCI), headed by Professor Gaston Tonna Barthet. Agreement on this alignment was reached on 14 February 1952 – not without considerable difficulties – and accordingly the Group began to call itself the Modern Art Circle.

Most members of the Circle were able to participate as a group in the 'Centenary Art Exhibition' held by the Malta Society of Arts, Manufactures, and Commerce at Palazzo De La Salle between 18 and 25 October 1952 in spite of objections raised by the still actively hostile opposition. In the Foreword to the exhibition's catalogue, the Curator of Fine Arts, Dr John A. Cauchi, remarked, by way of justification, that

In some cases the technique is novel and daring. True art is not a stagnant pool, but it moves with the times; and because of this, it is in continual evolution. We should not frown on certain works because at first they look to us somewhat unorthodox, but we should rather try and be sympathetic towards the artist who sometimes has been at pains finding out the means of expression most congenial to his personality.

The Circle, however, remained unsatisfied with the general presentation of their work and thus resolved to present itself to the public by organizing an event in which only the members' works were to be hung. On 17 January 1953, the Modern Art Circle launched its First Annual Exhibition on the premises of the Civil Service Sports Club, Hotel de Verdelin, Valletta. The eleven participants in this historic event for Maltese art were Oliver Agius (1910-82), Frank Baldacchino (b.1924), Joseph M. Borg Xuereb, Samuel Bugeja, Joe Calleja (later migrated to Canada), Antoine Camilleri, Hugo B. Carbonaro (1908-79), Jos. A. Caruana, John Fenech (b.1918), Frank Portelli, and Giorgio Preca; the last two were secretary and president respectively of the Circle. The exhibition catalogue, designed by Frank Portelli, was interspersed with an anthology of quotations from famous artists and critics on the nature of art.

The event created quite a stir and re-kindled old animosities so that the comments were generally adverse. An art correspondent, writing in the *Times of Malta* of 20 January 1953, sprayed his commentary with such jewels of irony as:

George Preca ... exhibited a series of abstract compositions to which various titles are appended. Even so late in the day, a proper appreciation of this out-moded style is an acquired taste ... Frank Portelli exhibited a number of problem-pictures in cubist manner ... It is hoped that he will soon get tired of his cubism as his undoubted talent deserves to be applied to something more convincing.

The same writer seems to be echoing the general reaction to this novel exposure to modern art when he opines that 'where the man in the street cannot see eye to eye with them at present is ... in the technique of their interpretations'.

Yet the occasion had also proved that the potential was there and that it was essentially a question of re-educating the prevailing decadent, stale taste. Within less than twelve months, the Modern Art Group, which had meanwhile severed its links with the MCI and resumed its old name, returned to the attack, launching its second exhibition, at the same venue, between 12 and 20 December 1953. The eleven original participants (except that J.F. Muscat had substituted Samuel Bugeja) were now flanked by three associate members – N. Camilleri, G.R. Hopson, and Toni Pace. Once more, the public reception did not prove encouraging, leading even to a minor polemic waged over newspapers' columns on the standard of the exhibits.

By then the movement was well launched on its course, better attended with each event organized by the Group. In fact, the opposing front began to weaken and eventually to crumble. When the 'Third Annual' was opened on 26 March 1955, it was marked by the entry of the sculptor Victor Diacono, while the

'Fourth Annual' held on 12 October 1956, proved a regular triumph with the participation of Esprit Barthet who had hitherto staunchly opposed the Group. Irrevocably he now threw his weight in favour of modern art, even going to the length of officially joining the Group which for the occasion was re-baptized Atelier-56.

VI THE MODERN RENEWAL OF MALTESE ART.

Independently of these events, Willie Apap, who spent his time between Malta and Rome, abandoned the trappings of academicism which he had brilliantly outgrown, to begin creating a series of great works that now constitute his chief claim to artistic fame. In fact, the increasingly mature progression of modern sensibility in Maltese art was sealed by the emergence of the next generation of artists, all committed from the beginning of their careers to explore the rich variety of modern sensibility and construct their own art on such a basis. These initiatives have given Maltese contemporary art its rich cosmopolitan character, often commingled with indigenous traits. Among the young Maltese artists who thus received their baptism of fire, one can single out George Fenech (b.1926), Harry Alden, Gabriel Caruana, Toni Pace, John Bonnici (b.1932), Alfred Chircop, Anton Agius, Richard England (b.1937), and Joseph Casha (b.1939).

In the field of sculpture, the emergence of Joseph Genuis (1934-70) and Edward Pirotta (1939-68) presaged an exciting future, a hope that was slightly blighted by the premature death of both these highly-gifted sculptors. The artists' association Atelier-56 remained active up to the early seventies, although with the passage of time its influence began to fade, presumably because it had fulfilled all the expectations it had set out to propagate. With Emvin Cremona producing his popular impastos, soon followed by his celebrated 'glass' series, there were no further dissenters of merit left on the scene.

This development was succinctly summed up by Renato La Ferla in his introductory note to the catalogue of the XIIth Annual Art Exhibition, held at the National Museum of Fine Arts in Valletta between 18 and 29 December 1969.

How does it feel [remarked La Ferla] to be a revolutionary after the revolution is over? Especially if the revolution has been a success and those who used to come to laugh in derision at what they used to think was madness, now came to stand in awe before what they had been told is creative expression.

As Malta entered upon a decisive phase of its long history — the acquisition of its political independence in 1964 — Maltese art had, thanks entirely to a supreme effort of its own artists, pulled itself out of the tormented artistic limbo into which it had sunk and languished after the fateful events of 1800. In the realm of art, too, little Malta was able to face the world, not as a culturally ailing Third World country, but as a valid member of the international community.

Dominic Cutajar

NOTES

Part One: 1800-60

[1] H.G. Schenk, *The Mind of the European Romantics*, 38.

[2] D. Cutajar, 'The Lure of the Orient: The Schranzes, the Brockdorffs, Preziosi and other artists', 101-36, where attention is drawn to a brief visit paid to Malta by William Turner on 7 May 1828 on board the *pacchetto a vapore Real Ferdinand* bound back for Naples.

[3] For a biography of Gianni, A. Ganado, 'Girolamo Gianni 1837-1895 — Two decades of landscape-painting in Malta'. For Vincenzo D'Esposito, D. Cutajar, 'Vincenzo D'Esposito — The sensibility of a Late Romantic in a Maltese setting'. Vincenzo D'Esposito was born in Naples on 5 March 1886; he was brought to Malta at the age of six months, where he practically spent the rest of his life. Exiled in 1940, D'Esposito died in Novara in September 1946.

[4] Cutajar, 'The Lure of the Orient', 111.

[5] Stefano Zerafa read his *Discorso* as an oration at the inauguration of the academic year on 1 October 1850. *L'Ordine,* ii, 68, (5 October 1850), reported: 'Il dottor Stefano Zerafa, professore di Botanica e di Medicina legale recitò un discorso archaeologico (sic) relativo alla scoltura, architettura e pittura nostrale che fu generalmente applaudito'.

[6] The report is entitled *Relazione dello stato delle scuole del Disegno nell' Università di Malta dal 1802 al 1850;* the unpaginated text is found in PAV, *Malta Miscellaneous Papers,* ii.

[7] This key passage in the original reads: 'A maggior intelligenza del nostro soggetto, credo proprio di dare in breve un'idea del progresso contemporaneo sul continente circa lo studio delle Belle Arti. Le arti cristiane hanno segnalato il primo movimento : esse hanno dato addosso al barocchismo il quale avea guastate non pur le arti, ma le massime ancora per ristabilirle. A Roma giovani

artisti dalla Germania salirano per contemplare muti e pensierosi gli affreschi del Vaticano, ed in questo intelletuale ritiro, nel quale consumarono ore intere del giorno, comparavano i procedimenti delle moderne accademie e dei moderni maestri e le loro dottrine; e tra gli altri oggetti della loro meditazione e le opere dell'arte moderna vedevano un'infinita differenza.'

[8] In the original: 'Premessa questa breve ed informe notizia, è cosa giusta il dire che del movimento in se, che doveva produrre una generale rivoluzione di idee riguardo lo studio delle arti stesse, qui fra i nostri non si sapeva nulla.'

[9] In the original: 'Gli artisti risorti a miglior vita davano in ogni genere opere meravigliose liberi dal barocchismo e dal lezzo del Voltarianismo, che in odio alla religione le avea infettate, queste opere spargevano una lieta novella.'

[10] For some information on Grognet's ideas, projects and works, D. Cutajar, 'The fascinating personality of Giorgio Grognet'.

[11] G. Calleja, 'Rocco Buhagiar Pittore'.

[12] *Malta Letteraria,* vii, (March-April 1910).

[13] *L'Arte,* i, 5 (1863), 3-5.

[14] *L'Ordine,* x, 449 (22 January 1858).

[15] *L'Arte,* i, 7 (February 1863), 3-4.

[16] *L'Ordine,* iii, 86 (8 February 1851)

[17] Ibid., iii, 52 (15 June 1850)

[18] *The Malta Times,* 15 August 1840.

[19] *L'Arte,* iii, 49, 4-6. In the original Dr Zammit's analysis reads: 'Il suo fare (referring to Zahra) si direbbe oggi barocco, e non manco forse d'esserlo nel senso accettato di questa parola; ma è esso perciò meno affine al vero, meno impressivo od artistico? Il compasso e la squadra portali nell'arte l'hanno assiderata. Un'esuberanza ermeneutica, poggiata a metafisiche sottigliezze proclamò nel genero sacro la scuola dello spirito, declamando contro il sensualismo della forma. Nella voga delle mummie, di stecche coperte d'un cencio e pieghe perpendiculari, nel gusto di figure tisiche e stentate − nella negazione d'ogni bellezza e d'ogni attrattiva si trovò la ragione del sublime, si appellò divino quel che il buon senso non direbbe che deforme. Questa pittura a geroglifici se giova alla contemplazione, non può essere capace d'un' impressione, non può rappresentare un bello se lascia supporlo. Nella povertà e grettezza dei modi, nell'astinenza del senso, nell'antipatia pel finito essa pretende rivelare un infinito. Il nostro artista (again referring to Zahra) non era di questa setta che venne dopo di lui, ispirata meno da un'elevazione ascetica che dalla sterilità d'un immaginazione costretta a trovare eloquente il silenzio, sublime la negazione, divino la miseria dell'arte.'

[20] Zerafa, *Discorso sulla storia artistica di Malta,* 33-4. No wonder that many of Busuttil's figures appear in danger of sloping off the canvas.

[21] PAV, *Blue Book, 1823* for the date of Michele Busuttil's appointment as Professore di Disegno. Also ibid., *Malta Miscellaneous Papers,* ii, for the *Relazione.*

[22] Ibid.

[23] D. Cutajar, 'Alberto Pullicino', for a brief biographical sketch on this eighteenth-century *vedutista.*

[24] For a biography of G. Pullicino, M. Ellul, 'Art and Architecture in Malta in the early 19th Century', 1-19.

[25] Here is the list of the holders of the post of professors or teachers of Drawing between 1800 and 1921.

Michele Busuttil

Giorgio Pullicino

Pietro Paolo Caruana

Michele Bellanti
Giuseppe Calleja
(Post vacant in 1893)
Giuseppe Cali
Giuseppe Duca

[26] Giuseppe Hyzler was born on 5 October 1787: PA, *Porto Salvo, Reg. Batt. 1787-98*, 40.

[27] PAV, *Arrivals*, xvi (unpaginated), 19 August 1822; Hyzler arrived on the Sardinian pink *Sant' Antonio* from Civitavecchia.

[28] For Minardi's intervention in Giuseppe Bonnici's work, *L'Ordine*, vi, 260 (16 June 1854); also A. Ferris, *Descrizione storica delle chiese*, 468. For Pietro Gagliardi's employment of his brother Giovanni, ibid., 263.

[29] For an outline of this complex affair, *L'Ordine*, iii, 87 (15 February 1851); ibid., 129 (6 December 1851); ibid., vi, 244 (17 February 1854); and ibid., 247 (10 March 1854).

[30] T. McGill, *A Handbook or Guide for strangers visiting Malta*, 59: 'the Malta Fencibles were for some years permitted to assemble for mass in this fine temple ... until with their arms and iron heels they had punched into irreparable ruin the beautiful mosaic pavement.'

[31] Some halls in the Magistral Palace were similarly converted, at first under the direction of Sir George Whitmore (1775-1862). According to *L'Arte*, ii, 31 (February 1864), 3 : 'Ci è grato ricordare le ricche decorazioni di cui il governo ha pensato, testè, fregiare il vasto salone da ballo del Palazzo ... opera del valente artista Sig. G. Sabbatini di Roma.'

[32] *The Malta Times*, 10 July 1840; the long comment in *Il Portafoglio*, iii, 114 (6 July 1840) looks like a justification written by Hyzler himself. It contains an explanation regarding the de Rohan monument erected on the design of Antonaccio Grech, brother of Giuseppe Grech. The original project submitted by the talented Giuseppe Casha was rejected − a circumstance that might account for Casha's reluctance to return to Malta.

[33] *Il Mediterraneo*, 805 (28 December 1853); ibid., 807 (11 January 1854). *Il Portafoglio*, 872 (11 January 1854); and *L'Ordine*, vi, 239 (13 January 1854).

[34] The part of the canvas added to the *San Giovannino* by Hyzler, as recently found out during restoration, represents a Romanticized rosy-tinged landscape, done with admirable taste − one must admit − although both paintings were of course 'falsified' by the additions. A more genuine use of a similarly Romanticized landscape appears in Hyzler's portrait of Sir Hilderbrand Oakes, now in the National Library of Malta.

[35] AOM 1358, despatch from the Order's ambassador in Rome, dated 14 September 1762, announcing the award in 1762 to Casha for the first prize in Sculpture. Also NLM, *Lib.* 1142, *Galleria Maltese*, entry no.629; also *Il Portafoglio*, iii, 114 (6 July 1840). There does not seem to be a single sculptural work of Casha in Malta.

[36] *L'Arte*, iv, 79 (22 February 1866).

[37] For Salvatore Busuttil's birth-registration − PA, *San Paolo, Reg. Batt. 1797-1809*, 30 January 1798, 56. For his death's report, *L'Ordine*, 278 (13 October 1854); the artist's death occurred on 19 August 1854; his last will was registered in the acts of Notary Giacomo Fratocchi, 13 November 1849.

[38] *L'Arte*, i, 10 (April 1863), 3-6; for Farrugia's return to Malta via Leghorn, PAV, *Arrivals & Departures* (1837), xliii, f.3010.

[39] For a biography of P. P. Caruana, A. Ganado, 'Pietro Paolo Caruana: the first lithographs produced in Malta', 49-60.

[40] *L'Arte*, ii, 28 (7 January 1864), 2-4.

[41] In this sense, Pietro Paolo Caruana can be considered as the prototype of a class of Maltese artists with an inverted artistic evolution, fading gradually away after a brilliant start; the most illustrious example is, of course, Antonio Sciortino. P.P. Caruana's obituary appeared in *L'Ordine*, iv (1 May 1852).

[42] D. Cutajar, 'The Lure of the Orient', 131-2.

[43] *L'Arte*, ii, 37 (May 1864); *The Malta Times*, 31 July 1840; *L'Ordine*, ii, 65 (14 September 1850); and ibid., iv, 162, 163 (24, 31 July 1852).

[44] The present writer has come to believe that Vincenzo was either a cousin or a nephew of Giuseppe Hyzler, adopted by the latter's aging parents just before he left for Rome in 1814.

[45] *L'Arte*, i, 5 (1863), 3-5. Also PAV, *Arrivals & Departures*, , xlix, f.412, and lxiv, f.475. Also Calleja's adulatory sketch in *Malta Letteraria*, iii. (January 1906), 3-9.

[46] There is some confusion about the generalities of this minor artist. For Antonio Falson's birth-registration, see PA, *San Paolo, Batt.1797-1809*, 441 (4 December 1805). Also *L'Ordine*, vi, 244 (17 February 1854), and 266 (21 July 1854).

[47] *L'Ordine*, vi, 260 (16 June 1854).

[48] For Henry Casolani's baptismal registration, PA, *Porto Salvo 1811-17*, 492 (14 October 1817); for his movements : PAV, *Arrivals & Departures*, lxiv, f.475 (12 July 1843) from Civitavecchia; ibid, lxx, f.994 (26 November 1844) to Italy; ibid., lxxiii, f.478 (1 August 1845) from Naples; ibid., lxxx, f.570 (26 May 1847) to Italy. NLM, *Lib*.1487, 1479 and 1480 contain pencil-drawings by Casolani. *L'Arte*, i, 7 (February 1863), 4, *apud* biography of Giuseppe Hyzler, there is the note: 'Si sono, oltre ai rimasti qui in paese, distinti a Londra i due suoi allievi Bonavia e Casolani'.

[49] For Amodeo Preziosi's baptismal registration, PA, *Porto Salvo, Batt.1810-1817*, 2 December 1816. For that of the brothers Frederick and Luigi Brockdorff, ibid., 6 April 1811 and 28 December 1812 respectively. For that of Luigi (Aloysio) Taffien, ibid., 9 September 1811; it is likely that Taffien returned to Malta later.

[50] I have examined this major development in nineteenth-century Maltese art at greater length in 'The lure of the Orient', 101-37, where it is indicated that 'a net division of interest in Maltese nineteenth-century art, between the traditionalists who sought a 'serious' renewal through the infusion of the Nazarener ideology – a group among whom the Hyzlers were the main protagonists – and those open to the Romantic impact seeking to fulfil it in the wider Mediterranean context.'

[51] For what appears to be the first notice of Gallucci, *L'Ordine*, x, 449, 22 January 1858; he was soon commissioned for the painting of the Mdina Cathedral dome; the fact that his brother was Bishop of Loreto appears to have commended his services as much as his art. The first mention of Gagliardi's work to appear in the local press seems to be a note in *L'Arte*, iv, 82 (April 1866), reporting a painting of his being commissioned and sent 'da Roma al molto Rev.Sig. il Canonico capitulare Dr. Don P. Pullicino'.

[52] For an informative biography of Mariano Gerada, E. E. Montanaro, 'The People's Sculptor'.

[53] For Vincenzo Bonnici, *L'Arte*, i, 6; ibid., ii, 28 (1864), 6; ibid., iii, 67 (22 August 1865).

[54] Several works of Carlo Darmanin are listed in A. Micallef, 'Carlo Darmanin 1825-1909 – Malta's foremost statuary'.

[55] For a summary account on Maltese sculpture, S. Zarb and M. Buhagiar, *St Catherine of Alexandria*, 215-23.

Part Two: 1860-1921

[1] A Neapolitan artist born in Barletta, whose expulsion from Naples where he was trained forced him to proceed to Florence where he came into contact with the *Macchiaioli,* and thence to Paris.

[2] Morelli is represented at the National Museum of Fine Arts in Valletta by a small canvas entitled *A Lady,* part of the Edward Caruana Dingli Bequest. Though it cannot, as a subject, provide hints at Morelli's more grandiose compositions, it gives sufficient insight into the Italian artist as the source of Cali brushware technique.

[3] V. Bonello, *La Madonna nell'Arte,* 48.

[4] E. Sammut, *Art in Malta,* 92.

[5] The *St Jerome* at the Sacred Heart Church in Sliema is widely considered as Cali's best representative painting of his first phase. Also belonging to the same period were paintings on the dome and ceiling of the parish church at Cospicua (1884) which were unfortunately replaced, except for those above the nave proper, by other paintings on canvas executed in 1929 by Virgilio Monti. The four prophets in the pendentives under the main dome, which must be considered as among the most powerful figures to have emerged from the hands of the artist, were luckily spared. See M. Buhagiar 'Xogħlijiet ta' Arti w Artiġjanat fil-Knisja ta' San Ġorġ', 59-91.

[6] In V. Borg (ed.), *Il-Knisja Parrokkjali ta' Ħal Lija,* Rafel Bonnici Cali relates that the German Consul, Baron von Tucker, considered Cali's painting of *Christ surrounded by Children,* above the main door of the parish church at Lija, as the most beautiful painting which he had ever come across.

[7] The only instance where these three representatives of the Cali family are shown together is the chapel of the Holy Crucifix in the parish church at Cospicua: Giuseppe painted episodes from the childhood of Christ on the dome together with four seraphim in the pendentives (1903), Ramiro has an altarpiece showing the Sacred Heart of Jesus with souls (1925), while Raffaele utilized *bozzetti* by Giuseppe to decorate the apsidal vaults with Passion scenes.

[8] For a contemporary account of the exhibition, H. Ganado, *Jien Inħobb Nitkellem Magħkom,* 78. The figure of 15,000 visitors, a substantial figure for an art event in Malta, is mentioned.

[9] Pisani's main ecclesiastical works are found in the parish churches of Siġġiewi and Nadur, the latter widely considered as the chief extant testimony of his art. In addition one must mention his decoration in the Dominican church of the Annunciation at Vittoriosa which, until totally destroyed during the Second World War, incorporated the largest piece of ceiling fresco in Maltese churches.

[10] Bruschi worked for a time in the Maltese Islands, among his more important works being the painting of *Our Lady as Queen of Heaven* (1880) in the Canons' Vestry of the cathedral in Victoria, Gozo, and the altarpiece showing the *Annunciation of the Virgin* (1886) at the cathedral in Mdina.

[11] V.M. Pellegrini writing an introduction to the artist for a retrospective exhibition held at the Society of Arts, Manufactures, and Commerce in December 1983.

[12] For a more detailed treatment, H. P. Scicluna, *The Church of St. John in Valletta,* 204.

[13] Minardi (1787 - 1871) was a vital formative element on several Maltese artists. Vincenzo Bonello writes : 'quasi tutti i pittori maltesi che fiorirono nel '800 uscirono da quella scuola'. *La Madonna nell'Arte,* 77.

[14] Among works in this vein could be cited the four figures of Deborah, Judith, Jahel, and Esther (1888) in the pendentives under the *trompe l'oeil* dome of the

Gozo cathedral.

[15] In 1979 Aldo Vella, son of the artist, compiled a pictorial biography to coincide with the second anniversary of his death. It was launched on the occasion of a retrospective exhibition at the National Museum of Fine Arts. Another exhibition followed in 1983 at the National Museum of Archaeology.

[16] In recognition of his long artistic activity, Gianni Vella was awarded a Gold Medal by the Malta Society of Arts, Manufactures, and Commerce on 22 December 1976.

[17] See E.V. Borg's Foreword to the catalogue of *Maltese Sculptures and Ceramics* for the exhibition held at the Gallerija Feniċi in March/April 1981.

[18] Sciortino held the coveted post of Director of the British Academy for 25 years.

[19] The plaster-cast is on permanent display in the courtyard of the National Museum of Fine Arts.

[20] Rodin's variegated figures gave a vague sense of the Impressionistic technique to which Sciortino was visibly drawn during this period.

[21] Sciortino is the best-represented artist at the National Museum of Fine Arts, thanks to the Deed of Donation, dated 11 February 1947, which states: 'It is the will of Professor Sciortino that the works of art donated by him to the people of Malta shall be housed at the Malta Museum and there exhibited to the general public.' The decorator Giuseppe Galea (b.1911) was instrumental in bringing to Malta the whole collection of works from Sciortino's studio in Rome.

[22] John Spiteri Sacco (b.1907), who for at a time was tutored by Sciortino at the British Academy in Rome, is practically the only artist to have aligned his style on a mild interpretation of Sciortino.

13

OLIVER FRIGGIERI

The Search for a National Identity
in Maltese Literature

The literary critic is hardly supposed to ignore or to underestimate the social and political factors that contribute to the formation of a collective consciousness. Such factors directly or indirectly enable an author to arrive at his personal degree of awareness and to discover the appropriate modes of self-expression. Although the aesthetic merit of a literary work does not depend either on the relationship between society and the writer, or on the degree of faithfulness with which the former is reflected by the latter, the search for relevance necessitates the recognition of the objective forces determining the author's subjective interpretation. It is possible to give a work of an eminently private and intimate nature a subtle political reading. On the other hand, such political content easily comes to the fore in the case of a work which is intentionally extrovert, meant to look at things in their proper empirical perspective and ignore or subdue the suggestions of introspection.

A scientific analysis of a literary product can exist, and is supposed to exist, without any reference to its social milieu, although social influence is a subconscious energy stronger and more far-reaching than even the will of the author himself. In a purely sociological and political account, like the present one, the critic adopts two intimately related, though distinct, criteria: (a) the establishment of a work's intrinsic literary value and its worth in terms of creativity and social relevance; (b) the detection of a harmony between aesthetic strategy and social commitment, with the consequence that, for the sole purposes of such an enquiry, the former is considered as an efficient instrument for the expression of the latter. Whereas literary merits are taken for granted, credit and emphasis are given to those features which qualify a work as a reflection of its own time and space dimensions.

In the adoption of such a scientific methodology, the critic should not forget that spiritual experience, such as literature is, can never be subservient to geographical demarcations or to superficial racial distinctions. Consequently he must insert the author's place of origin within the proper regional and continental context, thus considering the particular region or continent as the whole 'nation' of which the author's country of origin is just a component. Such a consideration is more than ever necessary in the case of tiny islands like Malta which, mainly owing to geographical limitations, have partly formed their identity through the conditions imposed by political colonialism.

The application of these principles in the analysis of the influence of British colonialism on the development of a national literature in Maltese implies a thorough defining of a set of linguistic relationships between English and Maltese, ultimately reducible to the social rapport between the colonizers and the native population, or the relationship between the old and sophisticated cultural tradition of Britain and the uncultivated and downtrodden popular culture of the Maltese, necessarily resolving itself into a psychological, violent confrontation between two highly disparate patrimonies. In the first decades of the nineteenth century Maltese literature gradually emerged into existence and attempted to assert itself. The orientation of European culture in the previous centuries hampered such a process; the Maltese popular heritage could only rise to a dignified level in so far as international cultural awareness developed a democratic approach towards the hitherto underestimated cultural expressions of the people.

I THE BIRTH OF A MALTESE NATIONAL CONSCIENCE

Colonial domination implied a psychological submission and the adoption of a peaceful attitude when faced by officialdom. The Maltese, profoundly embedded in a centuries-old Christian culture which greatly encouraged collective passivity and resignation, could hardly become instantly conscious of a different mode of being, and much less of a predisposition diametrically opposed to the one adopted since time immemorial. The active presence of the Order of St John in Malta guaranteed not only a certain degree of political security, especially from foreign invasions, but also the continuation of traditional behaviour; culturally, it ensured the adherence to the recognized canons of the Renaissance and neo-classicism which the Order had succeeded in establishing in the island in all the forms of cultural expression, particularly architecture, music, and literature. The official adoption of Italian, the language of high culture, is obviously the most significant development in this context.

The rising of the Maltese against the French, however, unequivocally marks an early form of popular participation in the new spirit of rebellion typical of modern Europe. Submission soon began to be called into question and the most tenuous feeling of patriotism started to creep in. The new democratic belief sweeping the continent was bound to reach the island eventually. The presence of Napoleon in Malta in 1798 manifested the principal paradox of Maltese modern history: on the one hand, his challenge constituted a threat to national security; on the other, it was a spark of rebellion which could serve as a subtle example to the people, at least to the few Maltese personalities gradually developing into unofficial leaders and authentic motivators of a modern awareness. Moreover, one should consider the vast activity carried out in the island by numerous Italian exiles in the first half of the nineteenth century, some of whom, including eminent writers and journalists, found refuge as well as understanding. Their example was soon bound to influence the Maltese.

This is the first important political conclusion to be drawn from the evaluation of the complex situation in nineteenth-century Malta: the traditional passivity of the people, directly reflected in the poetry and prose produced in Italian, came to be directly provoked by the political activities of Italian exiles on the island. The irresistible image of democracy which Britain managed to give of itself to the locals and to the outer world enticed many activists of the Risorgimento to develop to the full their plans in Malta. The traditional resignation conflicted increasingly with the modern sense of rebellion. This dualism soon had its impact on Maltese sensibility, and fundamentally contained all the ingredients necessary to form a confrontation of sorts between the culture of Britain and that of Italy, within the close confines of the Maltese colony. British culture primarily signified a political system which hardly conceded any effective constitutional rights to the Maltese; Italian culture resembled the ancient classical heritage of the country as a civilized entity. As time went by, the Language Question, itself an apparently odious and outdated controversy about two languages (Italian and English) in social conflict, and in no significant manner a debate on the (ignored) efficiency and utility of the native tongue (Maltese), was to develop into a complex political battle and to invest all sectors of society, finally becoming a quest for national identity.[1]

As far back as 1796, the solitary voice of Mikiel Anton Vassalli (1764-1829) had insisted on the social need to cultivate the *lingua nazionale* (which for him was Maltese, and not Italian) and mould it into a refined vehicle for popular education and the adequate development of an autonomous literature.[2] Vassalli received his education in Rome, where he published some of his works, and imbibed highly liberal ideas on the principles of popular participation in culture and of the democratic diffusion of knowledge. His illuministic spirit urged him to attach paramount importance to the function of the language of the uncultivated masses.[3] He envisaged Maltese as a unique (and most useful) document of the island's antiquity, worthy of the scholar's objective research and of the cultured people's refined adoption.[4] While admitting that, at a first glance, Maltese seemed undignified and abundant in barbarisms, he concluded that this was only the result of its having been neglected for such a long time.[5]

A cosmopolitan in the sense that he had travelled widely abroad, an authentic nationalist at heart and in his professed beliefs, Vassalli is the end-product of two apparently distinct, mutually exclusive European cultural movements, – Illuminism and Romanticism; in reality, he is the realization of a synthetic fusion of the fundamental tenets of both. He characteristically discovered the supreme value of the concept of *patria*, and arrived at a sort of political programme for the island in the light of his experiences abroad. He considered Malta as a spiritual and physical organism, the centre of interests wherein individuality is acquired and nurtured through the recognition of a national tradition, history, culture and, above all, language.[6]

The influence of such a rich and multidimensional figure as Vassalli was felt most in the first decades of the twentieth century, when Dun Karm (1871-1961) immediately transformed him into a national figure in a number of widely known poems like 'Lil Dun Mikiel Xerri' and 'Lil Ħaż-Żebbuġ Raħal Twelidi'. Ġużè Aquilina gave him a significant role in Taħt Tliet Saltniet and Ninu Cremona wrote his biography, which was later to be enriched by the research of other scholars. In Vassalli, Maltese writers saw not only an isolated scholar, completely misunderstood or utterly ignored in his times, but also a symbol of national awareness which was to animate the people in their fight for independence. Dun Karm attributed these merits in the final tercet of 'Lil Mikiel Anton Vassalli' published in 1933:

> iżd'għax ħabbejtha lil din l-art ħanina,
> u kont ewlieni fost in-nisel tagħna
> li ħsibt il-jedd li nkunu ġens għalina.†

The medium of communication which Vassalli did not have at this disposal was provided to his successors when the British Government conceded the right of the liberty of the press to the Maltese in 1839. Under colonial rule the press was rigorously controlled, and requests for the setting up of printing presses were not acceded to. Permission, denied to local citizens, was only granted to some religious institutions and to the Missionary Society of the Anglican Church which used to publish religious books for distribution in the Mediterranean, the Adriatic, and the Middle East.[7] This right was granted only following repeated requests by the Maltese[8] and in spite of the opposition of foreign Governments which did not agree with the diffusion of the printed word in their country. Their concern was not unfounded since the highly active Italian exiles in Malta were determined to make the fullest use of this facility; on the other

† But since you loved this gentle land / and were the first among our offspring / to conceive our right of becoming a nation.

hand, the social and political frustrations of the people could easily find the proper vehicle for public expression and communication. Maltese liberals could co-ordinate further and on a wider scale their hitherto isolated efforts.

Consequently many newspapers were published in Italian, in English, and in Maltese.[9] Journalism was to prove enormously effective in arousing popular interest in political matters and simultaneously in providing authors with an adequate means of communication. Writers and journalists (hardly distinguishable at this stage in the history of popular communication in Malta) began to assemble and to collaborate towards the same ideal which, as things developed further and the political situation became more complex first in Italy and later in Malta, assumed the nature of a twofold phenomenon: an Italian cause and a Maltese effect. The example set by the Italian exiles was to be assumed, at least on the level of awareness, by the Maltese writers, though it is fair to admit that the Maltese spirit was still led by its traditional sense of prudence in its confrontation with foreign rule. But there are subtle exceptions: Giorgio Mitrovich (1794-1885) is frequently reminiscent of Mazzini's passionate exhortations in his patriotic appeals to his fellow citizens.[10] It was a little early to expect the Maltese to be fully aware of the concept of an independent nation (a concept which is not only ideological but also economic), but Mitrovich's term *rigenerazione* (regeneration) is already a large step ahead, very near to the term *risorgimento* which is emblematic of the Italian movement. As the Italian journalists in the island spoke out in eloquent, unequivocal terms, so did the Maltese patriots who exploited any occasion provided by their foreign colleagues to give vent to their anger and to urge the people to become conscious of fundamental political rights.

The prophetic spirit of Mazzini, himself a man of letters who provided Maltese literature with some of its most typical patriotic images and patterns of phraseology, can be easily detected whenever the analysis of the local contemporary situation included the visualization of a future achievement.[11]

In due course, these sentiments were to be transferred from the domain of political discourse to the realm of literary production, and the main theme of Maltese literature was soon to become nationhood, a concept to be defined and expressed in the Romantic terms so typical of the times. This vision includes a historical and cultural evaluation of the ancient identity of the island, essentially composed of the religious tradition, the heroic events of the remote past, the enchanting beauty of the countryside, the moral and physical virtues of the Maltese (especially the village woman), and the Maltese language as the most distinctive feature of the national community. The discovery of the vividness and expressive richness of the Maltese language was supposed to be justified and finally accepted by the different sectors of society in so far as it coincided with the discovery of a relevant political and social thematic content, that is, of a set of themes wide and profound enough to embrace the tensions and aspirations of a subdued colonial people possessing a culture, a religion, a language, and a history, distinct from those of their rulers. It is superfluous to recall that nobody could then look at English as the most popular and useful medium of international communication; it was rather considered from a purely political standpoint — as the speech habit of the colonizers which, if imposed through legislation, could condemn politicians and most of the writers and men of culture to dumbness. From De Soldanis to Vassalli, Ġużè Muscat Azzopardi, Anastasju Cuschieri, Dun Karm, and Ninu Cremona, there is one unbroken line of cultural continuity: all of them had an Italian-orientated formation and produced many works in Italian. Subsequently, however, they passed on to the discovery of Maltese in a harmoniously natural manner, namely when the political and cultural situation matured enough as to render this choice purely linguistic and in no way cultural — an irresistibly natural, democratic step in their roles as faithful interpreters of their country's evolution.

II The Poets of the Nineteenth Century and Early Twentieth Century

Within the framework of Romantic ideology, and especially in terms of its nationalistic component, the recognition of the language amounted to a recognition of national identity. De Amicis' dictum — *dove non c'è lingua non c'è nazione* (where there is no language, there is no nation) — was shared by almost all the thinkers of nineteenth-century Europe. From cosmopolitanism of the Illuminists, the Romantics derived their own concept of cultural democracy; they soon realized that their political cause had to be focused on the concept of a nation, and no longer on the unattainable vision of the whole world as one nation. Popular unity could be attained on a national scale through the adoption of the vernacular or even through the transformation of the refined literary idiom into a faithful image of the popular speech habits. There is much to confirm that this awareness is the key-motive of whatever happened in Maltese literature during the nineteenth century, when writing in Maltese made huge strides on the journalistic and aesthetic levels, and the appreciation of the language gradually widened to assume the shape of a thorough evaluation of the country itself, now defined and considered primarily as a fully-fledged nation.

Patriotic sentiment really developed into a creed when the writers found their truest personality in its expression and divulged it among the people in various literary forms. In Maltese, and no longer in Italian, the writer could exploit in a modern direction the most uncontested principle in European aesthetics, that is the Horatian principle of *prodesse* and *dilectare*: literature is duty bound to teach and to give pleasure, or better, to be pleasantly instructive. The earliest exponent of this democratic approach is Ġan Anton Vassallo (1817-1868), Professor of Italian at the University of Malta and a poet of an admirably constant popular inspiration. He himself declared that he intended to teach the people with his works.[12] It was the people who made him dedicate himself to literature, and the people were the source of his inspiration. Utility and relevance, as well as enjoyment, are the over-riding concerns of his literary production.[13]

A prominent feature of his is the application of historical events and nationalistic sentiments to the contemporary situation. He sorts out significant landmarks in history and relates them to immediate experiences. Even in this respect, Vassallo shares the psychology typical of various Italian Romantic poets: through the evocation of remote events, and by relating them to identifiable contemporary conditions, the poet succeeds in being both relevant and prudent. His implications are frequently clear though they are always veiled under a thin layer of imagination which renders them ambiguous and open to various interpretations. Like most of his successors, he rarely, if ever, indulges in the direct speech typical of politicians.

Of all the epochs of Maltese history, Vassallo chose the period of the Order of St John and identified therein the characteristics of a colonial condition. The best example is provided by *Mannarino* which is subdivided into four sections. The Maltese patriot is depicted in four different moments of his life; he speaks to the Maltese people; subsequently, he is presented as a prisoner; then he speaks his mind in front of Bonaparte, who eventually closes the whole episode. Vassallo dramatizes patriotic sentiments by creating an imaginative event and placing it against a known historical background. During the reign of Grand Master Ximenes, the Maltese had suffered various political abuses, and popular discontent was considerable. The Order had ignored the claims of the people, and Gejtu Mannarino, a priest, organized a protest against the foreign rulers. Vassallo adapts historical facts to construct a political situation in which the people fight for their emancipation; relevance is reached in the typical Romantic manner, that is, through the depiction of a remote condition analogous to the contemporary state of affairs. The theme of national subjugation, the urge for rebellion and civil agitation against the irresponsibility and abuse of the foreign dominators, the prophetic vision of a free future, the appeal to the citizens to rise up and fight for their own liberation, and the solidarity amongst the Maltese forming one whole family of brothers and sisters, all faithful towards one same 'mother' calling them for battle: all these features are typical of the Italian model of patriotic poetry prevalent during the Risorgimento:

> Ilha wisq marida qalbi
> fuq li ġralha din il-gżira...
> F'kelma waħda rrid ingħidu
> aħna lsiera, Malta lsira!

> Naqilbuhom! Xejn la tibżgħu,

ej' ningħaqdu lkoll flimkien
u naħilfu li nġarrfuhom,
l-ewwel wieħed naħlef jien.[14]†

Various other poets, such as Richard Taylor (1818-1868),
Dwardu Cachia (1853-1907), and Ġużè Muscat Azzopardi
(1853-1927), all adopt the same literary technique to render past
events relevant and to trace parallelisms between the past and
the present. Altough not all of them express themselves with
the same intensity concerning colonial rule, they all make use
of poetry as a vehicle for the dissemination of anticolonial
feelings and for the forging of a collective self-confidence. These
poets filled page after page of the papers and magazines of the
period with verse which provided enjoyment as much as it
expressed national solidarity; as a group, they contributed
considerably towards the development of a national democratic
culture which, later, was to find its supreme expression in Dun
Karm, who was acclaimed national poet in 1935.

These sentiments were rarely combined with a direct political
action; the anticolonialism of most of the poets did not transform
itself into real rebellion. After all, the role of the poet is
exclusively verbal, essentially distinct from the politician's, and
should be simply assessed in terms of its literary efficiency. Most
poets have been, and still are, very jealous of their personal
identity and find it rather difficult to involve themselves in
political matters. On the other hand, there are instances wherein
a political personality, totally engaged in the fight for the rights
of the community, comes to discover *a posteriori* the intrinsic
force of the literary exercise and makes full use of it in order
to convey better a political message. In such cases, one should
rather speak of a politician who tries his hand at poetry rather
than of a poet who indulges in political activity. In other terms,
whereas there are poets who resent being political, since they
do not deem it fit to go beyond the confines of their own
definition, there are social leaders who fall in love with poetry,
or with any other literary genre, because they believe that it
can make them better politicians and provide them with more

---

† Long has my heart been sick / for what this island passed through ... / In a
word we have to say / we are slaves, and Malta's a slave! / We will overcome
them! Do not fear, / let's unite together / and swear to bring them down, / I'll
be the first to swear.

effective means of communication and emotional involvement. This is precisely the case with Manwel Dimech (1860-1921), who was eminently a political agitator, and who discovered that the verse form could serve him well in arousing national consciousness.

In this sense, *mutatis mutandis,* Dimech can be considered a rebel poet who combined action with literature. From a certain stage onwards in his life, it becomes very difficult to distinguish his contributions as a journalist, novelist, and versifier from his achievements as a social reformer and a ferocious opponent of the British colonial Government. It is equally difficult not to conclude that his persecution at the hands of both the Church and the Government was largely due to the nature of the content of his written output. In his verse, he makes full use of emotion and of various rhetorical devices to urge the people to rise against the colonial rulers. His patriotic poems have a strong religious feeling, and although they rarely reach any literary standards, nevertheless they somehow anticipate Dun Karm's patriotic poetry. There is an odd spiritual link, in this respect, between the two; Dun Karm was later to translate lyrical elements into an epic frame, to express with literary dignity identical emotions, and to submit the exuberance of passion to the equilibrium which art demands.

Dimech stands for freedom from foreign rule and for the complete emancipation of his fellow countrymen, whom he repeatedly urges to prepare themselves intellectually and to take immediate action. His poetry echoes the vision of a liberated *patria* proposed by the Italian poets of the Risorgimento (he himself wrote various poems in Italian), identifying the poet with the soldier and vice versa, and subordinates literary values to the political cause. Dimech himself is an example of the vast impact on the local intelligentsia made by the Italian intellectuals who found refuge in Malta. From the rebellious spirit of Italian culture he derived the fundamental concept that the writer and the politician should work hand in hand to attain, through different means, the self-same cause. In his case, as in the case of numerous Italian personalities of the period, the two dimensions are fused into one identity, to the extent that the political activity can be considered as the motivating force of the literary one.

These themes were further developed in the following decades, and it is mainly in this light that one can detect a sort of parallel relationship between the process of social and cultural emancipation of the Maltese language and political evolution. In making use of the language of the people, in direct or implied collaboration with the politician, the poet was setting the pattern of behaviour for the average citizen, now sufficiently conscious of his right to have his national culture officially recognized (the main requirement being the recognition of the ancient uncultivated idiom) and to obtain for his country a reasonable level of constitutional freedom:

> Jasar qatt! Jasar għalina
> qatt, le qatt! Il-mewt aħjar;
> iva l-mewt! O liema fina
> qiegħed jikbes qawwi nar?
> Triegħdu
> tbiegħdu
> għax ġejjin
> ulied Malta l-qalbenin.[15]†

III   THE HISTORICAL NOVELISTS

Like poetry, the narrative prose produced throughout the nineteenth century is partly aimed at tracing the existence and the essence of a national identity through the reconstruction of the past, and the recognition of its immediate moral relevance to the contemporary situation. The shifting of contemporary facts to the remote past was not merely a nostalgic adventure, but also a strategic measure whereby people were drawn out of their previous apathy and reminded of their valorous forefathers. The novelist aimed at identifying resemblances and parallelisms in comparing previous dominations with the contemporary one. In this respect one can detect the great impact exerted on Maltese prose by Italian Romantic literature. Whereas the Language Question focused on the conflict between two great linguistic traditions within the narrow context of a small island, traits of this conflict can also be identified in the

---

† Slavery never! Never slavery for us / no, never! Death is to be preferred / yes, death! Oh! What a fire fiercely burns within us! / Tremble / Be gone / for Malta's valiant sons / are coming.

literary field: the influence of Italian novelists served to help the Maltese novelist assimilate and adopt the typical narrative pattern of the historical novel and to apply it to the local situation. In other words, the Italian Romantic heritage was instrumental in enabling Maltese writers to find for themselves the appropriate methods of narration and forms of expression they badly needed to project their own anticolonial sentiments.

In reviving the memory of the heroic past the Maltese novelist wanted to revive forgotten national myths and dignify the rightful claims of the country. Historical experiences are idealized and rendered sacred, since religion and politics are conceived as one complex enterprise; in re-interpreting history emotionally and raising it to the level of perfection, the novelist could then pass on to relate the past and the present and to project both on to a new, different future which was fast approaching. In searching for an ideal *patria*, the novelist transformed past glories in a highly spectacular scenario which was bound to be viewed again in due course, namely when freedom from foreign rule was attained.

Structurally, such novels are reducible to a series of alternating episodes; on the one hand, sublime historical events are described in a manner which produces the admiration of the readers; on the other hand, the readers are invited to rouse themselves and perform their part in the fight for freedom. Again, the fundamental metaphorical nucleus characteristic of Italian risorgimental inspiration is present: the country is one whole family, the national heroes are the fathers and the *patria* is the mother, the people themselves are consequently brothers and sisters, sons and daughters. The logical sequence of events forming the basic plot is coupled with the gradual formation of a patriotic philosophy; fact and fiction, real heroes and legendary figures, popular customs and beliefs, and a set of moral qualities such as courage, faithfulness, solidarity, are all blended together to fabricate a 'national mythology', itself the ethical foundation for the country's claim to nationhood.

In this respect one can easily understand the great efforts made by various novelists to rescue from oblivion and reconstruct historical personalities like Dun Mikiel Xerri, Mikiel Anton Vassalli, Nazju Ellul, and Dun Gejtu Mannarino. They all assume the role of national leaders whose identity embodies the most characteristic features of the people. At the other end of the spectrum, there is a united people unanimously ready to follow the leaders. When such a stage is reached in the narrative pattern, there remains nothing for the novelist but to depict in the most negative manner the foreign aggressors who have now found themselves for the first time 'painted into a corner', courageously opposed by heroes who have grown from popular roots.

The Maltese historical novelists who wrote in Italian, like Ġan Anton Vassallo (*Alessandro Inguanez*, 1861; *Wignacourt*, 1862), Ferdinando Giglio (*La bella maltea ossia Caterina Desguanez*, 1872), Ramiro Barbaro di San Giorgio (*Un martire*, 1878), and Gaetano Gauci (*Il condannato al supplizio del rogo*, 1905; *L'ultimo assalto del Forte San Michele*, 1907; *Maria Valdez*, 1909; *Notte di dolore*, 1915) gradually created a social and literary environment which ultimately was bound to make them understand that the cause of national identity and constitutional emancipation could be best expressed in the language of the people, and no longer in the language of refined tradition. This psychological necessity was highly instrumental in inducing Maltese writers to appreciate the native language, not solely for abstract or sentimental reasons, but mainly for solidly practical ones: it was through Maltese that they could hope to be understood by the widest possible cross-section of the population, and it was also through the native tongue that they could attain a high degree of emotional and intellectual involvement. The use of Italian might convey dignity to the writer (and this is the primary reason why many politicians and men of letters had maintained that Italian was the language of Maltese national culture, since it could give a sense of superiority, or at least of self-confidence, when in conflict with the rich cultural tradition of Britain) but it did not in any way guarantee popular participation. It is within this context that one can understand the spate of linguistic 'conversations' which took place in the literary field throughout the period.

An ancient language which had gone on being spoken by the uneducated for many centuries without being taken care of either scientifically or politically, Maltese still needed to be rehabilitated in all respects (up to the 1920s, for example, the alphabet still had to be standardized); fundamentally, it lacked the backing of any respectable literary tradition. The twofold programme of linguistic reconstruction and patriotic self-expression in Maltese can be said to have been launched by Anton Manwel Caruana (1839-1907) whose *Ineż Farruġ* (1889) unifies stylistic achievement with patriotic idealism. Some of the linguistic and literary features of the novel brought about a certain approach to the problem of literary style: Caruana chose his lexical stock from the Arabic component of the language, whereas he constructed his sentences on the Latin pattern. *Ineż Farruġ* narrates the misadventures of a young Maltese lady who, before her marriage, is kidnapped by a Spaniard. Since the whole story happens during the period of Spanish rule, the abduction resolves itself into a complex image of the condition of the island (poetically always envisaged as a woman, or a mother) bereft of freedom. The sentimental motif, therefore, is not only fused with the political intent, but is transferred from the personal level to the collective one. The solidarity among the natives and the ruthless exploitation by the dominators are the two extreme points of reference which develop the novel in terms of conflict and transform it into a metaphor of the contemporary condition.

Ġużè Muscat Azzopardi is the undoubted protagonist in the cause of linguistic emancipation and political awareness. *Toni Bajada* (1878), *Viku Mason* (1881), *Susanna* (1883), *Ċejlu Tonna* (1886), *Ċensu Barbara* (1893), and *Nazju Ellul* (1909) evolve around a 'historical' protagonist radically transformed and actually recreated, set against an equally-modified historical background. This compromise enabled the writer to keep in view the authentically historical data and to adapt them imaginatively in a manner that is simultaneously pleasant and instructive. This narrative model was further developed by Ġużè Aquilina in *Taħt Tliet Saltniet* (1938) and by Ġużè Galea in *Żmien l-Ispanjoli* (1938) and *San Ġwann* (1939). The fact that these novelists chose their protagonists from among humble national heroes constitutes a political challenge, itself an example of the deep sense of democracy acquired by the writers in a period when the actual rulers of the country were foreigners. The sublimated reincarnation of these heroic figures counterbalanced the image of sheer power directly identifiable with the British Governors. Their substances are basically democratic and nationalistic; they play the role of the truest, legitimate representatives of the whole native community, and their personalities somehow impose themselves in direct opposition to the characteristic pattern of the colonial system. The complete identity attained between the central hero and the people betrays the consciousness of a proper parliamentary democracy which, in the political field, still had to make many strides to reach an acceptable form. Alongside the subtle concept of parliamentary democracy, one can detect the will of the country to reduce its dependency on the foreign Government. With the exception of Aquilina's *Taħt Tliet Saltniet*, one can hardly find this awareness expressed in a properly defined theoretical system, but there is sufficient ground to confirm that the basic aspects of democracy are shared and professed by all.

IV THE SOCIAL NOVELISTS

Whereas the historical novelists insisted on the necessity of attaining constitutional emancipation, the social novelists concentrated their efforts on the need for rehabilitating the more unfortunate and unprivileged strata of society. The historically orientated plot illustrates the urge for political freedom; the socially inspired plot resolves itself into an inquiry into the working-class condition. Since colonialism meant, in its broadest and most simplistic definition, an amount of power possessed by the foreigners and denied to the natives, the basic confrontation underlying all literary plots of the period 1900-50 (and, with significant modifications, also the plots of the following decades) is between an arrogant aggressor and a prudent victim. Manzoni had already divided humans into two opposite groups, the rich and the poor, who in political terms are the powerful and the powerless; in moral terms, they become the good and the bad respectively. Verga had slightly modified this distinction in speaking in favour of the oppressed and against the oppressors; his vision of humanity is reduced to a battle between the *vinti* and the *vincitori*.

Maltese literary awareness followed the path of the Italian masters and of others, like Dickens and Dostoevsky, who arrived at a moral interpretation of facts through a far-reaching analysis of purely economic and social conditions. Although it is possible to provide a critical reading of these texts in the light of partisanship, that is, according to the ideological leanings of the writers set against the background of local politics, one should not forget that all works, both historical and social, overlap in various senses and frequently identify economic problems with wider political ones, and vice versa. In other words, all writers are fully aware of belonging to a fortress colony and not to an independent nation, totally sovereign and responsible for the welfare of *all* the population. Priorities vary, and the shifting of emphasis is there the better to define the real core of each particular work; but the ultimate distinction, within which every other division could occur, was between the foreign rulers and the native inhabitants. Consequently, internal strifes tend to lose much of their intrinsic impact owing to their being overshadowed by the globality of the political situation prevailing in different degrees with all Maltese. This may be the reason why the sociological content provided by these novelists in their analysis of the workers' condition is frequently abortive in its conclusion, in the sense that it never touches the levels of popular agitation reached by foreign novelists. But they are strongly unanimous in their belief that the country needed a radically different approach to social problems. In this respect I choose to define them as 'reformists'.

Ġużè Ellul Mercer (*Leli ta' Ħaż-Żgħir,* 1938) , Ġwann Mamo *(Ulied in-Nanna Venut fl-Amerka,* 1930), John F. Marks *(Tejbilhom Ħajjithom,* 1937-38), Ġużè Bonnici *(Il-Qawwa ta' l-Imħabba,* 1938; *Ħelsien,* 1939), Wistin Born *(Is-Salib tal-Fidda,* 1939), Ġużè Orlando *(L-Ibleh,* 1948), and Ġużè Chetcuti *(Id-Dawl tal-Ħajja,* 1958; *Imħabba u Mewt,* 1961; *L-Isqaq,* 1962; *It-Tnalja,* 1964) assumed the role of keen, sensitive observers and critics of the working-class character, situation, and environment, and sought to detect in them the real causes and motivations of social and economic exploitation. More than ever before, the writing in Maltese identified itself with the feelings of the 'lower' classes which were still deprived of a decent standard of living. Consequently, the narrator's analysis revolves around the possibilities of employment, the conditions of work, emigration, poverty, and ignorance.

A great deal of this social inquiry relies on the principle, itself a residue of the beliefs promulgated by Illuminism and Romanticism, and later on by certain currents within the socialist spectrum, that no political and social emancipation can ever be attained if the minds of the workers are not enlightened through education. Almost all the novelists mentioned above insist on the urgent need to give the workers their legitimate right to educate themselves and to broaden their knowledge, particularly with reference to the moral justification of their right to adequate employment. Within this context, it is particularly important to recall the case of sedition brought against Ġużè Orlando in terms of the Seditious Propaganda Ordinance of 1932. Following a raid on his house by the police, Orlando, together with some of his close friends, were charged in 1933 with possessing 'seditious' literature.[16] The proceedings against him were held from April to August 1933, and Orlando was fined and condemned to two months imprisonment. Later on, he himself gave a detailed account of the whole episode:

During the trial conducted against me under the Seditious Propaganda Ordinance 1932 ... the Prosecutor, besides indicting me for all my writings and the entire history of my political activities since 1921 ... has also pointed me out as guilty for several writings and extracts from books found in my possession (among some 2,000 volumes which I own) by such prominent writers as Shaw, London, Sinclair, Webb, and Tolstoy. The court based its judgement on many of the incorrect statements made against me by the Police Prosecutor, and also admitted that such prominent authors, as mentioned above, are seditious, and condemned me to a term of imprisonment and a fine for the crime of having kept these writings in my possession.[17]

The social novelists are, of all the Maltese writers, the most directly involved in party politics, even if their works do not betray any sense of belonging to a particular bloc. This can be said with equal weight of most of the other authors writing in this period. It all points to the same direction: the main source of inspiration was the people as a whole, with emphasis shifting periodically from one social class to another, in opposition to the forces of a powerful colonial system.

V DUN KARM: THE VOICE OF DIGNIFIED NATIONHOOD

Dun Karm's poetry, which reached the highest peak of its achievement in the 1930s and 1940s, provides a harmonious synthesis of the two opposite positions, so often dealt with in isolation from each other in some of the works produced in the nineteenth century and in the first half of the twentieth. On the one hand, it professes respect towards the colonial rule, considered as legitimate and in certain aspects fruitful and beneficial (a feeling shared by other contemporary poets like Ġorġ Pisani) since, notwithstanding the demand for greater constitutional rights and ultimately for political autonomy, it had succeeded in maintaining order and tranquillity and in winning the sympathy of many of the people. On the other hand, it forcefully expresses the conviction that Malta is a nation, possessing its own identity, and which should go ahead on its way towards full independence. Mutual understanding and patriotic resolution, therefore, are finally fused into one wholesome awareness. An awareness of the natural limitations of the country is never missing in Dun Karm's perspective, but national dignity, based on the belief that the island has a very old history and a rich cultural tradition, demands that Malta should realize to the full its potentialities as a distinct geographical and cultural entity.

Dun Karm's typical pacifism is a proof of the influence of Manzoni on his spiritual and literary formation. Manzoni himself, as a Christian, had restrained the emotional content of his patriotic convictions and kept it aloof from any intellectual violence or *vendetta*. In this sense, Dun Karm is a forerunner of strategic attitudes adopted in politics by Boffa, Mintoff, and Borg Olivier; practically, his approach is characteristic of the sound policies which were to prevail later on in foreign relations. But Dun Karm, like any other true artist, is never directly political or, worse still, partisan. His main aim is to convey the image of a unified homogeneous community, and this is primarily confirmed by the catholicity of his inspiration. Whilst celebrating the glorious events of the past ('Il-X ta' Frar', 'Il-Għanja tar-Rebħa', 'Fil-Mużew', 'Nhar San Ġwann', 'Dehra tat-VIII ta' Settembru 1565'), the beauty of the local landscape ('Xenqet ir-Raba', 'Lil Ħaż-Żebbuġ Raħal Twelidi', 'Il-Libiena',

'Otia Aestiva', 'Żjara lil Ġesù'), and the value of the traditional
popular customs ('Lill-Mitħna tar-Riħ', 'Il-Għodwa', 'In-
Nissieġa'), he shows a great awareness of the working class and
of its central role within society ('Għanja ta' Malti fl-Amerka',
'Xenqet ir-Raba' ', 'In-Nissieġa', 'Kennies', 'Lid-Dielja', 'It-Tifla
tar-Raba' ', 'Ħaddiem'). 'L-Innu tal-Ħaddiema', published in
1912, is one of his earlier works in Maltese.[18] His profound
social awareness is rooted in the fact that he is at once constantly
conscious and proud of his rural origins, and that he often thinks
of the island as a whole as one enchantingly beautiful village.
But the central dimension of his complex personality is not
essentially social but national. His works, if seen as an
intellectual corpus, constitute a set of moral, cultural, and
historical justifications for Malta's claim to independent
nationhood.

His patriotism is guided by a deep sense of faith in history,
a tendency he inherited from a combination of Illuministic and
Romantic principles which were not altogether obsolete in
Europe by the time he was writing. 'Lil Malta' (1939) affirms
his absolute belief in a substantially distinct Maltese
nationality. The path leading to this final conclusion is, again,
historical. Continuity explains the present and indicates the
direction to be followed in the future. Dun Karm affirms that
he cannot fail to admire the cultural wealth of neighbouring
Italy, in the same way that he is bound to respect Britain for
her democracy. In this way he hoped to neutralize the polarized
extremities of the contemporary local mentality by recognizing
equally the cultural roots of the country (Italian) and the political
system adopted in the island (British). Mediation between
extremes, however, is reached by his professing the supreme
respect due only to his country, the only *omm* (mother) the
Maltese can ever have. 'Lill-Bandiera Maltija' (1946) indicates
again a healthy middle course: the two colours of the national
flag should not be mingled either with the green of the Italian
one, or with the blue of the British, since such an artificial
amalgamation would mean the loss of national identity. A
political interpretation of the sonnet would readily bring out the
poet's opposition to plans to integrate the island with either Italy
or Britain. In the manner that Italian Romantic poets strove
to discover in history the heroes who best embody the spiritual

heritage of the country, Dun Karm transforms Mikiel Anton Vassalli and Dun Mikiel Xerri into national figures whose personalities reflect what is intrinsically Maltese. The two sonnets of 1933 – 'Lil Dun Mikiel Xerri' and 'Lil Mikiel Anton Vassalli' – constitute a tribute to the two patriots, but are eminently a way of paying homage to the Maltese people who had given them birth and identity.[19]

It is very difficult to assess the enormous impact, cultural, political, and literary, which Dun Karm has exerted in his times and since his death in 1961 on the Maltese political outlook, on culture in general, and on the poets and novelists of the twentieth century. One can briefly say that he was highly effective in strengthening national self-confidence, on the one side, and in developing a healthy sense of prudence, practical wisdom, and discretion, on the other. Even in blending two apparently distinct and contrary instincts, Dun Karm is subtly adopting an attitude typical of the traditional Maltese character, proud of his identity and hospitable towards foreigners.

VI CONCLUSION

The history of literature in Maltese[20] mainly concerns the corpus integrating the sentiments and aspirations of the Maltese during the British colonial rule. Whereas the first efforts in verse form, and in simple narrative, descriptive, and devotional forms, go back to an earlier period, it is the nineteenth century which really marks the first significant steps towards a mature literary development. Such a situation could not but be characterized by a new awareness of the ancient identity of the country which had previously been either unsung, or ignored, or both. Consequently, the anticolonial feeling so typical of the nineteenth century was not a mere reaction to the obtaining state of affairs, but also a radical stock-taking, which the literary conscience was bound to embark upon with regard to the whole past.

The conflict between the two great cultural forces which exerted their fullest influence on this sensibility, the Italian and

English languages, expressed itself through the recognition and the emancipation of the popular language, traditionally looked down upon owing to its Arabic origin and to its being identified with the uncultured and with the socially depressed classes. The assertion of the language, implying (as the Romantic mode of thinking demanded) the automatic affirmation of ethnic, cultural, and political values, could be best executed by intellectuals who were well-versed in the foreign, and locally esteemed, speech medium. This is what had happened from De Soldanis and Vassalli, up to Cuschieri and Dun Karm. This process of mediation, however, is not lacking in points of contact with either of the two foreign cultures. Whereas Maltese national identity was to be consolidated through the radical modification of the central role traditionally played by Italian, it was the culture of the peninsula which formed the personalities of the Maltese writers themselves; most of them, in fact, spent long years writing exclusively in Italian before trying their hands at the uncultivated language. Vassalli wrote in Latin and Italian to prove the richness of Maltese, and Dun Karm had passed his fortieth year before producing his first lyric in the vernacular. This is a condition undergone by practically all significant writers of Maltese. The influence of English, or better, of British culture, was gradually put in a political perspective, as it looked like a threat to the affirmation of national identity, since English was seen as the speech medium of the colonial dominators, rather than an international language. Its imposition on the community signified a break with the traditional past and a landmark in the steady process of the island's Anglicization.

Time and the course of events healed these historical prejudices, but in the meantime the two languages were to be identified with different values which traditionally were completely alien to them. For instance, following the Second World War, Italian was not primarily considered as the classical language of culture but as the language of a country which had bombed the island; English was no longer emblematic of colonial domination, but began to be considered as the language of the country which had defended Malta, and as a necessary medium for international communication. Within this framework, one can already assess how sound and positive was Dun Karm's analysis of history in which he did not adopt a rigid, extremist position. In 1937 he himself summed up his belief, which can be tacitly attributed also to most of his colleagues:

> Io non sono stricklandiano oggi che scrivo in maltese, come non ero mizziano quando scrivevo in italiano. Io odio la politica e godo di non aver mai appartenuto ad alcun partito politico. Io sono maltese, solo maltese, e niente altro che maltese.[21]

The literary experience, stretched over such a long period, can, therefore, be considered from different angles. It can be evaluated as a coherent movement of self-consciousness which led the Maltese to affirm their identity and to seek the means to guarantee constitutional emancipation. It can be also looked at as a strategic instrument of opposition to the colonial Government, or as the portrayal of an alternative way of thinking and being under a foreign rule. On the other hand, it can be considered as an intriguing example of the dynamics of history since, while the Maltese writers decided to make use of the traditional Italian culture to give shape to and enrich in form and content the emergent Maltese literature, they found themselves exposed to the influences of British culture. Poets like Ružar Briffa (1906-1963), Ġorġ Zammit (b.1908), Ġorġ Pisani (b.1909), and Anton Buttiġieġ (1912-1983) all bear witness to a partially new mentality. Whereas they are conscious of their being Maltese writers, most of their cultural roots are embedded in the soil of British literature. Keats, Shelley, and Wordsworth, for instance, are frequently echoed, as are G.M. Hopkins, T.S. Eliot, Edward Thomas, and a host of other writers in the case of the poets of the post-independence period. When Malta finally attained full independence from Britain, the affirmation of national identity was an accomplished task, at least constitutionally and on the literary level, and new traits of self-awareness came effectively to the fore. Different anxieties and aspirations are not totally detached from those of the past, and various traditional thematic contents and forms are still alive, even if modified according to changing literary conventions and modes of expression. The responsibility of independent nationhood, however, is prone to develop traits of nostalgia as much as those of resentment towards the colonial past. Mixed feelings, therefore, give substance to the conviction that the basic

problem overcome during the British colonial domination – the
search for self-identification – is still the one which lingers on
in Maltese authors.

NOTES

[1] For further reading on these aspects of the Language Question, which
approximately falls within the period 1880-1939, H. Frendo, 'Language and
Nationality in an Island Colony: Malta', 26-7; O. Friggieri, 'Il-Kwistjoni tal-
Lingwa – Għarfien ta' Identità Nazzjonali', 25-42.

[2] 'La vivezza dell'espressione, le sentenze prodotte dal fervore della fantasia
maltese, la semplicità e la naturalezza attrattiva unite alle doti naturali della
lingua, benchè l'idee siano qualche volta ristrette, formano il bello delle nostre
canzoni. Sarebbe impresa molto degna che alcun de' nostri si mettesse ad
illustrare questo articolo'. M.A. Vassalli, *Ktieb il-Kliem Malti,* xix.

[3] 'In un secolo in cui le arti e le scienze han fatto progressi sì grandi ed
ammirabili, che quasi non restano fra di esse più dipartimenti da illustrare,
pareva che non si dovesse tralasciare incolto, senza dissottenerlo dall'obblivione,
uno de' più antichi monumenti, qual è la lingua maltese'. Ibid., vii.

[4] Ibid., xiii.

[5] 'Ma si coltivi prima, anche per un poco, e si vedrà che più d'ogni altra è
suscettibile di colture'. Ibid., xix.

[6] 'La coltura d'una nazione consiste nell'educazione, d'onde risulta la qualità
di sua morale; nella prudenza e politica nazionale, che la rende docile, affabile,
e sempre intenta al bene comune; nella coltivazione delle arti e scienze, poichè
da queste quelle si perfezionano, oggetto che aumenta l'attività nazionale ed
il commercio; e nella cognizione ed osservanza delle leggi, che tengono in pace
e tranquillità lo stato, e quindi producono la felicità e l'individuale sicurezza
... Da ciò rettamente deducesi che ove non si coltivi la lingua nazionale, ne si
scriva, quella nazione che la parli non può mai pervenire all'apice di sua floridezza
ed ingrandimento'. Ibid., xxi.

[7] K. Sant, *It-Traduzzjoni tal-Bibbja u l-Ilsien Malti,* 10.

[8] It is worth recording the efforts of Giorgio Mitrovich who, in July 1835, went
to London to fight for the cause of the Maltese people and to get in contact with
the British Cabinet. See G. Mitrovich, *The Claims of the Maltese founded upon
the principles of Justice.*

[9] Between 1838 and 1870 about 180 papers were published. See V. Bonello et
al., *Echi del risorgimento a Malta,* 30-110.

[10] The following extract is typical of Mitrovich's style: 'Il tempo della
persecuzione è passato. Levate dalla vostra mente ogni minima ombra di timore,
perchè si tratta di ricorrere ad un'assemblea di un popolo libero, che vi dà piena
facoltà di parlare apertamente, domandare e ripetere. Ora è il momento, miei
cari fratelli, e non dovete perderlo ... Siate certi che verrà un giorno che il popolo
maltese sarà reso felice, sarà liberato dalla sua schiavitù, ben trattato e
accarezzato. Il tempo della nostra rigenerazione si avvicina'. G. Mitrovich,
Indirizzo ai maltesi da parte del loro amico, 14-15.

[11] Mitrovich writes: 'La nazione dovrà presto trionfare, la riuscita di una causa
nobile e giusta, com'è la nostra, è certa; un altro poco, e vedrete'. Ibid., 24.

[12] See G.A. Vassallo, *Mogħdija taż-Żmien fil-Lsien Malti,* 5.

[13] The principles enunciated in these stanzas by Vassallo are shared by all the contemporary Maltese writers:

> Del popolo io son, ed a lui pegno
> d'amore do nel poco, dove arriva
> la penna cui mi diè povero ingegno
> onde fatti e costumi gli descriva.
>
> Non plauso d'accademia mi fa gola,
> non la scienza superba; sol m'aggrada
> quando al popolo servir possa di scola.
>
> Seria o giocosa la parola cada,
> greca o latina, vo' una cosa sola;
> che sparsa in vano ella giammai non vada.

Hrejjef u Ċajt bil-Malti, 7.

[14] Vassallo, *Mogħdija taż-Żmien fil-Lsien Malti*, 7, 10.

[15] *Il-Ħabib Malti*, 21-2.

[16] See *Malta Chronicle and Imperial Services Gazette*, 20 March 1933, 15.

[17] J. Orlando Smith, *The Sedition Case*, 4.

[18] See *Il-Ħabib*, 13 March 1912, 1.

[19] For a detailed account of the nationalistic component of Dun Karm's poetry, O. Friggieri, *Storia della letteratura maltese*, 222-4.

[20] For the purpose of this study no consideration is being given to Maltese literary tradition in Italian prior to the birth of literature in Maltese. A brief outline of the history of both languages is, however, relevant here. The Arabs conquered the island in AD 870 and laid the foundations for the formation of modern Maltese. Since the second Norman conquest in 1127, the language began to find itself open to various extra-Arabic influences, and has since grown into a rich medium owing to its being exposed to European influxes. See J. Aquilina, *Papers in Maltese Linguistics*. Maltese began to be written on a fairly wide scale in the seventeenth century and much more in the eighteenth and nineteenth centuries, but Italian had already established itself as the only cultural language of the island. One of the earliest documents in Italian dates back to 1409. See A. Mifsud, 'Malta al sovrano nel 1409', 243-8, and id., 'La cattedrale e l'università', 39-40. A basic conflict to be resolved was, therefore, linguistic: the native-speech medium of a European country had a Semitic origin, whereas its cultural content was Latin. The British period, largely coinciding with the influx of Romantic principles in the political and cultural fields, introduced a further conflict, namely between English and Maltese. Once the debate gathered momentum, it was bound to develop into a question of national self-awareness.

[21] Letter to Laurent Ropa, 21 May 1937 (Ropa Collection, 'Melitensia', Library of the University of Malta). Enrico Mizzi (1885-1950) and Gerald Strickland (1861-1941), Prime Ministers of Malta, favoured the use of Italian and Maltese respectively.

14

DENIS DE LUCCA

British Influence on Maltese Architecture anf Fortifications

The principal medium of British interests in the Mediterranean, following the establishment of the British Levant Company in Istanbul in 1581, was the presence of a well-equipped squadron of ships which required a series of strategically-placed shore bases to operate and control effectively. It is therefore understandable that the position and strong fortifications of Malta played an important role within the framework of Britain's Mediterranean policy after 1800. As the elaborate seventeenth- and eighteenth-century fortifications of the Knights had never been tested in action, the British in Malta inherited both them and several palatial buildings in a relatively undamaged state and were free to re-use or modify them according to the changed needs of nineteenth-century Malta. Between 1800 and 1850, several reports were drawn up by various members of the British Royal Engineers stationed in Malta – the intention of these reports was the updating of the defence potential of the existing fortifications through relatively minor additions, modifications, and alterations. After 1850, however, the introduction of long-range artillery mounted on steam-powered ships compelled the British to start thinking in terms of a change of policy based on the creation of a series of new forts outside the main lines of fortifications built by the Order. These new forts were purposely designed as containers of large guns and can be interpreted as Britain's response to the new technology which was introduced into the Mediterranean after 1850.

The actual history of British influence on military architecture in Malta started in the first decade of the nineteenth century, soon after the French garrison was expelled from the island and the old public works department of the Knights was re-organized on the basis of three quasi-independent sectors — the civil, the naval, and the military branches, the latter under the responsibility of the Royal Engineers.[1]

It would appear that the earliest proposal for enhancing the defence potential of the island came from one Colonel Dickens who suggested the construction of four powerful redouts on Corradino hill.[2] This proposal was suspended in 1813 by the new Governor of Malta, Sir Thomas Maitland; but fifteen years later Captain H. Jones of the Royal Engineers submitted a comprehensive list of recommendations for an improved defensive system.[3] Among other things, the latter recommended that the different Cottonera bastions were to be interpreted as separate fortresses with all curtain walls joining them neutralized as defence elements, this clearly in line with the new international military strategy of using a series of independent artillery forts, detached and outside the main lines of defence. In this respect it is interesting to see that Captain Jones also suggested the conversion of the Floriana Crown Works into a separate fort and the destruction of all coastal towers and batteries built by the Order. In 1843 Captain Widdrington forwarded a number of additional proposals,[4] among them the construction of a large raised cavalier in the middle of Fort Manoel, the replacement of Fort St Elmo with a new fort designed to contemporary specifications, and the building of a series of round towers to be positioned in each of the Cottonera bastions, similar to structures built by the Austrian army at Verona in Italy. As a direct result of the Jones and Widdrington reports, work was started on St Clement bastion at Cottonera[5] with the intention of converting it into a separate fort surrounded by a ditch and protected with casemated cannon. The new fort was also provided with accommodation for the garrison which became a model for similar quarters built on the island by the British Government.

In about 1860, Colonel Jervois of the Royal Engineers arrived in Malta and forwarded a number of proposals[6] to accommodate new armaments, including large Lancaster guns which were to arrive from the arsenals of England. Among other things, Jervois recommended the total isolation of Valletta by means of an excavated ditch connecting the Grand Harbour and Marsamxett. In addition, the engineer advised the construction of six powerful ring forts around the Grand Harbour and the placing of new beach batteries at St Julians, Sliema Point, St Rocco, and Delle Grazie. In view of the impact of Jervois' proposals on the environment, his suggestions were not carried out. As an alternative, however, four projects were done. In the first place, work had begun on the fortifications of the Victoria Lines, in continuation of a project undertaken by the Knights in the earlier half of the eighteenth century.[7] Secondly, Fort St Elmo was extensively modified after 1866 by the construction of several iron-throated casemates meant to accommodate new long-range guns. Thirdly, a series of casemated gun positions were built in front of seventeenth-century Fort St Lucian, and fourthly, a defensive line was constructed on Corradino Heights. The high ground of Corradino had also been the subject of extensive studies in the eighteenth century[8] owing to the fact that the advisers of the Order had always been particularly alarmed at the prospect of a potential enemy establishing positions at this high point overlooking Senglea and the deepest point of the Grand Harbour.

The second and more important stage in the defence programme for Malta was begun by the British early in the 1870s with the building of the first British fort on the island. Sliema Point Battery was a fan-shaped structure with casemated guns capable of firing far out into the open sea. Colonel Jervois' interest in the neo-Gothic style of architecture is clearly seen in the designer's decision to introduce neo-Gothic trappings to mask the functional nature of this war machine.[9] Following the building of Sliema Point, design and actual construction work was started on a number of forts, some of which were intended to stiffen the escarpment of the Victoria Lines – Fort Maddalena, Fort Mosta, and Fort Bingemma – followed by Fort Delimara and the excellently designed Fort St Leonardo. All these forts represented sophisticated work in the field of contemporary military engineering – their main purpose was to counteract the presence of hostile long-range artillery which could blow to pieces a complicated baroque fortress from about four miles away without actually coming into contact with the fortifications. This situation historically became obvious for the first time in the Franco-German War of 1870, when it was realized that only towns encircled with a calculated ring of detached forts could effectively put up resistance to invasion. In these changed circumstances, the numerous forts built on Malta after 1870 can be interpreted as sound British strategy aimed at keeping a potential invader well away from the vital harbour installations centred on Valletta and the Three Cities. Their design indicates that these forts were primarily designed to contain large guns and not to resist assault, as had been the case of the fortifications designed by the Order in the previous century. The only protection provided against assault were counterscarp galleries, low pill-boxes flanking the ditches, palisades, and barbed wire – on the other hand, full protection was provided for the guns and the men who operated them by means of carefully integrating the forts in the landscape, by various camouflaging devices, such as painting the guns in Maltese limestone colour and by the use of movable equipment to get all the guns rapidly out of view. These, then, were the principles of British military engineering in Malta in the last decades of the nineteenth century.

The fort-building spree was concluded in the 1880s when two large forts were built on the two opposite sides of the Grand Harbour, at Rinella and Cambridge, to accomodate a new invention – the 100-ton Armstrong rifled muzzle-loader.[10] This was a formidable weapon which was swung around, its muzzle was then lowered and a big shell, raised from underground by a pneumatic lift, loaded into it. The gun was then automatically returned to the firing position. The presence of such a complicated war machine in Malta after 1880 necessitated a fort which was exclusively designed to shelter and protect one gun from hostile ships and atmospheric humidity – as such, the two last forts built by the British in the nineteenth century can be described as elaborate and impermeable containers enclosing expensive and dangerous war machinery.

During the first years of British rule, few civil buildings were built owing to the fact that the British found a large quantity of undamaged buildings left by the Knights which were sufficiently large and well furnished to satisfy its requirements.

To quote three examples, the Governor found an extensive Magistral Palace in Valletta complete with all the ostentatious baroque trappings that were more than consistent with his high office; the armed forces established their headquarters in the Auberge de Castille; and the Lord Bishop of Gibraltar put up residence in the Auberge d'Aragon. What British Malta lacked in terms of civil buildings were Protestant churches and a suitable modern hospital to meet the needs of the Mediterranean Fleet stationed in the Grand Harbour — two problems which the British were quick to remedy.

In view of the above-outlined situation, British influence on civil architecture in Malta was in the nineteenth century far less than its impact on military architecture. This is understandable when one considers the fact that, whereas the latter was the exclusive responsibility of the colonial Government and conformed to a fixed policy of defence devised in England, civil architecture very much depended on the requirements and visual tastes of the Maltese. To the Maltese in general the rational and decorative qualities of the Catholic baroque idiom inherited from the Knights made much more sense than the 'pagan' Romantic architecture which the English and some of the Maltese pro-English intelligentsia of the time found so appealing. As a direct result of this clash of ideas, the built environment of the nineteenth century very much continued to shape itself on the basis of the baroque and vernacular traditions of the previous century and, at least initially, the English found it rather hard to communicate to the Maltese public the sophisticated architectural language of the neo-classical and neo-Gothic forms of expression which in England formed the main pillars of the Romantic movement after 1750.

In the circumstances, it is to the credit of the colonial Government that it was content to embark on a policy of introducing new architectural concepts by letting things be until a favourable occasion presented itself in the form of either building a 'model' specimen in the new Romantic style, or by infiltrating the public service with Maltese having a marked disposition to accepting and promoting the new ideas, or even by regarding promising young Maltese architects and artists through scholarships or patronage aimed at advancing their career opportunities. The aim of this subtle policy towards the introduction of new architectural ideas,[11] which reflected the political shrewdness of the Colonial Office in London, was the gradual conversion of many educated Maltese into accepting the 'spirit' of the Romantic movement, particularly that aspect which emphasized a philosophy based on the emotional side of man as opposed to his rational qualities. It was rather unfortunate that this policy took a rather long time to become effective. To judge by comments and reports in the local press, the initial neo-classical expression of the Romantic style of architecture between 1800 and 1850 was never really accepted by the Maltese whose conservative and practical way of thinking seemed to react strongly towards the Anglo-Saxon novelties. For five whole centuries they had looked towards Italy for inspiration. By contrast, the neo-Gothic expression, introduced after 1850, seems to have fared better because of its religious overtones, although one must stress that it reached the shores of Malta too late to leave a profound effect on the built environment.

The British influence on civil architecture in Malta in the nineteenth century has three aspects: the influence on architectural education, the formulation of new building standards, and the building of some fine architectural 'models', mostly situated on prominent sites to provide a source of inspiration to all who were disposed to be inspired.

In education, one of the very first achievements of the first British Commissioner of Malta, Sir Alexander Ball, was the reopening of the University and the appointment of Mgr. Francesco Saverio Caruana as its first Rector in October 1800.[12] Two years later, Mgr. Caruana introduced, within the framework of the University curriculum, a special school for the teaching of architecture, design, painting, and sculpture. This was meant to introduce Maltese young men to the basic skills associated with the above subjects and to that particular branch of the Romantic movement in architecture associated with the Roman academies as a suitable alternative to *barocchismo* which Caruana defined as the destroyer of pure art.[13] The first professor of drawing and architecture at the newly-restored University was Michele Busuttil, but as Busuttil was not an architect, two assistant professors were soon appointed to teach architecture and the arts. These were Vincenzo Dimech and Giorgio Pullicino, the latter being an architect who had studied at the *Accademia di San Luca* in Rome and a personal friend of the great eighteenth-century sculptor Antonio Canova.[14] With Pullicino's appointment, the link with the new trends of thought of the Roman academies was formalized in so far as the education of young Maltese artists and architects was concerned.

The impetus which the new British Government gave to architectural education was followed up in the middle of the century by the enactment of the so-called Police Laws aimed at improving building standards through the introduction of new sanitary regulations. Two indirect implications of the new laws were, first, an improvement in the quality of buildings based on English damp-proofing principles, proper ventilation, and superior interior lighting and, secondly, the introduction of the concept of geometric territoriality based on long rectangular plots with varying back-garden space, which soon led to the emergence of more regular streetscapes more in line with the row houses of England than with the traditional vernacular idiom of the older village cores.

The third and most important aspect of the British influence on civil architecture concerned the building of several 'models' which communicated to the Maltese public the merits of the two principal expressions of Romantic architecture — the neo-classical and the neo-Gothic. In England, neo-classicism resulted from a belief that architecture had attained perfection in its simplest and most primitive form of expression — James Stuart, one of its first pioneers, claims to have discovered this purism in the Doric antiquities of Athens. It is therefore not at all surprising that one of the earliest official monuments put up in Malta by the English follows closely the basic design format and detailing principles of Greek Doric. Sir Alexander Ball's monument in the Lower Barracca at Valletta (fig. 1), comparable to a similar one built in Corfu, was novel to Malta in two respects — in the first place, there was the novelty of its design, and particularly its details based on the exact archaeological information that English neo-classical architects enjoyed; secondly, there was its siting in the open landscape of the bastion. For the first time in Malta, an isolated monument to a revered hero was designed by Giorgio Pullicino exclusively

Figure 1. Front elevation of Sir Alexander Ball's monument at the
Lower Barracca, Valletta

to fit into an 'open' as opposed to a 'closed' context, thus militating against the baroque ideal of integration between buildings and subservient surrounding space.

Soon after Ball's monument, several other buildings were erected in the Doric style, among them the Main Guard portico opposite the Magistral Palace, the fine exedra at Fort St Elmo, Villa Frère at Pieta, the Old University entrance in Valletta and, perhaps the most important of all, the new naval hospital at Bighi, this representing an interesting conversion and extention exercise of an existing late seventeenth-century baroque villa.[15] The architect responsible for the design of Bighi hospital was Sir George Whitmore,[16] who was also the architect of the Palace of the British Governor on Corfu. As a major exponent of the *Pax Britannica* in the Mediterranean, Whitmore seems to have had two aims in mind when designing Bighi – first, to create a service hospital which was to be the best of its kind in the Mediterranean and, secondly, to adorn the entrance area of the Grand Harbour with a living symbol of the English Romantic movement. To a very large extent, Whitmore succeeded admirably in both aims as Bighi soon became renowned as a most efficient hospital where ether anaesthesia was actually used for the first time in 1847.[17] Aesthetically, the old villa was subtly screened by elegant Doric porticos which, coupled with the isolated setting in an open context, communicated to the Maltese public in no unclear language the ultimate ideals of English architectural thought at the time. Another important example of a baroque – neo-classical conversion was carried out within the Magistral Palace where an attempt was made, in the first half of the nineteenth century, to screen the baroque trappings of the interior with the purism of Greek columns.

After 1830, the neo-classical idiom manifested itself in a somewhat interesting adulterated form in two major architectural works – the Anglican Church in Valletta (1839) and the Mosta Rotunda (1833). The first building, originally designed by Richard Lankersheer,[18] developed faulty foundations which gave occasion to the anti-British press in Malta savagely to attack the occupation of all high posts by Englishmen, particularly architects like Lankersheer, who knew little about the local building materials. The second building, at Mosta, is remarkable because it was the only significant building of the nineteenth century that the Maltese designed and built for themselves in what can be explained as a unique popular interpretation of the neo-classical style. The architect of Mosta church, Giorgio Grognet de Vasse,[19] was basically a visionary interested in Atlantis. His main contribution at Mosta is that he was the only architect who successfully managed to combine three very different attitudes towards contemporary architectural expression: his own eccentric approach, visionary and ego-centred; the official attitude, with an obvious bias towards the purist solutions associated with the mother country; and, last but not least, the popular approach which clearly enjoyed all the rich trappings of a village *festa* celebration combined with that love for monumentality which was so necessary to boost the ego and sense of identity of the villagers. It is to the credit of Giorgio Grognet, despite considerable criticism, that his building at Mosta managed to blend the above ideals in an original way based on sound construction principles which no contemporary British architect practising in Malta could match. The Mosta Church was, in fact, a Maltese version of British neo-classicism − it is perhaps relevant to note that, soon after its completion, the people of Mosta continued decorating the building until its interior resembled the baroque interiors they were accustomed to for worship. It is also significant that the Mosta Rotunda is the only building in the neo-classical tradition which most struck the imagination of the Maltese; the few other buildings in this style are almost intruders on a culture that never fully accepted them.

The neo-Gothic expression of the Romantic movement began to infiltrate the Maltese built environment after 1850. To a far larger extent, the neo-Gothic expression of the Presbyterian Church in Valletta of 1856, designed by Giuseppe Bonavia,[20] was far more acceptable to the Maltese than neo-classical, presumably because Gothic was considered to be *architettura eminentemente Cristiana*[21] diametically opposed to the paganism of ancient Greek Doric. This mentality shows itself clearly in another neo-Gothic early 'model' − the Carmelite Church at Balluta, but then various contemporary sources defined the style of this building, also designed by Bonavia,[22] as *longobarda*, which suggests Italian, as opposed to Anglo-Saxon, associations.

The neo-Gothic idiom in Malta found its full expression in the works of a brilliant architect, Emanuele Luigi Galizia, who in 1869 completed his *chef d'oeuvre,* the Addolorata Cemetery.[23] This vast undertaking, which received favourable press comments, was the result of thorough research by the architect into the principles and details of English Gothic, both crystallized in the chapel situated at the salient point of the magnificent cemetery. The Addolorata scheme was followed by the construction of four large churches which echo its style, thus reflecting the popularity and influence of neo-Gothic in late nineteenth-century Malta. These churches were the Holy Trinity Church in Sliema (1866), the new church at Balluta (1876), the Methodist Chapel at Floriana (1880), and the Church of Our Lady of Lourdes, perched on the heights of Mġarr harbour in Gozo (1888). The Balluta and Mġarr churches, designed by Galizia as a physical manifestation of the Romantic spirit, indicate the hold of the new expression on popular opinion after 1880, presumably because of its close association with the pre-Reformation Christian Faith. It would, in fact, appear that at this time the obvious picturesque qualities of Gothic also started to influence the architecture patronized by the upper echelons of Maltese society. It is, in this respect, interesting to see that many noble and wealthier Maltese families seem to have been keen, after 1870, to build country villas in the neo-Gothic idiom, thus echoing similar activity in the English countryside with which the officers of the British garrison were so well acquainted. To all intents and purposes, it would seem that architecture in Malta towards the close of the nineteenth century was rapidly transforming itself into the subtle instrument of political influence that the British authorities had originally intended it to be.

The ultimate blend of civil and military architecture in the nineteenth century was sealed with the building of Sliema Point Battery (fig. 2) between 1872 and 1877.[24] The landward face of this container of guns looks more like a medieval castle than a nineteenth-century gun fortress. The walls are vertical and conspicuously defined by Gothic crenellations and, of course, pointed arches, thus using Romantic architecture to conceal an otherwise intensely functional edifice in the same way that Whitmore had used neo-classicism to embellish Bighi half-a-

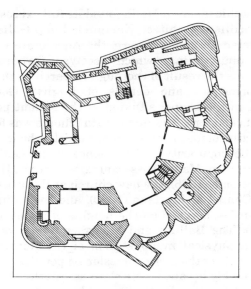

Figure 2. Plan of Sliema Point Battery

century earlier. In the circumstances of the late nineteenth-century, it would seem that the colonial authorities were anxious to conceal as far as possible the stark reality of the British military presence on the island with the civil and graceful lines of an architecture that was basically English, but not so English as to offend nationalistic popular opinion. In this respect, the neo-Gothic expression was eminently suited to perform this task as it gradually became associated with two very Maltese qualities which the British Colonial Office of the nineteenth century was wise enough not to meddle with — the Catholic religion and sentiment on one side, and the love of the Maltese for ornate beauty and intricate stone craftsmanship on the other. More than anything else, this perhaps best explains the ultimate acceptance of the architecture of Romanticism in nineteenth-century Malta and its influence on the Maltese built environment, despite initial resistance at all levels of Maltese society.

In the twentieth century, British influence on military and civil architecture in Malta was generally more indirect than in the previous century. The period 1900-1964 was marked by two

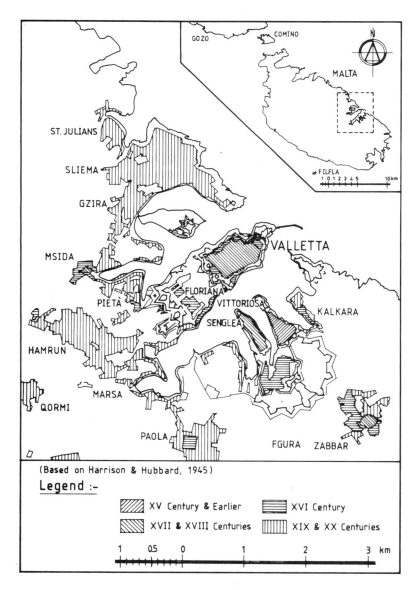

Figure 3. Growth of the Harbour area

world wars and, after 1912, by the gradual process of the withdrawal of the British fleet from the Mediterranean. The heyday of British imperialism was over and building activity in early twentieth-century Malta reflected this changed situation. In the field of military architecture, there was little achievement beyond the fact that coastal defences and establishments were brought to their final state of perfection and that three airfields consumed a substantial portion of land. What was, however, more important was the influence of Britain on settlement growth and architecture in the postwar period. Of particular interest in this context was the influence of a number of English consultant architects, engineers, and town planners who devised policies and master solutions following the widespread destruction caused by aerial bombardment. In the words of Governor Sir Edmond Schreiber,[24] Messrs Harrison and Hubbard submitted 'a plan which incorporates the requirements of modern traffic and amenities with a minimum of fresh demolition and the preservation of the characteristic features of the cities and towns in Malta's harbour area' (fig. 3). Details of this plan and its underlying philosophy are to be found in a voluminous report dated 1945. At a rather later stage, the conceptual influence of British town-planning discipline continued being felt through close contact between the local sphere of activity and several leading town-planning institutions and 'experts' in England. This led to the inevitable introduction, for better or for worse, of several Anglo-Saxon planning concepts in a Mediterranean island which, according to some, should have looked once again towards Italy for inspiration. Among these English conceptual influences, which can still be seen and felt in the contemporary built environment, one can mention the use of grid-pattern planning schemes as an illogical form of continuation of the historic organic villages, the introduction of detached-villa and front-garden concepts in an environment where land wastage is sacrilegious, and finally, the use of wide promenades closely following the contours of the coastal areas which are very strongly reminiscent of a Brighton or a Scarborough transported into the Mediterranean. One can, in addition, also mention innumerable facilities such as pubs, clubs, polo pitches, and turf, which remind one of a typical English environment. Together with the language, these then were the elements that represent the heritage of Great Britain in twentieth-century Malta — they can, among other things, be interpreted as the ultimate balance of the continental and Islamic influences of the previous centuries, and the one factor that made the built environment of Malta unique when compared with other Mediterranean islands.

NOTES

[1] *Rapporto del Comitato Speciale sull'Offizio dei Lavori Pubblici*, v.
[2] Castlereagh, *Letters of London*, 65.
[3] PRO, WO, 55/910, Copy of a Report addressed to Maj.-Gen. The Hon. F.C. Ponsonby CB, Malta, 4 April 1828, by Capt. Harry Jones, Royal Engineers.
[4] Ibid., Letter from Capt. J.S. Widdrington on the Fortifications of Malta, Garden Street, London, December 1843.
[5] Q. Hughes, *Britain in the Mediterranean*, 129.
[6] Ibid., 152.
[7] D. De Lucca, 'The Contribution of François de Mondion in the Architectural Development of Eighteenth-Century Malta', 79.
[8] Id., 'French Military Engineers in Malta during the seventeenth and eighteenth centuries'.
[9] PRO, WO, 32/33, Report of 1878, 4.
[10] Hughes, 167-8.
[11] M. Ellul, 'Early nineteenth-century Architecture', 16-25.
[12] K. Borg, 'Neo-Classical Architecture in Malta in the nineteenth century', 13.
[13] PAV, *Malta Miscellaneous Papers*, vol.ii, *Relazione dello Stato delle Scuole di Disegno nell'Università di Malta, 1802-1850*, unfoliated.
[14] Ellul, 20.
[15] J.F. Darmanin, 'The British Naval Hospitals at Malta', 153-83.
[16] *Rapporto del Comitato Speciale sull'Officio dei Lavori Pubblici*, (1829), 6.
[17] P. Cassar, *Medical History of Malta*, 97.
[18] *The Malta Penny Magazine*, 9 November 1840.
[19] Borg, ch.3.
[20] K. Buhagiar, 'Romanticism in the nineteenth century', 21.
[21] N. Zammit, *Esposizione di Industria Maltese nel 1864*, 98.
[22] A. Guillaumier, *Bliet u Rħula Maltin*, 487.
[23] K. Buhagiar, 'Neo-Gothic Architecture in nineteenth-century Malta', 9.
[24] A. Harrison, R.P. Hubbard, *Valletta and The Three Cities*, iii.

15

STEPHEN HOWE

British Decolonization and Malta's Imperial Role

We are still too close to the end of Britain's colonial Empire —
both too close in time and, perhaps, former colonizers and former
colonized alike, too close emotionally — to see it in clear
perspective. Historical research on British decolonization
remains in its infancy. In recent years, however, scholarly
discussion of imperial decline has widened considerably, become
ever more extensive and vigorous; stimulated both by the
opening up of official records under the 'thirty-year rule' and
by an outpouring of new interpretative work. Within Britain,
too, contemporary events like the Falklands War and the
continued precipitous decline of the British economy have
sharpened the perceived need to reappraise the colonial legacy.
Everywhere in the ex-colonial world also, the nature of that
inheritance is inevitably high on the political and intellectual
agendas.

This chapter surveys these debates, attempting a general
overview of the current state of historiography on British
imperial decline. It seeks to situate the fate of Malta within that
framework; though necessarily in tentative fashion, both
because of my lack of expertise (especially as compared with
other contributors to this volume) in Maltese history, and
because few of the general patterns now discernable in Britain's
'transfers of power' can be applied easily to the Maltese case.

The reasons for Malta's special place in the history of
decolonization are evident enough. She was almost unique
amongst British colonies in having a European population which
was not, however, a settler community of British descent — thus

racial attitudes and cultural preconceptions, amongst both colonizers and colonized, took unusual forms. She had a long-established, highly-sophisticated political élite, whose representatives evoked in turn the admiration, the exasperation, the bemusement — and on occasion, it must be said, the ill-deserved contempt — of British officials. During the twentieth century she also evolved a vigorous Labour and trade union movement, heavily influenced by, though also reacting against, British Labour's organizational and ideological models. There was, of course — perhaps the overridingly complicating factor in the equation — Malta's strategic position, and the corresponding dependence of the Maltese economy on British military spending. There was the role of the Church. And there was a set of ideological crosscurrents not paralleled elsewhere, with militant socialists demanding integration with Britain, arch-conservatives raising the banner of separatism.

The narrative of decolonization, too, had some unique twists in Malta: nowhere else in the British Empire was political integration with the metropole, so characteristic a feature of the rival French colonial model, seriously proposed; nowhere else was the onward march towards self-government thrown into reverse not just once (as happened in Newfoundland in 1931, Guyana in 1953, and very briefly in Zimbabwe in 1980) but three times — in 1903, 1933, and 1958. It is necessary, though, to establish some general propositions about British thought and action in decolonization before we can judge how Malta fitted into or departed from that wider framework.

I IMPERIAL DESCENT AND DISSENT

Asked to produce a list of causes for the end of British colonialism, most historians would respond with more or less the same entries. The decline of Britain's industrial economy, and consequent overstretching of resources exposed by global war; the rise of colonial nationalism; challenge from the USA, USSR, and perhaps the United Nations; growing anti-colonialist sentiment within Britain; the impact of military defeat in 1939-42 and financial indebtedness thereafter; the turn towards Europe in British political thinking; the conviction that formal colonialism was an increasingly uneconomic means of exerting influence or extracting profit; the breakdown of bargains earlier struck with 'collaborators' amongst the colonized – most or all of these would feature in every account. Yet a list is not an explanation, even if some early surveys of decolonization seem to have confused the two.[1] Nor is the single-minded – and perhaps simple-minded – espousal of one particular element in the complex a satisfactory procedure, popular though that has been among both the self-congratulatory British chroniclers of a supposedly voluntary, consensual disengagement and the vainglorious celebrants of nationalist 'revolutions'.[2] Only very recently have serious attempts been made to go beyond these simplicities and to construct more sophisticated models of decolonization.

The earlier monocausal explanations for imperial decline took three main forms. First, and most popular within Britain itself, was the view of decolonization as a planned, voluntary, and successful process of disengagement by British statesmen, gradually transferring power and transforming the colonial Empire into a free association of equals.[3] If this interpretation echoed the rhetoric of postwar British Governments, a second and sharply opposed view mirrored that of colonial nationalists. This saw decolonization as a result of a 'colonial revolution': the British were forced out by the nationalist upsurge of colonized peoples.[4]

Reacting against both these arguments, there was a growing tendency from the 1960s amongst scholars (mostly but not entirely on the Left) to see decolonization neither as a 'transfer of power' nor as a 'revolution' but merely as the replacement of formal colonial rule by a more insidious 'neo-colonialism'. What happened was merely a change of flags and faces at the top, leaving in place the essential structures of colonial exploitation.[5]

The problems with the first two views are obvious enough. British politicians and officials were neither as willing to surrender imperial power, as sagacious in planning disengagement, nor as successful in carrying it through as the 'transfer of power' interpretation suggests. The end of Empire may have been a less bloody and traumatic process for Britain than for France or Portugal, but a glance at Malaya, Cyprus,

Kenya, Aden, or numerous other violent passages indicates that it was hardly a smoothly consensual affair.

On the other hand, it cannot be denied that, especially after the mid-1950s, British Governments were ready, indeed eager, in many cases to hand over authority to suitable successors. This, and even more the revelations brought in subsequent years of the shallowness of many successor élites' political bases, call into question the often vainglorious claims of 'freedom fighters' to have forced the colonialists out. Some historians have indeed swung to the opposite extreme and characterized the conflict between British rulers and nationalist leaders in many colonies as petty theatrical posturing.[6] The third argument — that Britain sought to pursue a 'neo-colonialist' strategy, perpetuating influence by new and less direct means — is a more serious proposition. Yet too many of its proponents have rested on unexamined assumptions about the nature of Britain's economic interests in the colonies, have held an almost 'vulgar Marxist' view that economic interest simply and directly determined political calculation, and have virtually bypassed the political events of decolonization in their emphasis on economic continuities. Furthermore, if Britain's rulers did seek to adopt a 'neo-colonialist' strategy, it is far from self-evident that it was a *successful* strategy — a point to which I shall return.

If none of these simple explanations is now thought adequate by serious scholars (though, as we shall see, elements of all three have persisted, albeit perhaps in more sophisticated form), what has been offered to replace them? We may begin by summarizing the general theses on which there is substantial agreement, before turning to the rather more numerous claims about which historians have disagreed.

First, no one has seriously doubted that economic considerations played a major determining role in the loss of Empire: that there was *some* sort of causal relationship between the decline of the British economy and imperial retreat. In this sense all the major explanations of British decolonization are in some degree, as B.R. Tomlinson says, 'mercantilist'.[7] That apparently simple observation, however, itself raises a number of problems. One is that if, as is now generally agreed, the structural weakness of the British industrial economy, and its poor performance relative to major competitors, can be dated at least back to the 1890s,[8] why was it not until half a century later that territorial contraction began? Should historians be asking, not why the Empire fell, but − as Paul Kennedy suggests − why it lasted so long?[9] A resolution to part of this puzzle may be sought in the argument, widely accepted since it was first propounded by Ronald Robinson and John Gallagher in the late 1950s, that the later phases of British colonial expansion, especially Britain's participation in the partition of Africa, were themselves responses to and intended bulwarks against national decline rather than expressions of growing strength.[10] Yet this view yields an apparent paradox: it seems to be asserted that *both* the expansion and the contraction of Empire were products of decline and insecurity.

Attempts to resolve the paradox are considerably hampered by uncertainty and lack of information about the actual economic value to Britain of the colonial Empire in its latter stages. The question 'did Empire pay?' has of course been perennially contentious ever since J.A. Hobson argued in 1902 that colonies were a drain on the British national economy and profitable only to a minority clique of financial speculators.[11] Recently Lance Davis and Robert Huttenback have subjected the issue for the first time to sophisticated cliometric analysis − and intriguingly the answer they come up with is very similar to Hobson's early and crude approximation. During the period covered by their data, 1860-1912,

The British as a whole certainly did not benefit economically from the Empire. On the other hand, individual investors did ... probably at no time, and certainly not after the 1870s, were Empire profits sufficient to underwrite *British* prosperity. However, for the shareholders in the agricultural and extractive and the public-utility sectors − and perhaps others as well − where competition was blunted, or enforced property rights pushed potential competitors onto inferior lands, the Empire was important, and it was profitable.[12]

Unfortunately, we have as yet nothing comparable to Davis and Huttenback's study − or Marseille's work on the economics of late French colonialism[13]− covering the British Empire during the twentieth century. Therefore there are major gaps in our knowledge of the economic considerations underlying decolonization: for instance, only very preliminary work has been done concerning the impact of decolonization on trade between colonies and metropoles,[14] and research on British firms' attitudes to the transfer of authority has offered rather agnostic findings.[15] D.K. Fieldhouse's judgement on this latter issue is that

British business firms never thought very clearly about the prospects of decolonization ... none of the companies took any part in pressing for or against independence ... Big companies were confident that they could cope with changing situations by adapting their methods and activities.[16]

Perhaps more fundamental to our enquiry are official attitudes; the balance-sheet of Empire as perceived by the British Treasury and its effect on the eventual withdrawal from Empire. Here then seems to be an emergent consensus amongst scholars: but it is a consensus which once more presents us with a seeming paradox. This is that in the period immediately preceding decolonization, the years during and shortly following the Second World War, the colonies were seen as essential to the British economy, and their resources were used to subsidize it, to a greater extent, probably, than ever before − certainly far more than in the period dealt with by Huttenback and Davis. In other words, plans were apparently being laid to withdraw from Empire just when Empire was most directly valuable to Britain. The British economy was kept afloat during the war, its postwar reconstruction financed, the attempt to maintain its autonomy as against the USA pursued, and perhaps above all the position of sterling protected, substantially through the exploitation of colonial primary producers. This was accomplished through the sterling area 'dollar pool', hoarding colonial financial surpluses in London, through the compulsory purchases and fixed prices of marketing boards, and a variety of other physical and fiscal controls.[17] All this was at a time when wartime coalition and postwar Labour Governments were proclaiming a new, more development-oriented and less exploitative colonial economic policy;[18] but one estimate suggests that whilst the Colonial Development and Welfare contributed £40 million to development projects between 1945 and 1951, less than £240 million was flowing the other way.[19]

It would indeed have been surprising if ministers or the Colonial Office had been planning to divest themselves of the major dollar-earning colonies at such a time: but it is clear that they were not. Under both Coalition and Labour Governments, plans were indeed pushed forward during the 1940s for accelerated economic development and political devolution in the tropical colonies. Historians have disagreed over whether the major innovations here should be attributed primarily to Arthur Creech Jones and Sir Andrew Cohen in 1946-50, to Colonial Office rethinking during wartime, or perhaps further back to Malcolm MacDonald's tenure at the Office in the late 1930s.[20] All have agreed, on the other hand, that the new strategy was aimed at strengthening the imperial system through reform, not to dismantle it. For most colonies, especially in Africa and the Caribbean, self-government was seen as an objective only for the very distant future, and would in any case be self-government *within* the Empire. It was also explicitly stated that some colonies could never become politically independent, on account of their small size, their strategic importance for Britain, or the impossibility of their becoming economically self-sufficient. As we shall see, Malta was felt to fall into this category. The great exceptions were, of course, the South Asian colonies. India had always been different – more important economically, politically, and emotionally to the British than any other colony. Yet by the Second World War much of this value, historians now believe, had been eroded: as Tomlinson has powerfully argued, the British and the Indian economies were becoming less complementary with industrialization in the latter; the costs of the relationship to the British exchequer were rising sharply; and the strength of Congress meant that the political risks involved in seeking to 'bend' Indian economic policy back towards British needs would be enormous.[21] We cannot, of course, explain Britain's decision to quit India purely in terms of these changing economic relationships (still less can we do so for Palestine, where financial considerations barely entered into the complex conflicts among Zionism, Arab nationalism, US pressure, and Britain's search for continued regional strategic footholds)[22] but it is clear that India's economic value to Britain was no longer a decisive factor in decision-making.[23]

By the late 1950s, this was the case also for the African and other tropical colonies. The postwar position of heavy reliance on the colonial Empire did not persist long after 1951. The immediate crisis of the British economy was resolved, and Britain appeared to be sharing fully in the long postwar boom − though sharing as a more junior partner than hitherto, and in ways that concealed profound structural problems which were later to become apparent. It was a boom whose dynamic centre lay in relationships between the advanced industrial countries, so that Britain's traditional trading links with primary-producing regions seemed less important. Not only were these links considered less necessary as a safeguard against renewed world recession or (with falls in commodity prices and a general commitment to free trade under GATT) useful 'captive' sources of raw materials, but continued adherence to them might even isolate Britain from the associations offering the greatest potential for growth − which, Macmillan's Conservative Government came increasingly to believe after 1957, lay in closer integration with Europe. Meanwhile, disappointment with the performance of the Colonial Development Corporation, and Treasury fears about the long-term financial commitments its projects might involve, sharpened a wider pessimism in official circles about the prospects for rapid 'take-off' of the underdeveloped economies into self-sustained growth.[24]

In 1957, therefore, Macmillan took the apparently unprecedented step of commissioning a wide-ranging survey of the remaining colonies. He sought answers to three questions: were the colonies an economic asset to or a drain on the British State; which colonies' constitutional position was likely to alter towards independence and how quickly; and, most important, what would be the economic effect on Britain of independence for the remaining colonies? The conclusions suggested that the colonies were running a sterling deficit of £28 million, but a non-sterling surplus of £63 million. The surplus derived overwhelmingly from the Malayan area (£51 million) which was about to become independent; the major loss-makers were the East African territories (sterling deficit of £49 million) and the West Indies (£16 million). The cost to the British Government of the colonies (through the Colonial Development and Welfare Acts, the Colonial Service Vote, and the Colonial Development Corporation) was about £51 million per annum. Colonies which became independent would cease to be eligible for most of this money; therefore the more rapid the transition to independence the greater the savings for the British Government. However, given the likely pattern of future commitments to continuing aid after independence, and the countervailing factors that independent Commonwealth States would be less likely to bank sterling balances in London and to trade heavily with Britain,

the conclusion was drawn that the economic considerations were fairly evenly matched. Consequently, it was felt that the economic interests of the United Kingdom were unlikely in themselves to be decisive in determining whether or not a territory should become independent.[25]

So if economic considerations were 'neutral' – and as we have seen what little evidence we have on the thinking of private firms suggests that they took a similar view to the officials – other developments must have conditioned the nature and timing of these late decolonizations as of those in Asia and the Middle East earlier.[26] This is as we would expect: just as no historian has seriously doubted the intimate interconnection between British economic policy and decolonization, so no serious scholar – including Marxists – has sought to argue that narrow financial calculation was all-determining.[27] Here, though, the scholarly consensus begins to break down. Broadly, three types of change have been identified as significant, and academic support has been forthcoming to assert the primacy of each of them.

First we may note the possible influence of political and social change within Britain. This has several different strands. In the sphere of party politics itself, it has been judged important but not overwhelmingly decisive which party was in office in Britain during decolonization; there was, after all, a broad bipartisan consensus amongst the leaders and the 'moderate' wings of both Labour and Conservative parties over many of the general themes of colonial policy.[28] This consensus was never unchallenged or unconditional, and it frequently did not extend to India: it is generally agreed that a Conservative Government under Churchill, had he won in 1945, would have been far less willing to transfer power in India than were Attlee and Labour – it was probably on this issue that party politics was most significant in decolonization.[29] Later, and especially under Macmillan and Macleod, Conservatives proved willing to recognize the inevitability of decolonization — even if it has been argued that in so doing they were pursuing the illusion of reconstituting an 'informal empire' on the mid-Victorian model: a model which Britain no longer had the power to sustain.[30] Equally, it would seem that within the bipartisan framework the Labour Opposition was able to exert important informal influence on the decolonizing process, helping to accelerate and liberalize it.[31]

Standing somewhat outside the consensus were two similar but significant groups: the diehard pro-imperial Conservative Right wing, and the militantly anticolonialist Left both within and beyond the Labour Party. The first was increasingly marginal in its influence on colonial policy: though it was a sadly different story for its impact on immigration and race relations policies.[32] The latter was probably more important: I have argued elsewhere that it made a clear though subsidiary impression through its contacts with and assistance to colonial nationalist politicians, its lobbying and propagandizing role, and the energetic activities of its parliamentary supporters in exposing abuses of colonial power.[33]

The activities of such radical anticolonialist groups may alternatively be viewed as the forerunners or 'extreme' fringe of a more general trend: the growth of a liberal unease about and eventual rejection of the imperial mission in British society as a whole. It is evident that traditional beliefs in the moral worth of the colonial enterprise had long been eroding, especially amongst the educated middle class — it is unclear how far such beliefs had penetrated amongst the mass of the population in any case.[34] The 'moral disarmament' of imperialism was far advanced by the 1930s,[35] and by the 1950s few outside the aforementioned Empire Loyalist die-hards could invoke notions of the civilizing mission or the 'white man's burden' other than ironically. At the least, major psychological barriers against decolonization had been dismantled. Some commentators would add that the rise of a 'new middle class', oriented towards Little Englandism and secondarily towards Europe, pressurizing Governments to emphasize domestic consumerism and/or welfarism rather than overseas commitments, supplanted whatever political constituency imperialism had possessed within Britain.[36]

The second major pattern of change identified by historians as determining decolonization lies in the field of the superpowers and grand strategy. Here four major trends have been emphasized. One was pressure from the 'anticolonialism' of United States policy, especially during the Second World War.[37] Britain's increasing subordination to the USA made it impossible in the long run for her to maintain an independent imperial world role, though Ernest Bevin in particular, as Foreign Secretary in 1945-50, tried tenaciously to do so.[38] The Suez débâcle, according to this argument, was what brought home to British statesmen the reality of their dependence on the USA.[39]

Another and related claim arises from the Cold War. This was important in two ways: both in their fears that, unless concessions were made to colonial nationalists, they would turn in frustration to the Soviet bloc (a central theme of Macmillan's famous 'Winds of Change' speech), and in that nuclear weapons dramatically lessened the strategic value of colonies whose possession had been predicated on seapower. Malta is of course an important test case for the latter argument.[40] Also sometimes emphasized is Britain's turn towards Europe: the decision to seek entry into the European Community, reached in the late 1950s though not consummated until the early 1970s, spelt the death of the imperial, and the radical weakening of the Commonwealth, relationships.[41] Finally — and here of course the argument reconnects closely with the economic explanation — it is asserted that Britain was by the 1950s simply too weak to continue to be a world power: decolonization was merely one of the indications that British politicians had grudgingly accepted the realities of minor-power status.

The third line of interpretation argues that the really crucial changes took place within the colonies themselves. It builds on the 'peripheral' or 'excentric' theory of colonial expansion propounded by Robinson, Gallagher, and Fieldhouse and seeks to apply its lessons to the period of decolonization (thus, incidentally, resolving our first paradox about the relationship between imperial aggrandizement and metropolitan weakness).[42]

The argument is that the crucial factor in all imperial systems was the collaborative relationships established between

colonialists and sections of the indigenous population: that
indeed 'the nature of imperialism in any particular country is
shown in the balance of terms struck between the imperialists
and their local contractors ... the relativity of imperialism to
proto- and modern nationalisms can also be measured in the
changing balance of collaborative equations.'[43] This approach,
it is argued, provides the key to explaining not only colonial
expansion, when 'the breakdown of informal collaborations led
to an imperial take-over', but also its contraction:

When imperialists demanded more from their sub-contractors than their
people would tolerate, contracts could not be delivered and the system
became unstable ... And, at last, when nationalists succeeded in
detaching enough mediators from colonial regimes into a united front
of non-cooperation, their rulers either chose to leave or were compelled
to go. They had run out of collaborators, which fixed the time for the
transfer of colonial power.[44]

This breakdown of collaborative relations might have a variety
of causes. Changes in metropolitan policy might lead to new
demands being made of local agents which they could not meet,
whilst alterations in the structure of the world economy,
impinging on the primary producers of the colonial areas, might
have similar effects. Nationalist movements, themselves
mobilizing support from those discommoded by such economic
shifts even if the ideologies of their leaders had quite different
roots, would seek to build coalitions challenging those formed
by the colonial rulers — which of course by no means excludes
the possibility of the nationalists in their turn seeking to form
collaborative links with colonial rulers. Indeed 'transfers of
power' — other than through all-out armed struggle — depended
upon their doing so, and thus on nationalism becoming at least
on this level the continuation of imperialism by other means.[45]
However, it would be a mistake to assume that such transfers
necessarily reflect the success of what Tomlinson disparagingly
calls — in criticizing the work of John Darwin — the 'fancy
footwork' or 'change of technique' of would-be neo-colonialists.
This approach

does not distinguish clearly the nature of perceived British interests
in various parts of the empire, and ... it ignores the question of
underlying structural changes that in the end, negated the fancy
footwork of the British policy-makers ... Britain's strength as a neo-

colonial power has declined since 1945 just as her strength as an imperial power declined.[46]

The 'excentric' theorists, then, call for attention both to economic change at the global level and to the shifts in and strains upon collaborative mechanisms 'on the ground' in individual colonies. In contrast to other theories, they move the focus away from metropolitan policy-making, from political ideologies, and from military strategies: the true centre of the analysis – the true imperial metropole, as Robinson would put it[47] – is in the changing relativities of local collaboration. Thus we may now turn to investigate how much this and the other general approaches we have surveyed help in explaining British relations with Malta, and conversely how well, if at all, Malta fits into the patterns identified.

II MALTA: THE DILEMMAS OF DEPENDENCY

Our discussion of decolonization in Malta will follow the same pattern as the preceding survey of late British colonialism, looking in turn at economic calculation, the influence of political debate within Britain, strategic factors, and the patterns of collaboration and conflict within Malta itself. Running throughout will be stress on the reasons why, from British policy-makers' point of view, Malta could never be a candidate for independence. We turn then to look more closely at the attempted resolution to these dilemmas through the integration proposal – after the failure of which independence came, in British eyes, almost by default.

In a sense, the general debates on the profitability or otherwise of Empire are irrelevant to Malta: such considerations had played no part in the British decision to establish colonial rule, which was reached for purely strategic reasons. To use a favourite metaphor of the British Government itself, it was no more reasonable to expect the colonial administration there to be self-financing (as was demanded, albeit often unsuccessfully, of colonial governments elsewhere) than it would be to pose such a demand of a warship. Yet this by no means implied that the Colonial Office was not eager that Malta should be self-supporting – with self-sufficiency defined to include paying for facilities which Maltese politicians could quite reasonably argue met British, not Maltese, needs. In fact British officials were frequently parsimonious in the extreme. As Davis and Huttenback point out, such penny-pinching by the Treasury over colonial expenditure – sometimes carried to ludicrous extremes – was a general phenomenon; and as Balogh notes it was exercised in regard to Malta throughout the colonial period.[48]

There were recurrent attempts to find ways of raising more through local taxation: revenue was long raised through import duties on wheat – the inconsistency of which with Britain's general advocacy of free trade occasioned some diplomatic embarrassment – and means sought of curtailing local expenditure, with one Commissioner in 1877 even suggesting the closure of the University as an economy measure.[49] Inevitably, this stringency was most intense in times of peace, relaxed in periods of war or tension, so that the Maltese economy prospered or languished in inverse proportion to the stability of European peace throughout the colonial era. Dockyard employment was particularly vulnerable to such fluctuations, and the attempt to make Britain accept responsibility for maintaining a more stable employment structure became a major political issue, more especially with the rise of the Malta Labour Party (MLP) and its core support amongst dockworkers.

Malta, then, was in no direct sense an *economic* asset to Britain. As a market for British manufactures it was insignificant, it was recipient to very little capital investment other than that on defence-related infrastructure, and its exports were almost non-existent. In the eyes of the Treasury, it was a drain on resources: *per capita* subsidies to Malta ran for much of the colonial period at a level exceeded only by Gibraltar.[50] One commentator has been driven to comment that the position of Maltese Governments was simply 'inconsistent' in proclaiming anti-colonial sentiments whilst simultaneously demanding increased levels of economic aid from the colonialists.[51] Maltese politicians saw the situation very differently. To them, funds from the British were in effect rent for the use of facilities vital to Britain's defence needs, and inadequate rent at that: Malta should be viewed, in negotiations with Britain, not as a debtor but as a creditor.[52]

As will be seen below, however, the local politicians

themselves became deeply divided over how to handle this gulf of perceptions. For the British, the key fact was that Malta was overwhelmingly dependent on British Government expenditures, directly and indirectly; they could envisage no possibility of the islands being viable without these, and this served both as an absolute barrier to independence and as a trump card in any negotiations with Maltese ministers. Thomas Balogh, the British economist commissioned to draw up development plans for Mintoff's Governments, came to believe that this perception led to arrogant and short-sighted British Treasury attitudes in dealing with Mintoff. He suggests that they

showed a complete disregard of the susceptibilities of the Maltese. The subservience of the financial 'experts' of the Colonial Office translated itself into petty attempts to 'claw' back as much as possible of the subsidies, rather generously granted by their political chiefs. They were incapable of discussing seriously Mr Mintoff's social and economic proposals and making constructive counter-suggestions. He was confronted with brusque ultimata in his demands for British help.[53]

The general conclusion with regard to the economic influences on late British colonialism in Malta must then be that wider commercial considerations, and the attitudes of British business, were marginal in the extreme, but that public finances – namely British defence spending on and subsidies to the islands – were at the heart of the relationship. They were the subject at best of widely differing presuppositions, at worst of bitter conflict between British and Maltese leaders. Should they be viewed as indices of British generosity, or of Britain's vital need for Malta? The long-term answer would evidently depend on non-economic factors, above all, changing strategic patterns, but in the meantime there was a massive asymmetry in bargaining power – the British seemed to hold all the cards. Whether this balance of power could be shifted might depend in part on whether Maltese politicians could find supporters of their claims elsewhere – perhaps within Britain. Therefore we now turn to look at the handling of Maltese affairs in the British political process.

A variety of different groups and interests within Britain were potential actors in Maltese-related events. Most important would, of course, be the political parties, and it is on these and on interested groups within them that this account will centre, particularly the Labour Party which seems to have been much more active on the issue and which was, being in opposition during the crucial years, a far more free agent than the Conservative Party whose policy was that of the Government. We have already suggested reasons why British business interests were unlikely to be significant participants, but the relatively low profile of some others requires more explanation. This applies especially to the Maltese community within Britain. The 1966 census estimated a Maltese-born population in England and Wales of 31,580, but as the standard study of Maltese in Britain notes, perhaps half of these would have been children of British service personnel.[54] The remainder, though heavily concentrated in certain districts of London, did not form a particularly cohesive community and had few effective communal organizations. Many, indeed, sought to assimilate rapidly into the majority host population.[55] These factors are probably enough to explain the lack of political activity on Maltese issues amongst British-resident Maltese, even without invoking the alleged political fatalism which several scholars have suggested was characteristic of the Maltese colonial mentality.[56] Nonetheless, as Dench indicates, the majority of these migrants would have been MLP supporters,[57] and there was for some time a small but active UK branch of the MLP whose leader Arthur Scerri, later Maltese High Commissioner in London, participated intensively in British Labour Party circles.

Also standing somewhat aloof, though in this case no doubt more from prudence than through lack of organization, was the Catholic Church in Britain. Whereas in the earlier conflict between Lord Strickland and the Maltese Church, prominent English Catholics had intervened in attempts to mediate,[58] no overt stance was taken by British Catholics — nor, incidentally, by British Protestant Churches — in the Maltese politico-religious struggles of the 1950s and 1960s. It is true that Lord Perth, a British Catholic member of the Round Table Conference on integration, expressed sympathy with the fears of the Maltese hierarchy about the proposal, but it is not clear how far he was influenced by specifically Catholic appeals, let alone by any official Church view.[59]

In the more central arena of party politics, Conservatives seem to have undertaken little activity beyond support for British Government policy. The British Conservative Party had far less close 'fellow feeling' with the Maltese Nationalist Party (PN) than did British Labour with the MLP. There were no formal links between the parties, and many British Tories must have harboured residual suspicions about the PN because of its pro-Italian past and record of strong opposition to British rule. British Conservatives, like British officials (whose attitude to the various Maltese political forces is discussed further below) felt far more at home with the traditional Anglophilia of Miss Mabel Strickland, the *Times of Malta*, and the Progressive Constitutional Party (PCP). The later evolution of the PN towards the political philosophy of European Christian Democracy[60] was to bring it closer to the thinking of many British Conservatives.

Considerably more needs to be said about British Labour attitudes. The influence of British socialist traditions on the political thought of the MLP, and of Mintoff himself, is obvious enough to require no further comment here; though the details of its transmission and reception are an important subject for future research. It should, however, be noted that the nature of these influences was widely misunderstood in Malta. Already in 1947 Sir Paul Boffa's Labour Government was being accused by its opponents of a 'totalitarian' and 'Fabian Socialist' ideology,[61] whilst later Mintoff's 'Fabian' beliefs were to be attacked in clerical statements as if the label were effectively coterminous with Communism.[62] 'Fabianism' appeared to be understood by many Maltese to be a revolutionary Marxist philosophy rather than, as it was, an extremely gradualistic and explicitly anti-Marxist ideology of social planning and reform.[63] How far either Boffa or Mintoff can adequately be characterized as Fabians is, of course, another question altogether.

In any case, contacts between MLP and British Labour were of long standing,[64] and during the Second World War MLP representatives established regular communication not only with the British Labour Party but with the main Labour specialist group on colonial affairs, the Fabian Colonial Bureau (FCB).[65] British Labour leaders became enthusiastic supporters of the MLP's integration proposals. Labour's official statement

on the issue, *Malta to Westminster?*, lauded both the Maltese
people ('If their country and population were larger, and perhaps
wealthier, they could have become a Dominion') and Mintoff,
described as having had 'a most romantic rise to power' and as
having exhibited 'imaginative genius' in formulating the
integration idea. The British Labour Party hopefully predicted
that

The example of Malta may well be followed by other Colonial peoples
who, realising the loneliness and exposure of solitary statehood in the
twentieth-century world, choose to become a part of a wider
international family, sharing and contributing to a common standard
of life.[66]

The FCB, meanwhile, was offering detailed advice to the MLP,
on the latter's request, in gathering information to back up the
integration idea.[67] The Labour spokesman on colonial affairs,
Nye Bevan — also a participant in the Round Table Conference,
and charismatic figurehead of Labour's Left wing — took a close
personal interest. In a House of Commons speech he offered
perhaps the most original line of defence for the proposal.
Opponents of integration, he said, had objected that it would be
a 'constitutional fiction' — but there was a great deal in favour
of fiction in making constitutions. Operating with the
'philosophy of AsIf' (he was alluding to a once-famous book of
that title by the German writer Vaihinger), one could make
fictions grow into living realities.[68] Less welcome to many
Maltese ears were Bevan's reported remarks at a Governor's
cocktail party in Valletta, when he is alleged to have referred
to the Maltese 'breeding like rabbits', and said this must stop.[69]
Left-wing supporters of Maltese political demands were not
necessarily immune to the superior attitudes which aroused
Maltese resentment throughout the colonial period.

Nor were relations between British and Maltese Labour
always wholly fraternal. Increasingly after the failure of
integration and Mintoff's turn towards a militantly anticolonial
stance, undertones of exasperation crept into British socialist
politicians' references to the Maltese leader. Party leader Hugh
Gaitskell told Mintoff in June 1960 that, whilst British Labour
supported the MLP, it was unhappy that he had refused to meet
the Colonial Secretary.[70] Mintoff replied that this was only
because the British had imposed unreasonable conditions on the

talks, and in thanking Labour Left-winger Tom Driberg for lobbying Gaitskell on the MLP's behalf, complained that: 'It is evident, however, that the Colonial Department of your Party are bending themselves backwards into accomodating (sic) the Colonial Office', whilst Labour Commonwealth Officer John Hatch was trying to impose his ideas on the MLP rather than collecting data to give a fair picture of the Maltese situation.[71] Later, another Labour Left-winger, Ian Mikardo, commented that he had been 'nauseated ... by the condescending attitude to Mintoff of Slim Jim (i.e. Labour Colonial spokesman James Callaghan) and some of the others.'[72] Certainly Callaghan, Bevan's successor as the senior Labour figure dealing most directly with Maltese affairs, was critical of the MLP's intransigence, telling Mintoff that 'I think, with many of my colleagues, that the tactics of the Malta Labour Party have set back your own case.'[73]

Nonetheless — and despite the fact that after 1958 the MLP seemed to have smoother relations with the Left-wing pressure group the Movement for Colonial Freedom (in which Scerri became actively involved) than with the Labour leaders,[74] Labour continued to press the MLP's case. In September 1961 Callaghan, with senior Labour MPs Hilary Marquand and George Thomson, met privately with Colonial Secretary Ian Macleod to urge that the British Government must 'say quite clearly that Malta is in no different position from any other colonial territory in the sense that it will achieve in due course full self-government and independence' — though no 'target date' for this was suggested.[75]

It is impossible to assess precisely how great an impact the British Labour Party's lobbying on behalf of the MLP, and that of pressure groups like the FCB and MCF, may have had on official policy — partly because many of the relevant Colonial Office files are still closed, partly because such influences can in any case not be quantified. It is clear, however, that British Labour's strong support for integration helped push the Government towards acceptance — or to put it the other way around, that strong *opposition* from Labour would have been a major and possibly insuperable obstacle to the proposal. No British Government would have risked pushing through such a measure unless there were near-consensual accord to it at

Westminster. Similarly, it may reasonably be surmised that Labour pressure on Colonial Secretary Duncan Sandys when he announced to the Commons on 1 August 1963 the 'target date' for Maltese independence,[76] helped incline the British Government against accepting PN proposals on the religious clauses of the Independence Constitution. British Labour calls for a referendum on the Constitution (very much a second best for the MLP, which wanted fresh elections) may also have had an effect.[77] Conversely, Labour's failure — despite the protests of some back-benchers[78] — to oppose the rushing through of the Malta Independence Bill in July 1963, with a Constitution and accompanied by defence and financial agreements all of which the MLP opposed, and without new elections (for which, however, an unsuccessful Labour amendment did call) was seen by MLP supporters as letting the British Government 'off the hook'.[79]

In sum, then, although definite judgements are difficult, Maltese decolonization would appear to substantiate the claim of John Hatch, and the Opposition in Britain could have a significant if indirect influence on the direction of colonial policy. Two general attitudinal trends within Britain may also be noted as possible influences. One was the increasing secularization and liberalization of British social attitudes, which meant that British support, official or unofficial, was much less likely to be forthcoming for the Maltese Church's stance on the status of the clergy and the scope of moral regulation in Malta. Few, even amongst British Conservatives or Catholics, were sympathetic to the traditionally dominant place of the priesthood in Maltese society or to the argument that socialist or Labour beliefs were incompatible with religious observance. Although, as we have suggested, the Catholic Church of the metropole did not itself intervene in the dispute, English Catholics did express their disagreement with the Maltese Church. For instance, Michael de la Bedoyere argued at length in the *Guardian* that Malta's Independence Constitution was inconsistent with the new spirit of the Church after Vatican II,[80] whilst Labour MP Tom Driberg (despite his unorthodox lifestyle, a devout Catholic) pressed in Malta and in Britain the case that one could be both a socialist and a good Catholic.[81]

The other trend, of perhaps wider significance, was the gradual transformation of the concept of moral responsibility towards Empire. The classic Kiplingesque version of this, claiming a duty to guide 'primitive' peoples towards civilization, later transmuted into the doctrine of trusteeship, had had in any case only very limited purchase in Malta. Given that the Maltese population was seen as European, and thus placed at the 'civilized' pole of the racial hierarchy in which the colonialist ethos believed, and given also that Malta was explicitly held for its military value and not even pretendedly as a moral duty, the ethic of trusteeship could only be proclaimed in the more pragmatic form that British overrule was necessary to Maltese economic survival. This could not serve as an adequate rebuttal to demands for self-government or at least the extension of representative institutions; particularly not after Malta's resistance to intense Italo-German assaults during the Second World War added considerable new weight to the idea of a special moral responsibility towards the Maltese. Maltese heroism during the war became a major theme of island politicians in pressing their claims for British aid thereafter. Undoubtedly Boffa's or Borg Olivier's emphasis on this record, like their claim that Malta had in 1800 joined the British Empire of its own volition rather than through conquest,[82] betrayed a certain naïvety about the determinants of British policy. Certainly it contrasted sharply with Mintoff's more hard-headed focus on Malta's military importance; but the notion of a Maltese moral claim on Britain cannot wholly be dismissed. It was a claim increasingly felt to be incompatible with the exercise of even a benevolent despotism: by the mid-twentieth century Wellington's notorious assertion that Malta must be governed like 'the foredeck of an admiral's flagship' could not publicly be sustained. Colonial autocracy, in the changed moral climate, could be supported only in a markedly defensive spirit, or else denied — as in Eden's (false) assertion of 1943 that Malta had 'complete self- government', or Lord Hailey's 1945 claim that Malta was a pre-eminent demonstration that civil rights could flourish under colonial rule.[83]

The story of Britain's changing strategic needs can be told more briefly than that of political attitudes within Britain. Each successive development in British foreign policy during the nineteenth century made Malta ever more crucial as a military and naval base. Its importance was first underlined by use as a staging post and rear hospital during the Crimean expedition (1854-6), and grew after Britain lost the use of Corfu to Greece in 1864. The real turning point was the opening of the Suez Canal (1869) after which Malta became the vital central link in the chain of bases ensuring British naval dominance in the Mediterranean, influence in the Middle East, and above all the lines of communication to India. It was the point to which troops were concentrated and from which they were dispersed in crises as varied as the Anglo-Russian confrontation of 1878 and the annexation of Ashanti in 1896 – crises whose incidence became more frequent as the 'Scramble for Africa' and growing great-power rivalries pushed intra-European tensions outwards to North Africa and the Middle East. The results for Malta itself included not only an ever-greater dependence on British defence spending but an increasingly interventionist administration.

Malta's pivotal role in great-power strategies climaxed in the 1930s. The rise of Mussolini underlined both the islands' importance and their vulnerability: the Italian dictator had formulated as early as 1936 plans for a 'lightning' attack on the islands, which he believed would destroy British power in the Mediterranean within seven weeks.[84] The enormous weight of German and Italian air power brought to bear against Malta graphically demonstrated its centrality in the struggle for the Mediterranean – but the rise of air power was one of the factors which, after 1945, eroded Malta's value to Britain.[85] This was recognized rapidly by the new Labour Prime Minister, Clement Attlee. In early 1946 he argued that the new conditions of warfare, based on airborne striking power and in the last analysis on nuclear weapons, as well as the rise of colonial nationalism and Britain's diminished strength, meant that British dominance in the Middle East was increasingly precarious: and in British strategic thinking Malta was decidedly part of the Middle East rather than of Europe, however the Maltese themselves may have seen it.[86] Gladwyn Jebb of the Foreign Office spelt out what he thought were the implications of Attlee's view:

As I understand it, the Prime Minister's suggestion is that we should abandon all attempt to defend our communications in the whole of the Mediterranean and Middle Eastern areas. This would presumably entail the withdrawal of all our forces from the Middle East, and presumably in the long run from Malta, Gibraltar and Aden also.[87]

'In the long run' — by the late 1960s — this proved indeed to be the logic of British policy, but this massive contraction of British power came far more slowly, more reluctantly, and more painfully than Attlee's projection suggested. Foreign Secretary Ernest Bevin, allied with the military Chiefs of Staff, had a far more traditionally ambitious conception of Britain's Mediterranean role than the Prime Minister's 'Little England' vision, and in the short run they won the argument. Even British withdrawal from India — defence of which had provided an important part of the rationale for British bases in the Middle East in the first place — did not immediately and fundamentally alter the situation. British planners hoped both to keep India and Pakistan within the Western defence system[88] and to construct a new system of bases, centred on Suez and guaranteed now more by fostering local allies and less by formal colonial rule, which would to some extent 'fill the gap' left by Indian independence.[89] Thus Malta remained a crucial part of the chain.

Meanwhile three new actors were entering the Mediterranean drama. First was the United States, which already in August 1946 was pressing for base facilities in Malta.[90] When an American naval air unit was stationed there in 1951 it became a focus for MLP protest: Mintoff charged that the Maltese Government had been 'tricked' into accepting it, and raised the spectre of Malta as a target in nuclear war.[91] Later Malta became NATO's Mediterranean headquarters after 'protracted and bitter' negotiations with the Maltese Government.[92] However, the 'internationalization' of Malta as a military site was a limited phenomenon: Western Alliance leaders continued to see it as primarily a British rather than a more general NATO responsibility. The second external factor was even more limited in its direct impact on Malta: the rise of Soviet power was not reflected in the USSR's becoming an important presence in the Mediterranean. Yet naturally the fear that she might do so, and might seek influence in Malta as a means to that end, became a new component in the British determination that Malta could not become fully independent. In particular, despite the extreme weakness of Communist influence in Maltese politics (an influence for which both British officials and Maltese conservatives watched with more than a hint of paranoia),[93] fears of a future Soviet presence strengthened the growing British hostility to the MLP. As one British politician commented, the threat to offer facilities to the USSR was always a tempting bargaining counter for Mintoff, even if he had no intention of carrying out the threat.[94]

The repercussions of the third new actor's entry onto the stage were more immediate. If Maltese national assertion from the 1880s to the 1930s was linked, not least in British official eyes, with that of Garibaldi, Cavour, or later Mussolini, the Maltese nationalism of the 1950s-60s was seen in connection with that of Makarios, Nasser, and later, of Gadhafi. As the British were forced out of Suez by Nasser, and as EOKA sought to drive them from Cyprus, Malta's importance to British thinking shot up in two ways. First, actual or threatened loss of bases in the eastern Mediterranean meant that Malta might become, no longer a connecting link in the British defence system, but its front line. Second, the British fear that Mintoff, if frustrated in his demands on Britain, might ally himself with Nasser's Arab nationalism, or even emulate the tactics of Makarios and Grivas (as MLP rhetoric seemed more than once to threaten), was more urgent and more realistic than suspicions that he might turn towards Moscow. There can be no doubt that this was a major factor, perhaps *the* major factor, in Britain's surprising willingness to pursue integration. As Holland comments, 'Eden's determination to respond effectively to Nasserism in the eastern Mediterranean, and Mintoff's determination to dish his ecclesiastic enemies, came conveniently together.'[95] On the other hand, the Suez crisis itself demonstrated that Mintoff's main bargaining counter, the naval value of Valletta harbour, was one of rapidly diminishing value. Malta was the base from which the British fleet steamed for Port Said, as so many great navies had done since the Phoenicians – but the Suez adventure, swan-song of British imperial assertiveness, was also that of the traditional Mediterranean naval power on which Malta's importance had so largely rested. Phillip Darby aptly summarizes the lessons of the operation:

Viewed in wider perspective, the operation revealed the failure of the defence establishment to adjust to the changed conditions of the mid-fifties. The weeks of planning, preparation and re-equipment; a vast armada which eventually steamed from Malta ... all were legacies of the days of global-war thinking ... Such an approach had no place in a world of heightened sensibilities and ostensibly at peace ... In short, Britain found that many of her foreign bases were much less usable in times of crisis than under routine conditions.[96]

This did not mean that Malta was immediately perceived to be irrelevant in the age of nuclear balances and mobile airborne strike-forces: after all, Malta *had* turned out to be usable in a crisis, even if usable in the service of an archaic strategy. As the future defence agreements involving Britain, NATO, and Malta were to show, defence chiefs wanted to ensure that it would remain so – and one can only speculate what role Malta might have played in recent Middle Eastern and Libyan crises if it had been still a NATO base. Yet as the gradual winding down of British defence and dockyard establishments in Malta (if so erratic a process can be labelled 'gradual') were still more clearly to show, the islands were now *useful* (and decreasingly so) rather than *vital* to British strategy. The final withdrawal of British land forces in 1975 'had only a minor impact', since the British Army had become irrevocably European-centred after the 1966-70 termination of British commitments east of Suez.[97]

This consideration of the strategic influences on Malta's colonial status has indicated how heavily its fate was determined by the place of the 'fortress colony' in a chain of British fortresses. It would appear to confirm Hancock's view that 'There is surely no other community in the British Commonwealth whose domestic disputes are entangled so inextricably with the shattering controversies which divide principalities and powers.'[98] The statement, however, cuts both ways: the 'shattering controversies' must be seen in their interconnection with the 'domestic disputes'. The 1957 review of colonial commitments commissioned by Macmillan had acknowledged this when, after pointing out that financial arguments did not point decisively either for or against decolonization, it had been suggested that strategic factors also could not be viewed as all-determining since 'the maintenance of bases against the will of the local Government and people would seriously limit their usefulness.'[99] This was intended as a generally applicable point, but its resonance for Malta is especially evident. We turn next, and finally, to explore its implications by looking at the interaction of what one historian has dubbed the 'colonial dynamic' and the 'patriotic consensus' — though there was very little that was obviously consensual about it[100] — in Malta.

The first collaborative alliance the British colonial rulers formed in Malta was, obviously enough, with the aristocracy and clergy of the Maltese Congress who emerged as controllers of the revolt against the French. It was, however, only a co-operation of the most limited sort, as the British were committed to direct physical control of the islands and 'persuaded of the mischievous effects that would result from entrusting any portion of political power to a people so singularly unfitted to enjoy it.'[101] The exercise of such control was facilitated for Britain both by the almost uniquely high relativity of metropolitan might to local resources — probably in no other British colony was the balance of physical force, if it ever came to the test, so heavily weighted towards the occupiers — and by the homogeneity of Maltese society: 'Here there were no hinterlands to be defended, spheres of influence to be disputed, squabbling chiefs to be pacified.'[102] Yet that very centralization and homogeneity could be turned against the occupiers if they stumbled athwart fundamental indigenous values, and for that reason the British long remained aloof from the two issues most deeply absorbing local opinion — religion and language, both initially the great unifiers, later successively the great dividers, of Maltese national consciousness.

From the 1860s, as colonial interventionism deepened and local political activity, stimulated both by the demands of the rulers and by the external (especially Italian) incitements, revived, alignments emerged more proximate to the typical colonial pattern: a collaborative and an oppositional élite. The former comprised colonial civil servants, a commercial bourgeoisie dependent on military contracts, and part of the traditional aristocracy. The latter mirrored precisely the configuration of the nationalist élites then emerging everywhere in southern and eastern Europe — as in Ireland and later over much of Africa and Asia — lawyers, journalists, aspirant literati, feeling their upward mobility blocked by colonial structures and rallying, again characteristically of nascent nationalisms, around linguistic identity.[103]

From the 1880s conflict sharpened, with the 'language question' as its immediate focus, as colonial rule (especially under the impetuous hand of Joseph Chamberlain) sought more actively to remould the Maltese polity and as indigenous loyalties coalesced into partisan structures. The colonial impetus was expressed both through the drive for administrative and fiscal reform — opposition to which, under conditions of relative powerlessness, inevitably acquired the obstructive and 'irresponsible' character which could make *anti-reformista* a badge of national pride — and through the imperative of linguistic transmutation. Though it is going too far to speak of Britain calling up a 'stunted Maltese nationalism of the masses' as a counterweight to the pro-Italian élite,[104] official encouragement of English and, to a lesser extent, Maltese as against Italian helped make these not only languages of command but, paradoxically, languages of popular anti-élitism.[105] As the Maltese Labour Movement emerged into the arena after 1918 — the working-class presence being first explosively demonstrated in the *Sette Giugno* uprising of 1919 — class politics began to cross-cut the linguistic disputes of the élite. The workers' movement, eventually tightly secured by the MLP and the General Workers Union (GWU), may have been 'pro-British' in terms of the language question, and at least incipiently anti-clerical, but it was also hostile to both Imperial and Nationalist élites — even if the charismatic presences of a Fortunato Mizzi and a Gerald Strickland might for a time successively enchant it. There was thus, at least *in potentia*, a tripartite division which made the task of the British in building a stable collaborative alliance peculiarly difficult. And even as, for all the kaleidoscopic recomposition of political parties, these alignments coagulated into intense two-party rivalry (reflecting, as Boissevain argues, the polarity of 'ins' and 'outs', of rival patronages and clientages, in Maltese village society)[106] the complexities of island politics would continue to confound British attempts to control the processes of constitutional change.

Thus in the 'high noon' of British rule over Malta, Britain's 'sub-contractors' comprised two distinct blocs, loosely articulated under the leadership of Strickland: the Anglicizing commercial and administrative élites and the workers' movement, ranged against the pro-Italian professionals and their clients. The intersection of imperial strategies and local rivalries made this an increasingly unstable basis of support. The British made ever-increasing demands on their local allies, thus rendering it ever more difficult for the latter to deliver their side of the bargain without antagonizing their own followers − a difficulty exacerbated by the insensitivities of an administration which, being almost invariably headed by military men, was not noted for delicacy of political touch. Here as in every colonial situation, too, the position of collaborative leaders depended on their striking a fine balance between imperial and local identities; and Strickland failed to maintain that balance, becoming 'more pro-British than was good for Britain.'[107] His confrontation with the Church dramatized this failure, and British refusal unequivocally to support him in the showdown indicated their recognition of the dangers of putting all their money on one horse in so close a local race. These were lessons which the next generation of Maltese politicians were to take to heart.

The Second World War transformed Maltese politics, as the old-style Italianism died under a rain of Italian bombs − but Dr Schembri Adami spoke too soon when he argued in March 1945 that the war had killed the language issue and that politics would henceforth be about social class.[108] Some of the old battles continued to be fought under new banners, if only because of what Frendo describes as an inherent drive towards intense two-party polarity. Each party would then inevitably be a coalition, united around personalities more than programmes, cross-cut by allegiances or passions deriving from earlier phases of political conflict. Old issues never quite died, but were overlaid with new controversies − a classic recipe for political instability.[109] A classic arena, too, for the emergence of the individual strongman who could seek to wrench political debate into new directions by strength of will and populist charisma. In the interwar years Strickland had grasped for and won that role: after 1945 Mintoff sought, with uneven but sometimes dramatic success, to inherit it.

The ever-shifting complexities of Maltese political alignment between 1945 and 1964 cannot be summarized here − though they still await an adequate account.[110] We can only broadly map out the alternative stategies open to each of the main actors, and their results. For the British, the imperative was to seek out a new set of local collaborative partners with a sufficiently broad and stable basis of indigenous support to ensure the security of long-term imperial interests. Initially they looked to the Strickland family and the Constitutionalists, but although these retained an especially favoured place in official eyes (as evidenced by Colonial Office reliance on the *Times of Malta* for judgements on local trends, and by Britain's according a role to the PCP in the 1955 negotiations despite its electoral insignificance),[111] they were too lacking in local support to suit British needs. The new partners, after their sweeping victory in the 1947 elections, were Boffa and the MLP. Yet in order to sustain their local allies, the colonial authorities had to be seen to 'deliver the goods', in terms of both economic security and constitutional advance, which their supporters demanded. This the British proved time and again, and increasingly, unable or unwilling to do; beginning with their failure to give Boffa what he − and more stridently his party's emergent Left wing − asked for in 1949.

The Boffa-Mintoff split emerged directly from this British failure, but it reflected also a more fundamental divergence, between an 'inside' and an 'outside' track to dealing with the British. The first, the strategy of Boffa and later of Borg Olivier's PN as the latter moved away from the Nationalists' previous 'outside' agitational stance, emphasized seeking concessions from the rulers by close co-operation with and strongly proclaimed loyalty to them. The outside track was Mintoff's (though he was both too wily and too volatile a politician to adhere wholly consistently to it). It involved building local support through populist appeals and, with that support behind one, adopting an overtly confrontational approach to negotiation. Eventually the rulers, realizing that they had no alternative, would have to accept one as a partner: the outsider would become an insider − on his own terms − having outflanked and marginalized his indigenous rivals in the process. By the mid-1950s, apparently successful examples of this strategy could be pointed to in other British colonies, notably that of Nkrumah in Ghana. The climax of Mintoff's bid for this role was the integration controversy of 1955-7.

If the success of the inside track depended on being able to demonstrate to one's supporters that the approach won significant concessions from Britain, the outsider strategy required a double victory. One had both to convince Maltese voters that the stance worked *vis-à-vis* the colonial authority, and persuade the latter that one's local support was unshakeably strong. Mintoff half-succeeded in the first requirement – only half, because he failed to obtain an overwhelmingly attractive financial package accompanying integration – but lost on the second front. Clerical mobilization ensured so high an abstention rate in the integration referendum that, as Holland comments, the British 'saw the result as proof that Mintoff could not "deliver" his side of the Maltese bargain, and immediately downgraded him as a likely local partner for the future.'[112]

Here all the strands of the late colonial dynamic came together. The financial calculations of the British authorities underlay every move in the integration argument. Whereas at the outset 'The United Kingdom Government wryly accepted that, whatever course was followed, an increased financial burden must be expected to fall on them,'[113] the Treasury was determined to drive a hard bargain, resisting Mintoff's demands for a subsidy of £7 million per annum:

It had been assumed throughout the proceedings of the round-table conference, so the Lord Chancellor and the Colonial Secretary maintained, that Malta's need would not exceed a level of between £4 million and £5 million a year ... Mr Mintoff's proposal would have doubled the rate of increase. This was a wide gap to close.[114]

Internal British politics, too, clearly shaped events – the unique willingness to pursue integration was influenced both by a conception of moral responsibility towards Malta and by British Labour's enthusiasm for the proposal. Conversely, it was increasingly impeded by doubts, especially among Conservatives, about the long-term political as well as economic implications. What if the trio of Maltese MPs held the balance of power in a hung Parliament? What if politico-religious tensions within Malta produced an Ulster-type conflict, umbilically linked to the British polity – a fear which must have grown as those tensions sharpened in the struggle over integration itself?

The strategic situation was an omnipresent background factor:

Malta's military value, seen as making independence unthinkable, drove both British and Maltese opinion towards consideration of other routes. It also, especially after Nasser's nationalization of the Suez Canal, underwrote Mintoff's faith in the outside strategy, giving him what he believed to be a winning hand in dealing with the British. But finally, it may well have been the balance of local forces, the relative strength of political alignments within the Maltese polity and the partly consequent relative attractiveness of alternative partners for the colonial authorities, which most determined Malta's fate. Maltese politicians were always fighting on two fronts; calling on local support to strengthen their hands against the British, and seeking to use their relationships with the colonizers to defeat their local rivals. He who could most successfully juggle those demands would emerge as victor − but that very duality meant that 'victory' would mean different things to different actors and at different times. In 1964 the Nationalists looked like clear winners; the British had at the least successfully cut their losses and retained that much-diminished part which they still wanted of their strategic hold. Labour, angrily watched from the sidelines the transition to an independence they regarded as fraudulent, seemed to have come off worst: the outside track had failed. Yet a decade or so later the balance sheet looked very different, with Labour in power, a Republic proclaimed, the role of the Church decisively weakened, new and far more favourable financial terms obtained for the bases. 'Who won', it turns out, is a question whose answer would depend entirely on which side one took in Malta's intense partisan conflicts. The nature of decolonization ensured that the colonial legacy would remain a live controversy at least as long as any of the participants still breathed. Its divisiveness could not more poignantly be summarized than by posing the question, which is the date of Maltese independence − 21 September or 13 December? It seems still too soon, sadly, for Maltese to recall, as did the great poet of another small island, another ex-British colony:[115]

> That Albion too, was once
> A colony like ours, 'Part of the continent, piece of the main'
> Nook-shotten, rook o'er blown, deranged
> By foaming channels, and the vain expense
> Of bitter faction.

All in compassion ends
So differently from what the heart arranged:
'as well as if a manor of thy friend's ...

NOTES

[1] For instance R. von Albertini, *Decolonization*; and H. Grimal, *Decolonization*.
[2] For a more extended discussion of the historiography of decolonization, S. Howe, *Anti-Colonialism in British Politics*, ch.1.
[3] The most detailed presentation of this interpretation is D.J. Morgan:, *The Official History of Colonial Development*.
[4] Perhaps the most powerfully-argued expression of this view is that of the veteran West Indian Marxist writer C.L.R. James. See his *Nkrumah and the Ghana Revolution*. In the Maltese case, many of the writings of Mr Mintoff adopt a similar perspective.
[5] There is a huge literature expressing arguments of this kind; probably the most influential version has been that of Frantz Fanon, *The Wretched of the Earth*.
[6] As argued for instance by John Gallagher, *The Decline, Revival and Fall of the British Empire*.
[7] B.R. Tomlinson, 'The Contraction of England: National Decline and the Loss of Empire'.
[8] It is beyond the scope of this paper even to begin to summarize the literature on British economic decline; a good introduction is A. Gamble, *Britain in Decline*.
[9] P. Kennedy, *Strategy and Diplomacy 1870-1945*, ch. 8.
[10] R.E. Robinson and J. Gallagher, *Africa and the Victorians: the Official Mind of Imperialism*.
[11] J.A. Hobson, *Imperialism − a study*.
[12] L. Davis and R. Huttenback, *Mammon and the Pursuit of Empire*, 306, 312.
[13] J. Marseille, *Empire colonial et capitalisme français. Histoire d'un divorce*.
[14] Notably by E. Kleiman, 'Trade and the Decline of Colonialism'.
[15] D.K. Fieldhouse, *Unilever Overseas;* J. Milburn, *British Business and Ghanaian Independence*.
[16] Id., *Black Africa 1945-1980: Economic Decolonization and Arrested Development*, 9-11.
[17] Accounts emphasizing these aspects include: M.P. Cowen, 'The British State, State Enterprise and an Indigenous Bourgeoisie in Kenya after 1945'; M.P. Cowen and N.J. Westcott, 'British Imperial Economic Policy During the War'; J. Bowden, *Development and Control in British Colonial Policy;* A.E. Hinds, 'Sterling and British Policy 1945-1951'; S. Strange, *Sterling and British Policy;* D.K. Fieldhouse, 'The Labour Governments and the Empire-Commonwealth 1945-51'.
[18] Some scholars have continued to take a considerably more benign view of these Governments' colonial development strategies than do those cited in n.17; for instance, K. Morgan, *Labour in Power 1945-1951*, and J.M. Lee and M. Petter, *The Colonial Office, War and Development Policy*.
[19] Fieldhouse, 'Labour Governments and the Empire-Commonwealth', 98.
[20] The case for 1945-50 is made in Fieldhouse, ibid., and in R.E. Robinson, 'Andrew Cohen and the Transfer of Power in Tropical Africa'. The war as turning point is supported in R.D. Pearce, *The Turning Point in Africa;* Bowden,

Development and Control; and J.M. Lee and M. Petter, *The Colonial Office.* MacDonald and the 1930s are emphasized in J. Flint, 'Planned Decolonization and its failure in British Africa'.

[21] B.R. Tomlinson, *The Political Economy of the Raj.*

[22] Amidst a huge literature on the end of the Palestine Mandate, much of it intensely polemical, see particularly Wm.R. Louis, *The British Empire in the Middle East,* and M.J. Cohen, *Palestine: Retreat from the Mandate.*

[23] The reading on British withdrawal from India is equally vast. For the final phase, see especially R.J. Moore, *Escape from Empire.*

[24] Morgan, *Official History,* vol. iv: *Changes in British Aid Policy 1951-1970,* esp. ch.6.

[25] Morgan, *Official History, vol. v: Guidance Towards Self-Government in British Colonies,* 102. The reports are not yet available to historians, but their findings are summarized in ibid., 96-102.

[26] Though R.F. Holland argues that considerations of the cost of colonial subsidies did play a major role in accelerating the last stages of decolonization, 'The Imperial Factor in British Strategies'.

[27] It is striking, however, how little Marxist-influenced work there has been in recent years on British decolonization, other than studies looking at particular national independence movements – the research of Michael Cowen is perhaps the most important exception.

[28] Best traced in D. Goldsworthy, *Colonial Issues in British Politics 1945-1961.*

[29] British Labour attitudes to India have been more thoroughly researched than any other imperial aspect of the metropolitan political scene: see P.S. Gupta: *Imperialism and the British Labour Movement 1914-1964;* G.Fischer, *Le party travailliste et la decolonisation de l'Inde;* and M. Ahmed, *The British Labour Party and the Indian Independence Movement.*

[30] As suggested by B. Porter, *The Lion's Share,* 324-6.

[31] This case was first made by Labour colonial specialist John Hatch in 'The Opposition's Part in Colonial Policy', and is broadly supported by Goldsworthy, *Colonial Issues.*

[32] See for instance D. Humphry and J. Ward, *Passports and Politics,* or P. Foot, *Immigration and Race in British Politics.*

[33] Howe, *Anti-Colonialism.*

[34] J.M. MacKenzie, *Propaganda and Empire;* J.M. MacKenzie (ed.), *Imperialism and Popular Culture.*

[35] K. Robinson, *The Dilemmas of Trusteeship;* P. Darby, *Three Faces of Imperialism,* esp. ch.5.

[36] Stressed in R.F. Holland, *European Decolonization 1918-1981,* 208-10.

[37] Wm.R. Louis, *Imperialism at Bay.*

[38] Louis, *British Empire in the Middle East;* A. Bullock, *Ernest Bevin: Foreign Secretary.*

[39] L. Epstein, *British Politics in the Suez Crisis.*

[40] P. Darby, *British Defence Policy East of Suez.*

[41] Emphasized by Porter, *Lion's Share.*

[42] The 'peripheral' theory is put forward in Robinson and Gallagher, *Africa and the Victorians;* Fieldhouse, *Economics and Empire 1830-1914;* and Robinson, 'Non-European foundations of European Imperialism: sketch for a theory of collaboration'.

[43] R.E. Robinson: 'The Excentric Idea of Imperialism, with or without Empire', 271.

[44] Ibid., 272.

[45] This perspective has been most extensively employed in the study of

imperialism and nationalism in India: see A. Seal, *The Emergence of Indian Nationalism;* J. Gallagher, G. Johnson, and A. Seal (eds.), *Locality, Province and Nation.* The most interesting theoretical challenge to it in the Indian context has come from the 'Subaltern Studies' school: R. Guha (ed.), *Subaltern Studies,* i-iv.

[46] B.R. Tomlinson, 'The Contraction of England: National Decline and the Loss of Empire', 60-1. The target of the criticism is J. Darwin, 'Imperialism in Decline? Tendencies in British Imperial Policy between the wars'.

[47] Robinson, 'Excentric Idea', 271.

[48] Davis and Huttenback, *Mammon,* 15-20; T. Balogh, *The Economics of Poverty,* 281.

[49] H. Frendo, *Party Politics in a Fortress Colony: the Maltese Experience,* 6-10.

[50] And as J.M. Lee points out (*Colonial Development and Good Government,* 129) Malta was one of only three colonies — with St Helena and Somaliland — where the *entire funds* for development projects planned for 1955-60 would have to come from CD&W funds, none from local resources or loans.

[51] J White, *The Politics of Foreign Aid,* 88-9.

[52] See E. Dobie, *Malta's Road to Independence,* 143 — citing the Nationalist Party's 1950 election platform.

[53] Balogh, *Economics,* 280-1.

[54] G. Dench, *Maltese in London,* 27-9 and Appendices B and C.

[55] Ibid.; cf. his self-explanatory subtitle.

[56] Dench, 11-14, 107-11; E.L. Zammit, *A Colonial Inheritance,* 31-41. As these and other authors point out, such fatalism might be thought a perfectly rational response to colonial powerlessness.

[57] Dench, 20-1, 52-4.

[58] A. Koster, *Prelates and Politicians in Malta,* 93-112.

[59] Cmd.9657, *Report of the Malta Round Table Conference,* 21.

[60] As expressed in Partit Nazzjonalista, *A Declaration of Policy.*

[61] Dobie, 131.

[62] Ibid., 128-9.

[63] See the official history of the Fabian Society, P. Pugh, *Educate, Agitate, Organize.*

[64] Though as Frendo notes there were important early Italian influences also, and certainly the generally-recognized 'founder' of socialism in Malta, Manwel Dimech, was far more moved by Italian than by British intellectual influences: *Party Politics,* 148-51, 185-8.

[65] See the correspondence between Mintoff, Scerri, and the FCB, FCB papers, Box 174/2.

[66] Labour Party, *Malta to Westminster?,* 6, 8, 14.

[67] J. Ellul Mercer of MLP to Marjorie Nicholson of FCB, 17 September 1954, FCB papers, 174/4/ ff.1-2; Nicholson to Mercer, 1 October 1954, ibid., 174/4/ ff.3-4, and subsequent correspondence in same files.

[68] M. Foot, *Aneurin Bevan 1945-1960,* 506.

[69] Ibid.

[70] Gaitskell to Mintoff, 30 June 1960, copy sent to Tom Driberg by Mintoff, in Driberg papers, Box M8.

[71] Mintoff to Gaitskell, 7 July 1960, and Mintoff to Driberg, n.d. but *c.*7 July 1960, Driberg papers, M8.

[72] Mikardo to Driberg, 11 October 1961, Driberg papers, M8.

[73] Callaghan to Mintoff, 10 August 1961, ibid.

[74] Scerri joined the Mediterranean and Middle East Committee of the MCF in mid-1958. See committee minutes in papers of the Rt.Hon.A.Wedgwood Benn,

in private possession of Mr Benn, London. For the role of the MCF, Howe, *Anti-Colonialism*, chs.6 and 7.

[75] Callaghan to Mintoff, 18 September 1961, Driberg papers, M8.

[76] *House of Commons Debates*, 1 August 1963.

[77] Ibid., 17 March 1964.

[78] Ibid., 23 July 1964. See especially the speeches of Tom Driberg and Michael Foot (who said that the House of Commons has behaved in the most monstrous manner in the way in which independence has been given to Malta).

[79] As argued by D. Sammut, *Too Early for Freedom*, 49-53.

[80] Quoted in Sammut, 52-3.

[81] See Driberg's notes for speeches made in Malta during his 1961 visit, n.d. but *c*. November 1961, Driberg papers, M8.

[82] As several historians have noted, this belief (only half-true in so far as Britain would undoubtedly have occupied the islands whatever the attitude of the Maltese) came to form an important element in Maltese national self-perception under colonial rule.

[83] Quoted in Louis, *Imperialism at Bay*, 276 and 572.

[84] D. Mack Smith: *Mussolini*, 241-2.

[85] Montgomery's view was that if Britain could no longer use Egyptian bases, a minimal requirement for continued British domination in the Mediterranean was a strong presence in Libya and Cyprus as well as in Malta. Lord Montgomery of Alamein, *Memoirs*, 385-7. Mobility, and air, rather than naval, bases, he recognized, were now the key to control.

[86] Louis, *British Empire in the Middle East*, 27-35, 271-8.

[87] Quoted ibid., 30.

[88] This is most fully emphasized in A. Inder Singh, 'Keeping India in the Commonwealth: British Political and Military Aims'.

[89] Louis, *British Empire,* and Bullock, *Bevin, passim.*

[90] Bullock, *Bevin*, 315.

[91] See *Manchester Guardian* and *The Times*, 14 November 1951, and Mintoff's letter in *The Times,* 27 November 1951.

[92] M. Chichester and J. Wilkinson, *The Uncertain Ally: British Defence Policy 1960-1990,* 39.

[93] See for instance J.G. Vassallo to Rita Hinden of the FCB, 2 July and 9 July 1952, seeking confirmation for his (erroneous) suspicions that the Union of Democratic Control, whose literature was being circulated in Malta, was a communist 'front' organization. FCB papers 174/3/ ff.4-6. Examples of the fears – clerical and other – in Malta about 'communist' penetration could be multiplied *ad nauseam.*

[94] Richard Crossman to Hugh Gaitskell, reporting discussions with Mintoff, 2 December 1958, Driberg papers, M8.

[95] Holland, *European Decolonization*, 262.

[96] Darby, *British Defence Policy*, 98-9.

[97] Chichester and Wilkinson, *The Uncertain Ally.*

[98] W.K. Hancock, *Survey of British Commonwealth Affairs*, i, 406. Hancock's work remains the best overview of the British Empire between the wars, and includes some penetrating and even prophetic comment on Maltese affairs.

[99] Morgan, v, 102.

[100] Frendo, *Party Politics*. My indebtedness to – though also my doubts about the conceptual assumptions of – this fine book will be evident in what follows.

[101] The Royal Commissioners of 1812, quoted in Frendo, 4.

[102] J. Morris, *Farewell the Trumpets: an Imperial Retreat,* 152.

[103] Frendo, chs.1 and 2. For the typical pattern of nationalist élite

mobilizations, and the centrality of language, see especially B. Anderson, *Imagined Communities*, the most stimulating recent work on the subject.

[104] Hancock, *Survey*, 427.

[105] Frendo, *passim*. Some suggestive Indian parallels may be found in B. Cohn, 'The Command of Language and the Language of Command'.

[106] J. Boissevain, *Saints and Fireworks: Religion and Politics in Rural Malta;* id., *Friends of Friends.*

[107] Koster, *Prelates and Politicians*, 61.

[108] Schembri Adami, 'Who will support Labour?'.

[109] For an acute portrayal of such a politics of superimposed, cross-cutting controversies inherited from the past — though, in contrast to the Maltese case, expressed through multi-party fragmentation — see P. Williams's work on the French Fourth Republic, *Crisis and Compromise*. A striking example of the deployment of older controversies within new alignments is the scorn heaped by Mintoffians on the alleged inadequacy of Boffa's English-language skills — argued to be a partial cause of his failure to bargain effectively in London. E. Ellul, 'Dr. Boffa Brush Up your English'.

[110] The two — now old — accounts, Dobie's *Malta's Road to Independence* and Dennis Austin's *Malta and the End of Empire,* are flawed respectively by the former's virtually uncritical attitude to the British record and the latter's impressionism. For a recent survey of the postwar years, J.M. Pirotta, *Fortress Colony: The Final Act,* vol. i.

[111] Dobie, 142-4, 160-73; Koster, 151-9.

[112] Holland, *European Decolonization*, 262.

[113] A. Eden, *Memoirs: Full Circle*, 384-5.

[114] Ibid., 389.

[115] D. Walcott, 'Ruins of a Great House'.

16

PETER SERRACINO INGLOTT

Was Malta a 'Nation' in 1964?

'Nation' is notoriously a notion difficult to define.[1]
Nevertheless, in ordinary usage, it can be taken to imply three
basic components:

 a) A group of people are identifiably bound together in a
special kind of socio-cultural network, usually with reference
to a shared territory and language, as well as to economic
interests, religious norms, and moral values, together
constitutive of a common heritage;

 b) The basis of the common heritage is deemed to be a long
shared past, a strongly persistent continuity of the socio-cultural
matrix through time; history is, in other words, its determining
factor.

 c) The common heritage, in turn, is deemed to be a sufficient
basis for building upon it a political structure for the present
and the future; in other words, to constitute a title to autonomous
status as a State, to justify either a present structure of power
or its change, in order to resume a deeper, more atavic, and
hence more legitimate system. Nationhood is thus considered
to be a prior condition of statehood.

This more or less generally accepted account has been radically
contested, notably by Immanuel Wallerstein. He grants that the
past is a basic element in the concept of nationhood, but
questions whether it is the real past that counts most, or rather
the consciousness or picture of it that the group of people in
question have. While the past in itself is irreversible, the picture
of it in people's mind is quite susceptible to change, and indeed,
very often, it is an ideological construct.

Real history — according to Wallerstein — shows that

statehood has usually preceded nationhood. 'Is there a Belgian, a Dutch, a Luxemburg nation today? Most observers seem to think so. If there is, is this not because there came into being *first* a Dutch State, a Belgian State, a Luxemburg State?' Before that there was a single entity: the Burgundian Netherlands. Wallerstein points out that very few indeed of the States that are today members of the United Nations were nations at all, in the sense of identifiable socio-cultural units, a century or two ago. Most of them did not even possess a name or exist as administrative units. Only a dozen or so can claim to a continuity of existence both in name and as administrative units that goes back to 1450. Wallerstein indeed claims that all contemporary nations owe their present status to the new political structuring of the world-system that occurred around that date.

He admits that once this system was created, then movements claiming sovereignty for some segments of some States on the basis of nationalism did succeed in their aims. But he holds that, in most cases, (i) these entities already existed as administrative units (hence, in a sense, already as States) and (ii) they were only consolidated as 'nations' after they had become States. A 'State', in the modern sense of the word, finds it necessary to become a nation (i.e. foster at least a semblance of cultural and social unity) for two reasons. The first is the obvious one: the emotive strengthening of its inner cohesion. The second is the promotion of its rank within the hierarchy of States to which it belongs within the world-system by appeal to the merits of its 'national' past.

I think that Wallerstein's observations should be given the greatest weight in the consideration of what one's attitude to nationalism should be; it should be recognized as inevitable in the present world-system, but only within it, and it is not sacrosanct.

My own view on the matter, with reference to the question which I have been asked to discuss in this brief essay, is that the question of whether nationhood is prior to statehood, or vice versa, is a chicken-and-egg question. The essential defect in the current theory is that it assumes that there can exist a fully-fledged socio-cultural autonomy (nationhood) in the absence of (possibly as an aspiration towards) political autonomy (statehood). This is the view which I think it is necessary to deny, and replace with another view, before the question put to me can be sensibly answered.

The assertion of nationhood has always first been made in negative terms. A Corsican says: 'No, I am not a Frenchman;' a Maltese says: 'No, I am not British, I am not Italian, I am not an Arab.' But as long as this basic declaration lacks an effective political buttressing in the absence of some such framework as that of a constituted statehood, it is merely ideological discourse. It amounts to saying: 'We Maltese have different customs, a different past, other ways of relating to each other and to others, etc., than the British, the Italians, the Arabs.' But these cultural features are only the tips above the visibility line of a social iceberg, which cannot sustain its own consistency.

The assertion of cultural autonomy in a context of political heteronomy is merely the acceptance of a disintegrated social structure in which culture is conceived as spectacle and folkloristic elements are exploited in a quasi-farcical way. The cultural identity of a politically subordinate group tends inevitably to be defined solely by contrast to that of the politically dominant group, i.e. negatively. Local history can only be narrated in the invented idiom of the central power. Otherwise, the greater the economic dependence and the political centralization, the more the apparent manifestations of cultural autonomy must be regarded as largely phenomena of psychological compensation for political and economic frustrations, rather than as authentic expressions of a corporate self. Only access to political power can allow a group to speak its own language and define itself in its own chosen terms.

Consequently, any claim to the fullness of nationhood before a certain degree of political autonomy has been reached is bound to be largely delusive. However, the manifestations of a socio-cultural identity that are usually taken as the expression of nationhood are not insignificant. While they can only function effectively even as symbols if they are loaded with at least some political force, they are usually indices of some past experience of political autonomy, surviving relics of some lost measure of statehood, and, because of that, not wholly devoid of meaningfulness and political propulsiveness. Nevertheless, the danger is great of taking them not as memory stimulants and provocations to political action but as actual proof of the full existence of nationhood. National existence would then be identified with a nostalgia for the past, with being a peripheral museum, the repository of a disappearing folklore. But a true socio-cultural identity is rarely developed by self-enclosure and rejoicing in a group's ability to provide some marginal manifestation of exotic customs.

There is a second, more valuable aspect in the display of the traces of past statehood, apart from stirring political feelings of protest against present subservience. It renders testimony of the emargination of nation-states themselves in the present global setting, a testimony similar to that provided by groups of feminists or of the handicapped or of minorities within the nation-state itself. It speaks against the real subordination of nation-states themselves to the ever more homogenizing and overpowering world-system and its trans-State institutions. In fact, probably nothing has proved to be stronger in re-inforcing 'national' sentiment in colonized or quasi-colonized areas than the experience of emigration or exile or other exposure to the world-system where its workings are less concealed by intermediary powers than it is in a colony or an ethnic region by the colonizing or State power.

The thrust of my argument so far is that the accepted notion of a nation has gained currency as the correlative and parasite of the notion of the State as a really autonomous institution in the world, when in fact this notion of the State in the actual world-system is largely a legal fiction. Consequently, the question which I was asked to attempt to answer is only worth the attempt if it is interpreted to mean *not* 'was Malta in 1964 the name of a community with an established socio-cultural identity such that it could support political autonomy in a world-system of independent States', because this interpretation implies a usually unstated false premise, but rather: 'Did the people of Malta in 1964 intend to assume the corporate responsibility of deciding for themselves, within realistic limits, the role they wished to play in the world?'

Nationhood is not constituted, in my view, by the existence of a collection of cultural traits, relics, and themes, but rather by the existence of a corporate subject ready to accept the challenges of making history, rather than merely recalling it or posing as a worthy object for ethnographic study. Indeed, I do not think that a socio-cultural unit can be said to exist except inasmuch as it actually assumes upon itself the risks of existing corporately, of speaking for itself as a group, of speaking the common language analysed by the outside observer.

There are three remarks concerning the Maltese situation in 1964 which seem to me to be particularly relevant to answering the question as I have interpreted it – that is, as the question whether (in the light of subsequent rather than preceding events) in practice rather than by proclamation, the people of Malta in 1964 could be said to have intended to pick up a definite role in the world-system. These remarks suggest that the answer should be a clear 'yes'.

The first remark may sound paradoxical. It is that the basic structure of the 'development plans' launched by successive Maltese Governments after 1964 was radically altered by the popular response. The 'development plans', over the formulation of which foreign experts had exerted a notable influence, reflected the sequential scenarios which economists at the time upheld as projectable within the framework of the established order. The prospect was accordingly unfolded of an economy built on the classical tripod: agriculture, manufacturing industry, services – set out in that order. In fact, agriculture continued to decline; manufacturing never developed with the stability the planners hoped; but the tertiary sector continued to maintain the disproportionate size (in the eyes of those familiar with the patterns laid out by development theorists) it had for a long time possessed. I do not presume to say how much this was forced upon, or chosen by, the Maltese people; but there can be no doubt that it corresponds to a historically long-established socio-cultural tradition. In practically all their cultural expressions, the Maltese people have shown the same sort of originality as the Phoenicians of old (or that which Wittgenstein claimed for himself and the Jewish tradition in general), namely in composition or rearrangement, rather than in conception *ab ovo*. Thus, there is for instance a distinctive Maltese baroque Church architecture, but its distinctive originality consists in its brilliant fusion of baroque ornamentation with a classically static spatial organization; the Maltese language is itself extremely distinctive, and rich in potential poetic effects,

because of its fusion of a basically Semitic vocabulary and
morphology with a basically Romance syntax and overlay; the
Maltese village landscape is equally distinctive because of its
combination of the low, cubic North African type of houses with
the dome-dominated baroque church; and so on.

The Maltese have shown a preference for, and excellence in,
work as catalysts, brokers, middlemen, entrepôt traders,
interpreters, translators, even as what one might call cultural
transvestites (thinking, for example, of the Abate Vella's famous
forgery, or Pynchon's description of Paola, in his great
Melitensian novel, V). The two major economic successes of the
post-independence period were achieved, not surprisingly, with
Central Bank funds and in the tourist trade.

The second remark is that, after 1964, there seems to have
occurred a sharp polarization of the Maltese people into two
groups and, it is very tempting to say, almost into two 'nations'.
Superficially, it might seem as if two socio-cultural networks
have come into being, with different economic, religious, and
moral values.

I think that there was real danger of this happening for a
number of years, but the very fact that the danger was averted,
in the sense that nothing like a civil war broke out, is a strong
piece of evidence in support of the judgement that the people
of Malta firmly assumed the mantle of nationhood in 1964.

In fact, despite the exacerbated differences between the major
political parties, there is more reason to be surprised perhaps
at the extent of the declared agreement between them, for
instance, on neutrality in foreign affairs, on social policy and
economic democracy in local matters. In fact, the sharp conflicts
between them are rarely referable to principles, but rather to
their application. Even the undoubted opposition between the
two political sides vis-à-vis the Church has never been extended
to any explicit rejection of Christian inspiration by anyone.

A third remark is due on the subject of language. I think it
would be a blatant mistake to identify the existence of a nation
with that of a language of its own. Obviously, it would be absurd
to maintain any such thesis in general, as it would imply that
such countries as Cuba are not nations. I consider that it is a
positive sign on the way of the fulfilment of nation-statehood
that a language is not shabbily or poorly used, that like all tools

in the hands of true craftsmen it is kept clean and polished, because language is the primary means of expression of man and of culture. Clearly, sharing a language which is proper to a people is a major element in the constitution of a socio-cultural unit, and it is likely to loom particularly large in the negative phase of nationalist development to which I have alluded. But sharing, in addition to it, one or more international languages may be even more expressive of the identity of a nation which has consciously determined that the role it intends to play in the world-system is that of a bridge-builder and communication facilitator. I consider it to be a sign of attained nationhood not when a people has a language of its own, but when it has decided to define by itself the cultural conditions which will allow it to be what it wants. Exclusive emphasis on a people's own language might even hamper or hamstring the chosen course of development, the fulfilment of the desired role of the nation in the world, its scientific, technical, and cultural progress. Language is a means, not an end. It may well be that the expression of national identity is much more definitely shown in the conscious adoption of, say, bilinguism or trilinguism by all the citizens of a State such as Malta, rather than by any exclusive emphasis on the Maltese language.

NOTES

[1] See, for instance, F. Chabod, *L'idea di nazione;* H. Kohn, *L'idea di nazionalismo nel suo sviluppo storico.*

Civil Commissioners and Governors of Malta
1799 - 1964

Capt. Alexander Ball	1799-1801
Maj. Gen. H. Pigot	1801

CIVIL COMMISSIONERS

Sir Charles Cameron	1801-1802
Rear-Adm. Sir Alexander Ball	1802-1810
Lt.-Gen. Sir Hilderbrand Oakes	1810-1813

GOVERNORS

Lt.-Gen. Sir Thomas Maitland	1813-1824
Gen. the Marquess of Hastings	1824-1826
Maj.-Gen. Sir Frederick Cavendish Ponsonby	1827-1836
Lt.-Gen. Sir Henry F. Bouverie	1836-1843
Lt.-Gen. Sir Patrick Stuart	1843-1847
The Rt. Hon. Richard More O'Ferrall	1847-1851
Maj.-Gen. Sir William Reid	1851-1858
Lt.-Gen. Sir John Gaspard Le Marchant	1858-1864
Lt.-Gen. Sir Henry Storkes	1864-1867
Gen. Sir Patrick Grant	1867-1872
Gen. Sir Charles T. van Straubenzee	1872-1878
Gen. Sir Arthur Borton	1878-1884
Gen. Sir John Lintorn Simmons	1884-1888
Lt.-Gen. Sir Henry D. Torrens	1888-1890
Lt.-Gen. Sir Henry A. Smyth	1890-1893
Gen. Sir Arthur J.L. Fremantle	1893-1899
Lt.-Gen. Lord Grenfell	1899-1903
Gen. Sir Charles Mansfield Clarke	1903-1907
Lt.-Gen. Sir Henry F. Grant	1907-1909

Gen. Sir H.M. Leslie Rundle	1909-1915
FM Lord Mathuen	1915-1919
FM Viscount Plumer	1919-1924
Gen. Sir Walter N. Congreve	1924-1927
Gen. Sir John P. du Cane	1927-1931
Gen. Sir David G.M. Campbell	1931-1936
Gen. Sir Charles Bonham-Carter	1936-1940
Lt.-Gen. Sir William G.S. Dobbie	1940-1942
FM Viscount Gort	1942-1944
Lt.-Gen. Sir Edmond C.A. Schreiber	1944-1946
Sir F. Douglas	1946-1949
Sir Gerald H. Creasy	1949-1954
Maj.-Gen. Sir Robert Laycock	1954-1959
Adm. Sir Guy Grantham	1959-1963
Sir Maurice Dorman*	1963-1964

---

*and Gov.-Gen. of Independent Malta 1964-1971

APPENDIX II

Prime Ministers of Malta
1921 - 1964

Joseph Howard	October 1921 - October 1923
Dr Francesco Buhagiar	October 1923 - September 1924
Dr Ugo P. Mifsud	September 1924 - August 1927
Sir Gerald Strickland	August 1927 - June 1932
Sir Ugo P. Mifsud	June 1932 – November 1933
Dr Paul Boffa	November 1947 - September 1950
Dr Enrico Mizzi	September – December 1950
Dr George Borg Olivier	December 1950 - February 1955
Dom Mintoff	March 1955 - April 1958
Dr George Borg Olivier	March 1962 -

Bibliography

M and L in the bibliographical references below
stand for Malta and London respectively

ABELA, Gian. Francesco
Della descrittione di Malta isola nel mare siciliano. M 1647.
ABERCROMBI/,E.N., HILL, S.
'Paternalism and Patronage', *British Journal of Sociology,* xxvii (1976).
ABULAFIA, David
'Henry Count of Malta and his Mediterranean Activities: 1203-1230', in
*Medieval Malta: Studies of Malta before the
Knights,* ed. A.T. Luttrell. L 1975.
AHMED, Mesbahudin
The British Labour Party and the Indian Independence Movement 1917-1939.
L 1937.
AHN, Franz
*Handbuch de englischen Umgangs-sprache, mit deutscher und franzosischer
Vebersetzung.* Mainz 1848.
ALBERTINI, Rudolph von
Decolonization. New York 1971.
ANDERSON, Benedict
Imagined Communities. L 1983.
ANGAS, G.F.
A Ramble in Malta and Sicily. L 1842.
Anon.
Qari għall-Maltin, maħruġ mix-Xirka Xemia. M 1885.
Anon.
'Why Malta chose Britain', *The Times of Malta,* 25, 26 June 1975.
Appeals of the Nobility and People of Malta. L 1811.
AQUILINA, Joseph
Papers in Maltese Linguistics. M 1961.
ATTARD, L.E.
Early Maltese Migration 1900-1914. M 1983.
AUSTIN, Dennis
Malta and the End of Empire. L 1971.
AZZOPARDI, Francis
'The Appointment of Bishop A.M. Buhagiar as Administrator Apostolic of

Malta', in *Proceedings of History Week 1981,* ed. Mario Buhagiar. M 1982.
BADGER, G.F.
Description of Malta and Gozo. M 1838.
BALBI DI CORREGGIO, F.
Diario dell'Assedio di Malta. Rome 1565.
BALOGH, Thomas
The Economics of Poverty. L 1966.
BARTOLO, A.
'History of the Maltese Islands', in *Malta and Gibraltar,* ed. A. Macmillan.
   L 1915.
BARTOLO, Paul
X'Kien Ġara Sew fis-Sette Giugno. M 1979.
BASTID, P.
Sieyès et sa pensée. Paris 1939.
BAX, Mart
'Religious Regimes and State Formation: Towards a Research Perspective',
   Anthropological Quarterly, lx, 1 (1987).
'Wie tegen de kerk piest wordt zelf nat', over uitbreiding en intensivering van
   het clericale regime in Noord-Brabant, Antropo logische Verkenningen, i,
   2 (1982).
BERGER, E. (ed.)
Registres d'Innocent IV. Bibliotheque des Écoles Françaises d'Athenes de
   Rome. 1896-97.
BEZZINA, J.
Servizzi Publiċi f'Malta. M 1962.
BEZZINA, Joseph
'Asylum in Malta: A British offer to Pope Pius IX', *Melita Theologica,*
   xxxviii, 1 (1987).
'British Diplomacy and the election of Bishop Gaetano Pace Forno', in
   Proceedings of History Week 1982, ed. Mario Buhagiar. M 1983.
Religion and Politics in a Crown Colony: The Gozo-Malta Story 1798-1864.
   M 1985.
BLACK, A.
'Tourism and Migration: causes and effects in social change'. Paper read at
   the Conference on the 'Design and Analysis of Current Social Science
   Research in the Central Mediterranean': University of Malta, 1978.
BLOUET, Brian
The Story of Malta. 2nd ed. L 1972
BOISGELIN, Louis de
Ancient and Modern Malta. 2 vols. L 1804.
BOISSEVAIN, Jeremy
Friends of Friends. Oxford 1974.
Hal Farruġ: A Village in Malta. New York 1969; 2nd ed. New York 1980.
'Ritual Escalation in Malta', in *Religion, Power and Protest in Local
   Communities,* ed. E.R. Wolf. New York / Paris 1984.
Saints and Fireworks: Religion and Politics in Rural Malta. L 1965.
'Social Trends in Malta 1960-74', *Cobweb: Economic Journal* (Winter 1975).
'When the Saints go marching out: Reflections on the decline of Patronage',
   in *Patrons and Clients,* ed. E. Gellner and J. Waterbury. L 1977.
BONDIN, Ray
*Deportation, 1942: The Internment and Deportation of Maltese
   Nationalists.* M 1980.
BONELLO, Vincenzo

La Madonna nell'Arte. M 1949.
BONELLO, Vincenzo, FIORENTINI, Bianca, SCHIAVONE, Lorenzo
  Echi del Risorgimento a Malta. M 1963.
BONNICI, Alexander
  Maltin u l-Inkwiżizzjoni f'Nofs is-Seklu Sbatax. M 1977
BONNICI, Arthur
  'Abolition of personal and local immunities', *Rostrum,* iii (1957).
  History of the Church in Malta. Vol. iii. M 1975.
  'The Oath Question', *Melita Historica,* iv, 1 (1964).
  'Thirty Years to build a Protestant Church', *Melita Historica,* vi, 2 (1973).
BONNICI, J., CASSAR M.,
  Il-Vapur ta' l-Art − The Malta Railway. M 1987.
BORG, Karl
  'Neo-Classical Architecture in Malta in the Ninettenth Century'. Unpublished
  B.E.& A. dissertation, University of Malta. 1982
BORG, P.P.
  La questione matrimoniale in Malta. Naples 1900.
BORG, Vincent
  *Fabio Chigi, Apostolic Delegate in Malta (1634-1639): An edition of his official
  correspondence.* Vatican City 1967.
  Il-Knisja Parrokkjali ta' Ħal Lija. M 1982.
BOSIO, Iacomo
  Dell'Istoria della Sacra Religione et Ill.ma Militia di S. Gio. Gierosolimitano.
  Part iii. Rome 1602.
BOSWELL, David
  'Patron-Client relations in the Mediterranean with special reference to the
  changing political situation in Malta'. Paper read at the Conference on the
  'Design and Analysis of current Social Science Research in the Central
  Mediterranean': University of Malta, 1978.
BOWDEN, Jane
  'Development and Control in British Colonial Policy, 1935-1948'.
  Unpublished Ph.D. thesis, University of Birmingham, 1980.
BOWEN, E.G.
  Wales. L 1965.
BOWEN-JONES, H., DEWDNEY, J.C., FISHER, W.B.
  Malta: Background for Development. Durham 1961.
BRAUDEL, Fernand
  The Mediterranean and the Mediterranean World in the Age of Philip II. Trans.
  S. Reynolds. Vol. i. Glasgow 1972.
BRESC, H.
  'Documents on Frederick IV of Sicily's Intervention in Malta: 1372', *Papers of
  the British School at Rome,* xli (1973).
  'Mudejars des pays de la Couronne d'Aragon et Sarasins de la Sicile
  normande: le probleme de l'acculturation', in *Congresso de Historia de la
  Corona de Aragon.* Saragossa 1979.
  'Società e politica in Sicilia nei secoli XIV e XV', *Archivio Storico per la Sicilia
  Orientale,* lxx (1974).
  Un monde Méditerranéen: economie et societé en Sicile, 1300-1450. 2 vols.
  Palermo / Rome 1986.
BRINCAT, Joseph M.
  'Le Poesie "Maltesi" di Peire Vidal (1204-1205)', *Melita Historica,* vii, 1 (1976).
BROCKMAN, Eric
  Last Bastion. Sketches of the Maltese Islands. M 1975.

BUHAGIAR, Konrad
'Romanticism in the 19th century: A History of Neo-Gothic in Malta'.
Unpublished B.E.& A. dissertation, University of Malta, 1982.
BUHAGIAR, Mario
'Xogħlijiet ta' Arti w Artiġjanat fil-Knisja ta' San Ġorġ', in *Il-Knisja Parrokkjali ta' San Ġorġ, Ħal Qormi: Erba' Sekli ta' Storja,* ed. Joseph F. Grima. M 1984
BULLOCK, Alan
Ernest Bevin: Foreign Secretary. L 1983.
BUSUTTIL, Salvino
Malta's Economy in the Nineteenth Century. M 1973.
CACIAGLI, M., BELLONI, F.
A Contribution to the Study of Clientelism: The New Clientelism of Southern Italy. M 1978.
CAHEN, C.
'Dhimma', in *The Encyclopaedia of Islam.* Vol. ii. Leiden / London 1965.
CALLEJA, Giuseppe
'Rocco Buhagiar Pittore', *L'Arte,* iii, 64 (July 1865).
CALLEJA, Reno
'Maltese Gemgem', *Il-Ħajja,* 9 February 1973.
CALLUS, Philip
The Rising of the Priests: Its Implications and Repercussions on Ecclesiastical Immunity. M 1961.
CARDINALE, H.E.
The Holy See and the International Order. Bucks 1976.
CASSAR, Paul
'A medico-legal Report of the Sixteenth Century from Malta', *Medical History,* xviii (1974).
The Quest for Mikiel Anton Vassalli. 1981.
CASSAR PULLICINO, J.
'M.A. Vassalli in 1798-99', *The Sunday Times,* [M] 21, 28 February 1982.
Studies in Maltese Folklore. M 1976.
CASSOLA, Arnold
'On the Meaning of *Gueri* in Petrus Caxaro's *Cantilena'*, *Melita Historica,* iii, 4 (1983).
CASTAGNA, P.P.
Lis Storja ta' Malta. Bil Gżejjer Taħha. Facsimile Edition. M 1985.
CATANZARO, R., REYNERI, E.
'Job Holding and Class Structure in a Southern Italian Town' Paper presented at the conference on the 'Design and Analysis of Current Social Science Research in the Central Mediterranean': University of Malta, 1978.
CAVALIERO, Roderick
The Last of the Crusaders. L 1960.
Census of Malta, Gozo and Comino [1872]. M 1872.
CHABOD, F.
L'idea di nazione. Bari 1970.
CHICHESTER, Michael, WILKINSON, John
The Uncertain Ally: British Defence Policy 1960-1990. L 1982.
COHEN, M.J.
Palestine: Retreat from the Mandate. New York 1978.
COLVILLE, J.R.
Man of Valour. The life of Field-Marshal the Viscount Gort. L 1972.
COOKE, John H.
Sketches written in and about Malta. M n.d.

COSENTINO, G.
Codice diplomatico di Federico III Aragonese, Re di Sicilia (1355-1377). Palermo 1885.
COWEN, M.P.
'The British State, State Enterprise and an Indigenous Bourgeoisie in Kenya after 1945'. Unpublished paper.
COWEN, M.P., WESTCOTT, N.J.
'British Imperial Economic Policy during the War'. Unpublished paper.
CREMONA, A.
Vassalli and his Times. Trans. M. Butcher. M 1940.
CREMONA, J.J.
An Outline of the Constitutional Development of Malta. M 1963.
CRITIEN, A.
The Manderaggio. Notes, Historical and Other. M 1938.
CUTAJAR, Dominic
'Alberto Pullicino', *Property*, ii (March 1986).
'The Fascinating Personality of Giorgio Grognet', *The Times*, [M] 25, 26 April 1980.
'The Lure of the Orient: The Schranzes, the Brockdorffs, Preziosi and other Artists', *Hyphen*, v, 3 (1987).
'Vincenzo D'Esposito: The Sensibility of a Late Romantic in a Maltese Setting', *The Sunday Times*, [M] 1 December 1985.
D'AUTUN, Quintin J.
Insulae Melitae Descriptio. Lyons 1536.
DARBY, Philip
British Defence Policy East of Suez 1947-1968. L 1973.
Three Faces of Imperialism. New Haven 1987.
DARMANIN, A.
'Grumbling', *Problemi ta' Llum* (March 1978).
DARWIN, John
'Imperialism in Decline? Tendencies in British Imperial Policy between the Wars', *Historical Journal*, 23 (1980).
DAVIES, J.
People of the Mediterranean: An Essay in Comparative Social Anthropology. L 1974.
DAVIS, L.E.
Defence Outline of Future Policy. HMSO, Cmnd 124, 1957.
DAVIS, Lance, HUTTENBACK, Robert
Mammon and the Pursuit of Empire. Cambridge 1986.
DAVY, J.
Notes and Observations on the Ionian Islands and Malta. Vol. i. L 1842.
DEBONO, Paolo P.
Sommario della storia della legislazione in Malta. M 1897.
DE LUCCA, Denis
'The contribution of François de Mondion in the Architectural Development of Eighteenth-Century Malta', in *Proceedings of History Week 1981*, ed. Mario Buhagiar. M 1982.
'French Military Engineers in Malta during the seventeenth and eighteenth centuries', *Melita Historica*, viii, 1 (1980), 23-33.
DENARO, Victor
The French in Malta. M 1963.
DENCH, Geoff
Maltese in London: a case-study in the erosion of ethnic consciousness. L 1975.

382   BIBLIOGRAPHY

DENNIS, Nigel
  An Essay on Malta. L 1972.
  Development Plan for Malta, 1973. M 1974.
  'Dichiarazione dei Diritti degli Abitanti delle Isole di Malta e Gozo [15 June
    1802]', in *Human Rights Documentation in Malta,* ed. J.J. Cremona. M
    1966.
DIMECH DEBONO, Ġużè
  Il-Malti. M 1951.
DOBIE, Edith,
  Malta's Road to Independence. Oklahoma 1967.
DRIAULT, J.E.
  Napoleon en Italie. Paris 1906.
DUDLEY BUXTON, L.H.
  'Malta: An Anthropological Study', *The Geographical Review,* xiv, 1 (1924).
EDEN, Anthony
  Memoirs: Full Circle. L 1960.
ELLUL, Grazio V.
  'The French Invasion of Malta: An Unpublished Account', *Hyphen,* [i], 3
    (Spring 1978).
ELLUL, Edward
  'Dr. Boffa brush up your English', *Labour Views* (December 1949).
ELLUL, Michael
  'Art and Architecture in Malta in the Early Nineteenth Century', in
    Proceedings of History Week 1982, ed. Mario Buhagiar. M 1983.
  'Early Nineteenth-Century Architecture', in *Architecture in Malta,* ed. P.
    Calleja. M 1986.
ENGEL, C.E.
  L'Ordre de Malte en Méditerranée. Monaco 1957.
EPSTEIN, Leon
  British Policy in the Suez Crisis. Urbana 1984.
Esposizione documentata della questione Maltese. Vatican City 1930.
[ETON, William]
  Mr. W. Eton's Vindication of his Public Conduct in Malta. L 1809.
EVANS, E.W.
  The British Yoke: Reflections on the Colonial Empire. L 1949.
Exposition of the Malta Question with documents (February 1929 – June 1930).
  Vatican City 1930.
FANON, Frantz
  The Wretched of the Earth. Harmondsworth 1967.
FAVA, Peter
  'A Reign of Austerity: Economic Difficulties during the rule of Grand Master
    Ximenes', *Storja 78,* [i, 1 (1978)].
FENECH, Dominic
  'A Social and Economic review of Malta during the First World War 1914-1918'.
    Unpublished B.A. (Hons.) dissertation, University of Malta, 1973.
  The Making of Archbishop Gonzi. M 1976.
FERRIS, Achille
  Descrizione storica delle chiese di Malta e Gozo. M 1866.
FIELDHOUSE, D.K.
  Black Africa 1945-1980: Economic Decolonization and Arrested Development.
    L 1986.
  Economics and Empire 1830-1914. L 1973.
  The Colonial Empires: A Comparative Survey from the Eighteenth Century.

2nd ed. L 1982.
'The Labour Government and the Empire-Commonwealth 1945-51', in *The Foreign Policy of the British Labour Governments 1945-51*, ed. R. Ovendale. Leicester 1984.
Unilever Overseas. L 1976.
FIORENTINI, Bianca
Malta, rifugio di esuli e focolare ardente di cospirazione durante il Risorgimento Italiano. M 1966.
FISCHER, Georges
Le party travailliste et la decolonisation de l'Inde. Paris 1966.
FLINT, John
'Planned Decolonization and its Failure in British Africa', *African Affairs*, 82 (1983).
FOOT, Michael
Aneurin Bevan 1945-1960. L 1975.
FOOT, Paul
Immigration and Race in British Politics. Harmondsworth 1965.
FRENDO, Henry
Birth Pangs of a Nation: Manwel Dimech's Malta, 1860-1921. M 1972.
'Borg Olivier's Legacy', in *The Popular Movement for a New Beginning*. M 1981.
'Cultural Interaction and National Identity: The Maltese Case', *The Democrat*, 13 December 1986 − January 1987.
'Dimechianism'. Unpublished B.A. (Hons.) dissertation, University of Malta, 1970.
En route from Europe to Africa: Malta, her People and her History. M 1978.
'Freedom after Independence: A Western European or a Third World Model for the Maltese Islands?' Forthcoming.
'Il-Ktajjen tal-Kolonjaliżmu', *Il-Mument*, 18 September 1977.
Ir-Rieda għall-Ħelsien: Storja Kritika tal-Partit Nazzjonalista matul il-Kolonjaliżmu Ingliż. M 1980.
Ir-Rivoluzzjoni Maltija tal-1919. M 1970.
'Language and Nationality in an Island Colony: Malta', *Canadian Review of Studies in Nationalism*, iii, 1 (Autumn 1975).
'Language of a Colony: A Study of the Maltese Language Question'. Unpublished M.A. thesis, University of Malta, 1973.
'Lejn Storjografija Post-Kolonjali', *Illum*, November 1976, January-June 1977, August-October 1977, December 1977-January 1978.
Lejn Tnissil ta' Nazzjon: it-Twemmin Soċjo-Politiku ta' Manwel Dimech. M 1971.
'Maltese Settlement in English-Speaking Countries: The Australian Case', *The Democrat*, 27 December 1986.
'Messages from Mintoff's Malta: The Grenada of the Mediterranean', *Quadrant* [Sydney], xxx, 12 (December 1986).
Party Politics in a Fortress Colony: The Maltese Experience. M 1979.
'Religion and Ethnic Identity in the Maltese-Australian Community', in *The Ethnic Churches in Australia*, ed. Abe Ata. Forthcoming.
'Self Identity in the "British" Mediterranean: Gibraltar, Malta, Cyprus', in *World Island Nationalisms*, ed. G.W. Trompf. Forthcoming.
Story of a Book. M 1972.
FRIGGIERI, Oliver
'Il-Kwistjoni tal-Lingwa: Għarfien ta' Identità Nazzjonali', *Azad Perspektiv*, iv

(1981).
Storia della letteratura maltese. Milazzo 1986.
GALEA, J.
'Matthew Callus: a Myth?', *Scientia,* xi, 2 (1945).
GALLAGHER, J., JOHNSON, G., SEAL, A. (eds.)
Locality, Province and Nation. Cambridge 1973.
GALLICK, C.J.M.R.
'Issues in the Relationship between Minority and National Language: Maltese
reaction to non-Maltese speakers of Maltese'. Paper delivered at the meeting
of the Society for Applied Anthropology, held in London, 1975.
GAMBLE, Andrew
Britain in Decline. L 1981.
GANADO, Albert
'Girolamo Ganni 1837-1895: Two decades of Landscape-Painting in Malta', *The
Sunday Times,* [M] 5 January 1985.
'Pietro Paolo Caruana: The first Lithographs produced in Malta', in *Proceedings
of History Week 1981,* ed. Mario Buhagiar. M 1982.
GANADO, Herbert
Jien Inħobb Nitkellem Magħkom. M 1984.
Rajt Malta Tinbidel. Vols.i-iv. M 1974-77.
GAVIN, R.J.
Aden under British Rule 1839-1967. L 1975.
*Gian Francesco Abela: Essays in his Honour by Members of the Malta Historical
Society.* M 1961.
GODECHOT, Jacques
'La France et Malte au XVIIIᵉ Siècle', *Revue Historique,* ccvi (July-September
1951).
GOLDSWORTHY, David
Colonial Issues in British Politics 1945-1961. L 1971.
GOUDAR, Ange
*Reflexions sur la dernière émeute de Malthe, suivie des Remarques politiques
sur celles qui ont troublé les différents états de l'Europe à la fin de ce siècle.*
[Florence] 1776.
GRECH, Rose M.
'The Development of Land Transport in the Maltese Islands'. Unpublished B.A.
(Hons.) dissertation, University of Malta, 1976.
GRIMA, George
'The Constitution and Religion in Malta between 1921 and 1974', *Melita
Theologica,* xxxvi (1985).
GRIMA, Rita
'Malta and the Crimean War (1854-1856)'. Unpublished B.A. (Hons.)
dissertation, University of Malta, 1979.
GRIMAL, Henri
Decolonization. L 1979.
GUHA, Ranajit (ed.)
Subaltern Studies. Delhi 1982-5.
GUPTA, P.S.
Imperialism and the British Labour Movement 1914-1964. L 1975.
HANCOCK, W.K.
Survey of British Commonwealth Affairs, vol. i: *Problems of Nationality 1918-
1936.* L 1937.
HARDING, Hugh W.
Maltese Legal History under British Rule 1801-1836. M 1968.

HARDMAN, William
A History of Malta during the period of the French and British occupations 1789-1815. L 1909
HARLOW, Vincent
'The New Imperial System 1783-1815', in *The Cambridge History of the British Empire*, ed. J. Holland Rose, et al. Vol. ii. Cambridge 1940.
HARRISON, A., HUBBARD, R.P.
Valletta and the Three Cities. M 1945.
HATCH, John
'The Opposition's Part in Colonial Policy', *The Listener*, 25 April 1963.
HINDS, A.E.
'Sterling and British Policy 1945-1951', *Journal of Imperial and Commonwealth History*, xi, 2 (1987).
HOBSON, J.A.
Imperialism – A Study. L 1902.
HOLLAND, R.F.
European Decolonization 1918-1981. L 1985.
'The Imperial Factor in British Strategies from Atlee to Macmillan, 1945-63', *Journal of Imperial and Commonwealth History*, xii, 2 (1984).
HOPPEN, Alison
The Fortification of Malta by the Order of St John 1530-1798. Edinburgh 1979.
HOURANI, A.H.
Syria and Lebanon: A Political Essay. L 1946.
HOUSE, H. (ed.)
The Journals and Papers of Gerald Manley Hopkins. Oxford 1959.
HOWE, Stephen
Anti-Colonialism in British Politics. Oxford 1987.
HUGHES, Quentin
The Building of Malta during the period of the Knights of St John of Jerusalem 1530-1795. L 1956. 2nd ed. 1967.
HUMPHRY, Derek, WARD, John
Passports and Politics. Harmondsworth 1974.
HUREWITZ, J.C.
Diplomacy in the Near and Middle East. Princeton 1956.
JAARSVELD, F.A. van
The Awakening of Africaner Nationalism 1868-1881. Cape Town 1961.
JAMES, C.L.R.
Nkrumah and the Ghana Revolution. L 1977.
KENN, M.
A Spanish Tapestry. L 1961.
KENNEDY, Paul
Strategy and Diplomacy 1870-1945. L 1933.
KININMONTH, C.
The Brass Dolphins. L 1957.
KLEIMAN, Ephraim
'Trade and the Decline of Colonialism', *The Economic Journal*, 86 (1976).
KOHN, Hans
L'idea di nazionalismo nel suo sviluppo storico. Florence 1956.
Nationalism: Its Meaning and History. Princeton 1955.
The Idea of Nationalism. New York 1945.
KOHT, Halvdan

KOHT, Halvdan
'The Dawn of Nationalism in Europe', *American Historical Review*, lii
(1946-47).
KOSTER, Adrianus
*Prelates and Politicians in Malta: Changing Power-Balances between Church
and State in a Mediterranean Island Fortress (1800-1976)*. Assen 1984.
'The Kapillani: The Changing Position of the Parish Priest in Malta', in
*Religion, Power and Protest in Local Communities: The Northern Shore of
the Mediterranean*, ed. Eric R. Wolf. Berlin 1984.
'The Knights' State (1530-1798): A Regular regime', *Melita Historica*, viii, 4
(1983).
LA LUMIA, I.
'I quattro vicari', in *Storie siciliane*. Vol. ii. Palermo 1969.
LABOUR PARTY
Malta to Westminster? L 1956.
LACROIX, Frederick M.
'Malte et le Gozo', in *L'Univers, ou Histoire et Description de tous les Peuples*,
ed. M. D'Avezac. Paris 1848.
LAFERLA, A.V.
British Malta. Vol. i. M 1938.
LAURENZA, Vincenzo
'Garibaldi a Malta', *Archivio Storico di Malta*, iii-iv (1932).
LE ROY LADURIE, Emanuel
'The Event and the Long Term in Social History: the Case of the Chouan
Uprising', in E. Le Roy Ladurie, *The Territory of the Historian*. Trans. Ben
and Sian Reynolds. Brighton 1982.
LEE, Hilda I
'British Policy towards Religion, Ancient Laws and Customs in Malta, 1824-
1851', *Melita Historica*, iii, 4 (1963); iv, 1 (1964).
Malta 1813-1914: A Study in Constitutional and Strategic Development.
M 1972.
LEE, J.M.
Colonial Development and Good Government. L 1967.
LEE, J.M., PETTER, M.
The Colonial Office, War and Development Policy. L 1982.
Lettera di Giuseppe Mazzini ai Signori Tocqueville e Falloux. M 1849.
LEVI-STRAUSS, C.
Structural Anthropology. New York 1963.
LEWIS, G.F. (ed.)
Letters of the Rt. Hon. G. Cornwall-Lewis Bart. to Various Friends. L
1870.
LOUIS, William R.
Imperialism at Bay. Oxford 1978.
*The British Empire in the Middle East 1945-1951: Arab Nationalism, the
United States, and Postwar Imperialism*. Oxford 1984.
LOWE, C.J.
Salisbury and the Mediterranean, 1886-1896. L 1965.
LUKE, Sir Harry
Malta: An Account and an Appreciation. M 1960.
LUTTRELL, Anthony T.
'Girolamo Manduca and Gian Francesco Abela: Tradition and Invention in
Maltese Historiography', *Melita Historica*, vii, 2 (1977).
'Malta e Gozo: 1222-1268', in *X Congresso de Historia de la Corona de Aragon.*

Saragossa 1979.
LUTTRELL, Anthony T. (ed.)
Medieval Malta: Studies on Malta before the Knights. L 1975.
MAC GILL, T.
A Handbook or Guide for Strangers Visiting Malta. M 1939.
MACK SMITH, Denis
Mussolini. L 1983.
Mussolini's Roman Empire. L 1976.
MACKENZE, J.M.
Propaganda and Empire. Manchester 1984.
MACKENZE, J.M. (ed.)
Imperialism and Popular Culture. Manchester 1986.
MAINE, Henry S.
Village Communities in the East and West. L 1880.
MALLIA, Filipp
L-Isqof li Ħabbu Kulħadd. M 1982.
MALLIA-MILANES, Victor
Descrittione di Malta, Anno 1716: A Venetian Account. M 1988.
'In Search of Vittorio Cassar: A Documentary Approach', *Melita Historica,* ix,
    3 (1986).
'The Order of St. John 1793-1798: Impending Collapse of a Glorious Heritage.
    The despatches of Antonio Miari, Venetian Minister in Malta', *Hyphen,* iii,
    3 (1982).
Malta: Studies of its Heritage and History. M 1986.
MAMO, G.B.
Il-Għannej Kormi u il-Għannej Żeituni − Meta morna tal-Mellieħa. M 1913.
MANGION, Giovanni
Governo Inglese, Risorgimento Italiano ed Opinione Pubblica a Malta 1848-51.
    M 1970.
'Per una storia di Malta nel secolo XIX', *Studia* (1963).
MARSEILLE, Jacques
Empire colonial et capitalisme français. Histoire d'un divorce. Paris
    1984.
MARSHALL, David
History of the Maltese Language in Local Education. M 1971.
MAZZARESE FARDELLA, E.
I feudi comitali di Sicilia dai Normanni agli Aragonesi. Milan 1974.
MICALLEF, Albert
'Carlo Darmanin 1825-1909: Malta's foremost statuary', *The Sunday Times,*
    [M] *23 December 1979.*
MICALLEF, J.
Ħal Luqa, Niesha u Ġrajjietha. M 1975.
L-Istorja ta' Ħal Safi. M 1980.
MIÈGE, M.
Histoire de Malte. Vol. i. Paris 1840.
MIFSUD, Alfredo
'La Cattedrale e l'Università, ossia il Comune e la Chiesa in Malta', *La Diocesi,*
    ii (1917), iii (1918-19), iv (1919-20).
'L'approvigionamento e l'Università di Malta nelle passate dominazioni',
    Archivum Melitense, iii, 5, 6 (1918).
'Malta al sovrano nel 1409', *La Diocesi,* ii (1918).
Origine della sovranità Inglese su Malta. M 1907.
'Sulle nostre Decime', *La Diocesi,* i, (1916).

MIFSUD, E.
'Who are the Grumblers?', *L-Orizzont*, 29 November 1975.
MIFSUD BONNICI, R.
Ġrajja ta' Baned f'Malta u Għawdex. Vol. i. M 1956.
MILBURN, Josephine
British Business and Ghanaian Independence. New England 1977.
MINTOFF, Dom
'Isolation is No Answer', *The Times*, [L] 1968.
Malta: Church, State, Labour. M 1966.
Priests and Politics in Malta. M 1961.
MITROVICH, Giorgio
Council of Government in Malta. L 1858.
Indirizzo ai Maltesi da parte del loro amico. L 1835.
MIZZI, Enrico
Malta Italiana. Turin 1912. Extract from *Italia!*, (fascicolo 8), a monthly review
    published under the auspices of the Società Nazionale Dante Alighieri.
Per il VIII Settembre, 1565: Lampi e Fremiti di Vita Nuova. M 1908.
MIZZI, Fortunato
'Appello agli Elettori', *Malta*, 18 January 1887.
MIZZI, Fortunato, CACHIA ZAMMIT, Salvatore
A Statement of Claims and Grievances of the Maltese. L 1899.
MIZZI, Fortunato P.
Priestly Vocations in the Maltese Ecclesiastical Province 1911-1964. M
    1966.
MIZZI, Spiro
'Il-Karriera twila ta' l-Industrijalista Numru Wieħed ta' Malta', *Storja 78*,
    [i, 1 (1978)].
MONROE, Elizabeth
Britain's Moment in the Middle East 1914-1956. L 1963.
The Mediterranean in Politics. Oxford 1938.
MONSON, W.I.
Extracts from a Journal. L 1820.
MONTALTO, John
The Nobles of Malta 1530-1800. M 1979.
MONTANARO, E.E.
'The People's Sculptor', *The Sunday Times*, [M] 25 August 1985.
MONTGOMERY, Lord, of Alamein
Memoirs. L 1958.
MOORE, R.J.
Escape from Empire. Oxford 1983.
MORGAN, D.J.
The Official History of Colonial Development. L 1980.
MORGAN, Kenneth
Labour in Power 1945-1951. Oxford 1984.
MORRIS, James
Farewell the Trumpets: an Imperial Retreat. Harmondsworth 1980.
MUGGERIDGE, Malcolm (ed.)
Ciano's Diary, 1939-43. L 1947.
NASSAU, Senior, W.
Conversations and Journals in Egypt and Malta. Vol. ii. L 1882.
Nationalism: A Report by a Study Group of the Royal Institute of International
    Affairs. Oxford 1939.
NICOLAS, J.

'The Position of Women in the Maltese Economy 1900-1974'. Unpublished B.A. dissertation, Univerisity of Malta, 1975.

Ordinances enacted by the Governor, Laws made by the Legislature and other official Acts. M 1923.

ORLANDO SMITH, J.
The Sedition Case: Official Correspondence between Joseph Orlando Smith and the Imperial Authorities. M 1934.

PARTIT NAZZJONALISTA
A Declaration of Policy. M 1987.

PATTI, Giuseppe
I cento giorni di Garibaldi in Sicilia nel giornalismo Maltese. Messina 1972.

PETO, Gladys
L'Empire de la Méditerranée. Paris 1912.

PIPES, Daniel
Slaves, Soldiers and Islam: The Genesis of a Military System. New Haven / L 1981.

PIROTTA, J.M.
Fortress Colony: The Final Act 1945-1965. Vol. i. M 1987.

PISANI, Ġorġ
Il-Ġabra tal-Qamħ. M [1945].

PITRÈ, G.
Feste Patronali in Sicilia. Turin 1900. 2nd ed. Palermo 1978.

PLATT, D.C.M.
Finance, Trade and Politics in British Foreign Policy 1815-1914. Oxford 1968.

PLAYFAIR, I.S.O.
The Mediterranean and the Middle East: History of the Second World War. Vol.i. L 1954.

POPPERWELL, R.G.
Norway.

PORTER, Bernard
The Lion's Share. 2nd ed. L 1984.

POST, Gaines
'Two Notes on Nationalism in the Middle Ages', *Traditio,* ix (1953).

PRATT, Laurence R.
East of Malta, West of Suez: Britain's Mediterranean Crisis, 1936-1939. Cambridge 1975.

PRICE, Charles A.
Malta and the Maltese. A Study in Nineteenth-Century Migration. Melbourne 1954.

PRICE, J.H.
'The Malta Tramways', *Modern Tramway and Light Railway Review,* xxxiii, 392 (August 1970).

Problems of Parliamentary Government in Colonies. A Report prepared by the Hansard Society. L 1953.

PUGH, Patricia
Educate, Agitate, Organize: 100 Years of Fabian Socialism. L 1984.

QUINTANA, J.
Guida dell'Isola di Malta e sue dipendenze. M 1843.

RANSIJAT, Bosredon de
Journal du Siège et Blocus de Malte. Paris 1800.

Rapport fai par Daru. Paris 1803.

RENAN, E.
Qu'est-ce qu' une nation? Paris 1882.
'Report of the Commissioners of Inquiry August 1812 ', in V. Harlow, F.
  Madden, *British Colonial Development 1774-1834.* Oxford 1953.
RHODES, Anthony
The Vatican in the Age of the Dictators 1922-1945. L 1973.
RHODES, James Robert
Anthony Eden. L 1986.
RIGBY, B.L.
The Malta Railway. Aylesbury 1970.
ROBINSON, Kenneth
The Dilemmas of Trusteeship. L 1965.
ROBINSON, R.E.
'Andrew Cohen and the Transfer of Power in Tropical Africa 1940-51', in
  Decolonisation and After, ed. W.H. Morris-Jones, L. Fisher. L 1980.
'Non-European Foundations of European Imperialism: Sketch for a Theory of
  Collaboration', in *Studies in the Theory of Imperialism,* ed. R. Owen, R.
  Sutcliffe. L 1972.
'The Eccentric Idea of Imperialism, with or without Empire', in *Imperialism
  and After,* ed. W.J. Mommsen, J. Osterhammel. L 1986.
ROBINSON, R.E., GALLAGHER, J.
Africa and the Victorians: The Official Mind of Imperialism. L 1961.
ROWSELL, F.W.
'Malta', *Nineteenth Century,* iv (August 1878).
RUNDLE, S.
Language as a Social and Political Factor in Europe. L 1944.
RYAN, Frederick W.
The House of the Temple. L 1930.
RYAN, Frederick W., BORON, V.
Malta. L 1910.
SAMMUT, C.
'La Minorité Maltaise de Tunisie: Ethnie Arab ou Européene?' in *Actes du
  Premier Congres d'Études des Cultures meditérranéens d'influence arabo-
  berbère.* Algiers 1973.
SAMMUT, Dennis
Too Early for Freedom. M 1984.
SAMMUT, Edward
Art in Malta. M 1953.
SANT, Karm
It-Traduzzjoni tal-Bibbja u l-Ilsien Malti 1800-1850. M 1975.
SAVONA, S.
Report on the Educational Institutions of Malta and Gozo. M 1882.
The Necessity of Educating the People. M 1865.
SCHEMBRI ADAMI,
'Who will support Labour?', *The Dawn,* 28 March 1946.
SCHENK, H.G.
The Mind of the European Romantics. Oxford 1979.
SCHERMERHORN, Elizabeth
Malta of the Knights. Surrey 1926.
SCHNEIDER, P., SCHNEIDER, J., HANSEN, E.
'Modernization and Development: the role of regional élites and noncorporate
  groups in the European Mediterranean', *Comparative Studies in Society and
  History,* xiv (1972).

SCHROTH-KOHLER, C., KOLZEER, T., ZIELENSKI, H.
'Zwei staufische diplome fur Malta aus den Jehren 1198 und 1212', *Deutsches Archiv,* xxxiii (1977).
SCHUSTER, G.E.
Interim Report on the Financial and Economic Structure of the Maltese Islands. M 1950.
SCICLUNA, Hannibal P.
Actes et Documents pour servir a l'Histoire de l'Occupation Française de Malte pendant les années 1798-1800. M 1923.
The Church of St. John in Valletta. Rome 1955.
ŞEAL, Anil
The Emergence of Indian Nationalism. Cambridge 1968.
SEDDALL, H.
Malta: Past and Present. L 1870.
SHEBBEARE, John
Letters on the English Nation. Vol. i. L 1756.
SHEPHERD, E.
Malta and Me. L 1928.
SIEYES, E.
Qu'est-ce que le tier État? Paris 1789.
SILVERMANN, M., SALISBURY, R.F. (eds.)
A House Divided! Anthropological Studies of Factionalism. Newfoundland 1978.
SINGH, Anita Inger
'Keeping India in the Commonwealth: British Political and Military Aims, 1947-49, *Journal of Contemporary History,* 20 (1985).
SMITH, A.D.
'The Diffusion of Nationalism: Some Historical and Sociological Perspectives', *British Journal of Sociology,* xxix, 2 (1978).
SMITH, Harrison
Britain in Malta. 2 vols. M 1953.
SMITH, Harrison, KOSTER, Adrianus
Lord Strickland: Servant of the Crown. 2 vols. M 1984-86.
SNYDER, L.L.
Varieties of Nationalism: A Comparative Study. Illinois 1976.
STRANGE, Susan
Sterling and British Policy. L 1971.
STRICKLAND, Gerald
Malta and the Phoenicians. M. 1921. Reprint, M 1969.
TESTA, Carmelo
Maż-żewġ Nahat tas-Swar. 3 vols. M 1979-82.
The General: The Travel Memoirs of General Sir George Whitmore, ed. Joan Johnson. Gloucester 1987.
TOMLINSON, B.R.
'The Contraction of England: National Decline and the Loss of Empire', *Journal of Imperial and Commonwealth History,* xi, 1 (1982).
The Political Economy of the Raj, 1914-1947. L 1979.
VALENTINI, Roberto
'I Cavalieri di San Giovanni da Rodi a Malta: trattative diplomatiche', *Archivum Melitense,* ix, 4 (1935).
'Il patrimonio della Corona in Malta fino alla venuta dell'Ordine', *Archivio Storico di Malta,* v, 1-4 (1934).
'Ribellione di Malta e spedizione alla Gerbe come conseguenze dell'inefficienza

della flotta Aragonese nel Mediterraneo', *Archivio Storico di Malta*, n.s., viii, 3 (1937)

VASSALLI, M.A.
Ktieb il-Kliem Malti. Rome 1796.
VASSALLO, Edwin P.
Strickland. M 1932. English trans., in 2 manuscript vols., May Agius.
VASSALLO, G.A.
Ħrejjef u Ċajt bil-Malti. M 1895.
Mogħdija taż-Żmien fil-Lsien Malti. M 1843.
VASSALLO, Mario
'Religious Symbolism in a Changing Malta', in *Contributions to Mediterranean Studies*, ed. Mario Vassallo. M 1977.
VELLA, Andrew P.
Storja ta' Malta. Vol.ii. M 1979.
The Tribunal of the Inquisition in Malta. 2nd ed. M 1973.
VELLA, E.B.
Storja ta' Birkirkara bil-Kolleġġjata Tagħha. M 1935.
VELLA, G.
Codice diplomatico di Sicilia sotto il governo degli Arabi. 6 vols. Palermo 1789-92.
VELLA, W.
'Transport in the Maltese Islands 1850-1890'. Unpublished B.A. dissertation, University of Malta, 1969.
VELLA, Philip
Malta: Blitzed but not Beaten. M 1985.
VENTURI, F.
Settecento riformatore. Vol. iii: *La prima crisi dell'Antico Regime 1768-1776.* Turin 1979.
VIANELLO, C.A.
'Una relazione inedita di Malta del 1582', *Archivio Storico di Malta*, n.s., vii, 3 (1936).
WALCOTT, Derek
In a Green Night: Poems 1948-1960. L 1962.
WEINGROD, A.
'Patrons, Patronage and Political Parties', *Comparative Studies in Society and History*, x (1968).
WEINREICH, V.
Languages in Contact. New York 1953.
WETTINGER, Godfrey
'Agriculture in Malta in the late Middle Ages', in *Proceedings of History Week 1981*, ed. Mario Buhagiar. M 1982. Offprint, with minor modifications.
'Early Maltese Popular Attitudes to the Government of the Order of St. John', *Melita Historica*, vi, 3 (1974).
'Linguistic Pluralism and Cultural Change in the Maltese Islands during the Middle Ages', in *Le pluralisme linguistique dans la societe medievale: Colloque international, 1986.* Forthcoming.
'The Arabs in Malta', in *Malta: Studies of its Heritage and History.* M 1986.
The Jews of Malta in the Late Middle Ages. M 1985.
'The Militia Roster of Watch Duties of 1417', *The Armed Forces of Malta Journal*, 32 (1979).
'The Pawning of Malta to Monroy', *Melita Historica*, vii, 3 (1978).
WILLIAMS, Ann
Britain and France in the Middle East and North Africa, 1914-1967. L 1968.

WILLIAMS, Philip
Crisis and Compromise. L 1964.
WOODS, W.
Report on the Finances of the Government of Malta. L 1946.
ZAMMIT, Edward L.
  A Colonial Inheritance: Maltese Perceptions of Work, Power and Class Structure with reference to the Labour Movement. M 1984.
  'Adult Education: The Role of R[oyal] U[niversity of] M[alta]', *Journal of Educational Affairs,* i, 1 (1975).
  'Some Social Aspects of Maltese Development'. Paper read at the Seminar on 'Development: The Maltese Experience': Ruskin College, Oxford – Young Socialist League, University of Malta, April 1977.
ZAMMIT, Nicola
  Esposizione d'Industria Maltese nel 1864: Memorie. M 1864.
ZARB, Seraphim M.
  'Matthew Callus', *Scientia,* xi, 2 (1945).
  St. Catherine of Alexandria. M 1979.
ZERAFA, Stefano
  Discorso sulla storia artistica di Malta. M 1850.

Index